Fields of Learning

Culture of the Land: A Series in the New Agrarianism

This series is devoted to the exploration and articulation of a new agrarianism that considers the health of habitats and human communities together. It demonstrates how agrarian insights and responsibilities can be worked out in diverse fields of learning and living: history, science, art, politics, economics, literature, philosophy, religion, urban planning, education, and public policy. Agrarianism is a comprehensive worldview that appreciates the intimate and practical connections that exist between humans and the earth. It stands as our most promising alternative to the unsustainable and destructive ways of current global, industrial, and consumer culture.

Series Editor
Norman Wirzba, Duke University, North Carolina

Advisory Board
Wendell Berry, Port Royal, Kentucky
Ellen Davis, Duke University, North Carolina
Patrick Holden, Soil Association, United Kingdom
Wes Jackson, Land Institute, Kansas
Gene Logsdon, Upper Sandusky, Ohio
Bill McKibben, Middlebury College, Vermont
David Orr, Oberlin College, Ohio
Michael Pollan, University of California at Berkeley, California
Jennifer Sahn, *Orion* Magazine, Massachusetts
Vandana Shiva, Research Foundation for Science, Technology & Ecology, India
Bill Vitek, Clarkson University, New York

FIELDS

OF

LEARNING

The Student Farm Movement
in North America

Edited by
LAURA SAYRE AND SEAN CLARK

Foreword by
FREDERICK L. KIRSCHENMANN

THE UNIVERSITY PRESS OF KENTUCKY

Editorial and Sales Offices: The University Press of Kentucky
663 South Limestone Street, Lexington, Kentucky 40508-4008
www.kentuckypress.com

15 14 13 12 11   5 4 3 2 1

Library of Congress Cataloging-in-Publication Data

Fields of learning : the student farm movement in North America / edited by Laura Sayre
and Sean Clark ; foreword by Frederick L. Kirschenmann.
      p. cm. — (Culture of the land)
  Includes bibliographical references and index.
  ISBN 978-0-8131-3374-4 (hardcover : alk. paper)
  ISBN 978-0-8131-3395-9 (ebook)
  1. School farms—United States. 2. Agricultural students—United States. 3.
Agricultural education—United States. 4. Agricultural colleges—United States. 5.
Agriculture—Fieldwork—United States. 6. School farms—Canada. 7. Agricultural
students—Canada. 8. Agricultural education—Canada.
9. Agricultural colleges—Canada. 10. Agriculture—Fieldwork—Canada.
I. Sayre, Laura Browne, 1970- II. Clark, Sean.
  S533.F49 2011
  630.71—dc22   2011008596

This book is printed on acid-free paper meeting the requirements of the American
National Standard for Permanence in Paper for Printed Library Materials.

Manufactured in the United States of America.

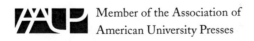 Member of the Association of
American University Presses

For the sustainable farmers
of the future

All studies arise from aspects of the one earth and the one life lived upon it.

—John Dewey, *The School and Society* (1900)

Contents

Illustrations

Foreword

FREDERICK L. KIRSCHENMANN

The fact that books, documentaries, and journal articles about food and farming are becoming increasingly popular is one indication among many that a food revolution is emerging in our culture. *Fields of Learning* makes an important contribution to that body of art and literature. These stories provide valuable historical information about the creation of alternative learning environments that will almost certainly become crucial in the decades ahead.

I suspect that everyone who ponders the stories in *Fields of Learning* will agree that they are delightful and inspiring narratives. They are well written and convey a sense of value that far exceeds what Robert Bly once called "the flat poetry of the universities." However, perhaps not everyone will agree that student farms are important. Indeed, as the stories themselves reveal, institutional support for student farms is often lacking. And so *Fields of Learning* also provides us with an opportunity to reconsider what we value in our universities as well as in our communities.

While the students and faculty actively involved in student farms strongly believe that the farms play a significant role in students' education, administrators responsible for deciding which academic programs are most important for a college or a university are more likely to question the cost and the need to devote valuable land resources to this purpose. Consequently, almost all these stories reveal tensions around the appropriateness and practicality of maintaining these farms as part of an educational curriculum. Do student farms provide a learning environment that is important enough to compete for scarce resources with academic courses in science and technology or art and literature?

This same tension is now emerging in our public schools with respect to school gardening programs. The terms of the debate were clearly articulated in an article by Caitlin Flanagan published in the January/February 2010 issue of the *Atlantic Monthly*. Flanagan takes strong exception to the popular trend of including school gardens in public school curricula. From her perspective, taking children out of classroom environments where they could be "reading important books or learning higher math (attaining the cultural achievements ... that have lifted uncounted generations of human beings out of the desperate daily scrabble to wrest sustenance from dirt)," and placing them instead in gardens where they perform menial tasks with their hands—an activity that is likely to turn them into "sharecroppers"—is a serious misstep.[1]

While the critics of student farms in the *Fields of Learning* stories do not go to such extremes, it is easy to see, given our current culture of agriculture, why thoughtful leaders in our academic institutions might question the wisdom of devoting land, funding, and course hours to teaching students how to farm. After all, the successful trend of industrializing agriculture during much of the twentieth century strongly suggests that we will need fewer and fewer farmers to produce all our food and fiber. Today, we still cite the heroic achievement of this strategy. While one farmer fed only 20 people in the 1950s, one farmer now feeds 150!

However, assessing the value of student farms from this perspective fails to recognize some very important present and future trends, trends that may well go to the heart of future national and global food security policies.

First, we have been ignoring some important data with respect to trends in the human capital available for our present and future agriculture production needs. Every five years, when the USDA conducts its agriculture census, the data appear to indicate that our farm populations have basically stabilized at around 2 million farms. Indeed, there was some euphoria in the popular media when the results of the 2007 census data were published, revealing that there was actually a slight *increase* in the number of farms—2.2 million, up from 2.1 million in the 2003 data. What is never mentioned in these media reports is that these data are still based on a 1974 definition of a farm. According to that definition, "a farm is any establishment from which $1,000 or more of agricultural products were sold or would normally be during the year."[2]

I know of only one journalist who has pointed out how misleading this definition can be when it is used to determine what is happening to actual farm populations. In a column published by the Prairie Writers Circle, Lisa Hamilton pointed out that, considering that she could "make $500" selling eggs from the four chickens in her backyard, if she got "four more hens," her "suburban home could qualify as a farm" by the USDA's definition since she then would have produced $1,000 in gross sales.[3]

When we actually break down the data from the 2007 census, what we find is that we now have only 192,442 farms producing 75 percent of total gross U.S. farm income. Even more troubling is the fact that 30 percent of our farmers are now over age sixty-five while only 5 percent are under age thirty-five. One simply cannot project these trends very far into the future without concluding that we are headed toward a very serious human capital problem in U.S. agriculture. So, without student farms and other opportunities to learn how to farm, where will the next generation of farmers come from?

A second reality makes this troubling set of statistics even more alarming. Like any other industrial enterprise, our present system of agriculture operates on the basis of three principles: specialization, simplification, and economies of scale. These principles, implemented to achieve maximum, efficient production and short-term economic return, achieve their intended purpose so long as cheap energy, surplus freshwater, and relatively stable climates are available. But, as we enter the twenty-first century, each of these resources is in steep decline. The era of cheap energy is over, we are drawing down our freshwater resources all across the planet at an unsustainable rate, and all indicators suggest that we will experience more unstable climates (more droughts, floods, and severe weather events) in the decades ahead. This suggests that we will need to redesign our farming systems if we are to maintain productivity. The large, specialized, simplistic, monoculture-based farming systems that now occupy so much of our agricultural landscape require enormous amounts of energy and water as well as stable climates to perform well.

Since those three critical resources are not likely to be available for much longer, we will have to begin imagining new farming systems. To maintain productivity, farming systems in the twenty-first century and beyond will have to use ecological principles rather than industrial principles, making our farms more resilient, self-regulating, and self-renewing. This will require a much more knowledge-intensive agriculture. And that transformation will require a new generation of farmers who are educated and motivated to transform agriculture from efficient input/output industrial operations to resilient, interactive ecological operations.

And this new agriculture will require more farmers. Richard Heinberg estimates that we will need 40–50 million people engaged in producing our food within the next half century owing to declining cheap energy resources. Whether or not this estimate proves accurate, it is clear that a far greater number of people will need to be involved in agricultural production than are today.[4] Student farms can play a major role in supplying the intellectual capital for this revolution in agriculture.

Third—and this is part of the good news—a new generation of young people is emerging throughout the United States, young people who are interested in farming and intrigued by this new agriculture. It is likely this new phenomenon that accounts for the slight gain in farm numbers between the 2002 and the 2007 agriculture census data. While we lost 224,190 farms during that five-year period, we gained 300,000 new ones, for a net gain of 75,810. Interestingly, these new farmers are a diversified group (30 percent are women, there is a 10 percent increase in the number of Hispanic farmers, and there are increases as well among African American and Native American farmers), and most have off-farm jobs, suggesting that they want to farm for lifestyle reasons.

I meet many of these new and aspiring farmers through our Young Farmer program at the Stone Barns Center for Food and Agriculture near Tarrytown, New York, and I am always deeply impressed by their commitment, their imagination, their enthusiasm, and their intellectual curiosity. They welcome the more complex ecological approaches to producing food, and they are exactly the kind of human capital we will need to address the challenges of the future. Also encouraging is the fact that, according to our records, 70 percent of the numerous apprentices and interns who have worked on our farms at the Stone Barns have subsequently found ways to become engaged in some kind of full-time farming.

Finally—and this is more good news—a food revolution is definitely already under way, and this revolution will provide many opportunities for the new generation of young farmers who want to farm. This revolution is driven by food-related health concerns, by food safety concerns, by production-related environmental concerns, and, more generally, by a growing desire for more trusting relationships throughout the food chain. The emerging generation fits this food revolution very well since these farmers share many of these same concerns and desires.

All these indicators suggest that student farms (along with many other existing and emerging educational opportunities to learn how to produce food in an ecologically sound manner) will have an increasingly important role to play in our future food system. Far from being a romantic, irrelevant throwback to yesteryear, student farms may, in fact, be essential in preparing our nation and our planet to become part of the food revolution of the twenty-first century. The stories featured in this book provide enormously valuable information for developing the additional student farms we will need in our immediate future to achieve that goal.

NOTES

1. Caitlin Flanagan, "Cultivating Failure: How School Gardens Are Cheating Our Most Vulnerable Students," *Atlantic Monthly*, January/February 2010, available at http://www.theatlantic.com.

2. *Farms and Land in Farms, Final Estimates, 2003–2007*, Statistical Bulletin no. 1018 (Washington, DC: USDA National Agricultural Statistics Service, February 2009).

3. Lisa Hamilton, "Let's Grow a New Crop of Farmers," Prairie Writers Circle, Monday, May 11, 2009, available at http://www.landinstitute.org.

4. Richard Heinberg, *Peak Everything: Waking Up to the Century of Declines* (Gabriola Island, BC: New Society, 2007), 47–66.

Preface

In the late summer of 2003, I began researching an article about student farms for NewFarm.org, the online magazine of organic and sustainable farming published by the Rodale Institute. I visited a couple of farms I'd heard about on campuses not too far away—Dartmouth College in Hanover, New Hampshire, and Cook College at Rutgers University in New Brunswick, New Jersey—and started asking around to find out about others. Most people I talked to—staff or faculty associated with a given student farm project, for instance—seemed to be aware of four or five others, but no one had a comprehensive list. "I know there's one at Hampshire College in Massachusetts," one person would tell me, "and I think there might be one at Cornell?" "There's a place called Berea in Kentucky that's had one for a long time," someone else would say. "I'd love to know more about it."

I posted a query to SANET, the Listserv managed by SARE, the Sustainable Agriculture Research and Education program within the U.S. Department of Agriculture. I discovered that the people at the Alternative Farming Systems Information Center, part of the National Agricultural Library in Washington, DC (and affiliated with SARE), had put together a bulletin titled "Educational and Training Opportunities in Sustainable Agriculture," but this was not quite the same thing. So I started assembling a spreadsheet with schools, names, acreages, and other details, adding to it as new leads emerged. By the time we were ready to post the article on the NewFarm.org Web site in January 2004—I had in the meantime been hired by NewFarm.org as a full-time writer and editor—I had a total of about thirty. My fellow editors and I decided to turn my spreadsheet into an online directory to accompany the article.

I was working for an online magazine, but it was with this project that I really discovered firsthand the power of the Internet—not just as simple research tool, but as a means of collectively, spontaneously generating information. Our online "Directory of Student Farms" quickly became one of the most popular pages within the New Farm Web site. At least once a week, it seemed, I would get an e-mail from someone in Minnesota or

Georgia or Idaho describing an existing or nascent student farm or garden and asking to be included in the directory. Because we were online, it was relatively simple and inexpensive to make updates. In time, the directory came to include more than eighty student farms in thirty-one states and four Canadian provinces.

This book is an outgrowth of that experience. It's easy to forget how much more powerful a simple Internet search has become since 2003 or how much more slowly personal and professional networks were assembled even a decade ago. These days, we have to remind ourselves that there are, in fact, forms of knowledge, ways of thinking and relating, even nuggets of information *not* available on the Web. Sometime around the summer of 2007, I started to think about the value of putting together a book about the student farm movement: to describe and share in detail what was at stake in the business of creating and maintaining hands-on farming projects (growing food and managing land) within an academic setting. So, in November of that year, I took a detour on the way back from a trip to visit some friends in Nashville, Tennessee, to see for myself the place that had often been mentioned to me as possibly the oldest student farm in the country: Berea College in Kentucky. Touring the farm in a well-used college pickup, admiring the greens in the hoophouses and the goats in the pastures, inspecting a student's homemade biodiesel brewer, Sean Clark and I began to plot out what such a book could look like.

After that, it was just hard work, for which farming is excellent preparation.

L.S.

Acknowledgments

This book has benefited from the input and support of numerous people. The Yale Agrarian Studies fellows of 2008–2009—Karen Hébert, Keely Maxwell, Alessandro Monsutti, and Nandini Sundar—commented on early versions of the book proposal and offered indispensable encouragement for the formulation of the project. Laura Lengnick, Suzanne Morse, and especially Damian Parr offered critical observations on the organization and rationale of the book as it took shape. Norman Wirzba, the series editor for *The Culture of the Land*, showed faith in the undertaking from the start; Steve Wrinn at the University Press of Kentucky was unfailingly communicative, knowledgeable, and humane as we progressed through the steps toward publication. Above all, we offer our thanks to all the contributors to this volume for their enthusiasm, persistence, and hard work. The process of watching their individual stories and insights develop was both challenging and rewarding; we hope they are all as pleased with the collective result as we are.

Laura Sayre would also like to thank everyone she interviewed during her research for the original student farm article, especially Scott Stokoe, Matt Steiman, and the student farm crew at Rutgers, as well as her fellow editors and writers at NewFarm.org (Chris Hill, Greg Bowman, Dan Sullivan, Amanda Kimble-Evans, and Cara Hungerford) and all the people who e-mailed in with additions, comments, or corrections for the online student farm directory. Sean Clark would like to thank the many Berea College farm students who have contributed to the project directly, by assisting with research, and indirectly, by sharing their personal perspectives on the value, effectiveness, and possibilities of on-farm education.

Publication of this book has been assisted by a grant from the Sue B. Hart Foundation, for which we are also grateful.

Introduction

The Student Farm Movement in Context

Laura Sayre

The past decade has seen the revival of an old pedagogical idea: find ing ways to combine liberal arts undergraduate education with hands-on, practical farming and gardening experience. Scores of largely student-motivated, student-run, on-campus farms and market gardens, ranging in size from less than an acre to dozens of acres, have been established at a wide variety of universities and colleges across North America. Typically, the goal is to provide basic training in organic production and marketing while linking to more formal academic work in agroecology, environmen tal studies, or other disciplines and, at the same, facilitating broader cam pus sustainability objectives such as the recycling of food wastes and the provision of local food for dining halls. Frequently, there is a community service element as well, as students grow food to be donated to local food banks, install gardens at nearby secondary schools, or host farm tours for elementary school groups.

The size and dynamism of this movement are truly remarkable. Fifteen or twenty years ago, on-campus farms were largely unheard of, with just a handful of programs in place at a few unique institutions. Today, the situation has changed radically: the 2009 College Sustainability Report Card, examining three hundred leading universities and colleges in the United States and Canada, found that 82 percent do at least some local food purchasing, 55 percent have food waste–composting programs, and 29 percent have community gardens or student farms on campus.[1] Although it is easy (and probably advisable) to be wary of such broad-based "sustainability" claims, the research conducted for this book suggests that there are, indeed, about a hundred, if not more, higher education institutions in

North America with on-campus farms or gardens of some sort, with more being established each year. From Minnesota to Idaho, from Quebec to South Carolina, college and university students are, in increasing numbers, putting up hoophouses, supplying salad greens to on-campus cafés, maintaining rototillers, selling radishes at local farmers markets, making compost, moving chicken tractors, tapping maple trees—in short, doing all the thousand things that go into small-scale organic farming and market gardening. Even ten years ago, these were not activities that formed part of your typical college education.

This transformation is being driven first of all by overwhelming student interest and demand. In the wake of books like Michael Pollan's *The Omnivore's Dilemma* and Barbara Kingsolver's *Animal, Vegetable, Miracle* and films like Morgan Spurlock's *Supersize Me* and Aaron Woolf's *King Corn*, students and young people are taking an unprecedented interest in where their food comes from and why it matters. They want to know why the standard liberal arts curriculum has so little to say about the modern agrifood system and what a curriculum would look like that did bring this central element of human existence under consideration. College and university professors and administrators, meanwhile, are responding to these demands. New courses with titles like "Food, Agriculture, and Society," "From Farm to Fork," "Food Politics," and (more directly) "Organic Fruit and Vegetable Production" are logging record enrollments. New sustainable food systems majors and concentrations are being established. Many of these courses and programs seek to incorporate some kind of experiential learning into their syllabi and look to campus farms and gardens as places to do so. In other cases, students are asking for and receiving small parcels of campus land to create gardens and grow food as an extracurricular activity, for instance, under the auspices of a student club. As a commentator in the *Chronicle of Higher Education* put the case in March 2008: "With the attention that colleges are paying to local foods and to sustainability, perhaps more institutions should offer basic lessons in agricultural skills, as a way to make students familiar with an important American industry, if not to make farmers out of them. Recently, scholars have worried that young people are disconnected from nature, so why not let students carve out a corner of the campus to start a small farm?"[2]

Why not indeed? The arguments in favor of student farming are many and will be explored at length in the course of this book. But, at their most basic level, they come down to this: in these days of obesity and diabetes, of high-pressure work and learning environments and total digital media saturation, it's good for students to put down their books (or close their computers) occasionally and get outside, to get some exercise, to learn what a real tomato tastes like and how to grow one, to put their hands in the earth, to learn how to wield a spade. Having a student-run farm or garden on campus enables universities to demonstrate their commitment to environmental ideals while letting students explore how those ideals might be applied in the real world. Student farms are at once seedbeds and test plots for agrarian values, all too necessary in our increasingly urban and suburban world.

But how exactly do universities and colleges manage these programs? What do they cost? How much land do they require? How do students or faculty go about setting them up? What do they look like in the winter—or in the summer, for that matter, when most students are away? What happens when key students graduate? What about livestock? Student-run campus farms sound great in principle, in other words, but how do they work in practice? And how can they be meaningfully and usefully integrated with the broadest possible range of courses in order to serve a diverse cross section of students and other members of the campus community, not just those with a particular interest in organic farming? Should every college and university have a student farm? *Could* every college and university have one? In today's academic climate, with food-and-farming topics gaining ground in anthropology, history, sociology, geography, political science, and many other fields, it may be less radical to propose the "centrality of agriculture," in Colin Duncan's phrase.[3] But, at the same time, this very popularity of agricultural issues lends new urgency to the cause of student farming experience as a *practical* matter. A research paper on, say, cut-flower production in Ecuador will take on a different aspect when it is written by a student who has herself spent some long hours in the hot sun at the end of a hoe.

Fields of Learning is the first book to profile this rapidly expanding movement and address these and other pressing questions. As a collection of essays by individuals directly involved with innovative college farm programs nationwide, it emphasizes practical details while also examining larger pedagogical concerns. It cautions against common pitfalls and honestly assesses ongoing challenges. While the shared aim of the editors and contributors is to convince readers of the multilayered value and rich interest of student farming, these are not mere puff pieces for the college viewbook: the authors describe setbacks and failures as well as triumphs and successes; they raise questions as well as providing answers. If the current

Figure I.1. Spring transplants in the greenhouse at the Dartmouth College student organic farm. (Courtesy Laura Sayre.)

student farm movement is to continue to flourish—as we believe and hope it will—it will do so by engaging in an active public and scholarly discussion of the means and ends of experiential food system education within university and college curricula. Discussions of student farming to date have taken place largely within the student farming community itself—for instance, at conferences organized by the Sustainable Agriculture Education Association, founded in 2006—or within the individual institutions where student farms are in operation.[4] The aim of this book is to extend those conversations to include a wider set of constituencies, including students of all kinds, academics across all disciplines, administrators, other college and university staff members, parents, food system activists, policymakers, farmers, farmworkers—in short, all citizens and community members with an interest in the twin futures of agriculture and education.

Toward that end, this book takes a broad approach, charting the student farm movement as it has developed, survived, and flourished in North America since the nineteenth century. Many readers may be unaware that the student farming tradition extends back this far or, indeed, that it is not entirely the product of the recent surge of popular interest in sustainable and organic food and farming. In fact, however, student farming has deep roots in North America, and an understanding of that history may be essential to ensuring that the current wave of enthusiasm for student farms doesn't turn out to be just a fad. It is our belief that the on-campus farming initiatives being set up today, in the early twenty-first century, can learn a great deal from student farms established fifteen, thirty, even a hundred years ago—both in terms of the everyday details of farm management and in terms of the larger institutional dilemmas of how to administer and integrate the lessons of student farming within the diverse objectives of tertiary education. It is surprising how many of the seemingly novel challenges and questions posed by campus-based farms today were raised as well by observers of the movement in its earliest decades. Similarly, this book considers examples of student farming at a diverse range of institutions, from large land-grant universities to small liberal arts colleges, from exclusive private universities to open-admission community colleges. One of the most interesting aspects of the student farm movement is that it cuts across institutional categories, cropping up with equal vigor in all these settings. Some aspects of student farming are characteristic of the type of institution in question; others transcend institutional factors and have more to do with geography or the age of the project.

What qualifies as a student farm? A full survey of all North American educational establishments that have or have had some kind of farm as a part of their infrastructure is beyond the scope of this book. The U.S. land-grant university system in particular, with its founding mission to "teach such branches of learning as are related to agriculture and the mechanic arts," occupies an important position with regard to the student farm movement without actually being synonymous with it.[5] While this book profiles four examples of student farms at land-grant universities, it in no way pretends to offer a comprehensive history of land-grant university farms. There are also a number of educational farm programs in North America operating at the middle school and/or high school level, within both the private and the public sectors, as well as a small number of independent, non-degree-granting entities, such as the Michael Fields Institute in Wisconsin, that offer formal training in organic farming and market gardening. For the purposes of the present volume, we decided to limit our focus to tertiary education and to accredited, degree-granting colleges and universities. Furthermore, we agreed on two essential, if somewhat loosely defined, criteria for student farming: first, there must be some level of student initiative or possibilities for student leadership associated with the farm; second, there must be a degree of attention and concern paid to questions of environmental stewardship and sustainability. (Note that the contributors to this volume tend to use *student farm* more or less interchangeably with other terms, including *college farm, campus farm, student organic farm,* and *student educational farm.*)

This book also adopts a case-study approach, with fifteen chapters profiling fifteen student farms at colleges and universities across the United States and Canada (see fig. I.2.). Each chapter is written by a faculty or staff member who either helped establish the student farm or has been directly involved with it for many years—in several cases, for more than a decade—and who is, thus, uniquely qualified to describe that farm's history, evolution, organization, and rationale. In addition, most chapters feature at least one short contribution by a current or former student reflecting on the myriad riches of campus-based farming, riches at once large and small, tangible and intangible, practical and intellectual, predictable and unforeseen. The specific goals of this collection are to instruct students, faculty, and administrators in the benefits and challenges of establishing and running campus farms; to contextualize and revitalize a tradition of hands-on, place-based pedagogy; to summarize the range of curricula related to on-campus farming projects and the range of management structures used to administer them; and to underscore the conviction that farming can be

Figure I.2. Student farms represented in this book.

both a valuable part of any undergraduate education and, for some students, a viable career path. As the stories in this book testify, young people from all walks of life find student farm programs to be enormously enriching, empowering, even life-changing experiences. Student farms convince some students that they want to be farmers, help others figure out what kind of farmers they want to be, and persuade still others that they want to pursue other careers and life choices to positively affect our contemporary food system. As such, the student farm movement promises to play a critical role in the formation of what some are calling *generation organic* or *generation O*, the next generation of sustainable farmers and the communities that support them. The essays in this book explore why and how that happens.

AGRICULTURE, EDUCATION, AND SUSTAINABILITY

What, then, is the proper relation between agriculture and higher education? What is the role of the former in the latter or of the latter in the former? It's a testimony to the radical nature of the subject that, outside the specialized field of agricultural education itself, the list of writers and thinkers to address these questions is relatively short. Progressive-

Figure I.3. Meat goats on pasture at the Berea College Farm. (Courtesy Laura Sayre.)

era thinkers like Liberty Hyde Bailey and John Dewey championed "the nature-study movement" in the early twentieth century as a way of introducing a reverence and a wonder for the natural world into elementary school education; school gardens were promoted as a practical, tangible way of connecting children to nature and to community and also as a way of bridging the gap between urban and rural.[6] Bailey was likewise concerned with the problem of educating farmers as a means of improving rural life; his long career at Cornell University included the founding of its College of Agriculture and the development of horticulture as a professional science. Bailey is a paradoxical figure, however, in that the agrarian ideals expressed in many of his writings would, in some sense, be undercut by the professionalization of the agricultural sciences he did so much to advance. Still, student farm advocates can find ample support for their cause in his prolific work. "We must understand that the introduction of agriculture into the schools is not a concession to farming or to farmers. It is a school subject by right," he argued in 1911. Nevertheless, he conceded, "The presumption is still against successful agriculture work in the literary and liberal arts institutions, because such teaching demands a point of view on education that the men in these institutions are likely not to possess."[7] For Bailey, the education of nonfarmers about farming was a future terrain, essential but less immediately practicable than educating farmers or schoolchildren.

Among Bailey's intellectual and spiritual heirs in the contemporary sustainable agriculture movement are Wendell Berry, Gene Logsdon, and Wes Jackson, all of whom—again paradoxically—have scathingly critiqued the land-grant and extension systems Bailey helped develop. From the perspective of the late twentieth century, the professionalization and institutionalization of agriculture as a science had gone too far, losing all sight of interdisciplinary education or the need to communicate with nonfarmers. This point was made powerfully as early as 1974, in a landmark article by André and Jean Mayer titled "Agriculture, the Island Empire." The Mayers argued that what they described as "the present isolation of agriculture in American academic life" held serious implications for the future of the earth and its people. For a variety of historical reasons, the Mayers observed, the utilitarian ideals embodied in the foundational structures of the United States for the development of agricultural expertise—including the Morrill Act of 1862, which established the land-grant colleges, the Hatch Act of 1887, which created the agricultural experiment stations, and the Smith-Lever Act of 1914, which authorized federal funding for cooperative extension—had given way to a gradual separation of theoretical and practical knowledge that was effectively insulating agricultural research from outside critique.[8]

The consequences of this separation could be seen in many spheres, the Mayers went on: in the breeding of crop varieties without regard for nutrition or taste; in the political isolation of "the farming interest"; in the elaboration of new "environmental studies" curricula with barely a glancing regard for agriculture. But the gravest outcome, in a nation with fewer and fewer farmers, was the cultivation of new generations of students with little idea of agriculture's profound importance: "The failure of our secondary schools and liberal arts colleges to teach even rudimentary courses on agriculture means that an enormous majority, even among well educated Americans, are totally ignorant of an area of knowledge basic to their daily style of life, to their family economics, and indeed to their survival. It also means that our policies of agricultural trade and technical assistance, as important to our foreign relations as food production is to our domestic economy, are discussed in the absence of sound information, if indeed they are discussed at all." Agriculture is so widely relevant to human concerns, in other words—to natural resource use and individual health, to economics and international relations—that it not only transcends traditional academic disciplines but also demands a level of basic practical familiarity even among those whose professional lives are unconnected to it. As the Mayers put it, "That colleges of agriculture seem anomalous at great universities such as the Universities of Wisconsin or California is more than a betrayal of history; it is an intellectual disaster."[9] (They might have added Bailey's institution, Cornell, to the list.) The argument went both ways, in other words: the study of agriculture needs to be enriched and questioned by the perspectives of nonagriculturists, and the lives and thinking of nonagriculturists need to be enriched and questioned by the study of agriculture.

From today's perspective, the Mayers' article appears deeply prescient: a powerful indictment of the disciplinary and cultural divisions that were increasingly coming to isolate food producers from the wider food-consuming public, simultaneously obscuring the political processes affecting the food system on both the global and the local level. Others, including Berry, Logsdon, and Jackson, would sound many of these same themes, further observing that the modern system of higher education as a whole militates against attachment to place—an essential feature of agrarianism—by presuming that the most promising undergraduate and graduate students will be educated in one location and then, in all likelihood, whisked away for a career somewhere else. But it was another member of the Berry-Logsdon-Jackson intellectual circle, David Orr, a professor of environmental studies at Oberlin College, who explicitly extended this line of thinking to propose the establishment of college farms as at least a partial remedy for this whole suite of problems. Working outside the land-grant system, Orr was more inclined to see the potential of small-scale, hands-on farming as a means of enriching a liberal arts education than to focus on the need to reform the land-grant system itself.

For Orr, the rich possibilities of college-based farming were an extension of his idea of ecological literacy: the belief that no student could be roundly educated without developing some sense of place, including a basic familiarity with the natural systems of his or her (in many cases adopted) local region.[10] In the short, provocative essay "Agriculture and the Liberal Arts," published in 1994, he noted that, in earlier eras, students' direct, familial experience with farming as a way of life had supplied precisely that level of ecological literacy that was now so palpably lacking. He proposed a heterogeneous list of the many benefits, both pedagogical and institutional, to be gained by including agriculture "as a part of a complete liberal arts education." College farms, he argued (I'm paraphrasing here):

1. can instill an ethic of work while promoting ecological awareness;
2. offer interdisciplinary field sites for the study of plants, soils, and other natural systems;
3. help revitalize local, rural economies;
4. protect biodiversity;
5. mitigate carbon impacts by reducing food miles and/or planting trees;
6. recycle yard and food wastes; and
7. teach problem solving and strategies for institutional change.[11]

It's interesting to note that Orr didn't include "teach students how to grow healthy food" as among the benefits of student farms. But let's consider these seven points. Speaking very broadly, point 2 is pedagogical, point 3 economic, and points 4–6 ecological. Points 1 and 7 are more complex and really speak to the shaping of individual minds—and, yes, bodies. They have to do with the formation of students' understanding of what is possible in the world, with negotiations of power between individuals and institutions, with the molding of responsibilities and expectations and obligations. Interestingly, for many of the contributors to this volume, these are the most fundamental lessons to be learned on a student farm.

The relation between agriculture and higher education, then, turns out to have far-reaching implications for the latter as well as for the former. On the one hand, student farms can be considered as a species within the genus *community farm,* itself a diverse grouping that Brian Donahue has justly characterized as "the schools of agrarianism"—places where people of all ages and from all walks of life can learn something about how food is grown, about what agricultural landscapes look like, about who inhabits them and why, and how things came to be this way.[12] On the other hand, the bringing of that diverse constituency into the farm fields threatens to pose fundamental questions about how those fields are managed, and, thus, about how agriculture in general is managed, and, thus, about a whole range of social and political and economic questions that are inextricably linked to agriculture. As Bailey put it, "Agriculture is not a technical profession or merely an industry, but a civilization."[13] As meeting grounds for the mutual interrogation of agriculture and higher education,

Figure I.4. A modular greenhouse at the Sterling College Farm. (Courtesy Laura Sayre.)

then, student farms become loci for the exploration of what we now call *sustainability*. A campus farm is where students can put their hands to the plow, figuratively and sometimes literally: a place where abstract intellectual discussions about sustainability are put to the test, where ideals yield to action. It is in that transition from theory to practice, that physical testing, that the most radical and compelling forms of learning take place.

The essays in this volume—and the student farm projects they represent—may not all explicitly address all these issues, but they all reflect a sense that student farms are somehow more than the sum of their parts and that it is this that makes them most valuable. Three themes that will recur in the following essays are worth pointing out here. The first is the issue of funding, or what might be called *the tension between production and instruction*. Many of the projects described in this book were launched with grant funding and have then, like all grant-funded programming, been faced with identifying new sources of revenue in order to continue their work. While some colleges and universities have found that student farms make excellent magnets for donor support, this situation can itself generate fresh challenges (e.g., if administrators feel that the student farm is drawing benefactor interest away from other projects deemed more vital). Managers of long-term student farm programs frequently find themselves having to argue that, as educational endeavors, student farms shouldn't be expected to pay for themselves any more than should basketball teams or history departments. (Another pertinent quote from L. H. Bailey: "To make a school farm pay for itself and for the school is impossible unless the school is a very poor or exceedingly small one.")[14] Younger student farms, on the other hand, are more likely to aim for financial self-sufficiency as a rationale for their continued existence. In this regard, the community-supported agriculture (CSA) model (in which farm customers pay an annual fee in exchange for a weekly share of the farm's harvest) has been crucial to many student farms' recent success. The CSA setup simplifies marketing in many respects, offers a fixed return relatively early in the season, and (at least in theory) creates a loyal clientele prepared to accept occasional crop failures or less-than-perfect produce.

In a sense, the issue of profitability falls doubly hard on student farms since many nonfarmers fail to understand the precarious economic terms of almost any contemporary agricultural enterprise. Simply put, it's not easy to make a living farming. On the one hand, starting a farm is like starting any business: it requires a certain amount of capital investment and the development and perfection of functional systems in order to reach a level of profitability or even to break even. Many business start-ups fail for all kinds of reasons, even those run by talented people with a promising new product or service to offer. Within the organic and sustainable farming community, five years is a generally accepted time frame for reaching that key profitability threshold, a time frame that may fall well outside the tolerance of the average benefactor or provost's office. On the other hand, many conventional farms today rely on federal subsidies to balance their books, the costs of production for many basic commodities—corn, soybeans, milk, sugarcane, cotton—frequently exceeding their farmgate price. A typical student farm must, therefore, attempt to establish a farming system that is a good deal more economically efficient than average, despite the fact that its primary purpose is the training of an inexperienced workforce. On top of all this, many student farms are sensitive about being perceived as unfairly competing with other area farmers in bringing their goods to market.

The second theme is intrinsically linked to the first and has to do with *striking a balance between student leadership and staff or faculty direction.* Should student farms be absolutely guided by students alone? For some, this would appear to be the essentially defining quality of a student farm endeavor. In practice, however, long-running campus farm programs usually find that some level of formal mentoring of students is essential. Student turnover and shifting student interests, the frequent overlap between spring planting and final exam periods, the need to negotiate among the varied priorities of different groups of students, and the concerns of administrators (with regard to issues like safety, aesthetics, and accountability) all lend weight to the establishment of a nonstudent student farm director of some sort. But, as will be seen in the following essays, these same faculty and staff directors remain highly conscious of the need to preserve spaces within the farm for the expression of student initiative and experimentation—not just for students' own satisfaction, but for the continued vitality of the whole project. Paradoxically, the longer a student farm is in operation, and the more firmly established it becomes on campus, it seems, the more likely students themselves are to lobby for the funding of a permanent staff position, despite the fact that the early years of the project, when students had to figure out everything for themselves, may be celebrated as having been among the most enriching. In a sense, student farms could be said to go through their own life cycle, with an early, slightly chaotic developmental phase followed by maturation into a more fixed form. The challenge is to maintain flexibility and preserve avenues for student input even as the operation grows larger and more complex.

The final theme of note relates to *the profound interdisciplinarity of student farming*. Although most student farms seem to find a home within environmental studies or agronomy/horticulture departments, others are housed elsewhere or exist independently. Regardless of a farm's departmental affiliation, moreover, participating students and faculty tend to come from all divisions of the college or university. College farms can be (and are) used as outdoor classrooms for courses in biology, economics, horticulture, animal husbandry, engineering, creative writing, history, anthropology, development studies, soil science, plant ecology, business management, and more. Remarkably, a survey of student farm managers and instructors conducted by Heather Karsten and her colleagues at Pennsylvania State University in 2007 found that the thirty-four respondents to the survey had taught a combined total of ninety-nine different courses to 2,965 students over the preceding three years.[15] If I had to guess, I'd venture that those roughly three thousand students represented dozens of different backgrounds, major fields of study, and future aspirations. As one researcher reporting on the University of Minnesota's new student farm project put it, "A student-run organic farm providing opportunities for experiential learning can uncover a population of students interested in growing organic food."[16] It's not necessarily clear, even to the organizers of a student farm, where the center of gravity of student support for the farm will eventually prove to be—and, indeed, that center may shift over time. This is just one way in which student farms challenge traditional disciplinary assumptions.

Among the three themes just outlined, the issue of interdisciplinarity, in my view, deserves special emphasis because it runs counter not just to prevailing ideas about agriculture and education but even to prevailing assumptions within the student farm movement. My own interest in student farms, it is perhaps worth specifying, originates not so much in direct experience with an on-campus farm project as in contending with its notable absence: I've never worked on a student farm (apart from a few days here and there), but I did a great deal of farming as a student. After spending three postcollege years at the Land Institute, in Kansas (where we had an intern program integrating organic gardening, agricultural field research work, reading and writing assignments, classroom discussions, regular guest lectures, and public programs), I spent most of my graduate school career working on an organic vegetable farm that is now one of the largest and most successful CSAs in the nation.[17] Most of my fellow graduate students and professors thought I was crazy, although a few came out to the farm to volunteer for an afternoon or became CSA members. Today, Princeton has a student-run garden, an on-campus farmers market, and a handful of courses relating to food and agriculture. It remains to be seen whether Princeton will take the next step and establish some kind of full-fledged food system studies program encompassing an experiential element.

It is an open question among student farm advocates whether the establishment of a student-managed organic garden at, say, Princeton University, Iowa State University, or Middlebury College represents the more radical step forward in the redefinition of food system education. For some observers, a primary distinction is to be drawn between student farms and gardens at schools *with* academic programs in agriculture and those at schools *without* academic programs in agriculture. Schools with academic programs in agriculture obviously have more immediate opportunities to link student farmwork to academic coursework. On the other hand, schools without academic programs in agriculture are in many ways freer to develop new linkages between the scholarly study of food, farm-

Figure I.5. February at the Hampshire College Farm Center. (Courtesy Laura Sayre.)

ing systems, and natural resource use (e.g., from the perspective of history, anthropology, geography, rural sociology, or American studies) and students' experience in the field (the real, physical field, the one with the soil and the plants in it). Students themselves can be extremely resourceful in pointing out these linkages: a group of students at Mount Holyoke College in Massachusetts, for example, strengthened their case for the establishment of a student garden on campus by pointing out that the school had created and maintained an extensive victory garden during and after the Second World War, providing a legitimating precedent in the eyes of college administrators. What unites agricultural and nonagricultural colleges and universities today, however, is that the majority of students at both now come to higher education without extensive previous farm experience, a situation that throws up for renegotiation most established assumptions about the role, structure, and objectives of agricultural education.

The student farm movement, in short, raises questions about pedagogy, about learning styles and methods, about the role of agriculture in contemporary cultural and economic life, about the organization of intellectual inquiry and academic thought. At its heart, it asks, Who should be farming? Who will be farming in the future? Where will new farming knowledge come from? How will old farming wisdom be transmitted and preserved? The widening crisis within mainstream agriculture on a global level has thrown all these questions up for debate. The deep diversity—this fertile chaos—within the goals and interests of student farming is, ultimately, one of its greatest strengths. It promises to reinvigorate higher education, public life, practical farming, and our collective future in the decades to come.

READING *FIELDS OF LEARNING*

As mentioned earlier, the essays in this book are organized chronologically by the year of each college farm's founding—those years being indicated by the date in parentheses following the name of each school in the chapter title. This arrangement highlights the historical unfolding of the student farm movement while revealing lines of influence and commonalities cutting across standard institutional categories (land-grant university, private liberal arts college, etc.). In engaging contributors, we sought to do justice to the diversity of programs and projects in operation and to represent the movement's geographic breadth while at the same time showcasing programs that have achieved a wide impact. There are, of course, many outstanding and influential programs in existence that, given space limitations, we were unable to include in this book. By way of partial recompense, and to illustrate the overall dimensions of the student farm movement, key information about every student farm project currently operating in the United States and Canada is included in the appendix to this book (although, given the dynamism of the movement, any list of this sort is necessarily provisional).

The body of this book is divided into four parts reflecting four phases of student farm development in North America. Part 1, "Roots," features farms established in the nineteenth century or the early twentieth, usually in near chronological proximity with the founding of their home institutions. The present volume includes essays describing student farm activities at Berea College, in Kentucky, where the farm has been a part of college life since 1871; at Wilmington College in Ohio, where the college farm dates to 1946; and at Sterling College in northeastern Vermont, which has had a farm since 1962. Other schools falling into this category include Deep Springs College in the high desert of eastern California (which has operated as part of a farm/ranch since its founding in 1917) and Warren Wilson College in North Carolina (originally founded as the Asheville Farm School in 1894).

To varying degrees, all these schools draw on a legacy of educational thought emphasizing a balance of physical and mental training. As early as the early nineteenth century, the manual labor school movement in the United States established farms and workshops at seminaries and academies in hopes of at once improving the scholars' health and helping defray the cost of their education.[18] Today, Berea, Sterling, the College of the Ozarks, and Warren Wilson are all federally recognized *work colleges*, a designation under which all students are required to participate in college-run labor programs, generally for ten to fifteen hours a week. By putting all students on a level playing field with regard to labor obligations, the work college system lends itself well to student farm activities, but work college farms still contend with many of the same challenges faced by student farms elsewhere. In chapter 1, Sean Clark, an associate professor of agriculture and natural resources at Berea College (and coeditor of this book), describes how the long history of the Berea College Farm reveals how few of the current tensions associated with student farming are really new: efforts to recycle food waste from student dining halls, for instance, met with practical difficulties a century ago, just as they do today. Clark's essay also shows how the larger historical and economic forces affecting agriculture in the United States over the past 150 years have necessitated a continual readjustment of the college farm's organization and rationale. Student farms must remain flexible to a changing agricultural landscape, he concludes, even as they seek to demonstrate new possibilities for sustainable farming.

Wilmington College, located in Wilmington, Ohio, and the subject of chapter 2, is one of a handful of *private* agricultural colleges remaining in the United States (others include Dordt College in Sioux Center, Iowa, and Delaware Valley College in Doylestown, Pennsylvania). Often operating with a strong religious affiliation, private agricultural colleges face an uphill battle in competing with their much larger and more numerous publicly funded counterparts, but they also enjoy advantages in being smaller and in some ways nimbler in their ability to respond to the changing needs of students and society. Colleges like Wilmington, in company with the land grants and the work colleges, were among the earliest to grapple with the nitty-gritty pedagogical dilemmas posed by student farm programs: How do you actually teach farming? How do you balance classroom time with field time? What kinds of reading and writing assignments are most useful? What about ancillary requirements, like language study or mathematics? Roy Joe Stuckey and Monte Anderson, former and current professors of agriculture at Wilmington, respectively, outline the history of the Wilmington College Farm, its role in the local community, and what it has meant to students over the years.

Chapter 3 tells the story of the Sterling College Farm, which in fact predates the college itself. Established in 1962 as an adjunct to what was then the Sterling School for Boys, the Sterling farm was originally conceived as a way of differentiating the school from its competitors as well as a means of cultivating discipline and practical competencies among its students. As Julia Shipley, former director of writing studies and faculty in sustainable agriculture at Sterling, explains, the experiment was so successful it managed to outlive the boys' school of which it formed a part. The Sterling farm became the central focus of a postgraduate program known as the Grass Roots Year, then a core element of Sterling College upon its accreditation in 1982. As a small (roughly one hundred students), environmentally focused college, Sterling has a unique ability to include the entire student body in its college farm activities, from doing farm chores to working with draft animals to managing the dining hall.

Part 2 of this book, "Back to the Land," includes farms established at colleges and universities during the back-to-the-land movement of the 1960s and 1970s. The most famous of these is undoubtedly the garden and farm complex established at the University of California, Santa Cruz (UCSC), by Alan Chadwick, a British expatriate, former actor, and expert gardener who arrived in Santa Cruz in 1967 and was commissioned to create a four-acre garden at the center of the University of California system's newest campus amid a background of widespread student unrest. (According to some reports, he was also an adjunct professor of English.) Transforming "a steep, south-facing hillside covered with chaparral" into a series of terraced beds managed according to what he called "biodynamic/ French intensive" methods, relying entirely on compost, hand tools, and hard work, Chadwick developed an informal apprenticeship system for the many students drawn to the beauty and purpose of the project.[19] Although Chadwick left Santa Cruz in 1972, the garden, farm, and apprenticeship model he founded were formalized two years later under the leadership of one of his protégés, Stephen Kaffka, and eventually developed into a six-month certificate course that has since trained more than a thousand students of all ages and many nationalities. The program gained important institutional reinforcement with the appointment of the agroecologist Stephen Gliessman to the UCSC Environmental Studies Department in the early 1980s. Now managed by the Center for Agroecology and Sustainable Food Systems (and operating independently of the university's degree-granting programs), the UCSC apprenticeship has had a deep impact on the sustainable agriculture movement as a whole. Its significance for today's student farm movement is evident, among other ways, in the fact that two of the contributors to the present volume—Tim Crews and Josh Slotnick—are graduates of the apprenticeship.

The essays in part 2 demonstrate how the winds of change buffeting the UCSC campus in the late 1960s and early 1970s were also making themselves felt elsewhere. The four student farm programs represented here—at Evergreen State College in Washington, at the University of Oregon, at the University of California, Davis, and at Hampshire College in Massachusetts—were all founded in the 1970s, but in distinct ways and with a variety of objectives. The stories of how these programs have developed and changed—and, above all, *survived*—over the past three to four decades offer useful lessons to newer projects just starting out. Founded in an era of mingled optimism and crisis, idealism and urgency, the 1970s student farms present instructive comparisons, as well as direct lines of influence, for today's efforts. Indeed, while in this volume we identify earlier origins for student farming, for some observers this 1960s- and 1970s-era phase represents the starting point of the contemporary movement.

At Evergreen State College, students created a farm in the first year of the college's existence. In the present volume, the faculty members Stephen Bramwell and Martha Rosemeyer and the farm manager and former Evergreen student Melissa Barker collaborate on a chapter describing how the first crop of Evergreen students discovered an old homestead in a forest clearing on the newly established campus and successfully lobbied for permission to renovate it, build a chicken coop nearby, and put in a garden. In the decades since, the farm has grown slowly but steadily, benefiting from, among other factors, Evergreen's intensive one-course-at-a-time academic structure. Greenhouses and other outbuildings have been designed and constructed as student projects, fields have been enlarged and enterprises added, and the farm as a whole has taken on an increasingly important role in the Evergreen curriculum.

The Urban Farm at the University of Oregon stands out among student farms as being the only such project (as far as we are aware) housed within a department of landscape architecture. Ann Bettman, an adjunct professor of landscape architecture at the University of Oregon and the faculty director of the farm for many years, recounts how the Urban Farm was established as part of a radical vision of how urban agriculture could reshape the small city of Eugene, connecting its residents to food production through a redesigning of the urban grid. Over the years, however, this grand vision has had to make room for more mundane concerns like how to balance efficiency and aesthetics in the layout of the growing areas, how to fend off university construction projects hungry for prime campus real estate, and how to organize a class that regularly draws up to one hundred students per term.

The founding of the Student Experimental Farm (SEF) at the University of California, Davis, represents a significant landmark within the movement: the establishment of the first student farm at a traditional land-grant university, a type of institution more commonly associated by the third quarter of the twentieth century with the promotion of conventional, input-intensive agriculture. Mark Van Horn, the director of the farm for more than two decades, explains how the project has emphasized the use of the SEF for graduate and undergraduate research while at the same time maintaining vegetable production, seed saving, and children's garden areas. In more recent years, the SEF has become central to the development of a new academic program in sustainable agriculture, an instance of how student farms can serve as incubators for curriculum development.

At Hampshire College, as at Evergreen, the establishment of an on-campus farm was closely linked to the school's identity as an experiment in alternative education, as Ray and Lorna Coppinger show in chapter 7. Founded in 1978, the farm was the focus of a handful of grant-funded projects conceived by Hampshire science faculty (Ray Coppinger among them) and designed to enable Hampshire students to engage in applied scientific research while considering the manifold problems of contemporary agriculture. Chief among these projects was the Coppingers' "livestock-guarding dog" research, a successful effort to promote the use of traditional European working-dog breeds as a nonlethal form of predator control for U.S. sheep producers. The dog project has since graduated, but the Hampshire College Farm Center remains as a diversified New England farm where students care for livestock, help manage a thriving CSA, make maple syrup, and pursue scientific and other academic research.

Part 3, "Coming of Age," reflects a maturation of the student farm movement in the 1990s. Dozens of student farms were established in this decade, making it particularly difficult to choose just four to include here: those at the University of Maine, at Central Carolina Community College, at Prescott College in Arizona, and at the University of Montana. In part, this efflorescence of student farming reflects a new level of institutional recognition for sustainable agriculture generally—as evidenced, for instance, by the creation of the USDA's Sustainable Agriculture Research and Education program in 1988. USDA programming was a source of both legitimacy and funding for faculty and students making a case for attention to agricultural values beyond the endless pursuit of increased production. The farm crisis of the 1980s—with its low commodity prices, falling land values, and staggering numbers of farm foreclosures—encouraged many within the agricultural establishment to reconsider their assumptions and to seek new routes for long-term agricultural viability. Forward-thinking farmers in many parts of the country began to develop low-input farming systems as a way of reducing costs and mitigating environmental and human health impacts. The idea of sustainable agriculture first began to hold its head high during this period.

The four student farms described in this section are based at four very different types of institutions. As Marianne Sarrantonio, a professor of sustainable cropping systems and the student farm faculty adviser, describes, the student farm at the University of Maine (UM) in Orono was an outgrowth of that school's new undergraduate major in sustainable agriculture (created in 1988, the first such program in the United States). After beginning their studies in sustainable agriculture, UM students asked for land to farm as a way of putting what they were learning into practice. The university agreed, and the outcome remains unique in terms of the level of independence granted to (or demanded of) the students. The Black Bear Food Guild receives relatively little official university support: students self-organize, receive minimum wage for their labor, and cover most of their own seed and other expenses (including land rent) from the sale of CSA shares. The arrangement is challenging but at the same time, Sarrantonio concludes, probably essential to the success of the school's sustainable agriculture program.

As a land-grant university, Maine was among the earliest to recognize what many other land grants have since been forced to acknowledge: that the pool of potential students for traditional agricultural programs was slowly drying up but that in its place was emerging a new demographic of young people interested in a different kind of farming and a different kind of education. If established agriculture programs are going to survive, they need to adapt to this new reality; otherwise, they may lose those students to institutions not traditionally associated with the teaching of farming. The remaining chapters in this section represent three such institutions. Central Carolina Community College created its five-acre Land Lab in 1996 as a way of meeting the emerging demand for vocational sustainable agriculture training in North Carolina and beyond. Conceived and developed by a coalition of local farmers, nonprofit groups, state university educators, and North Carolina cooperative extension personnel, the Land Lab (now known as the student farm) is the centerpiece of a two-year associate's degree in sustainable agriculture. Robin Kohanowich, the lead instructor for the program and the author of chapter 9, describes how students in the program value its emphasis on hands-on training and its strong ties to the local sustainable farming community. Many graduates have gone on to start farms of their own.

Prescott College, in Prescott, Arizona, is an environmentally oriented liberal arts college, another important type of school developing innovative approaches to the teaching of sustainable agriculture. In chapter 10, Tim Crews, a professor at Prescott since 1995, tells the story of how developing an educational farm was essential to his vision of Prescott's nascent program in agroecology. For Crews, the teaching of agroecological concepts and methods is the primary goal of the farm: optimizing the production and marketing of vegetables and other offerings must take second place. At the same time, however, Prescott has developed ancillary initiatives, like a network of on-campus vegetable gardens and a college-orchestrated regional CSA, to meet some of the other priorities associated with student farming, such as community involvement and exposure to food production for a wider segment of the student population.

The farm at the University of Montana is distinctive for its strong administrative partnership between the university's Environmental Studies Program and a local nonprofit called Garden City Harvest. Josh Slotnick, who has been involved with the PEAS (Program in Ecological Agriculture and Society) farm since its origins, emphasizes the importance of establishing a well-run farm, overseen by an experienced farmer, as a precondition for running an effective educational farm program. The PEAS farm thrives on its combination of community service and community involvement, production farming and student engagement, working a magic that, for Slotnick, is as much about cultivating an ethic of care as it is about teaching young people how to grow carrots—although it is that too.

The establishment of that transformative ethic, Slotnick argues, is what is truly radical about student farming.

Part 4 of this book, "New Directions," tracks a few of the many interesting developments in the student farm movement over the past ten years. If the 1990s phase of student farm establishment corresponds to the institutionalization of *sustainable* agriculture, the first decade of the twenty-first century witnessed the institutionalization of *organic* agriculture, represented first of all by the implementation of the National Organic Program standards within the USDA, creating a legally defined and enforceable label for organic foods. Although it is not possible for all student farms to be certified organic (usually because of space limitations and "buffer zone" requirements), for schools training students for careers in agriculture the teaching of organic techniques is becoming increasingly essential. In a workshop on organic horticultural education organized by the American Society for Horticultural Science in 2005, participants noted that traditional agricultural universities were developing undergraduate- and graduate-level training programs in organic agriculture in response to a variety of factors: declining enrollments in traditional agriculture programs; student demand for organic courses; a demographic shift in which even students in agriculture programs are less likely to have farming backgrounds, making experiential training more important; the remarkable expansion and success of the organic farming sector; and increased concerns about environmental impacts and sustainability. Fledgling programs generally feature a combination of classroom teaching and experiential training, a student farm or another facility as a central locus for that training, and "an applied marketing unit," usually a CSA.[20]

At the same time, the mainstreaming of organics has prompted many advocates to champion new goals for total food system sustainability, including the strengthening of local food networks, equitable access to healthy food for disadvantaged populations, and greater attention to global greenhouse gas budgets. Another new trend is the development of linkages by student farm and sustainable agriculture programs in the United States with parallel projects overseas, creating broader experiential opportunities for students, and taking advantage of cutting-edge work under way in many European and Latin American countries. The four programs represented in this section—at the University of British Columbia, New Mexico State University, Michigan State University, and Yale University—illustrate a range of possible responses to this new suite of challenges, each highly successful, and each promising even greater things to come.

The student farm at the University of British Columbia (UBC), in Vancouver, is unusual in that it was founded on the remains of the original UBC Farm, established in 1915 as part of the university's core mission to serve and train farmers in one of Canada's richest agricultural regions. By the end of the twentieth century, however, the university had moved away from its agricultural mission and had all but decided to pave over its remaining farm ground to build much-needed student housing in a city with some of the highest land values on the North American continent. In chapter 12, the UBC Farm program coordinator Mark Bomford describes how more than a decade of student and community activism has gone into saving the UBC Farm as a place to grow food, study agroecological relationships, educate young people, engage community groups, and much more. We should point out as well that, although this is our only Canadian example in the book, student farming is in evidence elsewhere among our northern neighbors. The University of Guelph in Ontario established the first North American undergraduate major in organic agriculture in 2005 and has since broken ground on a one-hectare on-campus center for urban organic farming to enhance hands-on learning opportunities for its students. College farms are also in operation in Nova Scotia and Quebec.

The OASIS project at New Mexico State University represents a valiant effort to make space for small-scale, organic vegetable production within a relatively conservative agricultural institution. Connie Falk, a professor of agricultural economics and the OASIS project leader, describes how she and a handful of other faculty and staff developed a course centered on the establishment of a one-acre CSA, keeping detailed records of inputs and outputs, and encouraging associated independent student projects that took the lessons of OASIS to other parts of campus as well as out into the greater Las Cruces community. Although the OASIS course and CSA had to be suspended after the grant that had helped get them started came to an end, students at the university are currently campaigning to get the student farm project reestablished.

Michigan State University's Student Organic Farm has grown dramatically since its founding in 2003, illustrating a different path forward for a land-grant university responding to the new world of organics. John Biernbaum, a professor of horticulture and the project's faculty adviser, worked with students to develop a forty-eight-week CSA based on extensive use of high tunnels (unheated greenhouses), maximum crop diversity, and continual soil building. While the production system has been enormously successful, the program is still experimenting with the associated curriculum setup, which currently includes a full-time certificate program in addition to a four-year concentration for horticulture majors.

Yale University is not the first Ivy League school to create a student farm—that honor is shared by Cornell University and Dartmouth College, which have both had active student farm projects in place since 1996—but it has certainly been the one to attract the most attention. Founded in 2003 with support from the celebrity chef and organic food advocate Alice Waters, the Yale Sustainable Food Project (YSFP) features a one-acre organically managed garden in addition to a vibrant series of lectures, workshops, and other public events highlighting the importance of healthful, locally grown food for all eaters. As Melina Shannon-DiPietro explains in chapter 15, the YSFP employs student interns to manage the garden and host events, funds food- and farming-related student research projects, and encourages the development of courses across campus that explore YSFP themes. It has also played a central role in the university's sustainable dining initiative, encouraging the use of fresh, locally grown and organic ingredients, and coordinates a freshman-orientation program putting students to work on area farms.

Taken as a whole, the essays in this collection illuminate the persistent obstacles as well as the remarkable triumphs of student farming over the past century and more. From one perspective, student farms are simply farms—subject like all agricultural enterprises to market pressures, infrastructural concerns, intergenerational conflicts, shifting definitions of best management practices, and the vagaries of the weather. From another perspective, they are absolutely unique: liminal spaces on the border between community and institution that are relatively insulated from the market, powered by the energy and enthusiasm of twenty-somethings, and enriched by the intellectual resources of academe. In this view, student farms can't help but break new ground—they are inherently positioned to challenge not just the nature of agriculture but also the nature of education. While existing student farm projects are remarkably diverse, successful campus farms share an ability to build on the specific strengths of their home institutions. As a number of the contributors to this volume point out, there is no single recipe for successful student farming. But the stories in this book present a rich and detailed series of examples of the many ways in which student farms are fostering a reintegration of culture and agriculture across North America and beyond.

NOTES

1. The College Sustainability Report Card 2009, Categories: Food and Recycling, http://www.greenreportcard.org/report-card-2009/categories/food-recycling.

2. Scott Carlson, "The Farmer in the Quad," *Chronicle of Higher Education,* March 28, 2008, available at http://chronicle.com/weekly/v54/i29/29a00401.htm.

3. Colin Duncan, *The Centrality of Agriculture: Between Humankind and the Rest of Nature* (McGill-Queen's University Press, 1996).

4. For details on the Sustainable Agriculture Education Association, visit http://sustainableaged.org. Another venue for these interinstitutional conversations is the Association for the Advancement of Sustainability in Higher Education, www.aashe.org.

5. U.S. Code Title 7, chap. 13, sec. 304 ("The Morrill Act").

6. See Ben A. Minteer, *The Landscape of Reform: Civic Pragmatism and Environmental Thought in America* (Cambridge, MA: MIT Press, 2006).

7. L. H. Bailey, *The Country-Life Movement in the United States* (1911), in *Liberty Hyde Bailey: Essential Agrarian and Environmental Writings,* ed. Zachary Michael Jack (Ithaca, NY: Cornell University Press, 2008), 128, 131.

8. André Mayer and Jean Mayer, "Agriculture, the Island Empire," *Daedalus: Journal of the American Academy of Arts and Sciences* 103, 3 (Summer 1974): 83.

9. Ibid., 84, 90.

10. See David W. Orr, *Ecological Literacy: Education and the Transition to a Postmodern World* (Albany: State University of New York Press, 1992), which includes a "Great Books" list for ecological education, broadly defined.

11. David Orr, "Agriculture and the Liberal Arts," in *Earth in Mind: On Education, Environment and the Human Prospect* (Washington, DC: Island Press, 1994), 117–21.

12. Brian Donahue, "The Resettling of America," in *The Essential Agrarian Reader: The Future of Culture, Community, and the Land,* ed. Norman Wirzba (Lexington: University Press of Kentucky, 2003), 47.

13. Bailey, *Country-Life Movement,* 128.

14. Ibid., 131.

15. Heather D. Karsten, Kathryn Bullington, and Nancy Ellen Kiernan, "Survey of US Student Teaching Farms and Their Educational Value," paper presented at the joint annual meeting of the American Society of Agronomy, the Crop Science Society of America, and the Soil Science Society of America, Houston, October 6, 2008.

16. Albert H. Markhartt III, "Organic Educational Opportunities at the University of Minnesota: The Role of a Student-Run Organic Farm," *HortTechnology* 16, no. 3 (July–September 2006): 443.

17. The Watershed Organic Farm, now Honey Brook Organic Farm, located on land belonging to the Stony Brook–Millstone Watershed Association, in Pennington, NJ.

18. L. F. Anderson, "The Manual Labor School Movement," *Educational Review* 46 (November 1913): 369–86. See also Herbert G. Lull, "The Manual Labor Movement in the United States," *Bulletin of the University of Washington, University Studies* no. 8 (July 1914), 375–85 (reprinted from *Manual Training Magazine,* June 1914).

19. Martha Brown, "Alan Chadwick Garden Celebrates 35th Anniversary," *Pacific Horticulture,* October–December 2003, 15–21. See also Jennifer McNulty, "Breaking New Ground: UCSC Celebrates 40 Years at the Forefront of Sustainable Agriculture," *UC Santa Cruz Review,* Fall 2007, 12.

20. M. Ngouajio, K. Delate, E. Carey, A. N. Azarenko, J. J. Ferguson, and W. J. Sciarappa, "Curriculum Development for Organic Horticulture: Introduction," *HortTechnology* 16, no. 3 (July–September 2006): 414–17. For more extended discussion of many of these issues, see also the recent study published by the National Research Council's Committee on a Leadership Summit to Effect Change in Teaching and Learning, *Transforming Agricultural Education for a Changing World* (Washington, DC: National Academies Press, 2009).

◆ Part 1 ◆

Roots

1

Berea College (1871)

The Work College Legacy

SEAN CLARK

Berea College, one of several federally recognized work colleges, has one of the oldest continuously operating student educational farms in the United States. All students at Berea participate in a labor program in exchange for a full-tuition scholarship, the Berea College Farm being one of the larger employers on the campus. While the work that the more than fifteen hundred students on campus do undoubtedly contributes to the institution and may reduce the need for some full-time staff positions, most of the actual costs of education are covered by the college's endowment rather than by the work the students do. In fact, although the labor program was an important means of keeping costs down in the early years, it is more often understood today as an integral part of student education. Throughout the college farm's 140-year history, it has helped prepare students for careers in agriculture and related endeavors, provided them with work opportunities and income during college, and functioned as a business. This multipurpose operation has been and continues to be a source of pride as well as tension for the college as a whole.

The Berea College Farm is located in a hilly region of Kentucky referred to as the "Knobs," situated between the Cumberland Plateau to the southeast and the Bluegrass region to the northwest. It comprises about five hundred acres of mostly contiguous land, dissected by the roads, railroad tracks, houses, and buildings of the small city that now surrounds it and the college that established it. About 90 percent of the farm's acreage is used for livestock, including cattle, hogs, and goats, or the crops grown to feed those livestock, such as corn, fescue, and alfalfa.

The remaining land includes about twelve acres for horticultural and field crops for human consumption and the steep wooded hillsides and riparian areas not used for production. The farm is a major feature in the area's landscape, blending scenic vistas of agrarian and natural beauty with elements of industrial infrastructure, sometimes decaying and inelegant, but still mostly functional.

The farm possesses an instructive heritage of agricultural experiences that mirror in microcosm many of those of the nation. That history in turn offers insights into the possibilities and limitations of educational farms as part of the curricula and infrastructure of colleges and universities. Today, financial and environmental uncertainties affecting society in general and higher education in particular are putting the farm under greater scrutiny. Faculty, staff, and students are debating the educational benefits and relevance of current management practices in the context of increasing agricultural industrialization, farm specialization, and economic globalization; students are asking why the farm doesn't grow more food for them to eat in the dining hall; and some faculty and administrators are asking why it costs so much to run. But, in looking back, we find that, in fact, all these questions and divergent expectations have been a part of the farm since its beginning.

ESTABLISHING THE FARM

Founded by abolitionists in 1855, Berea College began as a small school with a mission that continues today—to provide interracial and mixed-gender education to those with financial need and a willingness to work for the opportunity. The earliest years of the institution, immediately preceding the Civil War, were turbulent as local resistance to the school and its mission manifested itself in mob threats toward John Fee and his fellow founders.[1] Yet, with devotion to their cause, support from people and organizations in the North, and assistance from some local residents, including Cassius M. Clay, a well-known emancipationist from the region who provided some land and money, the founders operated the school until the beginning of the Civil War. In 1865, they returned from their temporary residence in Ohio, where they had relocated during the war, and reopened the school as the Berea Literacy Institute. Additional land was purchased, new buildings were erected, and the size and scope of the institution were expanded. In 1869, the first president of the college, Edward Fairchild, took office, and the first college class entered. In his inaugural address,

Fairchild stated that the college would do whatever possible to keep costs to students low and provide them with the means of self-support. According to Fairchild, almost anyone "who can show themselves competent and reliable can find all the work they can do."[2] At a time when half the U.S. population was involved with farming, agriculture must have seemed like an obvious and compatible source of employment for these students.

The earliest agricultural efforts of the college were modest. In 1871, a garden of about an acre and a half was established in conjunction with the college's boarding hall, and a few cows were kept for milk. A decade later, President Fairchild seemed neither impressed nor optimistic about the future prospects of farming at Berea. "Our students are engaged in making roads at Berea," he told a conference of college executives in 1881. "They have never tried to run a farm. I have seen student efforts to run a farm, but they have never amounted to much. I do not think it can be made successful. I would not undertake to run a garden with students. I can make a good garden but I have never seen a student who could do it."[3] Such a discouraging appraisal of student capabilities did not seem to bode well for the future of the Berea College Farm. But Berea's third president, William Frost, appeared more confident and enthusiastic, at least initially, about the prospect of farming as a meaningful and profitable endeavor for the college and its students.

Frost thought that it made little sense for the college to rent out its farmland to others while purchasing food produced hundreds of miles away and shipped in by railroad from Cincinnati. What was needed, he thought, was an expert, properly educated and thoroughly trained at a land-grant college, who could teach good farming practices, supervise and train students who would work on the farm to support themselves, and do whatever was necessary to improve the productivity of the college's farmland. While the search for this "scientific agriculturalist" was on, the college purchased additional land adjacent to the campus to expand the garden operation in 1895. (Some of this land is still part of the college farm today.) This investment coincided with a steep increase in student enrollment, providing a substantial labor force for horticultural crop production. Photographs taken during this time show teams of students, many from Berea's primary school, performing rigorous, manual field tasks such as hoeing weeds and harvesting, a sight that might generate shock and accusations of child exploitation today.

Though there was still no college academic program in agriculture, in 1897 Silas C. Mason, a graduate of Kansas Agricultural College (now

Kansas State University), was hired as the superintendent of grounds and professor of horticulture and biology. He was given enormous responsibilities for expanding and improving the farm, establishing a forestry operation, and cooperating with the farm manager on projects including fencing, road building, and field drainage in addition to teaching courses. It's hard to imagine a college administration today having similarly broad expectations for one employee. When Mason began his work, there were more than a hundred students (all male) engaged in farming and related activities for their jobs at Berea.

Two years after Mason's arrival, President Frost evidently was growing impatient with the farm as well as with Mason's progress in improving it. In an 1899 letter about the college farm, he wrote: "I am beginning to be disappointed that the farm does not bring in more. Last year we sunk a good deal in it, but this year it ought to do better than it is doing in the way of production. The cold frames and gardens ought to succeed, whereas they have been less productive than before we had scientific direction!"[4] In Mason's opinion, poor soil drainage was the main culprit limiting production; he recommended that the college invest in installing drainage tile. But Frost considered the cost too high and decided that such a project would have to wait until the college could manufacture its own clay drainage tile. More than a century later, poor drainage continues to limit the farm's productivity.

COMPETING PURPOSES

In 1912, two years before the passage of the Smith-Lever Act establishing the Cooperative Extension Service, a USDA special investigator named Frank Montgomery was appointed to Berea College to conduct on-farm demonstrations in the region. This predecessor to the county extension agent was technically not an employee of the college but did teach animal husbandry during the winter months, when area farmers were more likely to have the time to attend class. The college began offering a two-year agriculture diploma program through its School of Agriculture that included courses in agronomy, horticulture, forestry, animal science, and farm management. In an attempt to reach out to students unable to commit to a two-year program, fourteen-week short programs were also offered. According to a promotional pamphlet from 1914, the instructors of the School of Agriculture were "Christian men who have had practical experience and possess rare skills and ability in the different branches taught, and

Figure 1.1. Cultivating an area of the Berea College Farm currently known as the West Gardens with mule traction ca. 1915. (Courtesy Berea College Archives.)

to have them as instructors and friends is an inestimable privilege." The total cost for the program, including room and board, was less than $30 per term (three terms per year). The pamphlet also stated that "opportunities for self-help" were available, including positions in the shops, farm, and garden.[5]

Archived administrative reports and letters offer evidence about the conflicts that emerged between the farm as a business and its roles as a teaching facility and source of employment for students. In 1913, the college gardener was expected to provide a "cheap and abundant" supply of produce for the boarding hall while at the same time instructing students in the "science and art of gardening" and maintaining good records on "expenditures and experiments" in order to improve and pass on knowledge about gardening in general and the college gardens in particular. In addition, this person was expected to oversee maintenance of the campus grounds. Given all these demanding and sometimes conflicting responsibilities, it comes as little surprise that he struggled to operate the greenhouse profitably. The student workers were reportedly inexperienced ("green"), the cost of heating the greenhouse was too high, and the market for cut flowers was insufficient—"not enough deaths and marriages and the buying of expensive flowers by the students is prohibitive." Further, the labor program was inherently inefficient because the students worked for short periods in between classes. Half-day work periods were implemented for a while and were a "decided success" but apparently resulted in difficulties in scheduling and attending classes. The 1915 annual report of the college farm stated: "We might neglect the instruction of the boy in order to make our work pay. . . . We are sacrificing the opportunities of many a student because we are trying to make their labor pay in dollars and cents." High student turnover, inadequate supervision, and difficulty in marketing and selling products, even to the college itself, were frequently mentioned causes for the farm's financial problems.[6]

Local food enthusiasts and recycling advocates on campuses today will empathize with the problems encountered by those managing the Berea College Farm a hundred years ago. Many ideas that seemed simple and sensible in principle proved difficult to put into practice. For example, the farm maintained a small herd of dairy cows to supply milk to the boarding hall and hospital, but summer vacations led to an inconsistent demand. When the pastures were lush and the milk supply was most abundant, there were too few students to consume it. Exacerbating the situation, the boarding hall would often refuse to buy the milk in the spring when the cows were grazed on rye because of the "slight bitter taste" it reportedly caused in the milk. Unfortunately, rye was considered the only economical crop for spring pasture at the time. Hog production also suffered frustrating setbacks. The brood sows and piglets were typically fed kitchen scraps and food waste collected from the boarding hall. But, just as campus recycling programs today struggle with trash in collection receptacles, contamination of the hogs' food scraps with broken glass and other inedible debris caused gastrointestinal problems in the animals. Episodes of resource mismanagement, inadequate planning, and financial loss also occurred in the farm's horticultural enterprise, with complete crop failures due to planting too late, poor yields due to inadequate drainage and liming, postharvest losses due to delays in getting produce to markets in Lexington, and low prices paid for produce sold locally, especially when yields were high.[7]

Despite the sometimes frustrating conditions and apparent inefficiencies on the college farm, however, there was still recognition, at least by some, of the progress achieved and the resulting benefits to students and the region. Educating student workers on a farm required resources, such as compassionate and capable instructors and time for learning, and,

Figure 1.2. Student work crew in the college gardens ca. 1915. (Courtesy Berea College Archives.)

therefore, some losses beyond those typically factored into an agricultural business had to be expected. The farm not only produced crops and live-stock but also, more importantly, educated graduates who would lead more fruitful lives and make greater contributions to society. The dean of the college's Vocational School, Frances Clark, wrote in 1915: "The careful observation of the workings of Nature under our immediate conditions is the most effective means of improving our profits and pleasures. The young men who work on our College Garden have a great opportunity to see what can be done by improved methods and the most important thing is that they learn the principles, so that they can put them into practice on their own farms."[8]

As this sentiment suggests, the mission of the farm was understood at least by some to extend beyond vocational training in farming: the ulti-mate goal was the cultural enrichment of individual lives as a means of solving societal problems in the region. Although the 1915 annual garden report includes numerous summaries of crop yields and farm budgets, it also describes the farm as being one element in the broader education of students. History, literature, art, music, and science were also recognized as essential subjects that would help students "find enjoyment in living." The report expresses a concern that land resources were declining, the prospect of owning land disappearing for many, and the human population approaching a level that would exceed the capacities of the land to support it. Poor students from the region would need the skills and experience to find opportunities and make the most of them to ensure their independence and security. "The rapid increase in our population, together with our present destructive methods of farming, is forcing upon us this intensive farming," Clark lamented, adding, "It is certainly the desire of the Vocational Dean to not have any man work on the Garden who is interested only in his eight or ten cents per hour. One of the main objects of the Garden is to train young men how to practice proper methods of gardening and to show them how it is possible to feed a large number of people from a small acreage."[9]

REAFFIRMING ITS EDUCATIONAL PURPOSE

In 1923, more than fifty years after the first garden was established on campus, agriculture was finally listed in the Berea College catalog as an academic major for a bachelor's degree. This allowed the operations and expenses of the farm to be more easily justified as supporting the academic goals of the college, rather than simply providing student employment, enhancing vocational training, and supplying food products for college use or income generation. From now on, the farm would be the educational laboratory of the college's Department of Agriculture, where "good farming practices" would be demonstrated and taught. By the early 1930s, the farm had grown in size and complexity to include sixty acres of fruits and vegetables, a cannery, a landscape nursery operation, and a dairy in addition to hogs, sheep, poultry, and several hundred acres of field crops and pasture. Dozens of students worked in these enterprises, producing food that was used by the college and sold locally. The dairy operation in particular was held in high regard as an example of a successful, modern, and efficient business enterprise. Nevertheless, William Baird, a professor of agriculture and the department chair at the time, cautioned: "We must never feel that the production of milk for our boarding hall is the primary function of our dairy. It is a very important function, but the educational value of our dairy work . . . is a far greater mission."[10]

By this period, the college had also invested in a new building on campus to house the Department of Agriculture, which included dairy and animal husbandry laboratories, refrigerators, pasteurizers, bottling

machines, laboratory tables, slaughtering equipment, and cheesemaking equipment. According to promotional material, the three classrooms
were "admirably equipped with running water, laboratory desks, cabinets,
tables, etc." Over one hundred students were enrolled in college courses
in agriculture each year and at the same time working on the farm to "pay
their school expenses and gain invaluable experience."[11] There were eight
full-time employees, including a county extension agent who was based at
the college. The prominent status of agriculture at Berea College during
the 1920s and 1930s resulted in part from the Smith-Lever Act of 1914
and the Smith-Hughes Act of 1917. The former, as we have seen, established the Cooperative Extension Service, and the latter provided support
to educate and employ vocational agriculture teachers in public schools.
Both these laws generated support for the academic program and a wider
range of employment options for Berea College graduates. Farm numbers, size, and productivity had also been relatively stable in the United
States during the first three decades of the twentieth century, giving the
impression that the future would hold promising opportunities for those
wishing to make a living from farming. That, however, would soon begin
to change.

Practical Limitations

Technological innovations, greater use of fossil fuel–powered mechanization, and remarkable increases in farm productivity beginning in the
1930s and continuing throughout the rest of the twentieth century led to
unanticipated and lasting changes in farming both as a way of life and as
a source of employment. During this seventy-year period, the Berea College Farm would have to adapt to ensure its economic survival, and the
academic department would have to be responsive to maintain its relevance. In 1938, the farm's enterprises included a 75-cow dairy herd; a
creamery for making butter, cheese, and cottage cheese; a beef cattle herd
of 20 head; a sheep flock with 75 ewes; about 125 meat hogs; 350 acres
of farmland for pasture, silage, hay, and grain production; a flock of 1,000
laying hens; a newly added turkey production operation; and 60 acres of
vegetable gardens. The farm also oversaw 140 acres of campus landscape
and 5,600 acres of forest. Though impressive for a program with fewer
than ten faculty and staff members, the farm continued to wrestle with
many of the same problems that demanded so much attention when it
was first established nearly seventy years earlier: high labor costs, inex-

perienced student labor that required considerable supervision, and poor soil drainage, all of which translated into continued financial pressures. To overcome these challenges, it had to develop and invest in new, profitable enterprises and discontinue those that had become a financial drain on the college.

During the 1940s, the farm experimented with some nontraditional crops, including hemp for seed and belladonna for medicinal purposes, and established a small apiary for honey production, though none of these enterprises persisted for long. The Agriculture Department's vocational agriculture teacher program was popular and well regarded, though many of the graduates entered the military rather than careers in teaching. In the decades that followed, land-use pressures around the campus and town, as well as occasional vandalism, resulted in the relocation of parts of the farm—the livestock enterprises in particular—to a recently purchased tract of land about a mile from campus. This meant that students would need daily transportation to move between the campus and the farm, an additional burden for the farm. In 1966, the new department chair, Robert Johnstone, wrote that there had been an "inability or failure to clearly delineate between commercial and educational programs" on the farm and that the student labor program would have to be modified so that "students might be more productively and educationally employed." He continued, "The problems of scheduling blocks of time sufficient to permit the student[s] to be productive are difficult."[12] Three years later, he closed the dairy to cut financial losses. About a decade later, the poultry operation was discontinued for the same reason. In the 1980s, the farm quit producing tobacco (for ethical reasons) and gave over responsibility for maintaining the campus grounds to the nonacademic department responsible for facilities upkeep. Today, the college's forest, consisting of about eight thousand acres, is also under the management of a nonacademic Forestry Department consisting of only two staff members and loosely affiliated with the Agriculture and Natural Resources Department.

In addition to eliminating programs and giving up responsibilities, the farm also changed its approach to marketing. The amount and variety of foods sold to the campus food service (for student consumption) and to the college-run hotel, the Boone Tavern, had dropped off in the decades following World War II. The college had also discontinued its canning and baking operations. By the 1980s, there was very little food from the farm being used directly by the college. Crops were grown to feed livestock, and the livestock were sold live either at auction, to corporate meat packers in the region, or occasionally to individuals in and around town for home processing and consumption. Commodity market prices were often below the cost of production, so generating a profit, even with government subsidies, was no longer an objective. The goals of the farm had gradually shifted away from achieving institutional food self-sufficiency with the college's land resources to providing students with practical work experience on a farm while minimizing the amount of money lost in the process. Such a situation could not be sustained for long. In addition to the financial burden, there were legitimate questions about what exactly students could learn by working on a farm that used conventional equipment and inputs and the latest management recommendations from land-grant universities and cooperative extension—yet still was unable to generate a profit or even break even.

ADAPTING TO THE NEW LANDSCAPE

Like millions of other farms in the United States, the Berea College Farm struggled under the pressures imposed on it by a changing economy. In several fundamental ways, the college farm's transformation since the 1930s parallels those in agriculture across the nation. According to USDA statistics, the average farm in 1930 was about 160 acres in size and produced four to five commodities; in 2000, the average farm was about 460 acres and produced only one to two commodities. The number of farms in the United States declined from roughly 6 million to 2 million, and the proportion of the population involved in farming dropped from 20 percent to less than 2 percent.[13] During that same period, the Berea College Farm eliminated several major enterprises, including dairy and poultry, and substantially reduced the scale of others, including horticulture, in order to specialize in the remaining crop and livestock enterprises. The number of students enrolled in the B.S. program in agriculture declined by about half, and a decreasing fraction of incoming students arrived at the school already possessing significant agricultural experience. With so few graduates entering farming as a career in recent decades, at least full-time, and shrinking opportunities for employment in cooperative extension and vocational agriculture education, the farm has been faced with important practical and philosophical questions. Should it continue to rely so heavily on student labor when the prevailing trend is to mechanize? Which technologies should it adopt and on what basis? What can graduating students go on to do in agriculture, and how can the farm remain relevant to their needs?

In addition to the financial and employment obstacles in agriculture today, concerns over the unanticipated environmental and societal effects resulting from decades of agricultural industrialization now demand a place in public debate. The sustainable agriculture movement of the 1980s grew out of an effort to address the complex and interrelated economic, social, and environmental issues associated with the modern agrifood system that now produces most of what we eat. Berea College responded to these often-intertwined concerns and tensions by holding an agricultural summit in 1997 to explore possible new directions for the college farm and Agriculture Department so as to better serve students and to adhere more strongly to the college's mission, which includes promoting values such as equality, plain living, work with dignity, and concern for the welfare of others. A number of prominent thinkers and writers, including Wendell Berry, David Orr, and Dean Freudenberger, participated in the event and, not surprisingly, offered harsh critiques of the industrial food system and a call for higher education to provide leadership in changing it. The summit was a turning point for the academic department, which was renamed the Department of Agriculture and Natural Resources, and for the farm, marking the beginning of a cascading series of changes that continue today.

Choosing a Future

As the Berea College Farm looks toward the future, it has become increasingly apparent that maintaining one foot on each of two diverging paths is no longer a tenable position. The farm cannot serve as an example of a modern, industrialized, high-input system with the goal of maximizing output for an unpredictable commodity market while depending on government subsidies for financial survival—and at the same time demonstrate ecologically based practices that reduce financial vulnerability and environmental impact through crop diversification, integration of crop and livestock production systems, and the localization of food systems. But there is risk in choosing either path. To discard the industrial model that now prevails means that students may fail to gain skills and experiences deemed essential by agrifood corporations and industries, thus limiting their possible job opportunities. In fact, some alumni and faculty have criticized the farm's limited adoption of organic and low-input practices

Figure 1.3. The Berea College Farm has a strong emphasis on livestock production, especially beef cattle and hogs. Here, the student management team member, Peter Thiong, is with the farm's cattle herd in 2008. (Courtesy Berea College Department of Agriculture and Natural Resources.)

already, considering them unrealistic and even dangerous. Conversely, it seems misleading, or even dishonest, to continue portraying highly capital-intensive and resource-demanding crop and livestock production systems as an economically viable option for beginning farmers or as an ecologically sustainable means of food production for the decades to come. Ideally, in the spirit of free inquiry and a liberal arts education, we would offer students experiential opportunities within both models, particularly since there are uncertainties in choosing either. But, in attempting to balance two vastly different and contrary systems, we lose our ability to manage either as effectively as we should and, thus, handicap and limit the potential of both.

It seems prudent to consider the past 140 years of successes and failures for guidance when envisioning the Berea College Farm's possible futures. Doing so reminds us that the quest to meet budgets and income goals can cause us to lose sight of the fact that the primary purpose of the farm is to provide a practical learning laboratory for students. This fact shouldn't be used as a crutch or an excuse to explain away losses and inefficiencies; careless decisions and costly mistakes can't be tolerated. But it does give a high priority to designing the farm's operations and infrastructure to safely accommodate inexperienced workers and justifies efforts to make connections between class and farm experiences so that students have the opportunity to seek out explanations and solve problems on the basis of sound knowledge and practical experience, even if it costs more. In accounting for farm costs, there must be a distinction between those that are required for the business and those that are necessary to support student education. The farm's history teaches us that the enterprises need to be flexible and adaptable to respond to unanticipated external factors, such as changes in the price and availability of inputs, market demand for products, government policies and legislation, public opinion, and, now, a changing climate. This means rationally negotiating the farm's dependence on infrastructural, human, and natural capital in such a way that maintains some balance between short-term financial efficiency and longer-term resilience.

What does this approach look like in practice on the Berea College Farm? The fifty or so students who work there participate in all aspects of the farm's operations, at least initially. Though this policy isn't always popular with students and definitely isn't an efficient way to use the ten to fifteen hours per week they work (usually in two-hour blocks), this breadth of experience is necessary to demonstrate the interdependencies that exist among the different enterprises that make up the farm as a whole. Management decisions made for one enterprise almost always have some effect on the resources available for others, and it's important that students understand that. Later, with guidance from faculty or staff mentors, students can gain more specialized training in financial, resource, and marketing decisions and analysis as well as in supervision of an individual enterprise—selecting from beef cattle, hogs, goats, the feed mill, horticultural crops, or field crops—so that over the course of their four years they move from performing a wide variety of menial but essential labor tasks, like feeding livestock or weeding gardens, to more complex challenges, like analyzing and adjusting crop rotations and livestock genetics, purchasing inputs like seeds, semen, and equipment, establishing short- and long-term priorities for specific enterprises like production goals and marketing strategies, and testing new ideas with on-farm research projects.

In the late 1990s, all the horticultural production—about five acres of vegetables, fruits, herbs, and ornamentals—was transitioned to certified organic management after a small group of students pushed for it. A food waste composting operation, initially established as a pilot project, now generates over thirty tons of compost annually, compost that is applied to fields or used as a potting medium.[14] In 2008, a small fraction of the farm's field cropland was put under organic management, more than doubling the certified organic acreage. Several acres of certified organic corn and wheat are now being grown, ground, and sold as flour and cornmeal. Current plans call for transitioning much of the remaining pasture, hay, and row crop acreage to organic management over the next five years, a challenging endeavor that will require longer crop rotations with more legume-based, perennial forage crops and fewer grain crops. The ability to integrate grazing animals into the rotations will provide more management options for controlling weeds, utilizing forages efficiently, and cycling nutrients within the farm. This new management direction should encourage long-term resiliency and open up new crop production and marketing opportunities. Student-initiated changes in the farm's livestock production are also under way, including shifting part of the beef production enterprise from feedlot finishing on grain to intensive rotational grazing and transitioning the hog production from confinement feeding to an outdoor, pasture-based system. These changes represent instances of students seeking creative ways to reduce production costs, risk, and the ecological footprint of the farm.

Financial management and marketing, often less appealing to students than production tasks and historically left to faculty and staff to handle, have gained more prominent roles in the student labor program of late. Students now contribute their expertise and creativity to monitoring costs and sales returns and market testing new value-added products, including baked goods from the wood-fired brick oven, which was built by students in a course in 2009. The horticultural enterprise experimented with community-supported agriculture from 1999 to 2003, and, though consumer demand was high and students were enthusiastic, the program was discontinued because too few students remained on campus during the summer to benefit from this educational opportunity. Now the farm markets an increasing quantity of vegetables and fruits, as well as meats and other products, through its Web-based store, at the local farmers market, and to the college's dining hall throughout the academic year. Students are taking leadership roles in all this, and, in 2004, some even formed a group with

Figure 1.4. Students in the course "Bees and Beekeeping" involved in maintaining the small apiary at the college gardens. (Courtesy Frances Buerkens.)

interested faculty and staff called the Local Foods Initiative to push for more local foods in the college dining hall and to promote to the campus community the farmers market where the college farm sells much of its pork, beef, vegetables, fruits, honey, and mushrooms.

It would be misleading, however, to suggest that the students working on the college farm are uniformly passionate about food and the environment or share a single vision of what the college farm should be. More than half of incoming freshmen selecting agriculture and natural resources as their major aspire to become veterinarians when they arrive (though very few maintain that goal until graduation). They request a labor position on the farm because of the livestock but may have little to no interest in the horticultural enterprise or even in crop production in general. By contrast, the minority of students arriving with an interest in ecologically based agriculture and environmental studies are sometimes discouraged by the livestock-heavy focus of the farm, which they see as ecologically or ethically problematic, and often don't seek a position on the farm until their second or third year at the college, when they can choose not to work in the livestock enterprises and, instead, specialize more in what they like. But, increasingly, there are students who see and understand the important connections between the various crop and livestock enterprises, a stated goal of the curriculum, and are able to bridge differences and promote interactions and collaborations that rise above the varying interests and opinions surrounding the farm. In comparison to a decade ago, the cohort of students working on the farm today is more cohesive and cooperative and has a more obvious common desire to see the *whole* farm succeed and thrive. Nowhere is this more evident than at the local farmers market in mid-November, where students of the college farm sell chorizo (made with a recipe developed and taste tested by students) alongside certified organic greens, winter squash, and stone-ground cornmeal while offering ready-to-eat black bean chili (vegetarian or pork) with cornbread made almost exclusively from ingredients produced on the farm.

In some ways, the Berea College Farm is being restored to an earlier version of itself—a diversified farming and food business that supports the college and community while providing students with work, learning, and leadership opportunities. Dynamic collaborations among students, staff, and faculty, though visibly disharmonious at times, are critical for assessing ideas and steering the farm toward some common understanding of sustainability. Economic pressures are forcing the farm to be more financially self-sufficient so that it not only generates enough income for its annual operating costs but also contributes to staff salaries and capital infrastructure. Students are asking that it teach them relevant skills for an uncertain future. They are involved with crops and livestock from the time of planting or conception until consumption, in the process gaining an understanding and appreciation of the food system that was once common but that few people have today. And they are mastering the essential management skills required for a small farmer to operate a successful business. What students need and want to learn is continually changing, and the farm must be responsive and able to change as well. Many of the challenges that emerged soon after the farm was established 140 years ago—high labor costs, inexperienced student workers, unpredictable input and commodity prices, and poor soil drainage—remain core issues today. But the integral role of students in the farm's operation, along with a continuous, open, and purposeful pursuit of economically and environmentally sound practices, should enable the farm to continue functioning as a practical laboratory for learning and a relevant, realistic, and adaptable model of sustainable agriculture.

Experiencing Agriculture

Jennifer Boyle

Reading about agricultural ecosystems in my plant science textbook is not nearly as powerful as watching those principles in action on a frigid Sunday at the greenhouse. While Matt and I performed the classic morning chore of food waste recycling, we realized the starlings were as much a part of the process as the students.

Against the blinding white backdrop of yesterday's snow, the birds were dark blotches set into motion by the truck creeping down the driveway. Somewhere beneath their patterned feathers ticked miniature clocks that knew only how to measure mealtime. They swarmed over the compost piles until our approaching truck startled them into flight. Snow-outlined trees provided the starlings with temporary perches, while Matt poured the slop into oozing mounds, and I struggled to push the next bucket to the edge of the tailgate. As we drove away, the trees exploded with black shadows cascading en masse to the feast.

For a while the birds were sated. Matt and I washed the slimy buckets, sending the last remaining bits of food streaming in rivulets down the gravel driveway. Then we slung the cleaned containers onto an empty table in the greenhouse. We thought the job was done; but, in reality, the morning chores remained unfinished until that swirling cloud of starlings sunk to the ground and picked over our scraps. A limp lettuce leaf and some broken tomato pieces soon flew away, cradled in golden beaks. Determined to comprehend composting as a relationship uniting people and soil, I had overlooked the less romantic interactions with these scavengers. Apparently, even the leftovers of the leftovers are valuable in the agroecosystem of the greenhouse.

The starlings' role of recycling nutrients parallels our own. I learned this biological relationship in a classroom, read about it in the stuffy environment of my dorm room, but the lesson remained incomplete until I was confronted with the physical manifestation of the written knowledge. During my two and a half years at Berea College, I have often felt that I had an advantage over classmates who studied agriculture while working outside the department—sometimes behind a desk. When I walked into the classroom, straight from weeding in the high tunnels or trimming hooves at the farm, I carried with me more than the mud on my boots. My job filled me with questions that were answered by teachers and textbooks; and, conversely, my studies frequently anticipated the future knowledge I would need to perform tasks at work. When a test was placed in front of me, I thought of the time spent outdoors at the farm and greenhouse, interacting with the earth.

With a newly enhanced understanding, I paused in the greenhouse to watch the starlings materialize on the other side of the glass door, like friendly phantoms eager to complete the chores we could not finish ourselves.

After I witnessed this real-time illustration of nutrient cycling in the food chain, textbooks fell just a little in my esteem. I am thankful to work in the living laboratory of the college farm, where I not only learn but also experience agriculture.

Jennifer Boyle is majoring in agriculture and natural resources and writing at Berea College. She is from Barnegat, NJ, where she worked at a greenhouse and garden center for four years before coming to college.

NOTES

1. Shannon Wilson, *Berea College: An Illustrated History* (Lexington: University Press of Kentucky, 2006).

2. Edward H. Fairchild, presidential inaugural address, 1869, Berea College Archives.

3. Quoted in Elizabeth S. Peck, *Berea's First Century, 1855–1955* (Lexington: University of Kentucky Press, 1955), 113.

4. William G. Frost to Dr. E. H. Fairchild, February 7, 1899, Berea College Archives.

5. Berea College School of Agriculture pamphlet, 1914, Berea College Archives.

6. William L. Flanery, College Farm, Annual Report, 1915, 1–3, Berea College Archives.

7. Ibid., 6.

8. Year Book of Berea College Garden Department, 1915, 4, Berea College Archives.

9. Ibid., 8.

10. Berea College Department of Agriculture, First Annual Report of the Department of Agriculture and Allied Schools for the Year Ending June 15, 1932, Berea College Archives.

11. Department of Agriculture, *Glimpses of Berea College*, pamphlet no. 5 (Berea: Berea College, 1932).

12. Robert Johnstone, "Farm Activities of Berea College: Observations and Projections," internal report, April 1966, i–ii, Berea College Archives.

13. B. L. Gardner, *American Agriculture in the Twentieth Century: How It Flourished and What It Cost* (Cambridge, MA: Harvard University Press, 2002); R. A. Hoppe, P. Korb, E. J. O'Donoghue, and D. E. Banker, *Structure and Finances of U.S. Farms*, USDA Economic Information Bulletin no. 24 (Washington, DC: USDA, 2007).

14. S. Clark and M. Cavigelli, "College Composting Program Matures," *BioCycle* 46, no. 7 (2005): 35–38; S. Clark and L. Law, "Multipurpose Program at Berea College," *BioCycle* 41, no. 9 (2000): 69–70.

2

Wilmington College (1946)

Balancing Education and Profitability

MONTE R. ANDERSON AND ROY JOE STUCKEY

The primary purpose of an academic farm at any college or university should be to enhance agricultural learning through demonstration and research. At a private liberal arts institution such as Wilmington College, the purposes of an academic farm are sometimes expanded to include revenue for the college, food for the dining halls, and, at times, a location for students to work. Most land-grant colleges and universities, and their farms, have a common genesis in the Morrill Acts of 1862 and 1890. The farms at independent colleges, by contrast, were not mandated legislatively but have separate histories as to how their farms became part of their respective educational institutions. Usually, there is a common denominator of an individual faculty member or college administrator who championed the purposes of a farm for the college. To truly appreciate a specific college farm, one has to identify and understand the roots of both the college and its agricultural program. This chapter will provide a history of the farm system at Wilmington College, which has persevered since its founding in 1946 and continues to flourish today.

Wilmington College was established in 1870 by members of the Religious Society of Friends, commonly known as Quakers, in Wilmington, Ohio, about sixty miles northeast of Cincinnati. For its first seventy years, the college focused its educational endeavors on preparing teachers with classical studies in the liberal arts, social sciences, and natural sciences. Graduates pursued careers in education, business, and medical fields. In 1946, an enthusiastic, farm-minded sophomore, Roy Joe Stuckey, approached Dr. S. Arthur Watson, the college president, with the idea of purchasing a 247-acre farm that adjoined the college campus on two sides in order to start an agriculture program.[1] The objectives of the farm would be to demonstrate new farming techniques and best management practices to interested college students and the surrounding community. To pay for the investment of the land and the necessary operating expenses, the farm would provide food for the dining hall and generate income from the sale of surplus farm products. So, with these objectives and support from the board of trustees, the farm was purchased for $93 an acre with money borrowed from the college's meager endowment.

The newly purchased farm was, at first, scarcely a model of good agronomic practices. It was worn down owing to poor management. The fences needed replacement. The soil fertility was depleted, and the crop yields were below average. Even worse, Wilmington College lacked the money to buy machinery and livestock and make the needed repairs. But young Roy Joe Stuckey and President Watson were determined to show how a run-down farm could be brought back to health and productivity through careful application of the latest agricultural conservation strategies. Three years later, with a master's degree in agricultural economics and an appointment as the first Wilmington College director of agriculture, Roy Joe Stuckey remodeled the cow barn, set up a milk-pasteurizing system for supplying dairy products to the college dining room, initiated what would become the periodically held Soil Conservation Field Day, and started teaching a small number of agriculture courses. These activities became the foundation of a department that, sixty years later, has an annual enrollment of 150 agriculture students.

On August 16, 1949, the first Soil Conservation Field Day at Wilmington College was held. Over four thousand people attended the event, which was sponsored by Wilmington College, the Clinton County Agriculture Stabilization Committee, the Clinton County Soil Conservation Service, and the Ohio State University Cooperative Extension Service. During the event, local farmers watched as pastures were renovated, terraces were built, and crop strips installed. Local drainage contractors donated their work and built a substantial tile system running to a retention wall, called a *weir notch*. Another terrace was installed to demonstrate how to prevent soil from washing into and polluting the local creek with sediment. In one day, the old farm was, in a sense, made new. Community members were impressed that the college was utilizing resources for the public good and teaching students. The following year a prominent physician, Dr. Peelle, who was also a college board member, died and willed his

Figure 2.1. Roy Joe Stuckey (on the ground) instructing an intern, Milton Wright, from the American Friends Service Committee in the basics of farming, 1951. (Courtesy Wilmington College Archives.)

two farms, totaling 200 acres, to the college. The willed gift of the Peelle farmland increased the college's total farmland to approximately 450 acres. The conditions of the gift specified that the land be used for the advancement of the college farms and for student scholarship funding. Over the next fifteen years, a handful of other individuals and families would donate an additional 800 acres to the college, and the college itself would purchase another 200 acres.

Through field days, faculty laboratories, and student involvement, the Wilmington College farms were demonstrating new and approved farming practices to the community and bringing in new resources, including land, to the college. The 1953 Soil Conservation Field Day demonstrated soil conservation techniques as well as new wheat and corn varieties. Two other, much larger field days were held in the late 1950s with a focus on agricultural mechanization and technology. These field days were dubbed Farm-O-Rama and eventually evolved into the Ohio State University

Farm Science Review, which has now been held annually for nearly fifty years and has grown into one of America's largest agricultural extravaganzas. The Farm Science Review occurs every September and provides a venue where new agriculture techniques and products are demonstrated. There are company displays as well as field demonstrations and educational presentations. In 2009, there were over 138,000 people in attendance at the review.[2]

EVOLUTION OF THE FARM: REVENUE GENERATION

One of the basic goals of the initial land purchase was for the farm to be able to pay for the entire expenses of its academic agriculture department. To accomplish this task, the college expanded and diversified its livestock enterprises, primarily with dairy cattle and hogs. The hogs were sold at market price through local livestock yards. The pasteurized milk, along with an orange-flavored drink made from a concentrated syrup, was produced for the college dining hall and sold locally in the college's dairy store. After the needs of the dining hall and local customers were met, the surplus bulk milk was sold to a marketing cooperative in Dayton, Ohio. Herein was a flaw in the system: the milk provided to the dining hall was never formally purchased from the farm, so revenue was in-kind, and that does not pay the bills. Although the distribution of the milk to the dining hall did save the college money, there was not a cash transaction to show an impressive stream of revenue to critics. When times were good, the dairy and farm enterprises were considered a good investment; when cash flow was tight, the farms were considered inefficient. By 1964, the dairy processing plant was closed down, and all the milk was shipped out in bulk. The value added through processing milk at the college was eliminated. Four years later, the dairy itself was shut down. This closure corresponded to the transition in society away from locally supplied and distributed food to a regionally supplied and processed food distribution system and economy-of-scale principles.

The college also developed a well-respected swine enterprise in the 1950s. It researched the new leaner and more efficient hogs, which were replacing the older style, lard-type hogs. By 1956, the efforts had turned to the sale of meat-type sires to be certified by the Poland China Breed Registry Association. These sales, coupled with support from E. Kahn's Sons of Cincinnati, Ohio, a meat-processing company, gave the college a legacy of swine research and production that extended into the early 1990s.

However, just as the dairy became a casualty of later economies of scale, so too did the hog operation.

The changes in U.S. agriculture from the mid-1970s to the early 1980s, sometimes referred to as the *fencerow-to-fencerow mentality*, occurred as increasingly larger tracts of land were cultivated in an effort to improve farming efficiency. Farms began to specialize in either crop or livestock production, rather than a complementary mix of crops and livestock. The diversified farm of the past was replaced with specialized facilities and much larger operations. Wilmington College followed suit and began to farm larger and larger areas of land. In this process, pastures were replaced with row crops; fences were removed, making larger fields; and farming became more of a manufacturing process than a nurturing of the land's resources. The evaluation of success was based on revenue generated. By 1986, forty years after the initial farm purchase, the college had farmland holdings in excess of fifteen hundred acres, with a farrow-to-finish hog operation as well as a cow-calf beef enterprise. Operating decisions were based on the return on investment to the endowment funds and the size of the annual operating budget, rather than on providing an educational experience for students.

In this way of thinking, the farms needed to be a profit center for the college. Financial accountability was critical. If the Agriculture Department was to model the vanguard of the contemporary farming system, it needed to manage its farms in an aggressive, forward-looking manner, with both eyes kept continually on the bottom line. Students would be hired as workers and paid minimum wage. The farm manager would report through the business office, although still working closely with the academic department. The role of the farm was to be a production farm first and a teaching laboratory second. The farm manager would provide learning opportunities as long as the faculty scheduled and taught the laboratories in a way that didn't interfere with the timely completion of day-to-day farming operations. During the school year, there were about a half dozen students working on the farm, with the majority in the swine facility. At this time, the college moved to a semester-based academic calendar so that the students were in finals or finished for the year altogether around May 1, just when planting occurred in the spring. Therefore, most of the crop production was accomplished by the farm management staff. Throughout the summer, most students either returned home to work on their families' farms or accepted internships with local or national agricultural companies. The college farm system could not financially compete with the companies, but it did provide some initial training in research methods so that the students would be successful.

This was a transitional time for the Agriculture Department, the role of the college farm, and the agriculture industry at large. The faculty were forced to adjust instruction to accommodate a growth in student numbers from 85 in 1985 to 130 by 1992. The farm management team was showing students what was needed to operate a productive and profitable farm, while industry was showing students, through internships, the opportunities that existed off the farm and the importance of additional education. Industry was expecting an employee who had completed a greater depth and breadth of course work. Educationally, the student could no longer simply major in agriculture but had to complement his or her major with a minor in chemistry or business administration. Supporting this change were students who were less interested in working on the farms and more interested in opportunities and activities off the farm. For example, one spring and summer, seven students had internships with the Monsanto Corporation in St. Louis, Missouri. They worked extremely hard, learned a lot, and earned enough money so that they did not need to work during the coming school year. They focused on their studies, added course work in economics and chemistry, and changed from a production agriculture mind-set of returning to the farm to an agribusiness and agriculture science orientation, focused on working in private agricultural research and enterprise.

By 1995, the department had grown to 150 students. The farm background of the students had also changed, with over half the students arriving at the college with only limited or no farm experience. This demographic shift changed the way introductory courses were taught. No longer could a faculty member assume students knew how to operate a tractor or how to process a litter of pigs. And, although the production farms were financially successful, they provided work opportunities for only some 5 percent of the agriculture students. Addressing this situation required a redesign of the farm and Agriculture Department interface. Around this time, the department had acquired a thirty-acre farm within walking distance of the college. Peter Drake, an alumnus, industrialist, and college board of trustee member, committed funds to redesign it as a teaching laboratory, flexible enough to change without committing excessive resources beyond what the farm could return. The farm would report through the academic side of the college, and those responsible would accept the fact that this farm might generate revenue but would never cover all its expenses. It would

Figure 2.2. Dan Bowman, a Wilmington graduate and now the assistant farm manager, cleaning the sow outdoor breeding area at the Wilmington College production farms in the late 1990s. (Courtesy Wilmington College Archives.)

operate in a manner analogous to other laboratories, athletic facilities, or the college theater on campus. Academically, the animal and crop science courses became year-long sequences. This was an integrated approach to learning in which students would have laboratory experiences that paralleled what was occurring in the field. For example, in the fall, the students would monitor the fall breeding program of the sheep, and in the spring they would have lamb watch. All students would be on the farm for at least thirty laboratories within the crop and animal science classes. Faculty would know the skills the students had been taught and what they had mastered. This model helped prepare students without previous farm experience and engaged all students on the farm. The farm was managed by a farm coordinator who realized that success was defined not by profit but by student participation and success.

In 2000, the college was again faced with a huge reinvestment decision with regard to most of its farms' facilities and equipment. Even without the improvements, the farms now needed to generate a profit that exceeded

Figure 2.3. Harold Thirey, an associate professor, demonstrating to freshman students how to square and level a post in a board fence installation in 2009. The fence was enclosing a livestock heavy use area that is designed and installed to reduce erosion and pollution during times of high soil moisture. (Courtesy Wilmington College Agriculture Department.)

the value of the potential cash rents, which had reached $130,000 annually. The farms were purchased with funds from the endowment, and, like any other investment, they needed to return yearly to the endowment. The risk associated with the potential profit or loss was considered too great for the decisionmakers to accept. Therefore, after a feasibility study, the president and the board of trustees decided that it was economically less risky and potentially more profitable for the college to rent out the majority of the college's production farms, rather than managing them directly with college employees. The farmland holdings would be managed by the business office, which would oversee the cash rental and management of the farms.

At the same time, however—and again with support from the feasibility study—the Agriculture Department was allowed to keep the majority of the original farm that was purchased in 1946 (minus a large tract that has been diverted to campus expansion) plus three smaller adjoining farms acquired through subsequent gift and purchase. The new academic farm, known as the Barrett Farm (after a local family whose farm was purchased by the college in 1984), would be about three hundred acres and would be funded by the academic budget for use by its rapidly increasing number of agriculture undergraduates.

However, as these farms were refocused to academic experiences, once again, major investment was needed. The buildings and fences needed to be replaced and a reemphasis on soil conservation implemented. Starting in 2000, the college began redesigning the Barrett Farm for academic purposes.

REFLECTING ON OUR EXPERIENCE

On the basis of our sixty years of experience in farming at Wilmington College, we find that decisions are made differently in an educational environment when the question is profit centered rather than student centered. In the profit-centered paradigm, the college will have reduced expenses and become more profitable. Within most production models, labor is often the largest and easiest cost variable to reduce, and, in a college farm setting, this equates to student involvement. Across the history of the Wilmington College farms, when times were good and prices exceptional, the farm enterprises were praised. When the market cycle ebbed, the critics failed to remember the good times. This pattern highlights the fact that educational institutions should be focused on education rather than on profit. In fact, teaching and learning are the business of college. The times when the college farm assets were focused on revenue rather than on education came at the beginning of a cycle of prosperity that was all too soon followed by lower prices and, eventually, the elimination of the enterprise, as was the case in the dairy and swine enterprises. Wilmington College's farm history shows that, as the farms evolved into profit centers, such as the dairy-processing plant and the swine-production center, the goals of the farm changed: ultimately, the enterprise became an investment that needed to be managed, rather than a facility to enhance education.

The Agriculture Department still has field days to showcase new techniques in pasture renovation and management, and these serve as the venue for various seed company demonstration days. In the past ten years, the college, alumni, and community members and businesses have again invested substantially in the farm. There is a current line of appropriately sized equipment, three livestock facilities, and an equipment facility as well as new tiling and research plots managed in collaboration with multinational companies such as Monsanto, Pioneer, and Agrigold.

The college farm has also sought to be responsive to community needs in other ways. In May 2008, DHL Air Freight, the major employer within the five-county area that includes Wilmington, announced that it was closing its local sort facility. Over eight thousand people lost their jobs during the following year. In response to the resulting local food needs, and with support from the college administration and an anonymous donor, the Agriculture Department grew a limited variety of vegetables for distribution. Service to the community aligns with the mission of the college. Although vegetables had never been grown or sold on the farms before, a decision was made to grow tomatoes, corn, and potatoes. In addition, chickens, which up to this point were usually used for laboratory experiences, were produced. A couple of acres were taken out of field crop production and converted to vegetable production. This project contributed over 6,000 pounds of potatoes, 3,000 pounds of tomatoes, 50 chickens, and 150 dozen ears of sweet corn to community food banks. In addition to the food donation, intensive gardening opportunities were developed to teach individuals how to garden and prepare the food they produced. In 2010, the production of fresh vegetables will be expanded; the harvest will be donated to local food pantries with community outreach assistance from VISTA volunteers.

Moreover, following its success in the production of fresh produce in 2009, the Agriculture Department was approached by the company handling the college's dining service contract and asked whether it would be willing to sell fresh chickens and vegetables to the dining hall. While this is an exciting opportunity, it also raises questions about the future role and focus of the college's agriculture program. Although it may be profitable to produce more vegetables, sheep, goats, poultry, and beef for sale, we must keep the purpose of the farms foremost in our minds. Will the members of the Agriculture Department and college administration remember to keep the focus of the farms on education, or will they succumb to the temptation to look once again to the farms as profit centers and forget that educational institutions are in the business of educating, not in the business of making money?

LOOKING TO THE FUTURE

Perhaps, in these difficult economic times, a middle-of-the-road approach is the most appropriate. There is, after all, a movement currently afoot to grow and consume more local food and to get back to the land. The

Figure 2.4. Members of the Grow Food, Grow Hope Garden Initiative, a Wilmington College local food project, wash and pack tomatoes on the Wilmington College Farm for donation to area food pantries. (Courtesy John Cropper.)

Wilmington College farms are highly productive. In the 2009 crop year, the entire Wilmington College corn crop averaged more than two hundred bushels per acre, soybeans averaged more than fifty-five bushels per acre, and the potatoes yielded about twelve thousand pounds per acre. The livestock enterprises consisted of thirty brood cows in the cow-calf operation, thirty Boer goat nannies, and thirty meat-type ewes. All livestock are primarily grazed in a modified intensive grazing system, and the farms are self-sufficient with regard to the animals' pasture, supplemental grain, and hay.

As for the role of the farms in the educational process, we believe that the basic skills, such as machinery operation, feeding, and maintaining livestock as well as the planting and harvesting of crops, are critical for the students to understand the theory and practice of farming. Most students today do not have farm experience and, as a consequence, do not have the basic competencies and comprehension of food and fiber production requisite to a solid understanding of the agricultural sciences. With these basic skills, students will be better prepared to understand the challenges of food production and food security that will affect the world over the next fifty years.

The Wilmington College Agriculture Department presently enrolls 150 agriculture students and manages about three hundred acres. During the school year, all the students in the agriculture program are on the farms in class-related activities and laboratories. The farm hires twenty to thirty students during peak times of harvesting and lambing and also usually one or two to work full-time during the summer. The livestock numbers reflect a herd or flock size that fits into an overall student class size of thirty or a laboratory of fifteen, meaning that every student usually has an animal to work with.

The changes that have occurred in the Wilmington College farms over the years have mirrored many of the larger changes in agriculture in the United States in the second half of the twentieth century. In the 1940s, the farm was a diversified animal and crop farm; in the 1950s, it started to specialize in one or two species of livestock. By the 1960s, it eliminated its dairy enterprise because larger companies could process milk more efficiently. The 1970s found an expansion of row crop farming and further growth in the swine industry. In the 1980s, the farm continued to grow, but investment in larger equipment reduced the need for employees. The 1990s found the farm in an awkward position: too large to be small, but too small to be large. The decision was made to rent out most of the land rather than invest in becoming still larger. However, emerging simultaneously in the 1990s was an interest in smaller, more diversified, but efficient farming. The college's small farm for the twenty-first century will continue to focus on shaping the lives of students so that they can find good jobs and build successful, satisfying careers.

STUDENT REFLECTIONS

MILKING

HUGH SHAUDYS

Roy Joe approached my brother Edgar about milking the Jersey dairy herd, and he in turn recruited my roommate Roland Armstrong and me. A schedule was set up so two of the three of us would milk morning and night, seven days a week.

Roland and I milked almost three years. I never took any pay in cash, but hours were credited against my tuition. By milking two semesters and earning money at home during the summer months, I was able to attend and graduate from Wilmington in June 1953. For this, I will always be grateful.

The original barn was small, with a four-stanchion-type milk parlor. Hay storage was above the free-stall loafing pen. There was a separate milk house, which sometimes did not have a door, until the Dayton City Health Department insisted on one.

The combination calf barn with pigs was a separate building to the south of the dairy barn. We would pasture the herd out in early spring and late into the fall to save hay and bedding. I remember many times getting the herd from a faraway back pasture, only to find I had miscounted and had to go back for one or two, which were usually first-calf heifers.

Before modernization of the dairy plant for pasteurizing, milk was shipped to Dayton. Even without the door on the milk house, I don't remember any milk rejected because of a high bacteria count or mastitis.

When the milking parlor was built, the milk house also contained a pipeline milk system for transport of milk from cow to cooler. After the pasteurization plant was installed, milk was furnished to the college cafeteria located under Denver Hall. I remember delivering milk there, via pickup truck, at almost every hour of the day. The new dairy plant had a dormitory-type room above.

From the beginning, Roy Joe organized field trips. I went on those he arranged for a tour of various Clinton County farms—dairy, beef, hog, and cropping (soybeans and corn). I also remember a trip to Malabar Farm and hearing Louis Bromfield extol the virtues of organic farming and minimum tillage.

Hugh Shaudys graduated from Wilmington College in 1953.

COLLEGE FARM ECONOMICS

BOB STEINMETZ

One evening during orientation week, the freshman class was at a picnic at the town park, and I had no idea of how I would pay my college expenses. I was sitting on the ground when I heard a voice from above call my name. It was Roy Joe Stuckey. He asked if I would be interested in operating the dairy plant on the college farm in exchange for full room, board, and tuition. I was puzzled how he knew my financial situation, but, considering my circumstances, I did not hesitate to accept his offer.

There was a dormitory with six bunk beds, a kitchen, and a living room with desks over the dairy plant. The walls were covered with unfinished brown insulation board. There was an old floor model radio with a tuning eye. The only telephone was in Roy Joe's house. Heat came from a boiler in a storeroom on the floor below and at the front of the dairy plant. The boiler operated on low pressure during the winter for heating the building. It was switched to high pressure when steam was needed to pasteurize milk.

Our transportation around the farm and between the farm and campus was provided by an old World War II Jeep that had a black metal top and an old Pontiac station wagon that had a steel bed built into the back. The Jeep and Pontiac served us well, but they needed quite a bit of loving care and attention to keep them going because of their age. The Pontiac was, by nature, very heavy, and the steel cargo bed put the brakes to the challenge, especially when loaded with several cans of milk. It could often be seen lumbering along the rutted land between the dairy plant and the back barn, loaded with milk cans, nearly hidden in a cloud of dust.

During 1953–1954, we earned our room, board, and tuition by working three ten-hour days per week and half of each vacation. This seemed like a very good deal until we analyzed the arrangement and realized that we were earning about fifty cents per hour. Roy Joe must have done his homework earlier. The following year we asked for an hourly rate and received sixty-five cents per hour and still had spending money after paying our own room, board, and tuition.

We worked hard, and life was never dull. Evenings were usually spent studying.

Academically, we had common interests in the core courses we took together as well as the biology and chemistry courses most of us were taking. From time to time, we were engaged in serious philosophical discussion. These discussions were very interesting and entertaining as most of us had quite conservative backgrounds and we were experiencing a new world of knowledge.

We were well-known by neighborhood residents for our late-night roundups of cows that had escaped from the farm and wandered into nearby backyards. For some unknown reason, they always headed toward town. I best recall going through my future landlady's rose garden on Ludovic Street chasing one of the escapees. We spent a considerable amount of time repairing fences to prevent these escapes. We were always amazed how a herd of cattle could get through a three-foot hole in the fence and how much territory they could cover in such a short amount of time.

We ate our meals at the college dining room, which was then in the basement of one of the girls' dorms. On workdays, we would enter through the kitchen in our work clothes, and the cooking staff would fill our plates from the large kettles on the stove.

We sat near the kitchen, where second helpings were near at hand; we ate very well. Since all the milk and orange drink used in the dining room was processed in the college farm dairy plant, we would make deliveries at mealtime. We had a key to the kitchen so that we could make late-evening deliveries. It also gave us the opportunity to raid the walk-in cooler for leftovers when we worked late and missed an evening meal.

The dairy plant was very basic. It had a batch pasteurizer that held about 120 gallons, a manual bottle-washing machine, walk-in cooler, and three washtubs. A homogenizer and, I believe, a cream separator were added around 1956 or 1957. Three, sometimes four, batches of milk were processed in a three-day period each week. Approximately one hundred half-gallon bottles were produced for sale to the public from each batch, and the balance went into five-gallon cans for the college dining room. Several gallons of chocolate milk and orange drink, made from concentrate, were produced and bottled for sale to the public and placed in cans for the college dining room. Milk was available to the public on a self-serve system twenty-four hours a day at about thirty-five cents per half gallon. Customers paid for their purchases by dropping money in a locked cash box. The milk had a very high cream content because it came from our herd of Jersey cows. Milk not needed by the dairy plant was sold to a bulk milk buyer.

During the summer of 1954, Roy Joe made us an offer we couldn't refuse. He said that, if we could get, I believe, thirty loads of corn silage into the trench silo in one day, he would buy us all the Dairy Queen sundaes we could eat. We met the challenge by getting up before dawn the next day and working until late in the day without breaking for lunch or dinner. Much to our surprise, we were so tired that I don't believe anyone was able to eat more than one sundae. Had we been smarter, we would have postponed our reward until the next day.

Bob Steinmetz graduated from Wilmington College in 1957.

STUDENT REFLECTIONS

The "Academic Farms"

Tom Smith

I came to Wilmington College with an interest in agricultural production and only two years of farm experience. As part of the freshman agriculture class, we had to have a tractor safety laboratory on the college farm. This occurred in the field just behind the new equine facility. The tractors were all John Deeres, and they were very new, which was a new experience for me since all the other tractors I had run were as much as seventy years old. With the excitement created by these new tractors, I promptly sought an opportunity to work on the college farm but was unfortunately denied as they were hiring only students with a "work study" classification, which I did not have. So I sat by and watched the farm from a distance and partook only in class laboratory functions. I watched two farm managers go by, and, when the third came, I applied for a summer job and was hired. By this time, I had four years of farm experience, but it was limited to hay, cattle, sheep, and poultry. I was very eager to learn new things and to learn the "why it works" for all the things I already knew how to do.

I spent many long hours talking to Randy (the farm manager) and listening to his experiences and relating them to mine and to what we were doing on the farm. In the next two years, I learned to plant soybeans and corn, utilize fertilizer equipment, and even run the sprayer. I will never forget the first time I planted soybeans: it was with an International Harvester end-wheel grain drill (the only red equipment on the farm), and I didn't realize how far I had to overlap on each pass, so, when the beans came up, there were one-foot open patches between each drill pass for the length of the field (I called them *observation rows*, but Randy insisted they were rabbit runs!). The greatest experience I had was probably learning to operate the JD3300 combine. It took me about three weeks to fully understand the functions of the combine and how exactly it could take a standing plant and extract only the grain to a holding tank while spitting everything else out the back of the machine. I gained valuable learning through hands-on work on the farm in those two years in working with machinery, handling livestock, and in property maintenance.

And who could forget those times when Monte would join in with the farmwork! Often he would show up at the hay field driving his Volvo, get out, and come across the field to join us on the hay wagon. It was in these hot days that we spent many hours discussing various farming techniques and styles. But this is not to leave out Monte's favorite activity, trimming the feet of the sheep and goats. He would always make us meet him at the farm at seven in the morning to get started in the summer. I know of no other department chair that would stand next to you on the hay wagon or help you trim goat feet early in the morning.

The farm has changed a lot in my time at Wilmington College. When I entered as a freshman, the college was just closing the production farms, and I really didn't understand the value of these until much later, but I was caught up in the affair as I watched them auction off the farm equipment.

The academic farms are where I worked and were closer to campus. This farm had an old bank barn with a leaky roof and a partially rotted first floor; it was in need of some help! Another landmark building was the chicken coop, which sat down a long muddy pathway in the middle of a pasture. This building almost always had water on the floor, which we assumed ran into the back of it from the pasture or from the roof—or both. The water was at the back of the building, where we had to crawl along the foundation to stay out of the mud while at the same time being sure to watch out for the ram, who lived in the back half of the barn and was sure to come after you if you let him.

Fences on the farm were another story altogether; but, slowly and surely, through my time at the college, Monte led us on the fence brigade, and we had the opportunity to replace almost every fence on the college farm with new high-tensile electric fence, spaced so that we could mow around both sides of it and it would never become overgrown again. Progress continued as the back half of the farm received a long gravel lane that cut it in two for easy access and a new fence that we put in (the tractor-powered post-hole auger broke on the first hole, so we dug them all with a small two-man engine for the length of the fence!). A new beef-working facility was built to replace the old one that ran uphill along the bank barn. Unlike the muddy mess of the old facility, the new was flat, sat on a stone pad, and was covered with a roof. The beef facility boasted a gravel heavy-use pad that the cattle could use when it was too muddy to be on the pastures. The chicken house was the next building to get attention, and it did—it was leveled to the ground, never to be seen again, and definitely not missed by anyone. With the condition of the bank barn worsening, it was decided that it would cost the same to build a new barn as it would to renovate the bank barn, so it too was demolished. The new pole barn was built as a machinery barn, and the older pole barn was converted over for livestock. Following the conversion, we all said good-bye to the bank barn with donuts and coffee and a really big flame. The fire was so hot that you could feel it five hundred feet away, and the flames were so high you could see them from the back of the farm.

I will never forget nor regret the time I spent on the Wilmington College Farm. These were some of the best times in my life and some of the best learning experiences I have had. I truly appreciate the opportunities to gain hands-on experience and do feel sad for those who have not had or have not taken advantage of that opportunity. I still look at the production farms every time I drive by them on Route 68 and think how great the farm must have been in its time and how blessed those students were with all the learning opportunities there (with dairy, sheep, cattle, hogs, crops . . .), and I hope that many more future students will have the chance I had for such intense learning!

Tom Smith graduated from Wilmington College in 2004.

Notes

This chapter is based in part on Roy Joe Stuckey's *Agriculture at Wilmington College—Sixty Years and Beyond* (Wilmington, OH: Wilmington College, 2007).

1. Dr. Watson later established agriculture programs at two other colleges: William Penn College in Oskaloosa, IA, and Friends University in Wichita, KS. The program at Wilmington College is the only one of these three still in operation.

2. http://fsr.osu.edu/.

3

Sterling College (1962)

Working Hands, Working Minds

JULIA SHIPLEY

A new Sterling College student may arrive in September having never really thought about how food makes it to a plate. By the time she leaves Sterling, however, she will undoubtedly have harvested potatoes behind a team of horses; she will have washed carrots for the kitchen in a bicycle-powered carrot washer; she will have hauled buckets of food waste from the kitchen to the farm compost and eaten beans or cabbage or beets fertilized by that compost. She will have walked past the oats growing in a patch near the road and eaten oat bread baked in the wood-fired oven. She will have planted carrots and potatoes. Even though she may self-design a major in circumpolar studies or natural history, she will have lugged water to the beef cows, carried hay to the draft horses, dumped grain in the chickens' pan, and collected their eggs. Then, at some later point, she will have eaten the eggs and consumed the beef. Her exposure to agriculture happens constantly: in the classroom, in the dining room, and in the community in which her college is situated, a community now recognized as a hotbed of emerging agricultural entrepreneurs. Whether she wants to or not, while pursuing the path to her diploma in a self-designed major in one of the six areas of environmental studies offered at the college, she will have to pass through the Sterling College Farm, and, as a corollary to that experience, undertake a reexamination of what it means to eat.

The Sterling College Sustainable Agriculture Program evolved slowly out of a one-year program known as the Grass Roots Year in forestry, wildlife management, and agriculture, first put in place over thirty years ago. As Sterling College developed over the years into a two-year and, ultimately, a four-year undergraduate college, with a new continuous semester system, the agriculture program has gradually changed shape and purpose. But several key facets of the original program are still intact. All students, no matter whether they are "ag" students or not, will do farm chores at some point. The college does not use a food service company because, as a federally funded work college, it utilizes student help in the kitchen. In addition to serving a significant quantity of its own, college-raised food and buying much of the rest of its food from other local farmers, Sterling has maintained a food waste composting facility for thirty years. As a result, all students are exposed to the full cycle of food simply by showing up at mealtimes. The small scale of both the college (one hundred students) and its farm and gardens enables an intimate, hands-on experience. While Sterling doesn't pretend to churn out fully formed farmers, it provides students with key foundational experiences, tools, and resources that have proved to be effective in supporting students who want to pursue careers and/or lifestyles that involve agriculture.

It's Not a Farm, It's a Barn

What is now Sterling College, in Craftsbury Common, Vermont, was originally a boys' boarding school founded in 1958. In 1962, in the middle of the school year, the headmaster abruptly left, and Ted Bermingham, the man responsible for Sterling's foray into farming, found himself taking over the helm of a financially strapped, second-tier prep school located about thirty minutes from the Canadian border. As Bermingham, who has a degree in agriculture from Colorado A&M and a degree in history from Princeton University, cast about for ways to make Sterling different from other boarding schools, many of them more prestigious and most of them significantly closer to the metropolitan areas where potential students' families resided, he hit on the idea of acquiring a farm.

For the record, however, this tiny school with its unique sustainable agriculture degree did not begin with the idealistic impulse to "Let them eat what they sow." Bermingham is quick to point this out. "One thing I want to be clear about: there never would have been a farm if a guy [the school's first headmaster] hadn't left in the middle of the semester."[1]

One morning in 1962 as Bermingham was commuting to work, he heard an announcement about an upcoming farm auction on the radio. The farm—a house and a barn—was about a mile from the Sterling campus. The town of Craftsbury is a quiet cluster of white clapboard houses surrounding a town green (the Common). Flanked by undulating hills, several lakes, and open fields, this town of about one thousand inhabitants is the epitome of quaint New England.

As Bermingham recalls, the parents of one of the students loaned the school the money to buy the farm. "But," another myth Bermingham wants to debunk, "it wasn't a farm; it was a barn." He explained the difference: "This never was a working farm; it was a place for farm projects. The students of Sterling School were mostly suburban kids without farm backgrounds. The farm provided students with a work ethic, discipline, and responsibility. So the farm served the role of an orchestra or a football team. It was an organizing device, something for students to come together around and participate in. But, more than that, the farm provided an additional element to their education. When you work with animals, you are constantly learning from them. We never claimed we were training people to be farmers. But we exposed them to farming by attending the farm show and going on farm visits. At the same time, we never let down on academics."

The final year of the boarding school was 1972. A series of short courses were offered in 1973, and in 1974 the Grass Roots Year was launched. The Grass Roots Program, as it turned out, was the next key step in the evolution of Sterling College's Sustainable Agriculture Program.

THE GRASS ROOTS YEAR

The Grass Roots Program of Sterling Institute was a one-year, interim program for both male and female students who had finished high school. Though they didn't grow a lot of food for the school, the Grass Roots Year perpetuated the legacy of the Sterling Boys' School by enlisting student participation in campuswide and farm-related chores, facilitating the completion of farm projects, and maintaining close links with practicing farmers in the community. The course catalog from 1974 states, "Students are expected to become familiar by actual participation with such activities as: tractor and farm machinery use; lambing; hog and beef slaughter; fence building; horse breeding; calf raising; artificial insemination, castration, dehorning, and [tail] docking; worming; Christmas tree shaping; maple sugar gathering and boiling; shade tree planting and transplanting; log cabin building; use of a skid-horse; compass and map work; stream improvement; wildlife blinds and live-traps." By 1978, the Grass Roots Program had evolved into the broader, year-long Forestry, Wildlife Management, and Agriculture (FWM&A) Program, a mix of academic subjects linked to experiential environmental education. By 1982, the Sterling Institute had channeled the FWM&A Program into an expanded curriculum and was accredited to award a two-year associate of arts degree in rural resource management. By the fall of 1998, Sterling had launched its four-year bachelor of arts degree program with concentrations in sustainable agriculture, outdoor education and leadership, conservation ecology, and northern studies.

The original barn, which was located a mile from the central campus and served as a unifying device for the boys' school, has since been sold, and a comprehensive on-campus farm has taken its place. The Sterling College Farm now consists of two acres of vegetable gardens, fifteen acres of pasture and hay fields managed with both tractors and draft animals, one hundred acres of working woodlot, a thirty-nine-acre leased sugar bush for maple syrup production, a thirty- by eighty-four-foot high tunnel for winter food production, a composting facility, and two solar- and wind-powered barns. What was once a flummoxed headmaster's baiting device to lure students into Vermont's Northeast Kingdom and instill in them a strong work ethic has become a dynamic interdisciplinary teaching tool and an integral part of the Sterling student experience. As Drew Conroy, Sterling's farm manager from 1992 to 1994, summarized the relevance of the college's holistic, integrated approach to farm education: "You're all going to eat for the rest of your life."

Hence, while the basic goals of the Sustainable Agriculture Program are to open students' eyes, get them excited about farming, and equip them with knowledge, experiences, and an understanding of best organic and sustainable management practices, the faculty approach these goals with the understanding that not all the students will go off and pursue farming in their postgraduate lives. As Rick Thomas, the college's draft horse manager and a faculty member in sustainable agriculture, puts it, "I see us as educators of 'the Little Farmers That Could'–type market gardens of one to twenty acres, demonstrating and offering practical skills in small-scale agriculture." But, he concedes, this is still a teaching farm where students work, not a profit-driven independent agricultural enterprise. "Because we aren't an actual farm, there's no severe consequence if we don't produce enough eggs. The dining hall will acquire them elsewhere, and we'll go on. The consequence of failing here is minimized so the students can really focus on learning how to balance equations, make decisions, and problem solve."

Figure 3.1. Grass Roots Program students spreading manure with a horse-drawn spreader, 1975. (Courtesy Sterling College.)

DISTINCTIVE FEATURES

Throughout the transition from a boarding school into the Grass Roots Program and from the two-year associate's degree program to the four-year bachelor's degree program, and now on the brink of a distinctive continuous semester model, the core of the Sustainable Agriculture Program has included five essential elements: the work program, obligatory farm chores, the Farm Project, a focus on draft horse management, and connections to community.

The Work Program

One of the first things Ted Bermingham did as a new headmaster of the Sterling Boys' School was to create a work program whereby students had regular tasks to fulfill—such as washing dishes, cleaning the dorms, and sweeping hallways—in addition to their academic course work. This hands-on approach to maintaining the campus and the campus community through full participation has endured throughout the school's several incarnations. Ann Ingerson, the garden manager from 1981 to 1998, recalls, "The attitude around chores was: because you are part of a community, everybody needs to pitch in and contribute." The feeling was, "Work is good for you; it's important to work hard and be responsible for things."

In 1999, Sterling joined the Work Colleges Consortium, an independent association of seven federally funded work-learning-service colleges. This enables students to earn tuition stipends for their work on campus and service to the larger Craftsbury community. Therefore, all Sterling students, no matter what their field of study, may spend a portion of their academic day mulching blueberries at Brown's Beautiful Blueberries, a local pick-your-own operation owned by the octogenarian Arnold Brown, or gleaning surplus produce from a nearby vegetable grower for contribution to Salvation Farms, a gleaning project started by a Sterling alumna that has harvested tons of food for Vermont's food banks and pantries. Students also have regular jobs on campus that help facilitate the school's day-to-day operations, minimizing the need to hire extra kitchen, grounds, and maintenance staff. This gives students practical work experience and also a sense of ownership of their institution. All residential students work at least eighty hours each semester and earn a minimum of $1,650 toward their college costs. Additional earnings are possible through work-study positions, summer internships, and residence hall supervision. At the heart of this practice, the philosophy of Ted Bermingham's boys' school work program is still reverberating. Sterling College president Will Wootton states, "The value of this is it simply demonstrates on a daily basis what it takes and what it means to be a productive member of an active community."

Among Sterling College's work-learning-service jobs are the following:

breakfast prep cook;
long trail crew member;
catamount trail crew member;
computer support technician;
Craftsbury High School mentor;
farm resource specialist;
community service coordinator;
green bicycle baron/baroness;
greenhouse and hoophouse manager;
kitchen/garden liaison;

maple sugaring team member;
Mt. Mansfield watershed monitor;
plant science teacher;
assistant public school reading tutor.

Farm Chores

"I went and fed cows every day whether I liked or not. Whether it was bright and sunny, or blowing so hard I couldn't see, or thirty below—I went and fed cows," says Bob Langen '81 in the 1986–1987 Sterling College course catalog. In addition to their work-learning-service job at the college, no matter what their previous experience or future longings, all students at Sterling must take a turn bringing water to the horses, mucking out stalls, collecting eggs, and tossing hay to the sheep. This too is a legacy of Ted Bermingham's philosophy, brought to life with the purchase of the farm in 1963, of linking academics with the physical labor of taking care of living things. Margaret Ramsdell, a dorm manager whose husband, Robert, taught at the boys' school, recalls, "The farm provided the kids

Figure 3.2. A student rototilling in the garden. (Courtesy Sterling College.)

with something they had never been exposed to before—I saw students who had never been near anything dirty fall in love with this whole new world opening up for them." Ann Ingerson explains the value of required farm chores like this: "When you're responsible for something that's sentient, that will notice if you slack, it's a big thing." She adds, "I think it means more to a student who eats farm-raised food when they participate in growing and raising it." Drew Conroy also thinks linking all students to the farm is a great idea: "Getting eighteen-, nineteen-, twenty-year-old students out building fences, shearing sheep, moving hay, is a great outlet for youthful energy."

Farm Project

Though not directly inherited from the boys' boarding school, the Farm Project has been a staple of the college's curriculum since the first Grass Roots Year. For over thirty-five years now, its simple, effective goal, as described in the course catalog, has been to "provide first-hand contact with livestock management through purchase, management, and marketing of students' own animals." Following the approval of their individual proposals by the farm manager, students undertake full responsibility for carrying out their livestock project. In this way, as Drew Conroy puts it, students learn "the commitment, the twenty-four-hour care, the meaning of ownership" that no other course or experience could provide. One example is a student who is raising two different kinds of mohair goats to compare their quality for fiber production. The Farm Project has been expanded in recent years to include plant projects as well. Currently, for example, one student is developing raised beds of medicinal plants intended for preparation of herbal remedies for livestock.

Draft Horse Management

Since 1963, when Ted Bermingham became headmaster and Sterling acquired its barn, Sterling students have had the opportunity to care for and manage draft animals. The boys' school barn housed a few Thoroughbreds and Arabians belonging to faculty. Students were exposed to horses and horse care through daily chores. But it was Bermingham, who also owned and operated the Draft Horse Institute on his farm in Cabot, separate from the boys' school, who bridged both enterprises by bringing students to his farm two or three days per week. Using the equipment of the Draft Horse Institute, interested students could receive an education in using horses to skid logs and pull loads. Sterling is one of the few colleges in the United States where students can get hands-on training to manage a draft animal. Instead of teaching a single skill set, such as how to plough or how to drive a sleigh, Rick Thomas uses the "teamster model," which involves teaching students how to manage and use horses by focusing on the student-horse interaction. As he notes, "Then they can do anything they want, be it give sleigh rides, skid logs or plough." Six of Rick's students from the past three years currently own teams of horses.

Connections to Community

Craftsbury is located in rural Vermont's Northeast Kingdom. The college is situated in the midst of a working landscape composed of small-scale traditional family farmers and young entrepreneurial vegetable farmers, cheesemakers, and organic seed growers. Sterling students are both introduced to and encouraged to build relationships with the people and resources of this area. Their connections to the community come through classes like "Introduction to Alternative Agriculture," through opportunities in the work program, through the Internship Program, which requires them to complete a ten-week work experience, and through collective community events and celebrations, such as the annual January Farm Show held in Barre, Vermont.

THE CURRICULUM

The Sterling College mission statement reads, "The Sterling College community combines structured academic study with experiential challenges and plain hard work to build responsible problem solvers who become stewards of the environment as they pursue productive lives." Students pursuing a degree in sustainable agriculture participate in a series of required core courses that progress from the theoretical and scientific to the practical, including lab-based classes such as "Soil Science" and "Plant Science" and immersion courses like "Organic Vegetable Production." They can then choose from a variety of complementary courses to either diversify or reinforce a strand of interest. These courses include "Permaculture Design," "Draft Horse Management I: Driving Principles," "Farmstead Arts," and "Literature of the Rural Experience." The capstone requirement for a student to graduate with a degree in sustainable agriculture is to participate in either the Summer Farm Semester, a ten-week immersion experience offered at the college, or create a portfolio documenting animal, plant, and farm-power competencies.

CONFLICTS

Ned Houston, vice president of Sterling College and currently the longest-serving faculty member, has witnessed the arrival and departure of seven full-time presidents and nine farm managers. He's fond of referring to the institution as a dynamic, minute educational undertaking comparable in its miraculous existence to a bumblebee, "which because of its design should not be able to fly, yet it does." And, though the quandaries and conundrums facing this forty-seven-year-old agriculture program are far from unique, it is worth noting some of the perennial questions that Houston has seen plague the faculty in his thirty-plus years as an educator there. (Some of these questions, it should be noted, are addressed in Sterling's new continuous semester system, launched in the fall of 2010.) Houston smiles as he lists them: "The questions of: who does the work on the farm? Should we pay students? Is this work integrated into the college curriculum? Is it part of the work college tuition stipend?"

To illustrate this fundamental dilemma of labor, learning, and wages, Houston tells a story about how once, when students were working at Bruce Kaufman's Riverside Organic Farm as part of a course on organic vegetable production, a student complained, "How can we spend so much time on a two-credit course when it seemed like all we did was weed?" Houston holds the polarities out in front of him, one in each hand: "Two-credit course vs. it's all about weeds." He sighs. "These are the ag realities and how that translates into academics." He also notes what he calls the "punctuated acceleration of work" and how it defies the narrow schedule of a syllabus: "For example, haying, squishing potato beetles—things like that don't conform to predictable times; they happen when they happen."

Then there are the sometimes surprising dilemmas of food production for the college dining hall. These include, in Houston's words: "How often can we serve root crops, which most students aren't used to eating on a regular basis, even though, given our limited growing season, roots make the most sense to produce?" How much meat should be in our diet? Should we eat less meat that's organic or more meat that's conventionally grown? Should we feed organic grain to the hens and have organic eggs or feed conventional grain and save money? How do we weigh the educational value versus the consumable value of the food we grow? Houston observes, "Even though we've been doing it a long time, these are still big questions. The school garden has always been primarily an education tool more than

Figure 3.3. A student working with a young team of oxen. (Courtesy Sterling College.)

a food provider. How do you get production when the tool is education? If it's just production, we limit what students can do."

STERLING'S CARROTS RISE IN STATURE

The mission statement for the dining hall at Sterling College—a three-page document—proposes to manage the college's food system as an integral part of the school's educational program. Demonstrating a "living what we teach" philosophy, its goals include the development of cost-effective menus using Sterling-grown and locally grown food, the preparation of food and the composting of waste in an environmentally conscientious manner, and the use of these dining hall practices as a means of educating students about the effects of their food choices on the environment.

In some ways, the creation and implementation of the dining hall mission statement was a return to former food practices and philosophies. During the boys' school days, the kitchen was run by local women who simply translated their own mealmaking practices, with an emphasis on using what was local and available, into cooking on a larger scale. Back then, the school raised twenty lambs, five steers, and a litter of pigs that were butchered and kept in the East Hardwick meat lockers. The school cooks were adept at using every part of the animal to serve students hot lunches and dinners. Ann Ingerson recalls, "The drawback was there wasn't a lot of variety. It was wholesome and healthy, but not very exciting." Eventually, in the mid-1980s, the college contracted with a local catering service.

However, in the 1992–1993 academic year, three faculty members—Annie Volmer, Ann Ingerson, and Allison Van Akkeren—proposed to take the kitchen back from its contracted food service arrangement as a part of a long-range planning process for "Sterling 2000." Van Akkeren, who teaches nutrition and environmental education, among other courses, led the effort to reconnect the links between Sterling's academic program and its eating habits. Though it's been over a decade since the dining hall policy and management practices were overhauled, Van Akkeren remembers the time when the catering company was serving mostly packaged and highly processed food and was unable to incorporate all the produce from the Sterling College garden into the meals. Lamenting how the fresh garden carrots would languish unused until they turned to mush, she summarizes, "Ultimately, we realized the best way to meet our objectives was to have a Sterling-run kitchen."

The first component was to develop the dining hall menu to make optimum use of Sterling-grown and locally produced foods when available. The kitchen manager now incorporates Sterling's meat, eggs, vegetables, and fruits into the meals. During the fall semester, nearly 80 percent of the vegetables used by the dining hall have been grown in Sterling's gardens. In 2009, the college produced about eight thousand pounds of produce and thirty-five hundred pounds of meat. Additionally, the college purchases vegetables, eggs, apples, apple cider, yogurt, dry beans, wheat flour, beef, cheeses, butter, ice cream, and milk from a variety of local sources. It bakes its own bread using bulk supplies of whole-wheat flour. This choice alone saves enormously on plastic bags, preservatives, and shipping.

Van Akkeren notes, "Yes, it's more work: on Monday morning you've got to call in the yogurt so it comes to Squash Valley on Tuesday, or we won't get it on Thursday. Locally sourced food means one more call to make, and one more delivery truck that potentially won't get here on time, and one more check to write." It can also create tensions as different members of the campus community debate food choices. "Food is personal,"

Figure 3.4. Student work crew positions in the kitchen are always brightened by food preparation, especially cookiemaking and baking in the new wood-fired outdoor bread oven. (Courtesy Sterling College.)

says Van Akkeren, citing the complaints over the purchase of a $60 bucket of tahini—the price of a single meat-based meal for the college.

However, the comprehensiveness of the mission has enabled the college to go above and beyond locavorism. Van Akkeren says, "It includes trash, laundry, equipment purchasing—the whole environmental picture. Little things like how long we leave the hot table on and researching the issue of unplugging the coffee machines versus leaving them on." In fulfilling the vision of a more sustainable dining hall, Van Akkeren got rid of the bubbling "sugar water" machine, slashed the paper products budget, reduced the number of fridges to lower electricity usage, cut back on meat meals, and eventually stopped serving dessert at lunch. She says that, within the first year of implementing the mission, the school was able to reduce garbage to just one big bag per day (compared to the days when it took two people to haul the multiple bags each day to the dumpster). Overall, total kitchen expenditures were decreased by 44 percent.

Now, instead of relying on an external food service staff to produce the meals, the dining hall operates with a kitchen manager, a few cooks, and a band of student workers who do everything from contacting local growers to preserving foods, cooking meals, and washing pots. Interestingly, the dining hall jobs have become some of the most sought-after positions in the work program. "This kitchen—as in any household—is the hub of activity on campus," says Christina Erickson, Sterling's first sustainability coordinator, in the nominating essay that garnered the Sterling kitchen a Governor's Award for Environmental Excellence.

HOLISM

A Sense of Plate is what students are calling a new group on campus that meets weekly to further enhance awareness about food and agricultural issues. But the name also refers to the unofficial and indelible curriculum a Sterling student receives, otherwise known as "breakfast, lunch, and dinner." Everything that a student experiences outside the dining hall—whether it's emptying the compost buckets, or gathering sap, or studying next to a tray of leek starts situated in the library window—is quietly and overtly coming together to inform her understanding of her meal.

This holism is at the heart of Sterling's Sustainable Agriculture Program. The fiber arts course enriches students' understandings of plant and animal fibers and how they are used to produce cordage, yarns, and felts. Using wool from Sterling's lambs and dyes made from the college's garden plants, students begin to acquire the skills to produce their own clothes as well as understand the environmental and social impacts of their T-shirts and jeans.

"A Reverence for Wood," a shop class that has been offered by the college for more than twenty-five years, provides instruction in the use of woodworking tools and construction techniques; each student is offered guidance in the design and execution of a wood project. The farmstead arts course, created for the Summer Farm Program, borrows the same structure, helping the students take raw farm products, such as milk and maple syrup or beeswax and calendula flowers, to craft finished products like ice cream or hand salve.

Rick Thomas celebrates the college's emphasis on providing a holistic experience: "This is a place where a student who needs boards is going to learn how to go out, cut the tree, skid it out with horses, mill it, and then, if there's time, we'll go to the blacksmith shop and pound out our own nails."

THE CONTINUOUS SEMESTER

As its next step toward campus sustainability and the integration of the college farm and the academic curriculum, as of fall 2010 Sterling College as a whole moved to a continuous semester system. This will enable all students to take a full semester's worth of courses over the summer months. These are the months when garden production is in full swing and when heating and lighting usage can be kept to a bare minimum, enabling better overall use of the campus resources. This will also expose students who may not be enrolled in any agriculture courses to the rhythms and pulses of the growing season as they will walk by the planted gardens, see the horses drawing harrows in the field, or share a room with a sunburned, exhausted Summer Farm Semester student.

As a parallel strategy that mirrors making the best use of college and climatic resources, the school's livestock management approach is assuming an even more seasonal emphasis. "Since we're basically in growing zone 3"—meaning that winter temperatures can dip to minus fifteen below and colder—"our new livestock model is 'in the freezer by November' so we're not carrying animals through the coldest part of the year." This is Rick Thomas's oversimplified explanation for how the college is solving some of its perennial agricultural education quandaries.

In addition to streamlining livestock to essential breeding stock and draft animals for the winter months, the school is also working to enhance connections with local farmers. For example, in the spring, the college will borrow twenty pregnant ewes from Neil Urie, the owner of Bonnie View Farm in nearby South Albany, Vermont. The students in the animal science class will then be exposed to the prebirth, birth, and postbirth processes. Then the milking ewes will go back to Neil for milk production, and Sterling will keep the lambs to grow out and feed the school. In the fall, those lambs will be sheared as part of an ag tech class, and that wool will be used in the college's fiber arts curriculum. Meanwhile, students enrolled in the Summer Farm Semester will learn about pasture management, vaccinations, hoof trimming, etc. on a relatively small and manageable animal. The college also plans to use rabbits, male goats, and piglets as part of its three-season animal management model.

HARVEST

There are no departments at Sterling College: no English Department, no Agriculture Department, no Biology Department. Though the faculty are recognized for their areas of expertise, they are not grouped into departments lest the students perceive a disconnect, an illusory rift between disciplines. As the former director of writing studies and faculty in sustainable agriculture, I can testify to how thoughts can be cultivated and harvested as readily as carrots and tomatoes. My goal was to find ways for students to take the raw materials of their concerns, passions, and curiosities and turn them into essays and poems, proposals and research, or batches of pesto, jam, butter, and cheese, depending on which course I was teaching that day.

Students are encouraged to make connections that bridge across their courses, that connect theory with their experiences. That is the essence, the manifestation of the school's motto, "Working Hands, Working Minds." In this environment, a student in "Exploring Alternative Agriculture" reaped personal insight from the academic exercise of reflecting on the course reading in "Permaculture" following a visit to the permaculture nursery. She noted in her journal, "The most powerful aspect of Permaculture to me so far has been the fact that embedded in a discussion of what to place where, how to create a gray water system on a sloped property, etc., is a section devoted to Attitudes in Permaculture . . . and that underlying attitude is this, 'Disadvantages can be viewed as "problems" and we can take an energy-expensive approach to get rid of the problem, or we can think of everything as being a positive resource.' That attitude is one of the most useful tools for life that I have ever come across."

The smallness of the school enables students to implement changes at the cellular level within both the institution and themselves. As a project for "Exploring Alternative Agriculture," a participant could elect to research the distance a particular food item travels to end up in her mouth. One student, Julie Almeter ('08), chose to research chicken. In doing so, she learned about the lives and deaths of factory-raised and -processed poultry. Inspired by this assignment, she researched and compared the costs with those of other poultry processors. This led to a Farm Project whereby she acquired two hundred Cornish cross meat chickens, raised them on grass and organic feed in mobile units, and processed them with a team of students for the commencement day meal.

The Sustainable Agriculture Program at Sterling itself has evolved organically. From Ted Bermingham's institution-rescuing and responsibility-inducing *barn* to the diverse and vital present day *farm*, the components of which permeate the entire campus, the Sustainable Agriculture Program is the legacy of a few very good and enduring ideas. These ideas first served high school students from urban environments, but the adaptation, expansion, and development of them as the school became a college have given students access to fundamental experiences that they can carry with them as they progress into other fields, whether those are the fields of their own market gardens or the fields of another kind of work altogether.

Andrew Webster, a student who graduated from Sterling in 2006 and was selected to give a commencement address, began his remarks by cataloging what he had *not* learned at Sterling College: "I don't really know how a telephone works, or a photocopier, or a CD player. . . . I don't know the solution for feeding an overpopulated planet. I don't know how to stop global warming. I don't know what's going to happen when we run out of oil. I can't begin to fathom how it is that a species of plant or animal is going extinct at a rate of at least one per day." But, against the weight of this cumulative powerlessness, he offered what his Sterling College degree in sustainable agriculture had provided:

> I know how to start a fire in minus-five-degree weather.
> I know what it feels like to walk in snow up to your waist.
> I know how to feed a piglet.
> I know what it's like to have to get up early for farm chores when you've got a million other things on your mind and your bed is really warm and cozy.
> I know what it's like to kill, butcher, and eat an animal that you've helped raise since it was born.
> I know the names and some of the uses for just about every plant on the path from here to the lower dorms.
> I know what it's like to sit in a community meeting where every person is valued. It's a pretty amazing feeling.
> I know three different ways to safely cut down a tree.
> And I know what songs they sing in the sugarhouse during the late night maple sap boils.
> In case it isn't clear, what I'm trying to say is that size matters. What I've learned in the past four years is that, the closer we can get to our primary sources of our strength, the happier, the wiser, and the more capable of making good decisions we will be.

NOTE

1. This quotation and all others for which a source is not identified are taken from interviews or personal correspondence with the author.

◆ Part 2 ◆

Back to the Land

4

Evergreen State College (1972)

Interdisciplinary Studies
in Sustainable Agriculture

STEPHEN BRAMWELL, MARTHA ROSEMEYER,
AND MELISSA BARKER

The organic farm at Evergreen State College in Olympia, Washington, came into existence during an era of change. The decades of the 1960s and 1970s raised many questions, among them one about the safety and sustainability of industrial agriculture. In 1972, inspired by the back-to-the-land movement, faculty and students founded the Evergreen State College organic farm, giving physical form to their dreams of a better world. The creation of small, diversified, organically managed farms offered a way of connecting rising generations with the agricultural and practical living skills that would sustain land and community.

The history of the organic farm at Evergreen State College also illustrates the linkages between alternative approaches to agriculture and alternative approaches to education. Evergreen opened its doors in 1971 in the vanguard of a movement promoting experiential education and the breaking down of disciplinary barriers. Manifesting this approach, students in one of Evergreen's first classes, an environmental design program, discovered that a derelict homestead on Lewis Road, bordering the Evergreen campus, was college property. The Lewis Road farm captured the imagination of many students in this class. Bent on farming the property, through the winter of 1971–1972 they scoured agricultural texts for information, invited an extension agronomist to help with planning, and held fifty-person meetings that culminated in the submission of a successful farm-development proposal to Evergreen's Board of Regents.

By the early spring of 1972, these students and others had knocked down moldy wallboard in the Lewis Road farmhouse, pulled remnant old-growth stumps from the ground, and mapped out Evergreen State College's first organic garden. On a shoestring budget of $800, secured through an Evergreen grant for student projects, the farm students started their first season by building a chicken coop and putting in a garden. Eventually, these efforts would lead to what is currently a five-acre farm serving a forty-eight-hundred-member student body.

EVOLUTION OF A STUDENT FARM

In its forty years of existence, Evergreen has earned a national reputation for innovative education based on a high level of individual freedom and academic challenge.[1] Its unique curriculum features several mutually supportive components: instead of classes, it has full-time interdisciplinary *programs* taught by small teams of faculty with a diverse range of disciplinary qualifications. Students take one program (such as the Ecological Agriculture [Eco Ag] Program) at a time for a minimum of sixteen contact hours per week. These programs often continue for two to three quarters. Usually more than one faculty member teaches a program, and with a student-faculty ratio of twenty-five to one, program sizes range from twenty-five to seventy-five students. The faculty team approach, where all faculty members are present at all class sessions, allows both inter- and intradisciplinarity, with an emphasis on synthesis. Evaluation of students is also somewhat novel as written evaluations are used instead of a letter or numeric grading scale. Additionally, teaching at Evergreen strives for a nonhierarchical learning community fostered through potlucks, seminars, frequent use of case studies, and ample opportunities for student teaching.

The structure of programs at the Evergreen farm is best understood in the context of the teaching and learning model at the college as a whole. *Learning contracts* at Evergreen are essentially independent studies organized by a student or group of students and proposed to a potential faculty sponsor who is then responsible for guidance and final written evaluation. The group of students that submitted the original farm-development plan in the winter of 1971–1972 was organized as a group-learning contract supported by a faculty member.

Through the remainder of the 1970s, over twenty individual and group learning contracts utilized the Evergreen farm. In the early 1980s, the multiquarter, faculty-planned Eco Ag Program was developed as a way of instituting a coordinated interdisciplinary curriculum that utilized the farm but was not directly responsible for its management—this task still fell to the farm caretakers, students who lived in the farmhouse and worked part-time on the farm. Meanwhile, independent learning contracts continued to satisfy the primary labor needs of the farm. This changed in 1985 with the hiring of a part-time farm manager and the establishment of a three-quarter, full-time practical farming program. This was called the Practice of Sustainable Agriculture (PSA) Program and was taught by the farm manager.

Over the years, the ground-level appearance of the Evergreen student farm took shape in the context of both considerable academic freedom and relative physical obscurity. As a non-land-grant institution established two or three decades prior to the emergence of mainstream interest in sustainable and organic agriculture, Evergreen saw its farm programs evolve with few well-defined curricular expectations. With respect to physical obscurity, the farm lies at the end of a wooded trail from upper campus. Along the way, salal, huckleberry, and sword fern crowd the understory of a towering second-growth forest of Douglas fir, alder, and western red cedar. After a fifteen-minute walk through this lush ecosystem fed by fifty-plus inches of rain per year, the trail emerges in a five-acre clearing. An exploratory intellectual climate and remoteness help explain the cacophony of production fields, experimental projects, unique infrastructural elements, and other manifestations of creative energy that greet the visitor to the Evergreen farm: student initiative, curricular open-mindedness, and an ad hoc approach to farm infrastructure development have all informed the Evergreen farm look.

On the farm itself, the teaching model focuses on small-scale farming techniques. The growing area is composed of about two acres of annual crops, a half acre of perennials, and another half acre of peripheral open space at the shady transition from field to forest that is kept in grass for livestock production. Fields for annual vegetable crops are rotated through growing beds running north-south, with the shadier pasture at the southern end. Perennial crops raised on the farm include apples, kiwis, wine grapes, plums, hazelnuts, chestnuts, walnuts, pears, Asian pears, and figs. A chicken coop adjacent to the orchard houses one hundred laying hens and fifteen ducks. The use of moveable electro-net fencing allows the chickens and ducks to range free in the orchard understory during the growing season and over the entire farm in the winter. Next to the pole barn are two beehives and the colorfully painted composting toilet, complete with a jigsawed crescent moon.

Faculty and students have carried out research on the farm, such as breeding vegetables for local, organic conditions with the nonprofit Organic Seed Alliance and wheat and quinoa variety trials with Washington State University. Community gardens provide students and community members with twelve- by twelve-foot plots to grow vegetables for their own consumption.

The northern end of the fields is hemmed by a series of greenhouses, the farm workroom, a walk-in cooler, shaded food-processing tables, a storage shed topped by a wooden gnome, a toolshed, a garage housing farm supplies and the biofuel facility, and a pole barn for fencing material, tractors, and cultivation equipment. On the periphery of this, along the driveway to Lewis Road, is the composting facility and Demeter's Garden, a student-run permaculture demonstration site.

Drawing on these diverse resources, students at the farm learn to grow and sell a full complement of products, including organic vegetables, tree fruits, berries, herbs, fungi, chicken and duck eggs, small livestock, vegetable seeds, grains, and processed foods from the value-added kitchen. To help facilitate this education, the Center for Ecological Learning and Living (CELL) was created in 2003 to bring the associated operational units of the farm to one management table. These units include Demeter's Garden permaculture demonstration site, the community garden, the biodiesel group, the medicinal plant garden, the compost facility (including both vermi- and forced-air composting systems), the farmhouse, and main fields (including both program and research fields). The stated mission of CELL is to combine ecological design and building with organic agriculture to address the broader goals of sustainable living. Keeping all the farm units synchronized has not been easy. Nevertheless, forty years has resulted in a workable suite of teaching facilities that continue to evolve out of our students' dreams of a better world.

ROLES AND REASONS FOR THE FARM

As a reaction to industrial agriculture, student demand for a practical, locally based small farming program far and away has been the primary reason for the Evergreen farm's existence and continued success. Wendell Berry has noted that a function of "industrial education" over the years has

Figure 4.1. Freshman orientation brings new faces to the Evergreen farm. Somewhere amid ear buds, head scratching, and sunglasses are future farmers. (Courtesy Evergreen State College.)

been to "preserve and protect an ignorance of local people and places."[2] In his mind, an economy capable of mining soil organic matter or creating junk food is possible only when decisions are sufficiently removed from impacts. This is how the worst of global and national economies operate. By contrast, in a local economy, people are more likely to ask and answer such questions as, "Did *I* do that?" "What will this do to *our* water supply?" or, "Is this healthy?" Participants in this economy will be less likely to accept damaging outcomes.

The education at the Evergreen farm teaches students about the power of local people and places. Students can become frustrated with political discussions on campus because global political problems tend to exceed the human scale. By comparison, when a student manages the on-campus farm stand, he or she is helping provide vegetables to the campus community in a way that directly substitutes for vegetables imported from California or elsewhere, sidestepping the industrial food chain with all its petroleum dependency, trade inequities, and pollution woes. The acquisition of local knowledge returns student choice, student action, and student impact to a scale that can be immediately experienced and valued. Year after year, students get excited and become proud to stake out a victory against ecological dismay, food insecurity, and corporate excess by means of a freshly pulled carrot, a pair of muddy boots, or a newly washed egg.

Developing a sense of order and tangible meaning in their lives is

Figure 4.2. A student in the Practice of Sustainable Agriculture Program harvests tomatoes. Farm workdays are busy and group intensive, but students also find time for reflection while tending the crops. (Courtesy Evergreen State College.)

another reason that the Evergreen farm attracts students. Some of the reasons students give for their involvement at the farm include "to form a personal relationship with the food I eat," "to run a self-sufficient homestead," "the conventional food system is ecologically unsound," "to be outside," "to feed my family," and "farming is a way I can understand life."

The motivations of student farmers at Evergreen vary from the more obvious, immediate desire to farm or garden to long-range interests in teaching or working for food justice. Many students are older and returning to pursue a second career or to satisfy a personal desire for self-sufficiency. Many motivations have a common denominator in what could be called *contextual knowledge*. Such knowledge is difficult to classify but tends to be practical, applied, immediate, traditional, interdisciplinary, hands-on, local, and collaborative. It also spans a common fissure in modern education in that it can be both applied and theoretical. Whether brain tanning a sheep hide or analyzing the chemical composition of carotenoids in late blight-tolerant heirloom tomato varieties, students link the applied and the theoretical around tangible issues. A question that can be answered through a contextual approach might be, Can heating coils wound through *this* static aeration compost pile heat our greenhouse? Good answers involve both theory and application.

So, while student backgrounds and motivations are varied, a key strength of the Evergreen farm is that it can provide the context of local needs and interests and the engagement that comes with an experiential, place-based education. The more theoretically based component of the work provides the contextual science while also providing some transferable skills for future educators, policymakers, and social justice advocates.

What to Teach: Curricular Choices and Questions

One thing we have found at the Evergreen farm is that existing curricula to teach sustainable farming and food system topics for today's student are relatively underdeveloped. Surprisingly, perhaps, this remains the case despite the current interest in healthy food, organic agriculture, and sustainability. Evidence of this is apparent if one compares the volume of curricular material available to an introductory social or natural sciences educator to that available to an introductory sustainable agriculture educator. Because of this, a developing student farm program must answer fundamental questions that are essential to providing a high-quality education in agriculture. Some questions we have asked ourselves at Evergreen over the years (and are still asking) illustrate how and why our current farm programs have taken shape:

- What is the length of the program (measured in quarters)? Should it follow the farming season?
- How do on-farm and in-class components of the education fit together?
- What are the goals of the curriculum? To train farmers, to use agriculture as a vehicle for general education, to learn life skills, to train social justice advocates, all of the above?
- Which agroecological systems will the farm teach?
- How much class time and how much farm time will the program include?
- How will the farm balance production with education?
- How will the farm balance the teaching of farming for the present with the teaching of farming for the future?
- What mode of in-class and in-field instruction is used, what

learning objectives guide the curriculum, and how are students evaluated?

- What is the balance between natural and social sciences that is necessary or that time permits—for example, how much time should be devoted to horticulture and how much time to agricultural policy issues?
- To what extent should the instructor follow a set curriculum versus taking advantage of immediate on-farm teachable moments?

At some periods in its history, academic programs related to the Evergreen farm have tracked the farming season (spring, summer, fall); at others, they have followed the standard academic calendar (fall, winter, spring). The obvious challenge is that the two do not align. Complicating this situation at Evergreen is the concept of faculty rotation, in which no one faculty member teaches the same program year after year. Grounded in the perhaps idealistic antidepartmental sentiment prevailing at the time Evergreen was founded, faculty rotations can frustrate year-to-year continuity, particularly given the importance of attention to seasonal cycles on a farm. When the farm program has operated in line with the farming season, faculty have had difficulty rotating in and out of other academic programs that track the academic calendar. Nevertheless, balancing in-class time with farm time may be easier at the Evergreen farm than at other institutions owing to the full-time commitment that students make to the programs they are enrolled in. An approach to education that connects theory to practice on a farm is certainly helped by enjoying a twenty-eight-hour per week student commitment. On Tuesdays and Thursdays, students spend nine or more hours on the farm, while two four-hour windows of classroom time are available on Mondays and Wednesdays.

The long hours are certainly challenging to students, but we find that the combination of actual farming and complementary in-class instruction provides a broader, more holistic education than that provided by traditional academic programs. The cornerstone of this effort is utilizing agriculture as a form of experiential education. Additionally, the important life skills of timeliness, responsibility, and following through on a task until completion are reinforced for students. Farm tasks themselves require coordination, stamina, figuring out how to deal mentally with repetitive tasks, and the organization of work for physical efficiency and ergonomic safety.

With respect to the outcome of Evergreen farm programs, familiarizing students with the basics of human subsistence is a great jumping-off point for a variety of undertakings. Not all the students will go on to farm in the Pacific Northwest, but a student farm–based education can be both a vehicle for *learning how to learn* and a fundamental beginning for many livelihoods. Among former Evergreen farm students are a significant percentage of the local food and agriculture community, including farmers, small-scale food processors, and agricultural policy food activists. Others are found farming elsewhere, working in food justice, urban agriculture, organic and environmental regulation (including the current deputy administrator of the USDA National Organic Program), and community garden and farmers' market management, working as sustainable chefs and entrepreneurs, teaching at all levels, and simply living as engaged citizens. Taken as a group, former students have played a significant role in the renaissance of farming and local food economies in western Washington and around the country.

Choosing farm-based curricula speaks to a central challenge of sustainable agriculture today: How can educational farms balance ecological integrity, social well-being, and economic viability? Some ideal ecological practices remain too expensive given the contemporary cost balance in farming of land, labor, and capital. Consequently, it falls to student farm programs to teach both more ecologically based programs for food production that will be needed in the future and current agricultural systems. As Ann Clark and Jacinda Fairholm describe it, "Ours is a future of full-cost accounting, where the requirement that product price reflect all costs of production shifts the balance in favor of local production and consumption, reacquaints the producer and consumer, and so breaks the power monopoly of specialization, consolidation, and globalization which otherwise awaits organic as well as conventional farmers. . . . New farmers will have to recapture their roots as self-directed, independent, and self-reliant information seekers and decision-makers—rather than being dependent upon paid consultants and distant experts."[3]

Reflecting this rebalancing of input pricing, the Evergreen farm has made shifts in its production plan linked to increasing costs (if not yet full-cost accounting) of farm inputs. From the 1980s forward, the predominant production model on the farm was that of an organic mixed-vegetable direct-marketing farm; in 2004, we adopted the community-supported agriculture (CSA) model as part of our production. Introduction of the CSA production system was tied to the efflorescence of this farming system throughout the United States. This approach provides reasonable

Fig. 4.3. A farm student brings food wastes to the farm for composting. Campus wastes can be used to move toward closing fertility cycles on small teaching farms. Distinctions between production and education can be necessary. (Courtesy Evergreen State College.)

assurance of economic security through advance payments, proximity of production to consumption, and farmer-citizen connections. However, direct marketing is not enough to address full-cost accounting and rising input prices.

For all its benefits, an organic, direct-marketing production system can (though not in all cases) become reliant on fertility inputs to balance nutrients lost off the farm as crops are sold. Typical amendments promoted in the primary farming texts and used in some of our programs include seed meal, lime, rock phosphate, kelp meal, and industrial confinement animal manures. Additionally, the production of eggs from laying hens, a cornerstone of many small-scale, diversified, and on-farm market stands, relies on organic feed, the ingredients of which are typically sourced nationally or, in the case of many farms in western Washington, internationally from Canada. Curricularly speaking, alternatives to input-intensive approaches are not always practicable on small-scale diversified vegetable farms, yet teaching alternatives to these approaches is imperative to future farming practices capable of weathering climate change, escalating fertilizer costs, and expensive future transport.

The offshoot of this is that our student farm programs strive to strike a balance between emulating sustainable agriculture production models and pushing the ecological paradigm for agriculture further than may be financially viable at present. Our teaching farm should draw on expertise from, but not mimic too closely, the skills and patterns in the broader sustainable agriculture community. The obstacle to practicing this is that educational institutions (Evergreen included) draw from the proximate pool of expertise among farmers and educators in the sustainable agriculture community. Therefore, we can end up in the paradoxical situation of both striving to exceed, and being dependent on, the sustainable agriculture knowledge appropriate primarily to *current* economic paradigms. Our programs strive to address this issue.

CURRENT EVERGREEN FARM PROGRAMS

Of the three agriculture and food system–related programs currently in place (PSA, Eco Ag, and Food, Health, and Sustainability), the PSA Program is the one that consistently stewards the farm. PSA is designed to provide students with interdisciplinary natural science course work complementary to practical farm management. Currently, PSA meets for eight hours a week of academic work (lecture and lab) and twenty hours a week of hands-on practicum. For the last several years, one full-time PSA faculty member has teamed with the full-time farm manager and several paid student employees serving twenty-five student farmers for a nine-month, three-quarter program. As the farm relies on PSA students for farm labor throughout the growing season, academic work seeks to provide more in-depth scientific understanding of farm ecology and decision-making. Examples of questions we address are: How are irrigation rates calculated? How do soil tests translate into nutrient management planning? What management skills are critical to substituting living mulches for plastic mulches? In the spring, soil sampling and nutrient management planning are a key part of the class. Students study nutrient cycling, interpret soil tests, and assess the nitrogen contributions of various cover crops and soil organic matter. In the winter, business planning and farm planning are examined. Students figure out how to plan a twenty-week CSA, assess crop varieties, learn about plant breeding for agricultural biodiversity, and study enterprise budgets and cash-flow analysis.

Specific topics in this program are determined by the skills and knowledge brought by the farm manager and the PSA faculty but also by frequent guest lecturers. The program recently has incorporated talks by representatives from the Washington State Department of Agriculture Organic Program, Washington State University's Small Farms Program, and sustainable business faculty at Evergreen.

Additional agricultural programs that use the farm, although to a lesser extent, are Eco Ag and Food, Health, and Sustainability. Both are nine-month, full-time, team-taught programs. The Eco Ag Program is broader in geographic focus than is PSA and uses ecological lenses to analyze agricultural systems. It involves a strong emphasis on ecology and soil science, with more focus on lab science and research. Teaching *systems thinking*—not just for agricultural production but for food systems more broadly—is a major goal of the program. Additionally, social science approaches and topics, particularly agricultural history and policy, are a strong focus. Having a grasp of U.S. agricultural history is critical to understanding why we are asking questions about agricultural sustainability. From the colonization of North America through to the most recent farm bill, Eco Ag students read and discuss about six books per quarter in a seminar format.

Having faculty with complementary backgrounds coteaching the Eco Ag Program is ideal—for example, a plant/soil ecologist teaching with a veterinarian. In this program, both faculty are present for all activities and engage with each other's respective disciplines, thus modeling learning and research behavior for the students.

The Food, Health, and Sustainability program, or "eco-gastronomy," focuses on the chemical behavior of biological molecules at the nexus between food quality, nutrition, and health. The genetics and evolution of humans and their foodstuffs tie these themes together. The class primarily uses the farmhouse kitchen facility for weekly cooking lab exercises to illustrate scientific principles involved in food preparation and food quality, for example, the assessment of the swelling of starch grains with the cooking of a potato or fat crystal formation in tempering chocolate.

Field trips are also an essential component of the Evergreen farm programs. Single and multiday farm field trips form a cornerstone of our students' farming and food systems experience. Workshops and field trips expose students to such topics as hydro-powered, stone-ground wheat milling, arc welding, ecological pest management, applied botany, grafting, basic construction, soil quality testing, and a myriad of other subjects. It is generally on field trips that the full picture of sustainability as a balance between ecological and human health, economic viability and social justice—all within the context of ground-level experimentation and farmer innovation—is fully grasped.

Management of the Student Farm

In the early 1970s, the Evergreen farm was managed by students and community members through a farm board. The board was composed of selected student groups, farm-oriented faculty, administrators, and interested community members. In contrast, since the mid-1980s the farm has been managed by a single college staff member, the farm manager, who is also involved in teaching PSA. The transition to decisionmaking by a farm manager facilitated operations but also somewhat compromised broad community representation among some groups that the farm seeks to serve.

The farm manager brought continuity to the farm and academic and practical guidance to students. The first farm managers were in charge of overseeing all farm operations and delivering an academic curriculum. In 1987, the half-time farm manager taught the first full-time farm management program (PSA). The overwhelming job of managing both students and the farm was soon recognized, and the farm manager's contract was expanded to a three-quarter-time position. Many of the same problems the farm is currently facing were also relevant during this time, such as ensuring continuity between rotating programs and faculty, securing funding, providing adequate care for farm livestock, maintaining a sense of the overall farm vision, and managing the delicate balance between student initiative and a set farm plan.

Beginning in 2003, a part-time faculty member began working with the farm manager to deliver the experiential curriculum of PSA. The position has expanded into a full-time visiting faculty position, and another permanent faculty member in sustainable agriculture was recently hired to rotate into teaching PSA. Up to this point, it has been the responsibility of the farm manager to orient the new visiting faculty to the PSA curriculum. The hiring of a permanent faculty member will help the farm manager, allowing the faculty, instead of the farm manager, to take responsibility for curriculum continuity.

The farm manager, with the faculty, creates on-farm seasonal teaching activities for students following the production schedule of a small-scale diversified farm. The farm manager oversees the entire organic farm, which includes annual and perennial field planning and production, marketing and sales, orchard management, on-farm research, beekeeping, biodiesel production, vermi- and aerated compost production, value-added food processing, organic and salmon-safe farm certifications, mushroom log cultivation, small livestock and egg production, and student projects.[4] In addition to the students enrolled in the PSA Program, the farm manager is assisted by paid student employees. The student employees are an essential part of farm management, especially for vegetable production, marketing, and composting. The number of students employed and hours worked is dependent on the college's financial situation and varies from one to three part-time positions. The employee positions allow dedicated students to gain further farming experience, and many student employees go on to run their own farms.

The management of student-designed and -built infrastructure also falls to the farm manager. The farm is rich in student-designed agricultural facilities that are great assets but also require management to function properly. Student-initiated projects are funded and implemented in a number of ways. By drawing on the diversity of expertise on campus, we have gained wide support for student initiatives. Many student projects have come and gone at the farm, including a weather station, a milk cow, a straw bale shed, and a solar greenhouse. Some of the most important still in existence are the following:

- The twenty-four-hundred-square-foot farmhouse was designed and built by students in the mid-1970s. It is the most prominent of the student projects and is currently the main academic teaching facility. Within the structure is a one-thousand-square-foot class-room, a seven-hundred-square-foot kitchen that is a certified food-processing facility, and a caretaker apartment.
- The compost and vermicompost facility was built in 2002. We currently compost all farm wastes, though, in the past, we have composted all campus food wastes (not including the main campus dining hall). The compost facility was the product of sustained effort over a period of three years, at the end of which a student successfully procured donations from an outside organization as well as campus sources.
- The biodiesel and biofuels facility began as an independent project within the PSA Program in 2004 and was completed through a group contract. Three students built the original facility in a corner of the farm's garage. The facility has seen many upgrades in the last six years and continues to attract student interest. The current funding is provided through the college's Clean Energy Committee and has expanded to include the design of a farm-scale wood gasification and biofuel algae production unit.
- Two student-designed toolsheds were recently built by students on the farm to house and secure farm tools for the community gardens and Demeter's Garden. These areas of the farm are student coordinated and are not usually part of an academic program. The students worked closely with the campus's Facilities Services, the health and safety officer, and the Campus Land Use Committee (CLUC).
- The freestanding composting toilet started as a project through the Eco Ag Program and was completed via an independent student contract. Again, the students worked closely with the campus's Facilities Services, the health and safety officer, CLUC, and the local health department.
- Two large, permanent hoop-style greenhouses were funded by Aramark, Evergreen's food service provider. The project was initiated by a student intern who was working with Aramark and taking the PSA Program.
- The welcome sign and kiosk for Demeter's Garden permaculture site were designed as part of a group project in PSA. The sign and kiosk were funded by a foundation activity grant and were built by students in collaboration with the college's facilities department.

Figure 4.4. The farm manager, Melissa Barker (with one of the farm's laying hens), in front of the original homestead barn on Lewis Road. (Courtesy Carlos Sanchez.)

Financially, day-to-day production at the farm relies on an operating budget derived solely from farm sales to the campus food service, a student-run café, the campus farm stand, the farm's twenty-share, twenty-week CSA, a campus office produce delivery program, and on-farm sales. Maintenance of the farm's various outbuildings, partial payment of utilities, and staff and faculty time are supported by the college. Academic goals and the desire for less tedium on the part of the students can conflict with the need to maintain a steady flow of farm operating funds.

Overall, the farm is a diversified and continually changing entity that needs consistent management to maintain curricular continuity and balance student creativity and initiatives. The farm manager works with students to foster and develop projects that contribute to the farm and help further its educational and sustainability goals. He or she also interacts with the campus and the greater community by selling produce, leading farm tours, and hosting on-farm activities. Challenges for the farm manager include balancing a wide range of tasks (from paperwork to farm management to on-farm teaching), orienting faculty, fund-raising, and completing the farmwork with student labor while trying to make each task a learning opportunity. Hiring a permanent full-time farm manager has led to a more successful student experience and enhanced community involvement. An effective farm manager has been critical to the educational experience of the many students working and learning on the Evergreen organic farm.

INTERACTION WITH THE COLLEGE AND BROADER COMMUNITY

From its inception, the farm has been conceived as a project of the college, not just the purview of any particular agricultural program. Over the years, many programs have focused on or contained some specific component at the farm—from art, medicinal plants, and agricultural research to sustainable design and the building of the farmhouse. Different administrative units of the college have contributed funding for buildings and expertise. In some years, there has been enthusiastic participation from programs across disciplines. In other years, the fifteen-minute walk to the farm has seemed very long indeed, with the result that the farm is perceived as a world apart.

This separation from the main campus can be both positive and negative. The lack of an institutional feeling has made the farmhouse, with its kitchen and wooden decks, a destination for end-of-the-quarter potlucks, workshops, and retreats. Escaping through the woods to the farm has been attractive for programs and individuals alike. On the other hand, the distance of the farm from upper campus can also result in an out of sight, out of mind mentality with respect to maintenance needs. The farm buildings are sometimes neglected by Facilities Services when it comes to cleaning and care, and it is often unclear who is responsible for the maintenance of student or program projects. All these factors contributed to the decision to create the CELL as a way of facilitating communication and cooperation between those who are managing the farm on a day-to-day basis (the farm manager and student farmers) and other, more occasional users of the farm. Continuity remains a key challenge.

With respect to the broader Olympia community, since 1981 the farm has sponsored the one-day Harvest Festival in October. This event features tours, live music, apple cider pressing, children's activities such as a vegetable toss, and various educational exhibits, including one hosted by Fungi Perfecti, a mycoremedial and mycomedicinal business started by a former student. A larger extension function for the Evergreen organic farm—the publication of organic gardening bulletins or the staffing of a hotline, for instance—has often been suggested. However, since Evergreen is neither a research nor an extension school, this has been difficult to justify under a teaching mission. The farm answers a number of inquiries weekly concerning the topic du jour—from biodiesel production to chicken raising—but without adequate staffing.

One of the purposes of CELL is to assist the farm manager in evaluating proposed projects on the farm. It also has provided a venue for discussion of the activities of two prominent student clubs with access to land at the farm: Demeter's Garden and the Community Garden. The coordinators meet regularly with CELL to discuss their ideas. A challenge for a grassroots organization such as CELL is to gain a place on the college's administrative chart.

ACCOMPLISHMENTS, CHALLENGES, AND FUTURE PLANS

The greatest accomplishments of the Evergreen farm are the contributions of our students to both local and national sustainable agriculture movements and the consistency and steady growth of farm program offerings. Additionally, the growth of infrastructure over the last four years has been significant as our students are supported in realizing their ideas.

Challenges include farming in an increasingly tall forest, the buildup of soil-borne plant pathogens in fields, the asynchronicity between the agricultural calendar and the academic schedule, the lack of facilities to accommodate larger classes on-site, and chronic understaffing. The trade-off between the educational and the business nature of the organic farm provides dynamic tension: faculty, staff, and student employee salaries are paid through the academic division of the college, but the farm's operational budget comes directly from the farming enterprises. A recent program that focused on developing a community vision and consensus for the farm's future suggested expanding the farm's field area. A green, sustainable agriculture and food lab was designed by a student program and is now being built, and a third agriculture faculty has been hired. At Evergreen today, it is possible to dwell on continuing challenges to our agriculture programs, but we also recognize that a few decades of farm classes and site development have resulted in significant accomplishments.

Despite the challenges a school might face in creating a student farm, our experience at Evergreen since the early 1970s suggests that there is wisdom in making a learning laboratory out of a farm and in integrating agriculture into a broader liberal arts education. Experiencing the results of student empowerment, and creating space for the emergence of a healthy group process, is one of the more magical experiences of being an educator.

Ultimately, student farms are an agrarian version of experiential education, with its many transformations through physical exertion, team building, tactile and gastronomic experiences, and encounters with the basic, gritty underpinnings of human sustenance. In this way, on-farm education grounds theory in practice and inspires students to passionately engage with the world on its quest for sustainability.

STUDENT REFLECTIONS

THE IMPACT OF A STUDENT FARM

MARYROSE LIVINGSTON

Eco Ag was my first introduction to poultry, specifically a laying flock of ducks and chickens. It was a wonderful hands-on thing to do my own butchering. It was also my first exposure to raising pigs. We fed them on bakery waste. A person on the grounds crew, a grumpy old German man, said, "You can't do this with pigs, you'll have worm problems." We ignored him, and we raised really good pork, which we custom cut and sold to the college staff. I fell in love with pigs. We now raise pigs on our farm in the same way as we did at Evergreen because it was really fun. I had never done vegetable production before either, and I loved those workdays where the whole class seeded carrots or weeded beets. I was the lead fencer on the main field—I built that outer fence. I had worked on farms before coming to college, so I had some practical knowledge. But I don't think I would have been able to raise poultry and pigs without the experience of having done it on the student farm. That practical knowledge is so vital to paving the way for people to step out on their own. It was the same with the cider press: here at Northland we bought the same one we had at the student farm. I think it's extremely important for students to have a place for hands-on learning. You can't sit in the classroom and learn this.

Maryrose Livingston attended Evergreen from 1987 to 1991, taking Eco Ag with Pat Labine. She now runs Northland Sheep Dairy in upstate New York with her partner, Donn Hewes, selling sheep's cheese, wool, grass-fed lamb and beef, and whey-fed pork.

Notes

1. http://www.collegesofdistinction.com; National Survey of Student Engagement, 2006, 2007, 2008, 2009, nsse.iub.edu.

2. W. Berry, "The Agrarian Standard," in *The Essential Agrarian Reader: The Future of Culture, Community, and the Land,* ed. Norman Wirzba (Lexington: University Press of Kentucky, 2003), 23–33, 25.

3. E. A. Clark and J. Fairholm, "'New Farmers' Need Skills Ag Schools Don't Offer—Yet," *New Farm,* October 2002, available at http://newfarm .rodaleinstitute.org.

4. "Launched in 1995, Salmon-Safe works to restore water quality and Salmon habitat in Pacific Northwest salmon watersheds, . . . by evaluating farm operations that are endorsed by our independent professional certifiers and promoted by the Salmon-Safe label" (http://www.cascadiapermaculture.com/salmon.html).

5

University of Oregon (1976)

Designing for Change

Ann Bettman

The Urban Farm has been both a class and a place at the University of Oregon since 1976. The farm itself is a one-and-a-half-acre plot of land on the north edge of campus. The Urban Farm class is a four-credit course offered through the Department of Landscape Architecture but open to all university students. The farm's goals are to teach students to grow organic food and to encourage them to become advocates for sustainable farming practices as a means of protecting the health of our air, land, and water. This chapter describes the origins, evolution, and current structure of the University of Oregon's Urban Farm project from the perspective of someone who has been intimately involved in that project for more than twenty-five years.

Urban Farm Histories

The 1970s

The old four-square farmhouse sat on the banks of the Willamette River in the middle of a cherry orchard. When you look at the 1937 aerial photograph of the site, you can see the dotted geometry of the fruit and nut orchards all along the river, just south of a gravel mining operation. Later aerial photographs show how the university and the Riverfront Research Park buildings gradually replaced most of the agricultural land.

In 1974, Richard Britz was hired to teach in the Landscape Architecture Department even though he was an architect without formal landscape training. Those were the days when something like that could happen—an architect teaching in the Landscape Architecture Department! Richard arrived in Eugene with a full-blown vision of "the Edible City" in his head. In 1975, he officially named the old student garden plot across Franklin Boulevard the Urban Farm. The term *Urban Farm* doesn't seem so strange now, but back then it struck people as an oxymoron. I wasn't involved in the farm during Richard's years, so I can offer only what I have pieced together from his stories and notebooks, from my interviews with his students, and from direct observation of the scene. Richard never bothered to ask for permission to expand the small garden into the Urban Farm; he just did it. There weren't any protracted negotiations or drawing up of memoranda of understanding. In the late 1970s, hordes of hungry students fed on the idealism and activism that the Urban Farm represented. In the summer of 1977, Richard was able to secure a VISTA worker to work the farm during the summer, and that helped make the farm into more than just a spring farming class.

Richard often recited the litany of modern-day horrors: agricultural roots to the land severed in favor of industrialization, immigration to the cities for jobs, the centralization of capital, urban chaos, eroding farmland, decaying city and town cores, dominance, dependence, unequal exchange, greed, and the widespread loss of dignity and spirit. Students were all too familiar with the "Problem"; what they wanted, and what Richard gave them, was a vision of hope and an inspirational project. Richard believed that growing food was one of the first steps toward making communities more self-sufficient and more livable. Showing aerial photographs of Eugene's city grid, he pointed to the vacant areas in the centers of the blocks that were unused and, thus, wasted. The land area at the farm was equal in size to the center of a typical block. Richard proposed reorganizing the city around the block unit to maximize urban food production, increase density, increase energy efficiency, and build community. The Urban Farm was a political, economic, and social model.

The peak of the Britz years at the farm came in 1978 when these concepts were explored and drawn up in a joint architecture/landscape studio with G. Z. "Charlie" Brown of the Architecture Department. Carefully rendered designs showed the gradual transformation of a West Eugene neighborhood block, starting with a critical mass of block residents forming a homeowners association to buy the commons and build a farmhouse. Later phases showed complete on-site recycling of wastes, the use of photovoltaic cells for the production of electricity, and the conversion of parts

Figure 5.1. Students making compost. (Courtesy John Carson.)

of the streets into spaces for recreation and growing plants. Charlie taught students to use analysis and design matrices to address social issues. The studio was an interdepartmental success, and the large-scale model of the block filled the Architecture School lobby for a festive, standing-room-only review.

Richard's systems diagram of the Urban Farm showed the functional relation of the parts to the whole in terms of energy flows. Animals were an integral part of the farm, although there were many chicken and rabbit deaths owing to raccoons, dogs, and probably passersby. There was a comfrey/rabbits/rabbit manure/compost/garden beds cycle and a similar buckwheat/chickens cycle. One of Richard's friends was Mike Gravino, a Buckminster Fuller groupie, who started a successful business called Garbagio's to collect food waste from local restaurants. The food waste was then fed to the worm bins at the farm, and the earthworm castings were added to the compost, which was then spread on the vegetable beds.

Richard always taught the urban farm class in addition to his regular teaching responsibilities. The good part of that was that the farm was integrated into the studio culture of the school, but the downside was that Richard was overloaded and his performance, though inspired, was sometimes spotty.

The last years of the 1970s in the department passed under a tenure-decision cloud. In 1979, Richard went up for and was denied tenure. Jerry Diethelm, then head of the department, urged Richard to reapply the following year, publicly stating that, if Richard didn't get tenure, then he, Jerry, would step down as department head. Richard was again denied tenure, and Jerry stepped down. The real reason Richard was denied tenure was never clear, and maybe no one ever really knows the reasons behind decisions like that. There were a lot of theories. Richard titled his tenure case "Under Siege," which had an inappropriate tone in those post-Vietnam times. Richard was often late for class and occasionally wouldn't show up at all. And then there was the undeniable fact that he was not an officially credentialed landscape architect. Probably it was a combination of these things. Richard left the university in 1981. A handful of stalwart believers tried to carry on, but, without Richard's charisma and energy, the farm languished. Finally, in desperation, the last graduate teaching fellow plowed the whole place under and walked. The Urban Farm was dead.

The 1980s

But the farm wasn't dead. Ironically, it was a small group of students specializing in interior architecture (the design and construction of interior spaces) who conceived, raised money for, and built the modest greenhouse structure that helped keep the farm alive. I was teaching the plants program and occasional landscape studios at the time, and it saddened me to see the department not take advantage of this precious small piece of university land. It also saddened me to see Richard's academic love child die. In the winter of 1983, I interviewed everyone who had been involved with the farm and put together a slide show for the department with the purpose of either finding someone to take on the responsibility of taking care of the land or recommending that it be given back to the university. The department's response was, "Great! Let's see you do it."

Maybe it was fortunate that my first years coincided with the Reagan era. There was no doubt that, by 1983, the exuberance of the 1970s had come to a grinding halt. Among University of Oregon students, business and making money were in, and community, veggies, and tie-dye were out (or as out as tie-dye ever is in Eugene). My first Urban Farm classes attracted twenty to thirty students, so I scaled down the area of annual vegetable beds and focused on developing perennial flowers, shrubs, and trees that demanded less annual reinventing. I learned that I had to take on this project in my own way—which, given the times and my own personality, was a little quieter and fuzzier than Richard's style of leadership. So it was probably a good thing that the classes were small in the beginning because it gave me a chance to learn how to lead a group of people to action gradually.

As I was trying to get a handle on the day-to-day class teaching and management, I was also faced with campus land-use politics, and I spent most of the 1980s trying to protect the farm from becoming a building site. Defending the farm was a good way to learn about it. Open land on the university campus, as is true almost everywhere, was seen as buildable space. In the mid-1980s, the Riverfront Research Park was looking for a building site and spotted the Urban Farm. After many meetings and many letters, the Architecture Department came to my aid, citing pattern 24 from *Pattern Language,* called *sacred sites:* "People cannot maintain their spiritual roots and their connections to the past if the physical world they live in does not also sustain these roots." The design of the University of Oregon campus is based on *Pattern Language,* as described in *The Oregon Experiment.*[1] When the architects explained that you shouldn't build on a sacred site, the Riverfront Research folks backed off, setting their sights on the land farther east. But it was only a year later that the Architecture Department itself looked acquisitively at the Urban Farm land, this time quoting pattern 109, *long thin house:* "The shape of a building has a great effect on the relative degrees of privacy and overcrowding in it, and this in turn has a critical effect on people's comfort and well being." The Architecture Department decided that the northern half of the Urban Farm would be an ideal building site for its long thin woodshop. In exchange for the loss of our farm area, they gave us a strip of land to the west, across the bike path. This was not a good land swap from our point of view because it made for a long thin Urban Farm, but at least it set the precedent that we were entitled to expand in some direction. Simultaneously, Lawrence Hall was expanding its library, and that resulted in the removal of the fourth floor greenhouse we had been using. We were promised a replacement greenhouse at the Urban Farm, although that promise has yet to be honored.

Those were painful times for me. It felt like a personal defeat and a lack of recognition that the Urban Farm was a viable class. The Landscape Architecture Department was unable or unwilling to defend its program. Clearly, the university in general and the Architecture Department in particular had no qualms about building on prime agricultural soil. They did not understand that only 1 percent of the soil in the Willamette Valley is class I soil. (Class I, II, and III soils are all considered prime agricultural soils, but there is a major difference: class I soil can grow three times as much as class III soil with far less energy input.) Nor did they recognize or defend the educational value of hands-on learning. True, the farm did not look like the rest of campus; vegetable crops are not well-behaved ornamental landscape plants. The farm did not look like Vaux-le-Vicomte—it was exuberant, out of control, and downright messy sometimes. But it was alive.

Finally, in frustration, I took the break that I needed and turned my teaching attention elsewhere. Steve Solomon was a local vegetable garden guru who had started the Territorial Seed Company up in the Lorane Valley southwest of town. In this phase of his life, Steve was a back-to-the-land survivalist. Lorane has heavy clay soil and a much shorter growing season than the Eugene area. Steve had often told me that, if he had the soil that we had at the farm, he could Grow (with a capital *G*, as he would say) *stupendous* vegetables. So I asked him whether he would be interested in teaching the class for a couple of years while construction of the woodshop was under way. He confidently took it on, writing out a list of demands and conditions. He was adamant about not wanting to get paid for the position, and that gave him the leverage to do whatever he wanted to do. He was not part of the landscape faculty and felt beholden to no one.

In retrospect, Steve was a good choice. In the first place, he really did know how to grow vegetables, and we learned a lot from him. We have been using his *Growing Vegetables West of the Cascades* ever since.[2] We learned that we needed to be fertilizing more. In the purity of the 1970s, we thought that all you needed was compost. I wanted to grow vegetables naturally because much of my professional work as a landscape architect focuses on native plants and restoration, and it took me a while to appreciate that most of the vegetables we like to eat cannot be treated like native plants. After all, our favorite vegetables are hardly native to this area. (Potatoes are from Peru; broccoli, kale, and parsley are from Europe; spinach and garbanzo beans are from Asia; peanuts, peppers, tomatoes, green beans, corn, some squash, and pumpkins are from Central and South America; asparagus, leeks, and fava beans are from northern Africa; watermelon, okra, eggplant, and basil are from the African tropics. North America's only contribution to our vegetable gardens is the sunflower.) And, on top of that, we all want nice, big vegetables. We had always prided ourselves on being organic, but, in truth, our vegetables were often scrawny. Fertilization with Steve's recipe for organic fertilizer has made a big difference.

The other Solomon legacy was that I started to understand more clearly the things that the farm had been doing well. Steve wasn't concerned about the Urban Farm as a place. He lobbied (unsuccessfully) to cut down the glorious black walnut trees that ring the farm so that the beds could get more sun, and he didn't have the time or the inclination to see the farm as a social community. In fairness, he was commuting to the farm from his own farm in Elkton, about an hour's drive away. The Urban Farm had grown out of the Department of Landscape Architecture, and, as such, it has always been first and foremost a place, a place for people as well as vegetables. But, all things considered, it was a good trade: the Solomon years provided a needed boost for the farm's productivity, and, after two years, I had regained my enthusiasm and was eager to pick up the shovel again.

The 1990s

When the 1990s rolled around, Reagan was out, and students were once again interested in the farm and the environment. The Environmental Studies Program at the university was launched in 1995 and rapidly gained momentum. A graduate student in landscape architecture, Kelly Donahue, did a master's project on campus farms at six West Coast universities: Santa Cruz, Berkeley, Evergreen, Humboldt, San Luis Obispo, and the University of Oregon. She visited all six schools and documented how those that were formed and flourished in the 1970s suffered enrollment losses in the 1980s but were making a comeback in the 1990s.[3] The pattern was the same across the board: environmentalism was back in.

In the fall of 1991, construction of the woodshop was complete, and we assembled a team of interested landscape students to form an Urban Farm master plan class. We designed the entrance, the trellis, the main path, and the retaining wall that was necessary to accommodate the grade change that had resulted from placement of the woodshop. The landscape architecture professor Cynthia Girling taught a design/build landscape studio that winter and spring. Cindy (as she was known then) had been involved in an Urban Farm project in the mid-1970s, building raised beds with basalt retaining walls for a garden at Ya-po-ah Terrace, a local retirement community. She took on this new farm project with her characteristic thoroughness and gave the farm its first hardscaping elements, which made a big difference: the project created a sunny, hot microclimate on the upper terrace and formalized the farm. The farm was no longer just open land; it had a recognizable structure and was now an official place on the University of Oregon campus map.

Figure 5.2. Ann Bettman, a former director, looking over the beds. (Courtesy Lorri Nelson.)

Reviewing my old class notebooks reveals a fascinating evolution of people management strategies. Organizing even a small class of twenty or thirty inexperienced students in the garden is a challenge. In the 1970s, with his large classes of seventy to eighty students, Richard based his organization on the hierarchical, military model, but, in the 1980s, with initially smaller enrollments, I revised this organizational strategy. Early on, I had assistants to help me teach the class, but, later, as the one or two assistants gained more experience, we divided the class into separate groups. By the early 1990s, the management strategy of one teacher and a couple of student helpers had to be revised and expanded. I remember drawing many diagrams on the chalkboard with Richard and having long discussions about the relative merits of guerrilla tactics compared to hierarchical organizations. Given his general predilection for guerrilla-style warfare, I am surprised now to recall that he urged me to adopt the hierarchical model. But trying to work hierarchically was fundamentally against my nature. After the thrill of having enrollments of 100–125 students in the mid-1990s, I finally came to my senses and limited spring and fall class size to eighty students and evolved a system with six team leaders with thirteen to fourteen students per team. Even with the large enrollment numbers, registration for the class usually fills on the first day, and the demand is always larger than we can accommodate.

When I stepped down as director and became one of the six team leaders, the farm took on a whole new feeling and outlook for me. I loved thinking about how to set up this wondrous hands-in-the-earth experience for people, and I also needed to be directly teaching students myself. The other major factor that affected my outlook and the success of the farm was that I decided to make the farm a more primary focus in my life. Until 1997, I taught the farm class only in the spring term but was responsible for the farm for the entire year. In the fall of 1997, the team leaders and I wrote an EPA grant to fund a farm manager. We did not get the grant, but, shortly thereafter, I rearranged my teaching schedule and made a full, year-round commitment to the Urban Farm, integrating the educational goals of the class and the logistics of the farm manager role.

ENTERING THE TWENTY-FIRST CENTURY

The farm in the first seven years of the new century largely refined the model that had been developed in the 1990s: a large, hands-on, general education class offered to all university students. What got better and better in this new decade were the team leaders—both as individual educators and as a cohesive team. As the director, I coordinated, nurtured, mentored, and learned from the team leaders. We all made decisions about farm logistics and class goals together. Over the past ten to fifteen years, there has been an "all-weather" group of team leaders: Harper Keeler, Lauren Bilbao, Tom Bettman, and Lorri Nelson (listed in order of appearance at the farm). Harper is a graduate of the landscape program, Lauren is a certified social worker, Tom is a retired physician, and Lorri is an architect and graduate of the landscape architecture master's program. There have been a half dozen other outstanding team leaders who have worked at the farm for shorter periods of time, most of them graduates of the Landscape Architecture Department (including Linda Pauley, Heidi Schroeder, and Kelly Densmore). Most of us have been gardening for many years—in most cases, decades. The combination of a core of experienced hands and some new blood is optimal. The continuity of the team leader group is a tribute to those individuals' dedication despite minimal financial compensation for their time and expertise (still only $850 a term). My dedication to the farm was always directly related to the pleasure of working with the team leaders and their enthusiasm. When I officially stepped down as director in the fall of 2007, Harper Keeler stepped in as acting director.

LAND, DESIGN, AND INFRASTRUCTURE

The Urban Farm facilities include approximately one hundred four- by fifteen-foot raised beds, a permanent greenhouse/toolshed, a sixty-tree mixed-species orchard of semidwarf fruit trees, a composting area, and a large plastic grow house. The shape of the farm is a backward L, with the east/west portion constituting the original part of the farm and the northern half-acre portion known as the *back 40*. It has been important, though sometimes difficult, to remind university administrators that the Urban Farm is a classroom that deserves and requires investment and upkeep like any other classroom.

The design of the Urban Farm growing areas has a fascinating evolutionary history, one that parallels that of the social organization. The basic productive unit of the farm has almost always been the four- by fifteen-foot raised bed. An arm's length is about two feet; the four-foot bed width enables a person to work the bed from both sides without having to step onto the bed and compact the soil. Keeping soil light and fluffy so that roots can penetrate and soil micro- and macroorganisms can breathe is one of a vegetable gardener's main jobs. The length can vary, but, when there are a lot of people working the garden, bed lengths of about fifteen feet ease traffic congestion.

The overall layout of the farm has gone through many transitions. The 1980s saw a lot of experimentation owing to my reluctance to accept the rigid grid of the 1970s. For a few years in the early 1980s, the northern half of the garden was in perennial flowers. Students loved and beneficial insects thrived in these long beds of brilliant blooms. In the Solomon years, these beds were planted to row crops. Steve thought that it was important for students to learn that some vegetables are more nutritionally demanding than others; some vegetables can do quite well in lower-maintenance, farm-style rows. Another early bed configuration was a basket weave of four- by fifteen-foot beds, thereby varying the north-south, east-west orientation of the beds and providing a visually more interesting layout.

In the spring of 1986, I thought that the farm could be a more organic-looking place, and I threw out the four- by fifteen-foot unit altogether. My theory then was that students should be able to determine their own bed shapes and that they could work in small groups of four or five students to determine what vegetables they wanted to grow and how they wanted to grow them. It was a philosophy of letting students find their own questions and answers. I was also at that time very enthusiastic about environmental art and showed the students slides of places like the great Serpentine Mounds to inspire them. The combination of these interests resulted in an experiment in earth art. The students lovingly patted the soil into all kinds of wonderful organic bed shapes: chevrons, circles, waves, and cul-de-sacs. My favorite was done by a group of women who shaped their beds into stylized but definitely recognizable female genitalia. On May Day of that year, one student read the ley lines of the farm and climbed high up into the three black walnuts to tie yellow streamers down to what he determined to be the center point of the farm's energy. The center was right in the middle of that lovely female earth art. That year, the farm looked its best in the spring before summer's luxuriant chaos set in. Later in the season, it was almost impossible to drag hoses, construct cloches, or move people through such a freeform maze. But it was fun while it lasted.

The following year, we formalized the energy center of the farm with an old square wooden platform that we dragged up from the edge of the Mill Race. We realized that we needed a place to be *in* the garden. Vegetable gardeners often forget to make a place for themselves. We planted a circle of perennial flowers around the square platform and then erected thirteen red poles in the center of the flower circle. The circle imagery was important because so much of gardening is about circles and cycles. We are very attuned to the ebb and flow of solar cycles. The number 13 represents the typical number of lunar cycles in the year. The red color celebrates menstrual cycles, and the poles are an obvious phallic reference. The Red Pole Circle continues to serve as the heart of the farm.

After the woodshop was built and the 1990s energy flowed back into the farm, it became clear that we needed more land to accommodate classes of 100–125 students. Expanding onto the back 40 was a major coup, tripling our land base. The back 40 was originally enclosed on all four sides by a chain-link fence topped with rolls of concertina wire. We were instructed to leave the fence protecting the biology greenhouse, and we did, but we immediately tore down all the other fences and, over the next couple of years, planted hedgerows around the perimeter.

The old or original part of the farm with the red poles is used intensively by so many students that it is best used as a laboratory for learning about a diverse range of vegetables that can be grown in our temperate

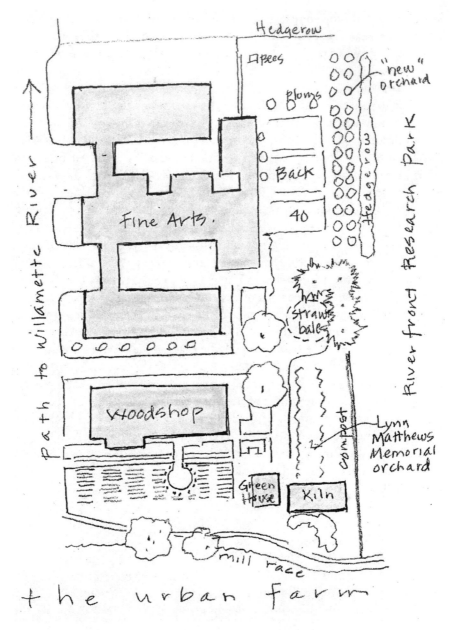

Figure 5.3. The Urban Farm plan. (Courtesy Ann Bettman.)

maritime climate. We think of the back 40 as being the farm part of the Urban Farm where we can have larger beds. For many years, we grew the high-demand crops: garlic, potatoes, and beans. More recently, the back 40 is more highly designed and maintained and now has a plastic grow house in addition to thirty fruit trees and a group of bee hives that the University of Oregon pollination ecologist and Oregon State University entomologist manage for us.

The Urban Farm grows food according to best organic, sustainable agriculture practices; all the food grown is given to the students as direct feedback for their efforts. No synthetic fertilizers or pesticides are used, but the beds are amended at every planting with organic fertilizer (a mix of cottonseed, alfalfa seed, rock phosphate, kelp, and lime) and compost. Compost is the heart of the farm's fertility program. The campus delivers truckloads of leaves in the fall, while a commercial soil company delivers fresh manure from a couple of small local farms to make compost. The majority of the composting is done in simple five- by five-foot bins constructed out of wooden pallets. Everything that comes from the planting beds is processed through the compost system. None of the beds have ever been fallowed, but the beds are cover-cropped, and there is an increasing interest in composting in the beds themselves, especially in the fall as the beds are prepared for winter.

The farm is also the site and the beneficiary of an eight-foot-in-diameter plastic composter that processes food waste from the university cafeterias. It takes a lot of carbon-dense material to process the kitchen scraps, but the resulting compost product is a good soil amendment, and the arrangement makes for a good demonstration of appropriate waste management. Compost tea, made in a five-gallon container aerated by an aquarium pump, is applied directly to the beds. A standard agricultural feed trough is used to demonstrate vermiculture, and worm castings are used to augment potting soil.

FARM PEOPLE

The fact that the Urban Farm class is offered through the Department of Landscape Architecture reflects my firm belief that the education of landscape architects and the profession of landscape architecture should more fully embrace the agricultural landscape. Agricultural land constitutes a large portion of the landscape and has a major impact on our water and soil resources, air quality, biodiversity, and the health of us all. Commonly used tools like geographic information systems enable us to correlate health statistics, geography, and agricultural land uses, and landscape architects have the graphic abilities to make these connections visually coherent and compelling to the public. Landscape architects can take leading roles in educating the public about the use of chemicals in the landscape, species diversity, habitat, water quality, wetlands, biofiltration swales, detention/ retention ponds, and groundwater dynamics—all issues that can be considered in an urban farm context.

But the farm serves more than the landscape architecture students at the University of Oregon; students from all over the campus take the Urban Farm class. A large number of farm students are in the Environmental Studies Program; the rest come from a broad range of other departments. Most of the students have never gardened before. It is shocking to realize how many students have never planted a seed, done physical work, or learned how to use simple tools. On the other hand, most of the students already have values in line with the farm's. We are, to some extent, preaching to the choir, but I think that it is more a matter of helping students think more clearly and articulately about what they profess to believe.

One of the outstanding resources of the Eugene area is the local organic farm community. The farm's connection with area farmers dates from the 1970s. The Organically Grown Cooperative (OGC) was originally a discussion group that met at the Urban Farm once a month for five years. It was a group of former Urban Farm students who had gone on to start farms; most were renting land, and they found themselves in the position of competing with their friends. They got a VISTA grant and started coordinating crops and setting minimum prices. Today, OGC (now Organically Grown Company) is a major business and the leading distributor of organic produce in the southern Willamette Valley.

Every term, we take a field trip to one of the area's many thriving organic farms. The list of farms for field trips includes Wintergreen Farm, NettleEdge Farm, Horton Road Farm, Hayhurst, Creative Growers, and Full Circle Farm. We make enough time for a tour and labor exchange. We've planted potatoes at Wintergreen, weeded the pasture at Full Circle, and harvested beans and planted garlic at NettleEdge. Sometimes we are able to make a more concerted effort: we spent three days raising three greenhouses with Richard Wilen at Hayhurst.

We also make field trips to Grass Roots Garden and Springfield Youth Farm, two gardens managed under the Food for Lane County umbrella. Food for Lane County is our local food bank, and it is one of the model food security organizations in the country. Grass Roots Garden grows organic vegetables to distribute to our county's hungry people, and Spring-field Youth Farm pays at-risk high school students to learn to grow organic vegetables to be distributed by the food bank. Every term, we visit these programs and lend a hand doing whatever needs a labor blitz.

For many years, we scheduled three or four sessions a term to all meet indoors in a classroom for formal lectures. Topics included sustainable agri-culture, pollination ecology, bees, OGC, the San Francisco League of Urban Gardeners, genetically modified organisms, biodynamic agriculture, the his-tory of agriculture, school gardens, garden planning, the history and current status of organic agriculture, the politics of meat, season extension, herbal-ism, garden gurus, and the history of the Urban Farm. More recently, we have concentrated the lecture series in November, in the fall term, after the garden has been put to bed, and we have expanded our use of reading and writing assignments. We ask students to read and write reports on books by Masanobu Fukuoka, John Jeavons, Wendell Berry, Wes Jackson, Ruth Stout, Bill Mollison, Gary Paul Nabhan, Michael Pollan, Helen and Scott Near-ing, David Mas Masumoto, Clive Ponting, Michael Ableman, Gene Logs-don, and others. We also have a good video collection.

One class day every term celebrates the sun's journey through the year with an earth-based ritual. May Day in spring term, Halloween/the Day of the Dead/Samhain in the fall, and August 2 or Lammas Day, an early harvest celebration, in summer term mark the midway points between the equinoxes and the solstices. This pause to connect with other agricultural cultures and celebrate the term's accomplishments is for some the highlight of the term.

The farm has also become active in promoting and building school gardens. Eugene's School Garden Project grew out of two Urban Farm students' belief that every school should have a garden. The School Gar-den Project is now an active nonprofit organization that helps manage gar-dens in twenty schools in the Eugene/Springfield area. One of the farm's team leaders, Lorri Nelson, teaches a one-week school garden seminar at the beginning of every summer that is open to the community and especially caters to teachers who are interested in starting school gardens. Urban Farm students also intern with the Farm to School Program, help-ing elementary school students learn where food comes from.

THE FINANCIALS

The Urban Farm was initiated by a faculty member and has always been faculty led. It was an overload class for the six years that Britz was full-time faculty, and it constituted half of my own half-time appointment in the Department of Landscape Architecture for the twenty-five years that I was director. In the fall of 2007, I stepped down, and one of my most experienced team leaders, Harper Keeler, took on the role of interim director. My directorship was an informal affair, but the Landscape Architecture Department is now in the process of establishing an official director of the Urban Farm as a university position. In 2008, the department received a large endowed gift that is tied to an estate. While this funding will provide a stable source of funding for the Urban Farm for years to come, we are currently seeking bridge funding for the interim funding of the director position.

The Urban Farm is the only student farm offered by a Landscape Architecture Department in the country. The Department of Landscape Architecture's commitment to the farm has provided critical funding and continuity of leadership for the program for more than three decades. In return, the Urban Farm class generates a large number of credit hours for a department that is otherwise studio based, with low faculty-to-student ratios. The Urban Farm class is essentially a stand-alone class; while it is supported within the department and within the university, it is not part of a coordinated academic program in sustainable or urban agriculture. The fact that it is so successful makes it an interesting model for other schools in the early stages of class or program development.

In addition to the Landscape Architecture Department's support, the Matthews Foundation has provided generous financial support for the farm for many years. In the 1980s, Jolene Matthews of Seattle established the Lynn Matthews Foundation to honor her daughter's interest in the Urban Farm. The foundation has grown over the years and has been critical to the farm's survival, especially during the lean years of the 1980s. The foundation continues to fund the major portion of the team leaders' salaries.

The third piece of the financial picture is the class fee of $30 paid by each student each term to cover material costs: tools, fertilizer, manure, straw bales, and some plant starts. Seeds are donated by a local garden store run by a former Urban Farm team leader.

Urban Farm Futures

The Urban Farm has been around for a long time. There have been challenges in the past, but it has survived and grown stronger owing to its multiple constituencies and, most noteworthy, the enthusiastic support of the students. Continued growth of the Urban Farm is, I believe, both inevitable and desirable. Harper Keeler is pursuing his master's degree in landscape architecture while serving as interim director of the farm. While the issues that fired up the farm in the 1970s remain relevant, today's increased public awareness of food and farming issues suggests that the farm may be able to benefit from a time of reflection and reinvention. Future directions will probably involve a tighter relation with a more advanced urban agriculture studies curriculum of some kind as well as greater physical and academic recognition of the farm's potential on campus. What will remain constant is the enthusiasm of the students because, in the end, the farm's success comes down to what the students learn. At the farm, students learn by doing. They learn about the soil, that soil is alive, and they learn about composting and how important it is to be good stewards of the soil. They learn what crops grow when and about crop diversity and varieties. They learn how to germinate seeds and how they really have to care for those seeds that they put in the ground if they want them to grow. They learn how to manage water and irrigation. They learn how, what, and when to harvest and what to do with all the food after they harvest it. Students learn to work, learn how to use tools, and learn that physical labor can be elegant. They learn that it is fun and often much more efficient to work with other people. And they learn by reading, discussing, and thinking about how most of our country's food is grown and how their own personal and their country's relation with food could be improved. Students are incredibly hopeful and eager to learn about solutions and the contributions that they can make for all the problems they see around them. For thirty-five years, the Urban Farm has inspired, informed, and nurtured their precious energy, and I'm confident that its impact on students' lives will continue to grow long into the future.

STUDENT REFLECTIONS

LEARNING AND TEACHING

HARPER KEELER

The first time I took the Urban Farm class, a guy named Steve Solomon was teaching a summer session. At that time, Steve had recently sold the

Territorial Seed Company and was enjoying (he might say enduring) the notoriety he received from publishing *Growing Vegetables West of the Cascades.* Steve was pinch-hitting for Ann Bettman, who was on sabbatical, and he was mostly into holding court, as it were. He had a favorite spot under one of our majestic black walnut trees where he liked to sit and wax poetic about his travels and the joy of growing your own food from seeds that you saved yourself. It was a pretty popular gig, and I remember thinking that this was what school in the summer was supposed to be like. There was one problem, though. It was summer, and in Eugene it doesn't rain in the summer. We had a limited number of hoses, and Steve decided that, if "we" could run a trench the length of the garden, "we" could drop in some PVC and easily have a new water source. Long story short, I spent the next couple of classes in the trench. If not for our fantastic flood plain loam, it would have been a tough job, but I recall getting to the end of a hundred-foot trench without hitting a stone larger than a golf ball. Such is the wealth of the Willamette Valley.

My work was not lost on Steve. Toward the end of the summer session, he took me aside and rather sheepishly told me that he was never really comfortable with getting paid for teaching young folks how to grow their own food. After looking both ways, he slipped me an envelope containing a couple of hundred bucks "for the effort." I later heard that he had refused to be paid for the course, so I could conclude only that he had paid me out of his own pocket.

I don't think he would mind that I'm spilling the secret—he asked me to keep it between us—because it gets to the essence of the Urban Farm. We don't do it for the money. I've been around for over fifteen years and would rather not think about the number of hours when I probably should have been at work instead. It's the same with all the team leaders at the farm. We're a bunch of talented, probably overeducated folks who do it because we have to. There's a spirit here that is undeniable, and every time you see a student harvest his or her favorite vegetable for the first time, you get paid in spades. Teaching at the Urban Farm: it's what we do.

Harper Keeler received his B.L.A. from the University of Oregon in 1995 and spent the next fourteen years working in the public sector while teaching at the Urban Farm. He is now the director of the Urban Farm and pursuing a M.L.A. degree.

STUDENT REFLECTIONS

MEETING THE URBAN FARM

RENEE WILKINSON

I would be making one of the biggest gambles of my life by returning to graduate school. With this one small decision, I would, in fact, be agreeing to live three thousand miles away from my spouse, quit a lucrative job I enjoyed, uproot my carefully cultivated garden, pack up my urban chickens, and leave all my friends behind—all this to pursue something I felt would lead to a richer, more meaningful life, one where I would create places in the world for people to interact with nature and each other. I wanted to make something lasting.

I came to visit the University of Oregon before making a final decision. The faculty in the Landscape Architecture Department seemed knowledgeable, wise, and approachable. They even seemed to genuinely like each other. Meeting them gave me peace of mind that they would work hard to nurture and support my academic journey.

I toured the campus and tried to imagine myself living in this place. And then I made my way to the Urban Farm.

My mind began to spin when I realized that this was a department that also teaches students to grow their own food, to support and respect the local agricultural system, and to understand that our lifestyle choices affect a much larger environmental system. I realized that this was a place where students become inspired, digging together among rows of vegetables with the smell of herbs and rich humus wafting around them. Whether they are business students or landscape students, they can actually do something in their own small corner of the world that can make a difference in their lives and the lives of others.

And that was not so different from my own small corner of the world, where I was trying to decide whether this gamble would work out—whether I would ever be able to do that much good by pursuing a passion. In that moment as I stood at the Urban Farm, a place so full of hope and inspiration, I decided to roll the dice.

Renee Wilkinson earned a B.A. in journalism at the University of Oregon in 2001 and is currently pursuing a master's degree in landscape architecture.

Notes

1. Christopher Alexander et al., *The Oregon Experiment* (New York: Oxford University Press, 1975); Christopher Alexander et al., *A Pattern Language: Towns, Buildings, Construction* (New York: Oxford University Press, 1977).

2. Steve Solomon, *Growing Vegetables West of the Cascades* (Seattle, WA: Sasquatch, 2000), originally published as *The Complete Guide to Organic Gardening West of the Cascades* (1981).

3. Kelly A. Donahue, "Urban Farms: An Evaluation Framework for Alternative Academic Programs" (M.A. thesis, University of Oregon, 1995).

6

University of California, Davis (1977)

Moving from the Margins toward the Center

MARK VAN HORN

It's 10:30 on a Thursday morning in April, and the sun is starting to get pleasantly hot on the students' backs as they dig, cut, and bunch more than a dozen kinds of organic vegetables for the Market Garden's community-supported agriculture (CSA) program. Those students who helped with the harvests that supplied fresh produce to the student-run Coffee House restaurant and filled sixty CSA baskets each week during the long winter are grateful for the warmth, blue sky, and drying soil in a way that the newer students can't quite fully appreciate. Nonetheless, everyone working in the Market Garden on this morning feels the joys of spring and collective accomplishment as they hurry to finish the harvest by noon.

The Market Garden occupies about one fifth of the twenty-one-acre Student Experimental Farm (SEF), located on the western edge of the central campus of the University of California, Davis (UC Davis). Other areas of the SEF are abuzz with activity this morning as well. Over in the one-acre Ecological Garden, thirty-eight second graders from a school in Sacramento are looking for worms, harvesting greens and carrots for a salad, feeding chickens, or singing "Dirt Made My Lunch" with a handful of student interns who are their hosts for the morning's Children's Garden Program tour. Meanwhile, out in the research fields, a graduate student has been adjusting the planter she is using in her study of the impacts of dif-

Figure 6.1. A Market Garden intern harvests spring kale for the Monday CSA baskets. (Courtesy Karin Higgins.)

ferent cover crops on soil food webs; in the afternoon, she'll be in the lab processing soil samples. A hundred yards to her south, two students from Project Compost have just pulled up to the compost windrow in their electric utility vehicle to add six thirty-gallon containers' worth of dining facility kitchen waste to the pile.

By this sunny morning in the spring of 2007, the SEF was beginning its fourth decade of students farming, gardening, composting, researching, and serving schoolchildren, farmers, and other communities. More than thirty years earlier, the SEF had evolved out of the efforts of a group of students who had set out to transform at least part of the university's agricultural education and research agenda and activities. Their efforts were part of a larger student movement that had begun even earlier. By 1970, widespread student concern about a range of environmental, social, and political issues had led to unprecedented levels of student activism in California and elsewhere. Many students at UC Davis, one of the largest and most diverse land-grant university campuses in the country, were particularly concerned with the growing environmental and social problems associated with modern agriculture, and they expected that exploring and finding solutions to these problems would be an important part of the university's agenda. They were disappointed by the relative lack of attention they saw being given to such issues on campus and began a discussion to focus more attention on the problems of agriculture and their potential solutions.

Several students started working with supportive faculty and others to address these issues, and, in 1973, the group organized a conference to explore and critique land-grant university research priorities and their social impacts. In 1975, a group of these students offered for the first time a course entitled "Seminar on Alternatives in Agriculture" that examined problems associated with modern agriculture and alternative approaches to solving them. A number of students became active in a community-based group called the Alternative Agricultural Resources Project. The conference, course, and activities of the community group drew the attention of significant numbers of students and others in and around Davis. This helped broaden and deepen the discourse on pressing contemporary agricultural issues such as increasing farm size, agrichemical pollution, farm labor, concentration in agriculture and the food industry, water policy, organic farming, and, particularly, the university's roles and positions relative to such issues.

By 1976, public pressure was building on the university to make significant programmatic changes relevant to these issues, and students were discussing the idea of a student-run program that would explore and help develop alternative agricultural systems and practices as well as provide new educational opportunities for students. The students envisioned a program that would offer new courses, seminars, and conferences; support student research projects; and operate a student farm where students could engage in a wide range of field-based activities. The student farm idea built on UC Davis's land-grant university mission, and the students' vision included activities in all three areas of land-grant responsibility: education, research, and extension. A group of students, including many from the 1976 "Alternatives in Agriculture" course, developed a proposal to create the Agricultural Alternatives Development Program (AADP) and the SEF, which would serve as a place for experiential learning; alternative (now more commonly termed *sustainable*) agriculture principles and practices; and student initiative, creativity, and exploration. In the summer of 1977, these students presented their proposal to the dean of the College of Agricultural and Environmental Sciences (CA&ES). The dean approved the proposal for the AADP and SEF, assigned more than twenty acres of university farmland to the SEF, and allocated the program a budget that included support for some graduate student research assistantships, a few students to work on a farm crew and other general program support positions, and some operating funds.

The SEF's flat, deep, alluvial sandy loam soil on the west side of campus had made it an excellent site for tree crops research and teaching for many years, but those activities had recently moved to a new and larger facility further from the campus core. The students realized that this land was a treasure. Besides the naturally productive soil, there was a surface irrigation system, some small remnant blocks of olives, figs, and almonds, a 1930s wood-frame field house, and greenhouse, shade house, and shop space that the SEF could share with the adjacent plant science teaching facility. The field house included two offices and a large workroom and could serve as a place for meetings, workshops, and social gatherings ranging from impromptu discussions and debates to potluck meals and barn dances. Importantly, the SEF was less than a ten-minute bike ride from the center of campus and had great neighbors. Besides the twelve-acre plant science teaching facility to the south, to the north were over six acres of community gardens and a recently established twenty-eight-member cooperative student community that included large gardens and other community spaces. The SEF's west boundary was a state highway, and to the east were several acres of open space habitat.

The students quickly put the land to good use, starting numerous field-based agroecological and agronomic research and demonstration projects. Individually and collectively, the students involved in the SEF had very diverse interests, and their projects reflected that diversity. During the first two years, there were field studies focusing on a wide range of topics, including cover crops, intercropping, compost utilization, no-till vegetable production, windbreaks, biological control, beneficial insectary hedgerows, and wind energy. In addition, a number of community-based action and research projects were initiated to serve groups such as farm-workers, local farmers, and students interested in apprenticeships on working farms. During this period, the SEF and the AADP continued to foster the exchange of ideas and organize educational programs for students and the broader community. These included an annual conference on women in agriculture, a draft horse workshop, and gardening workshops and field days. In addition to continuing to organize the "Seminar on Alternatives in Agriculture," the students worked with collaborating faculty to offer several other courses. In 1977 and 1978, these included a course focusing on ethical questions and planning criteria in international agriculture development, another on the origins, genetics, development, and uses of corn, and a third on organic farming. The organic farming course attracted fifty-five enrollees, twenty of whom participated in the optional field-based laboratory.

The laboratory activities of the organic farming course resulted in the creation of a small garden that quickly evolved into an ongoing project called the Demonstration Garden (later renamed the Ecological Garden). During this period, other small groups of students formed to grow crops together on a somewhat larger scale elsewhere on the SEF for a season or two. Two of these students became interested in marketing the vegetables they grew to help support the SEF financially. They worked for many months before finally receiving administrative approval to start the Market Garden and sell vegetables to the on-campus Coffee House. Other students working individually and in small groups also started educational projects focused on various aspects of agriculture, including chickens, fish, rabbits, grapes, and composting. Depending on student interest, the life span of these projects varied considerably. Some, such as the Ecological Garden and Market Garden, became core projects of the SEF, but others, such as the rabbit project, disappeared after a relatively short period. In some cases, smaller projects were incorporated into larger ones, such as when the chicken project became part of the Demonstration Garden.

In still other cases, a new project grew out of an existing one, as when the Children's Garden Program evolved out of the work of an undergraduate student working in the Demonstration Garden who started offering spring tours to classes of local grade school children. All these projects allowed the SEF to serve larger numbers of students, including those who—although they may not have had the interest, knowledge, or ability to initiate such projects—eagerly participated in them once they had begun.

In short, the SEF grew out of the interests and efforts of a relatively small group of dedicated students with the support of some key faculty members. During its establishment and shortly thereafter, SEF remained largely a student-driven effort. The agricultural alternatives that were explored by students were not restricted to alternative methods and systems of production—they also included alternative economic, social, and political arrangements and systems as well as new methods of learning and teaching. In their efforts to develop these alternatives, the students formed collaborative relationships with certain faculty members and others on campus with whom they shared common interests, and, thus, the SEF developed important allies within the faculty and administration. The knowledge, skills, and understanding that the students developed through those experiences allowed them to learn not only some of the technical aspects of agricultural production and research but also how to communicate and work with others, how to build organizations, engage in political processes, make decisions, and manage resources. The early period of the SEF thus provided an exceptionally rich learning environment for those involved.

Initially, SEF operations depended largely on students' volunteer efforts. Funds from the CA&ES and external grants helped support a number of research projects, but much of the activity at the SEF and its overall operations were being run primarily by student volunteers. However, the students quickly concluded that the level of managerial effort required to keep the SEF as a whole running smoothly was beyond what volunteers were willing or able to provide and that a farm manager was needed. They requested, and received, funds from the CA&ES dean's office that allowed them to hire a full-time manager beginning in the spring of 1978. By the mid-1980s, three additional CA&ES-funded, part-time staff positions had been created to help manage the SEF's field-based educational projects and general operations. The creation of these positions had several important impacts on the SEF. The staff positions enhanced the stability of the SEF and the efficacy of its operations, facilitated an increase in the number of students involved in its various projects, and improved the technical quality of the knowledge and skills being acquired by students. However, at the same time, some of the sense of ownership and decisionmaking authority and responsibility was transferred from the students to the staff.

The creation of the field-based educational projects and staff positions helped the SEF serve increasing numbers of students with diverse interests, backgrounds, and skill levels. Another strategy that helped attract additional students was the creation of new opportunities for students to engage with the SEF via formal courses. With the notable exception of the "Seminar on Alternatives in Agriculture," all the courses that had been developed by students in the early years had been short-lived. However, from the mid-1980s through the 1990s, the SEF developed a number of courses that were offered annually for a decade or longer and in which the enrolled students participated in SEF field activities on a weekly basis. These included an intensive summer sustainable agriculture internship, a course on organic crop production practices, and a course that prepared students to help lead Children's Garden Program tours. Such courses attracted many students who would not have become involved in the SEF's less formal, but otherwise very similar, learning opportunities. In the early phase of this process, the SEF relied on collaborating faculty who served as instructors in these courses. In 1990, in addition to my position as the SEF manager, I received a lecturer appointment, which greatly facilitated the SEF's ability to offer formal courses and formal internships. At the same time, the SEF and its staff continued to collaborate with faculty in several ways, including serving as a site for field-based laboratory activities, offering courses in various departments, and giving guest lectures.

Sustainable agriculture was gaining prominence and credibility both in California and nationally by the mid-1980s, and developments at UC Davis reflected this shift. In 1986, the University of California's statewide Sustainable Agriculture Research and Education Program (SAREP) was established on the Davis campus to focus on research and extension activities related to sustainable agriculture. This, along with the inauguration of the USDA's (similarly named) Sustainable Agriculture Research and Education (SARE) program in 1988, created significant new funding opportunities for this type of work. These funding opportunities made it possible for graduate students in disciplines such as soils, crop sciences, entomology, and agricultural ecology to complete thesis and dissertation projects at the SEF from the mid-1980s through the mid-1990s. These projects were often linked with the SEF's educational activities and helped many interns and students enrolled in formal courses learn about various aspects of sustainable agriculture research and its links to actual farming practices.

The increased funding for sustainable agriculture research and extension activities also led to new research efforts elsewhere on campus, including two large-scale, long-term interdisciplinary cropping systems studies that were started in 1988 and 1993. Although these studies were established at much larger research facilities on campus, previous student-led research projects at the SEF provided information and ideas that were important in the development of these latter projects. Thus, during the SEF's first decade, it was the focal point of sustainable agriculture research on the UC Davis campus. However, as the amount of relevant funding grew, so did the number of UC Davis sustainable agriculture research projects elsewhere on campus or in farmers' fields. Consequently, while the overall level of sustainable agriculture research and extension activities at UC Davis increased during the 1990s, the number of research projects at the SEF actually declined during the decade. Today, the SEF remains an important site for sustainable agriculture research on campus, although the program now focuses more strongly on education and the current level of research activity at the SEF does not match that which existed two decades ago.

For students who do conduct research at the SEF currently, their experiences are different from those of their peers doing projects at other facilities on campus because student researchers at the SEF are typically also partly student farmers or student technicians. That is, unlike at other research facilities on campus, student researchers at the SEF are encouraged to participate in all aspects of the management of the crops or systems used in their studies, and the SEF staff works closely with these students to help them learn the necessary skills to participate in this way. While this creates additional work for both the student and the SEF staff, it has a number of significant potential advantages for the student. For example, he or she typically gains practical skills and a better understanding of farming as well as the confidence that these can foster. Students can also gain an increased knowledge and understanding of the changes that occur in the field during the season, a comprehension of the connections between principles and practices, and an appreciation for both the farmer's and the scientist's perspectives. Such benefits have been important to many SEF alumni as they have moved into careers in agricultural extension, research, production, and related areas.

Figure 6.2. Graduate students collect data in a multidisciplinary cover-crop study. In the background, Project Compost's windrow is covered to protect it from heavy winter rains. (Courtesy Damian Parr.)

Two final distinguishing features of research at the SEF are the program's open-door policy and its emphasis on organic farming systems. As a CA&ES-wide program, the SEF allows researchers from any UC Davis department, graduate program, or undergraduate major to conduct field-based research using its facilities, provided that that research is consistent with the SEF's focus on sustainable agriculture. In addition, researchers from other UC campuses and institutions have used the SEF as a research site. Many researchers from both UC Davis and beyond are attracted by the SEF's long history of organic management. Since its inception in 1977, the SEF has used organic practices as the default management method in its fields, and most or all SEF research fields are under organic certification at any point in time. This has benefits of particular interest to those working in disciplines such as soil science or pest management as the fields have received regular organic inputs and no synthetic pesticide applications for over three decades. This history has allowed researchers to conduct projects on certified organic ground in collaboration with a staff with many years of experience in organic management. At the same time, there are many researchable questions important to sustainable agriculture that may involve procedures that do not comply with organic certification. For example, SEF student researchers have compared legume cover crops with synthetic nitrogen fertilizers in a multiyear interdisciplinary study. This research was possible because SEF policy permits certain SEF fields to be removed from organic certification to allow for such a research project. At the conclusion of such research projects and the cessation of the use of any noncompliant practices or materials, the land is again managed using organic practices and is recertified following the three-year waiting period required by USDA organic regulations.

CHALLENGES, PAST AND PRESENT

The SEF has faced a wide range of challenges over the years, including some related to what students have been interested in learning and exploring. While the SEF always has maintained opportunities for students to explore many types of agriculture, it has focused primarily on alternative agriculture, and this focus has led to negative perceptions of the SEF by some faculty and students. From the inception of the SEF, its focus on alternatives represented a questioning of the methods, systems, assumptions, and philosophies of agriculture that were dominant on campus, and this questioning has led to occasional tensions. However, from the earliest days, faculty sponsors have been required for all student projects conducted at the SEF. This faculty involvement has enhanced the students' learning experiences, increased their accountability to both the faculty and their fellow students, and ensured the scientific rigor of the students' work. This rigor has been particularly important when students have explored unconventional ideas and practices because it has made their research findings and their resulting recommendations more credible. Indeed, a number of student research projects conducted at the SEF have made significant contributions to the development of improved farming practices (e.g., related to cover cropping and enhancing biological control) for organic and other ecologically oriented producers. However important and rewarding such successes are, it is important to note that they were made possible by a combination of creative, unconventional student ideas and solid scientific investigations conducted with faculty support and guidance. Thus, even as once-controversial ideas—such as organic farming—become more accepted within the agricultural and academic communities, it is important that the SEF continue to foster student exploration of new ideas and practices, including those that are controversial and may be unwelcome in some circles.

Other challenges have related to how students learn at the SEF. The SEF always has maintained a strong emphasis on experiential, field-based, practical, and student-directed learning. While some, including key faculty, have valued this type of learning since the SEF's inception, others have seen it as not sufficiently academic to be included in a university education. Some faculty have even actively discouraged students from participating in SEF activities. Fortunately, field-based knowledge and skills are now valued more by many faculty, and they see the SEF as providing important opportunities for students to gain experiences that are essential to their learning processes.

As in most learning environments, differences in students' needs, interests, backgrounds, aptitudes, and skills have occasionally led to tensions at the SEF. While these differences have often led to significant social learning among students, they have also created challenges. For the staff and advanced students who work to facilitate students' learning, working with students with different skill levels and aptitudes can be particularly difficult in practical field situations. However, by strategically grouping certain students together, less advanced students can often learn from their more advanced peers. In its early years, there were few in-field mentors at the SEF, so the farm naturally attracted mostly self-directed learners. Such students typically learn through experimentation; they are often focused more on the experiential learning process than on the products of that process. Conversely, the main interests of many other students are on particular products and outcomes, such as acquiring specific knowledge and skills. Both types of interests are quite common, and both are integral to the goals of the SEF. In practice, the different types of interests can either complement or conflict with one another. Thus, sometimes it is advantageous to link the two, while other times it is best to separate them. For example, the main activities in the Market Garden are related to students gaining a wide range of practical skills and knowledge used in small-scale organic crop production and marketing. However, students are often interested in experimenting with variations on the Market Garden's production practices and systems. When such experiments are relatively small and simple, they can provide valuable learning opportunities, not just for the students conducting them but for all the students working in the Market

Garden. Larger and more complex experiments would conflict with the Market Garden's main objectives, however, and are, therefore, conducted outside the Market Garden, in one of the SEF's research fields.

There are also several important issues related to students taking risks and making mistakes in their learning processes. Mistakes provide important opportunities for learning, but our educational systems often fail to take advantage of them for this purpose. In fact, educators often penalize students who make mistakes, regardless of whether they learn from them or not. Within an experiential learning context, students should be not only allowed but in fact encouraged to experiment with new ideas, and this necessarily involves taking intellectual risks. Students involved in such endeavors need to be given guidance and supervision, as well as trust, by their mentors. Although it may require more staff time and other programmatic resources, staff and faculty should strive to promote and nurture students' explorations without controlling them or suppressing their creativity. Finally, particularly in agricultural (and similar) settings, it is important to distinguish between intellectual risks and risks that involve the safety and well-being of people or animals or possible damage to equipment or facilities.

In addition to the educational value of students engaging in the practical aspects of agricultural production and marketing, such activities can also produce revenue. Income that is essential to the functioning of the SEF is generated via the Market Garden's sales activities, and the Market Garden is managed to be economically productive and efficient. This situation provides an important level of realism in the Market Garden, and the project's educational and income-generating goals are complementary in this way. However, this situation can also create tensions between the program's educational and financial goals. At the SEF, education is prioritized over income generation, and the Market Garden's level of production is limited so that the SEF's educational goals are not compromised.

Several of the challenges faced by the SEF have developed with changes in students' situations and interests. Economic pressures on students have increased significantly since the 1970s. Many students now work while in school and have little, if any, time for strictly volunteer activities. In response to these and other factors, the SEF has placed increasing emphasis on formal academic credit internships and paid student positions to make participation in SEF activities accessible to as many students as possible.

The level of student interest and the specific topics of their interest have changed over time as well. In addition to responding to these changes with new SEF projects, programs, activities, classes, and other strategies, the SEF has also helped foster new student projects that are consistent with its goals. Since 2000, it has supported two new student-initiated efforts, Project Compost and Students for Sustainable Agriculture (SSA). Project Compost is a project of the associated students that collects preconsumer kitchen waste and other organic wastes on campus and composts them at the SEF with SEF equipment and supervision. It also conducts diverse compost education programs in the community. While the SEF has been involved in farm- and garden-scale composting for over twenty-five years, Project Compost's activities have significantly increased the number of students involved and the amount of compost being generated at the SEF as well as the level of campus and community awareness and activity around composting and related issues. SSA is an organization of undergraduate and graduate students "working to engage the campus and larger community in a socially just, ecologically balanced, and economically viable approach to agriculture." Students in SSA have organized many successful educational events; conducted an assessment of the campus food system and successfully lobbied for changes to increase its sustainability; and served effectively on a number of campus committees related to campus sustainability policy, faculty recruitment and hiring, and curriculum development. These examples illustrate that, much like students in the 1970s, today's students have diverse interests related to sustainable agriculture—ranging from the biophysical and technical to the socioeconomic and political—and are eager to learn, in part, by organizing and taking action to create positive change in their world. As such, the support of the SEF for these student efforts has been a logical extension of its historical roots and helped keep it relevant to students' evolving interests, concerns, and needs.

The SEF and the Curriculum

During its early years, the connections between the SEF and the formal agricultural curricula on campus were limited. The SEF mostly attracted students who were particularly interested in environmental and social issues related to agriculture, sustainable agriculture practices and theories, and experiential learning—none of which received much emphasis within existing, formal agricultural programs. However, the SEF did attract students from a wide range of undergraduate and graduate programs. Interested undergraduates in traditional agriculture majors found a place where they could learn practical skills and try to apply principles discussed in the classroom. Many of these students had moderate or strong interests in sustainability issues and found opportunities to explore these issues at the SEF. Undergraduates in environmental sciences were often attracted to the SEF because it was a place on campus where they could be involved in managing an ecosystem, albeit a highly modified one. The Children's Garden Program attracted a fairly distinct group of students whose main interests often were related to agricultural and environmental education, child development, or related issues. Students from a wide range of agriculturally related graduate programs came to the SEF to conduct M.S. or Ph.D. research projects in sustainable agriculture or to become involved in other SEF activities. However, for students in all these groups, SEF involvement has always been voluntary, and there has not been a degree program that required students to participate in SEF activities. Similarly, although for many years there have been courses relevant to sustainable agriculture (e.g., courses focusing on the ecology of crops, insects, soils, and weeds and those focusing on agricultural sociology, labor, and cooperatives), UC Davis did not offer a formal undergraduate curriculum that allowed students to focus on sustainable agriculture in the 1970s and 1980s.

Beginning in the early 1990s, however, as sustainability issues were becoming more prominent in California agriculture, a new agricultural systems and environment (ASE) undergraduate major was developed at UC Davis, with input from the SEF staff. The ASE major included a specialization in sustainable production systems and an introductory course on agricultural ecosystems that I cotaught with another instructor. At the same time, sustainability issues were discussed with increasing frequency in agriculture courses, although many faculty remained skeptical of sustainability concepts. Following the development of the ASE major, there was a period of expanding interest in sustainable agriculture at the undergraduate level, and the sustainable production systems option maintained an enrollment of twenty-five to thirty students throughout the 1990s. Students in the major as well as others could participate in the SEF's range of activities and courses, they could take other courses in agroecology and sustainable agriculture, and they could interact with faculty involved in sustainable agriculture research efforts. However, without the development of additional undergraduate courses focusing specifically on sustainable agriculture, enrollment in the sustainable production systems specialization began to decline after 2000.

A more significant effort to develop a major focused on sustainable agriculture began in 2004, following a report to the CA&ES dean. The committee submitting the report, on which I served, had reviewed the college's existing sustainable agriculture programs and activities and made recommendations for strengthening them and developing new ones. Its first recommendation was to develop "an undergraduate curriculum in the sustainability of agriculture, with tracks emphasizing the natural sciences and social sciences." Soon thereafter, another committee composed of faculty, staff, and students from many disciplines, departments, and programs, including me and students involved in SSA and the SEF, was appointed to develop a formal proposal for a new major. The student members were included after a group of students, including individuals involved in the SEF and SSA, successfully lobbied the faculty for representation on the committee. These students often played critical roles and made several important contributions to the work of the committee.

Early in the curriculum-development process, the students and some other committee members convinced the full committee to begin by focusing on the broad requirements for academic and professional proficiency in sustainable agriculture. To help identify those requirements and design a major that would help students meet them, the committee looked to several sources. Prominent among these was the SEF's thirty-year history, which provided the following insights and lessons:

- Students can understand and appreciate the diverse connections between agrifood system practices and theoretical principles, particularly through firsthand experiences in field situations. In addition, students' understandings of principles and practices are mutually reinforcing.
- Understanding agricultural sustainability requires learning to view agriculture from many perspectives, and, in the proper environment, students can be quite capable of such learning and understanding.
- Most students can develop the ability to critically analyze agricultural systems and solve complex problems related to them, particularly if they are given appropriate guidance and support.
- Students have many different learning styles and ways of learning. This diversity can be used as an advantage to help them learn in new ways, particularly if they are given opportunities to work together and learn from their peers.
- Students' needs and interests are continually changing, as are many

factors related to the university and society. Therefore, academic programs need to be dynamic and adaptable to remain relevant.

Another rich source of information for the curriculum-development process was a national survey conducted by a group of faculty and student committee members.[1] The survey asked participants what knowledge, skills, and experiences are necessary for students to have when graduating from a sustainable agriculture undergraduate major. Four stakeholder groups participated in the study: academics working in sustainable agriculture from throughout the United States, currently enrolled undergraduates in majors focusing on sustainable agriculture and closely related fields at U.S. institutions, alumni of such programs, and agriculture and food system practitioners working in California.

There was a high level of consistency within and among the four stakeholder groups' answers to the survey questions. Highlights of the survey results for each question can be summarized as follows:

- The content covered should include both disciplinary and interdisciplinary course work in specific social and natural sciences, with a focus on integration and application of knowledge.
- Students should develop skills in logic and analysis, interpersonal and communication skills needed for working effectively with diverse stakeholders, and specific professional skills for working in various aspects of the agrifood system.
- Significant and diverse on- and off-campus experiences, including practical course fieldwork, field trips, and internships, are essential to students' understanding of real-world practices and their links to principles learned in the classroom.

Following the stakeholder survey, the committee combined the suggestions, ideas, and concepts contained in the survey results with those in existing reports and literature on sustainable agriculture and education, along with those from historical experiences at the SEF and elsewhere, to develop a set of seven principles for the major. These principles focus on interdisciplinary breadth, systems thinking, skill development, experiential learning, linking the real world with the classroom, community building, and adaptive curriculum management. Using the principles as a guide, the committee worked to design a major that would produce graduates who possess a comprehensive understanding of agriculture and food systems

Figure 6.3. Student interns transplant onions in the Market Garden. (Courtesy Pat Vellines.)

and are prepared to work in complex real-world situations to enhance the sustainability of these systems. All students in the major would develop a broad understanding of agricultural and food systems and sustainability, and this breadth would be complemented by the depth all students acquire by focusing their studies within one of three academic tracks in the major: agriculture and ecology, food and society, or economics and policy.

At the heart of the curriculum are several common preparatory, applied production and common core courses that will allow students to develop a shared knowledge base and social network. The common preparatory and applied production courses will provide all students in the major with disciplinary training in agricultural, environmental, social, and economic sciences and applied knowledge and skills related to agricultural production. In addition, within each track, students will take additional preparatory courses to provide them with more in-depth disciplinary training relevant to that track. The interdisciplinary common core classes begin with an introductory course in sustainable agriculture and another in food systems and progress through two upper-division courses focused on the economics of sustainability and agroecosystem management. Students will also take track-specific, upper-division classes to focus their advanced work on particular areas. The culmination of the curriculum will be a two-quarter capstone sequence in which students from the different tracks will work together on team projects to analyze and solve problems using real-world case studies.

The major will employ a wide range of both traditional and nontraditional teaching concepts and methods. The common core courses and other learning experiences in the major are structured so that students will develop diverse and increasingly more advanced practical and professional knowledge and skills as they progress through the major. Experiential learning is integrated into many aspects of the curriculum, including the core courses and internships, and direct experience with food production practices is provided in the applied production courses that all students must complete. Additionally, each student will be required to complete one or more substantial internships in a wide range of possible settings, including farms and ranches, food system businesses, government agencies, nonprofit organizations, and research entities.

The SEF will play important roles in the new curriculum. It will be used for field-based laboratory and other class activities in at least three of the core courses and as a site for numerous internships and individual projects by students in the major. In addition, the SEF director is a coinstructor for the introductory core course in sustainable agriculture and will continue to contribute, along with other SEF staff, to the continued development of the sustainable agriculture curriculum in the future.

The major's diverse educational methods and activities are designed to meet its similarly diverse educational goals and objectives. The faculty, staff, and students involved in the major recognize that such an effort will involve challenges. Frequent assessment and adjustments will be necessary for the ultimate success of the major and the students it serves. Such adaptation and evolution of the major can be seen as a continuation of the evolution of sustainable agriculture education that began at UC Davis more than a generation ago.

In the mid-1970s, a group of students created the SEF to address what they perceived to be important gaps and flaws in agricultural education and research programs at UC Davis. The SEF was student driven, largely student managed, and dedicated to experiential learning, alternative agriculture principles and practices, and student initiative, creativity, and exploration. The students' goals included the creation of research and education efforts at UC Davis that would contribute to the development of more sustainable agriculture practices and systems in California and throughout the world. Over the years, the SEF and sustainable agriculture education at UC Davis have evolved and matured in many ways. Sustainability is now an important focus of UC Davis teaching, research, and outreach efforts in agriculture (and other areas). Thus, there has been significant progress toward reaching the students' original goals.

Yet the work of creating a more sustainable agriculture is far from complete, and important questions about the SEF, sustainable agriculture, and experiential education at UC Davis remain. Perhaps the most radical and significant aspect of the SEF was related not to sustainable agriculture, or to experiential learning, but to the students' coming together with the goals of directing their educational endeavors and transforming their university. How can the progress that has been made toward these goals so far be used to stimulate, and not stifle, more progress? How can a student farm that is no longer student run help students develop and exercise leadership? How can a formal undergraduate major help students identify their own educational objectives, which may or may not fall neatly within a university-approved curriculum, and facilitate their own empowerment to meet those objectives? Continually asking and addressing these sorts of questions will be critically important to the continued development of sustainable agriculture education at UC Davis and to ensuring that the SEF stays true to its original spirit, principles, and purposes in the future.

STUDENT REFLECTIONS

FARM INTERNSHIP JOURNAL, NOVEMBER 2009

SARAH GOODMAN

I usually go to the farm on Tuesday and Thursday mornings, but today a Wednesday class was canceled, which meant I could go. There was frost on the ground again until about midway through the morning. The ground looks beautiful with frost; it doesn't look real sometimes, just a light dusting of white powder that sits nicely on top of the big leaves of the plants and the dirt. To start off the morning, I grabbed a hoe with this guy Kaiya, and we went into the greenhouse to hack away at the weeds. Before I knew it I was sweating even though there was frost on the ground outside. We talked about the student occupations, the protests, all the fascinating things going on throughout the campus recently.[2] We both were active in some of the occupations and fighting for the right to have an affordable and diverse education. It's places like the farm that really add so much to my education and balance in life in general, and it's the opportunity to learn at places like the farm that are behind my shouts and chants at these protests. It is really an amazing opportunity to get to come to the farm and grow our own food and then go off to class! After the weeding, which took forever but was really satisfying when done, the two of us went on a quest to pick turnips. Turnips smell incredible when they are cut from their leaves, kind of like spicy cabbage. Well, this was the dirtiest I have ever gotten on the farm. Not only were the pathways in between the beds covered in gooey, slippery mud; the frost on the surrounding plants was melting so every time I bent down to grab a new turnip I would get muddy *and* wet . . . I loved it! The pinnacle of this experience was when I was ready to head back to the main shed with my box of turnips and, as I picked up the box, the entire bottom gave way and every single turnip fell out of the box and into the mud. At this point, I just took a breath and sat down in the mud to carefully salvage each poor turnip. The best part was walking into geology class covered in mud, arms sore from carrying a giant box of turnips. Life is good.

Sarah Goodman was a senior in international relations at the University of California, Davis; she graduated in 2010.

NOTES

1. N. Khanna, D. Parr, C. J. Trexler, and M. Van Horn. 2005. "Informing the UC Davis Curriculum Development Process: A Delphi Study of Sustainable Agriculture Stakeholders" (Davis: University of California, Davis, 10 January 2010), http://studentfarm.ucdavis.edu/samajor/UCD_SOE_Ag_Report.pdf.

2. The protests and occupation were part of student activism that occurred at UC Davis and several other system campuses in 2009 in opposition to the largest fee increases in the history of the University of California.

7

Hampshire College (1978)

The Agricultural Liberal Arts

LORNA COPPINGER AND RAY COPPINGER

Most people today don't think of Massachusetts as an agricultural state. How quickly we forget that once it was a breadbasket, shipping tons of foodstuffs back to England. The Connecticut River valley flowed with waving wheat until the Hessian fly put an end to it at the beginning of the nineteenth century. The wool business—gone by 1830—was enormous on the hillsides until the government changed the tariff laws and cheap land opened up beyond the end of the newly built Erie Canal. How quickly we forget that the Redcoats in Boston marched to Lexington and Concord because the large farm population there was hiding guns and powder to be fired as the first shots of independence, heard round the world. The leaders of our emerging democracy—Washington, Adams, Jefferson, Madison, Monroe—were all farmers who supported education. In the developing societies in Massachusetts, if there were more than fifty families in a town, then a school was required. The first four-year college in this country (Harvard, founded in 1636) was in Massachusetts; an agricultural land-grant college, now the University of Massachusetts, was established in 1863.

CREATING A "NEW COLLEGE"

Hampshire College was created in the late 1960s as an experiment in alternative education. The reason for creating a fifth college in a valley rich in colleges (within a ten-mile radius are Amherst, Mount Holyoke, Smith, and the University of Massachusetts) was to help solve a wider crisis in American higher education related to both quality and quantity. With increasing pressure from postwar high school graduates for places in four-year colleges, opportunities for gaining a high-quality, cost-effective education were scarce. The intent of Hampshire's curriculum was to teach students to teach themselves by providing a framework within which students read, wrote, studied, explored, questioned, and experimented—but were not constrained by the traditional academic pathways of distinct majors or disciplines. The first students arrived in the fall of 1970.

The Farm Center at Hampshire College grew from several perspectives that coalesced in the mid-1970s. First, the college was situated on eight hundred acres of farmland in the fertile Connecticut River valley. Second, the nascent environmental movement inspired students and faculty to tackle real-world problems that were affecting the quality of life. Finally, the designation *experimental,* which the college's founders had prescribed for their new institution, pointed firmly to a new departure in higher education and challenged students and faculty to find the way. Even though, at the start, Hampshire consisted of three reasonably traditional schools—the Schools of Humanities and Arts, Social Science, and Natural Science—these were only supposed to be administrative entities. The real action was slated to take place in programs.

Two formalized programs were in place at the very beginning— Human Development and Language and Communication. Faculty in each of the three schools were expected to participate in at least one of these programs by attending the weekly all-college program seminar, and they were expected to offer a course on some aspect of the program. The course work would provide information for the main seminar, which would, in turn, feed an expansion on some topics back to the courses. It was a good system. It turned out to be an imaginative way to teach and also encouraged a sense of community. Within a program, tremendous intellectual and instructive activity circulated.

The model was ideal for supporting the Environmental Quality Program (EQP), which began a year later. Surprisingly, in retrospect, there had been little attention paid to environmental studies during the creation of the new college. Original planning documents date from the mid-1950s, just when Rachel Carson was beginning to write *Silent Spring,* the book that set the stage for the environmental movement in the United States.

The EQP was about environmental problems but was never intended to fix them. In academics, a course in Shakespeare is about the author's work and not about how to rewrite it. Affectionately known as *De rerum natura* (after the first-century-BC Roman philosopher Lucretius's famous poem *On the Nature of the Universe*), the EQP consisted of once-a-week seminars, the satellite courses typical of a program, and a new series of once-a-week evening guest lectures. The guest lecturers covered a variety of subjects: sewage problems in New York City, DDT and soft pelican eggs, fish ladders in the Connecticut River, in short, any regional or national environmental topic. The invited speakers might be architects, engineers, political scientists, or researchers from law, medicine, physics, chemistry, or biology. The lecture series complemented and broadened the perspectives of the various satellite courses while at the same time introducing undergraduates to a range of contemporary issues. Researching those issues in multiple disciplines led students to multiple methods of inquiry. This kind of immersion fit perfectly with the college's overall goals of motivating learning and modeling how to learn.

What emerged from the EQP was the realization that many of our largest environmental problems stemmed from agricultural practices. Soils were being eroded because plowing reduced not only fertility but also the water reservoir stored within that soil. Pesticides were leaching from fields into streams, killing fish and wildlife, and endangering human health. Agriculture was a monster that chewed up the soil, polluting adjacent habitats, creating ever-expanding irrigation systems, and using so much water that some rivers no longer even made it to the sea. The air we breathed caused cancers, lung diseases, and allergies. Agricultural products poisoned us directly with residues in the food itself. If that wasn't bad enough, the food we ate had lost much of its taste. It was processed beyond recognition, fattening us without providing adequate nutrition.

It was a confusing time for both students and professors in an experimental college. We suspected that technological advancement was a cause of environmental degradation, that scientists were part of an industrial-military complex that was forsaking the basics of a good quality of life. Students in small liberal arts colleges tended to be antiscience. They didn't believe that atoms were for peaceful purposes or that electricity could be too cheap to meter. Nuclear bomb testing and the mortal threat of those bombs, coupled with the unwinnable war in Vietnam, made it all too clear what scientists had done for us. Besides, chemistry and physics were too hard to learn unless you were really smart, dedicated, and persistent. Advances in agriculture were driven by the economics of growing food for export to foreign nations to supplement military hardware as a means to equalize the balance of payments. But USDA scientists were not thinking about health and nutrition. Rather, they were selecting for crops that yielded big harvests and that could withstand mechanical harvesting, processing, and long-distance shipping.

TEACHING SCIENCE IN THE LIBERAL ARTS

Indeed, those of us thinking about new ways to teach science in the liberal arts knew that we had to be academically creative. Most students in our science courses were simply trying to satisfy their science requirement. They had come to Hampshire to be screenwriters or historians. Many biology majors were preprofessionals, anticipating medical school. Our love of science was confounded by the high schools, which typically made science courses into a hard and dull memorizing of facts and formulas. One high school teacher interviewed said that he would like to make his advanced-placement biology course interesting but that there "just wasn't enough time." Advanced placement was an interesting concept in itself in education. Pass the advanced-placement biology course, and you'll never have to take biology again. The carrot was that, if you enrolled in a liberal arts college, your advanced-placement course would satisfy your collegiate distribution requirement. When students got to Hampshire, they were dismayed to find that they still had to take science. They didn't believe us when we said it would be interesting and fun. Few people at that time realized that science was a language in which, in the late twentieth century, an educated person had to be fluent.

Meanwhile, the farmland surrounding Hampshire's small campus kept attracting the attention of faculty and students. Population studies were done in adjacent frog ponds and vernal pools. The chemistry of pond water was analyzed. Soil samples were taken. Woven in with these activities were several serious attempts by students to launch a farm program. Usually, the ideas clustered around communal living and working together and the wouldn't-it-be-great-to-grow-our-own-food approach. Many students were intrigued by the perennial grain crop studies at Wes Jackson's Land Institute, the organic approach at the Rodale Institute, the rethinking of food, water, and shelter at the New Alchemy Institute, and the back-to-the-land, living-the-good-life farm of the Nearings in Vermont and then Maine. Some Hampshire students interned at these centers and brought what they had learned back to Hampshire. By the early 1980s, they had created on campus a "greenhouse mod," adding a solar greenhouse to one of the communal dormitories, and growing their own vegetables. They experimented with hydroponics for the veggies and built a small pond for raising tilapia. In time, they acquired major funding from the Pew Memorial Trust to add a three-story bioshelter extension to the science building, where they engaged in aquaculture, growing a lot more tilapia, and studying the integration of ecological systems. Other students built a windmill out of a fifty-five-gallon steel drum just to see if it would work.

But, in the 1970s, agriculture was not seen as a plausible area of study within the liberal arts curriculum. Early attempts to launch a working/ studying/research farm did not have all-college support. A farm meant growing food or animals. A liberal arts education meant the larger, intellectual topics: Does Darwin's theory of natural selection hold up today? Discussion of agricultural problems had not yet taken its place in undergraduate colleges. Hampshire's farm ideas were not funded either internally or externally. On campus, the farm-based projects were seen to be in competition with other programmatic tracks, which were considered by many of the faculty as having greater lasting social value. Issues of equality for women and racial minorities were the important topics of the day.

Neither were we farmers, nor was our goal to train farmers. The University of Massachusetts (UMass), just three miles away, was the state's land-grant agricultural college. Future farmers went to UMass. Our attempts at Hampshire to start an agricultural program seemed far outside the interest of our UMass colleagues.

Besides, there was no money.

CULTIVATING RESEARCH AND EDUCATION

And then, in the mid-1970s, several projects were created by Hampshire science faculty that qualified as bona fide science/agriculture studies and that had some money attached to them. Quite by chance, they all centered on sheep. While we were trying to fit a money-attracting program around our belief that sheep would be a good-sized animal for liberal arts undergraduates, the sheep industry released its "Blueprint for Expansion of the American Sheep Industry." We connected with an extension agent for sheep (in New Hampshire; Massachusetts did not have one), who advised us about a potential flock. One of our adjunct professors, Paul Slater, had just finished a master's thesis titled "How Shall We Preserve Our Family Farms?" Paul had also raised sheep, and sheep figured in his answer to the question posed by his thesis. "As ruminants," he wrote, sheep "can use marginal lands unsuited to crop production to produce food and fiber on a sustainable basis while supplementing small farm incomes."

At about the same time, Professor John Torrey, a Harvard botanist, arrived at our door asking whether we would be interested in providing land for experiments with nitrogen-fixing alder bushes as a source of animal forage. This was exciting, for it seemed to dovetail with Wes Jackson's ideas of developing perennial polycultures. We said yes, thinking that this would be an excellent use for some of Hampshire's farmland and could lead to interesting student projects. It did, and our rationale for adopting sheep became even stronger.

And then came the breakthrough. In 1972, President Nixon had signed an executive order that forbade the use of toxic chemicals on federal land for predator-control programs. As a result, publication of the sheep sector's "Blueprint for Expansion" coincided with reports of a serious decline in sheep production owing to predation by coyotes and free-roaming dogs. Producers were clamoring for nonlethal methods of limiting predation.

A major center for the study of ruminant production, both in the 1970s and today, is the Winrock International Livestock Research and Training Center in Arkansas. The president of Hampshire in 1976 was Charles Longsworth, who suggested to us a visit to Winrock as a way of finding out more about predation on sheep. There the subject of nonlethal methods came alive. A staff researcher and sheep producer named Hudson Glimp told us of claims coming out of Texas that large European sheepdogs were having some success at protecting sheep there. What could be better than to go back to the Old World and study the dogs of traditional pastoralist cultures? We would bring back ideas—and puppies—to study their potential in the New World.

With such compelling evidence that Hampshire needed a farm to nurture these sheep-oriented projects, a proposal for the New England Farm Center was presented to the college in November 1978. It would encompass three projects, to start: sheep for New England pastures, livestock-guarding dogs for nonlethal predator control, and nitrogen-fixing plants for pasture improvement. A start-up grant for the dog project was obtained from Winrock; Susan Mellon of the Mellon Foundation provided a three-year challenge grant; and that, in turn, was matched by William Dietel at the Rockefeller Brothers Fund. These gained us a budget line in the business office, and we were official.

Within the next ten years, we had raised over $1 million in grant money. During this time, Hampshire's third president, Adele Simmons, provided constant moral and academic encouragement. She initiated several funding projects, two of which—with Control Data Corporation and the USDA—funded research for three years each.

Figure 7.1. Students bottling maple syrup. (Courtesy Hampshire College.)

The projects all counted as alternative agriculture: unusual ways of solving current agricultural problems. They suited Hampshire's desire to serve as a good corporate citizen, to avoid the ivory tower image, and to operate in the real world with innovative solutions. Problems from far away were brought into the Farm Center and studied. For example, one might think of rangeland as a perennial polyculture of grasses. But there is a problem with grass in big open country—on our western ranges or the South American pampas, for example. Grasslands need to be fertilized. Essentially, to raise beef, sheep, or wool on the range is to convert grass into some kind of protein and then export that protein to some faraway market. Every one of those protein molecules, or chains of amino acids, has nitrogen atoms attached to it, and that nitrogen is continuously taken from the land. Slowly, or, in some cases, rapidly, the grassland deteriorates and eventually turns to dust. The only way to fertilize—unless a better strategy can be found—is an expensive process involving quantities of fossil fuel.

The Farm Center projects fit well into Hampshire's academic program, designed as a sequence of Division I, II, and III courses leading to the bachelor of arts degree. In Hampshire's planning document, *The Making of a College,* the first-year "Div I" is proposed "to give students direct experience in conceptual inquiry in the company of faculty scholars who have a command of disciplines with which to approach subjects and problems they are really interested in."[1] In practice, this resulted in students choosing a topic for in-depth research—and, the more hands-on, the better. This worked particularly well in the School of Natural Science, as students developed questions that could be answered with a simple experiment. For example, they tested nitrogen-fixing plants, including woody dicots such as alder. Conceivably, alder would never need to be replanted, and it fixes nitrogen. So the students read papers, asked questions, and hunted in the fields, finding species that could survive in different habitats such as the upland, the lowland, the wetlands, and the dry land. The campus had it all. Would sheep eat it, and, if they did, would they destroy the habitat? Each question led to that first-year, project-oriented Div I examination, or a senior-year, longer-term research study and the Div III thesis, and often even to a peer-reviewed scientific publication.

CONNECTING PEDAGOGY AND AGRICULTURE

Then we discovered that our rationale for teaching about agriculture in the liberal arts college had already been put into words—eloquent, scholarly words by two giants in nutrition and education. A paper had been published in 1974 called "Agriculture, the Island Empire." It was written by André Mayer and Jean Mayer and published in the prestigious journal *Daedalus*. The article did two exciting things for us. It confirmed our view that agriculture was not beyond the scope of a liberal arts college. "The present isolation of agriculture in American academic life is a tragedy," the Mayers wrote. And they validated our use of agriculture in teaching biology, animal behavior, botany, chemistry, geology, and astronomy— all sciences that had arisen because of the needs of agriculture. Indeed, they argued, agriculture "was the first science—the mother of sciences; it remains the science which makes human life possible, and it may well be that, before the century is over, the success or failure of Science as a whole will be judged by the success or failure of agriculture."[2] They contended that children who know Shakespeare but nothing about their food could not be considered educated. It was a wonderful argument, and it made sense to us. All the disciplines could be involved, all who were interested in the environment, any of the Hampshire faculty. Studies of our food and water—even the world's food and water—were an exciting prospect for the work of a liberal arts college.

There was more to engage us in the Mayer paper. Farming activities are a great way to lure kids into science. Most college students are interested in one or more aspects of reproduction—and agriculture is all about reproduction. The antiscience student of the 1970s was not antireproduction. Studying sheep, lambs, dogs, puppies, and even the fortunes of alder shoots is fascinating for students. The questions we were asking were new. And the answers were *needed* by farmers. Students progressed through Hampshire, asked big questions, found out the answers to little questions, and wrote up their studies and sometimes published them in scientific journals. We had found a way to attract students to science, to get them to practice real science and enjoy it, all the while learning.

Our farm became a favorite center of activity. All students are required to pass a Div I exam in science, and many chose a farm-related project. Working on the farm was favored by many students on work-study. In the years since the farm's establishment, the enthusiasm of the students for the outdoors work and physical labor at the farm has trickled back onto the main campus, with the result that professors of social science, humanities, arts, and cognitive science have joined those in natural science in paying attention to the rich living resources of the farm. Students jostled to be assigned to overnight lamb watch. They helped deliver lambs and puppies. They tackled onerous chores—happily. They took charge of medical schedules and nutrition analyses. They spent hours in the science labs and hours on a shed roof clocking dog behavior. They worked one-on-one with their professors, almost as colleagues. Hampshire's Div I program, the "freshman" year, fosters this collegial relationship as students learn the methods of inquiry used by researchers. As the first-year introduction to methods of learning at Hampshire College, the Div I curriculum has excelled at fostering the successful engagement of students. Students are immediately immersed in the professional inquiries of their professors. The Div I year is when many would-be future writers or architects discover the fascination of science. Many go on to graduate school, Ph.D.s, M.D.s, D.V.M.s, and entire careers in scientific fields.

Among the courses taught at Hampshire right from its beginning were ecology, ecological modeling, environmental values, ecosystems analysis, organic farming, and the evolution and behavior of domestic animals. Concurrently, the more standard undergraduate biology courses were available: genetics, microbiology, plant anatomy and physiology, organic chemistry, neurophysiology, and biochemistry. By the mid-1970s, students were getting more sophisticated in their approach to the problems of agriculture, and, for many years, courses with such titles as "Biosocial Human Adaptation," "The World Food Crisis," and "The Future of Agriculture in New England" attracted dozens of students. "The World Food Crisis" was taught by a social scientist and a biologist and aimed to combine "natural and social science perspectives on the current world food situation with particular emphasis on New England, the United States, and Third World agriculture." Topics within this course included technological change, export orientation, agribusiness, the use of fossil fuels, human population, small farmers, "the feasibility of efforts to revive rural communities around a small farmer base," and "the promise and pitfalls of Green Revolution technology."[3]

Courses offered now at Hampshire reflect the need of students to understand problems facing world populations, including agriculture. A sample includes the following:

> Advanced Topics in Terrestrial Ecology
> Agriculture, Ecology, and Society
> Agriculture, Food, and Human Health
> Biomass Energy
> Farming in America
> From Generation to Generation: Seed Saving in Sustainable Agriculture
> The Microbial Farm
> Pesticide Alternatives
> Soil: Science and Society
> Sustainable Agriculture and Organic Farming
> Sustainable Agriculture: Local, Organic Food Production and the
>   Urban/Exurban Interface
> Sustainable Agriculture Seminar

Related courses are also available through the Five-College Consortium:

> Horticulture (Smith College)
> Plant Biology (Smith College)
> Plant Ecology (UMass)
> Soil Chemistry (UMass)
> Sustainable Agriculture (UMass)
> Tropical Agriculture (UMass)

Hampshire's original array of the three academic schools has metamorphosed many times, and now they are found within broader programs. The

Environmental Studies and Sustainability Program meshes the Schools of Natural Science, Social Science, and Art. In 1992, faculty of Hampshire and several other institutions founded the Institute for Science and Interdisciplinary Studies, which, in a sense, reflects the embryonic ideas in the original EQP. One of its goals is to develop research to study economic crises of agriculture. The Agricultural Studies/Farm Center Program mixes intellectual, political, scientific, and cultural studies. Faculty in the Schools of Cognitive Science and Natural Science have joined together to advise students studying animal behavior and cognition. Two recent projects from the program are "Domestic Sheep: A Two-Part Bioacoustic Study" and "Apple Maggot Fly Responses to Sticky Red Spheres."

Concurrently with this development of courses, the Farm Center was defining its landscape and objectives. Located a ten-minute walk from the library, past a dormitory, along a forest path, and across a field, the farm's office/farmhouse, barns, pastures, sugar shack, community-supported agriculture (CSA) distribution barn cum root cellar, hoophouse for winter greens, kennel/offices, irrigation pond, compost pad, and weather station are located on the north side of the main campus. The series of original farm managers had been hired mainly to take care of the sheep and dogs in the original research projects, but, by the early 1990s, both projects had been successfully finished, and the Farm Center looked for new appropriate goals. The college had kept the farm manager position filled, and, in 1990, the manager hosted the summer conference of the Northeast Organic Farming Association (NOFA) at Hampshire. The weekend in August brought families, tents, camper vehicles, and enthusiasm to campus dormitories and fields. Three days of workshops, exhibitions, demonstrations, markets, and games raised the profile of Hampshire's farm in the wider agricultural community. It was a center for studying about agriculture!

Then, as is typical for this college, a student-generated project helped keep the farm on the map. The students designed a CSA program to produce organic vegetables for thirty shareholders. Shareholding was initially limited to the Hampshire community—students, faculty, staff—but, very quickly, the CSA grew to two hundred shareholders from the Five-College community, and the original small garden area expanded to fifteen acres.

One of the attendees at the NOFA conference in 1996 was Leslie Cox, who had grown up on a large, progressive dairy farm, earned his B.S. in agricultural education at Cornell with a concentration in farm management, had worked in various states as a farm manager and teacher of agriculture, and was amazed to see sheep grazing on the Hampshire campus. He found out later that the manager's job was open and applied for it. Under his expert direction, the Farm Center has evolved into a real farm, but a small-scale one relevant to a liberal arts college. Currently, the livestock consists of fifteen to twenty ewes, six to eight milking cows, six to eight beef cows, twenty-five chickens, twenty-five turkeys, nine to ten pigs, and about three llamas for predator control. Leslie bales six thousand bales of grass hay a year; together, pasture and hayfields for the livestock occupy seventy-five acres.

In 1998, the farm hired another full-time professional, Nancy Hanson, as manager of the CSA. Nancy is a fourth-generation farmer from a Connecticut dairy farm with a degree in plant science from the University of Connecticut. She manages the CSA on fifteen acres, with three acres usually in cover crops each year. She also manages summer interns, work-study students, and volunteers, scheduling the workload to coincide as much as possible with the academic year. The CSA's distribution of vegetables, herbs, and flowers begins in early September.

One of the advantages of a student farm, of course, is the number of students available to do the chores. One of Hampshire's perennial problems has been to find enough jobs on campus to employ the number of its students eligible for work-study. The farm has taken up the slack: Leslie gets forty-five to fifty-five applications every fall. He accepts them all, meets the students at the barn, and tells them about the 7:00 A.M. chores and the 7:00 P.M. chores. Very quickly the applicants sort out for themselves whether 7:00 A.M. is a valid part of their day. During the school year, two students work full-time with the livestock and maintenance chores, and three or four work part-time during the busy times of haying, lambing, or sugaring. Many others work an hour here, two hours there.

The two managers schedule the farming chores according to the availability of students. The annual cycle of planting, weeding, harvesting, marketing, haying, maintenance, sugaring, milking, and logging is kept within the scope of the small farm and the relatively inexperienced student workers. The managers run the operations on a seasonal cycle familiar to any farmer. At any time, faculty or students can lend a hand with the ongoing activities. Marketing is focused solely on the Five-College community so that local commercial farmers are not threatened by Hampshire's farm. Recently, the farm has applied to the state for a grant to acquire cheesemaking equipment in order to create a demonstration of what can be done on a small scale. Information will be disseminated to interested local farmers.

Pedagogy and agriculture are well joined at Hampshire.

Figure 7.2. A student feeding the chickens. (Courtesy Laura Sayre.)

THE BOTTOM LINE

The greatest challenge to the Hampshire College Farm Center has always been funding. Who funds all the activities? It is still often difficult to get across the idea that the farm is about agriculture and not about plant and animal husbandry: it's not just about getting the chores done; it's about illustrating larger agricultural issues while getting the chores done. Early on, some administrators saw the farm as a good way to manage an acreage that it was our moral obligation to manage. Often, they saw potential dollars in produce or thought that the farm should be financially self-sufficient. That always created—and still does—an internal conflict because our job is to teach and to learn the culture of agriculture, not just to grow crops and sell them.

Changes in college administration brought financial managers who thought that it might be easier and cheaper to turn the farm into lawns, parking lots, and recreation areas. In almost every budget crunch, the administrators look to the farm as an obvious place to cut expenses. No one interested in the pedagogy of science would suggest that we close the science classrooms or labs, but the same people would suggest closing the farm.

The Farm Center was never part of the original college plan. It was never designed as an integral part of the new college. It was a program. As a program, the expectation was that it would be administered through the schools (Humanities and Arts, Social Science, and Natural Science). No budget line was ever prepared. The 1978 proposal for the Farm Center gained its stature solely from the *funded* projects it described. Since day one, the business office was anxious to know whether we could at least break even with the sheep on the farm. Running a commercial sheep farm for profit is difficult but not impossible. Making money on sheep at a college while accommodating student projects probably is impossible. It's hard for a business office to balance the cash outflow with the knowledge inflow.

Although the Farm Center has existed for over thirty years and presents a shipshape, organized, productive face to traffic along Route 116 in South Amherst, it exists on a precarious administrative and even academic ledge. Many Hampshire faculty still have the image of a farm as a place to do farming, not teaching, and, therefore, not relevant to a small liberal arts college. But other faculty have supported the combination of academic and agrarian ventures. They encourage student projects and write grant proposals for farm-based investigations. Some money for overhead is available to the college from grants, but this is neither a large nor a reliable funding source. As a result, thanks to the college's continuation of the farm manager's position and hiring of a CSA manager, the Farm Center in the 1990s began to focus seriously on earning a steady income through the sale of farm products and services.

Farm Center land now grows more than thirty different vegetables, flowers, and herbs for over two hundred shareholders. These are distributed once a week from early September through late November, at $300 a share, in a purpose-built barn. In the summer, local kindergarten through twelfth-grade students attend the Farm and Garden Camp, which was created and is led by the Farm Education Collaborative of Western Massachusetts. The farm runs the School-to-Farm Program, creates and mentors apprenticeships, and holds workshops on weaving, beekeeping, natural fiber dyeing, and maple sugaring. And, thanks to the endeavors of the farm manager and the input and enthusiasm of the students, the Hampshire farm these days has many small enterprises that help support it: sheep, dairy cows, beef, pork, turkeys, chickens, eggs, firewood, maple syrup, honey, and cordwood. Besides increasing the cash flow to the farm and college, these outreach activities extend the college's corporate citizen endeavors locally.

During the 1980s, the Farm Center had hosted an annual summer conference for sheep producers (Sheeposium, of course), and, from 1990 to 2007, NOFA brought hundreds of people to campus for three days.

Currently, the net cost to the college of the Farm Center is about $140,000 annually. A little over half of this is salaries. The CSA more than pays all its own expenses (minus salaries); farm expenses run about $18,000 short. The goal is for both programs to pay for themselves, minus the salaries of the two managers, who are on the staff of Hampshire College and who participate in some teaching and advising of students. This goal seems reasonable. Farm faculty are writing proposals for funding of pilot research/demonstration projects. The staff want to increase the sales of meat and the number of CSA shareholders. The farm is looking to expand into cheese, yogurt, and ice cream. And, although the final product is not for sale, the growing of hops at the farm results in several experimental beverages, and the spent grain is recycled to happy pigs and chickens. The dean of natural science, Chris Jarvis, writes, "I was awarded an NSF grant to teach students to ask questions and pursue answers in brewing science and it bought me a small brewery (very small, 15 gallon vessels, but high tech nonetheless)! We teach cheese making at the 100 level to introduce [students] to fermentation (using milk from the farm) and the cheese-making course and organic chemistry are the pre-reqs for Zymurgy, the course in brewing science! And our beer is very good!"

EVALUATING THE FARM CENTER

Word filters from the admissions office that several students have chosen Hampshire specifically because of its integration of academic liberal arts with an agriculture program and working farm. Word has also filtered from several parents who visited campus during a fall "Parents and Friends" weekend that the sight of sheep grazing along one side of the long entrance driveway was an unexpected and totally enjoyable surprise.

Are the students successful? Is the faculty? Is the farm? Yes, the students progress through their four years of self-selected and self-directed studies, choosing hands-on agricultural projects that are framed by academic inquiry, scientific methods, responsible use of materials, and the presentation of results. Sometimes their studies take them far afield. They have traveled across the country visiting the Hampshire livestock guarding dogs in situ on farms and ranches in thirty-eight states and collected data on their behavior and their working environment. In British Colum-

Figure 7.3. A student making yogurt. (Courtesy Hampshire College.)

bia, where sheep were being used in forest clear-cuts as an organic way to keep weeds cleared until the replanted trees were tall enough to outcompete them, a student went with a guarding dog to help protect the sheep. The Canadian government had mandated that, if there were going to be sheep grazing the weeds on the clear-cuts in the high country, then there needed to be a shepherd with them and also a livestock-guarding dog. We sent dogs and students.

Yes, the faculty are teaching science—to enthusiastic science majors and nonmajors alike. We teach that area of science called *hypothesis testing*. We teach experimental design, we teach methods of inquiry, and, most of all, we teach students *how* to learn. As the new college matured, the needs of the students for faculty to teach agriculture studies increased. The Schools of Natural Science and Social Science and the new School of Cognitive Science have each hired faculty expressly (although not exclusively) to participate in farm activities. We added a reproductive physiologist, international experts in food and nutrition, and several animal behaviorists. Which professors are active at the farm at any given time depends on the interests of the students. In a recent semester, four disciplines were profiled: botany, politics and environmental studies, ecology and entomology, and microbiology. The range of academic subjects is worldwide, from detecting stress in vocalizations in sheep in Ireland to agricultural policy in Africa. Think of any agricultural problem you can, and chances are a Hampshire student has investigated it.

The original research project at the farm, investigating whether Old World livestock-guarding dogs could protect New World livestock, expanded from a few sheep farmers in Massachusetts to a nationwide and international program, eventually keeping records on fifteen hundred dogs. By the early 1990s, the project had passed into the hands of the livestock producers themselves. In the spring of 2008, sheep and goat producers in Texas welcomed us back to their ranches and told us that, without the dogs, they could not stay in business.

Dozens of farm-based research projects continue. To mention just one, in the first decade of the twenty-first century, Dula Amarasiriwardena, a professor of chemistry, and his students published papers about remediating arsenic pesticides in apple orchards, measuring lead content in maple syrup, and teaching environmental analytic chemistry in a project-based lab study. As a result, to mention just one outcome, Vermont wrote new legal requirements for maple syrup production.

Thus, the results of student and faculty work in the field of agriculture at our small liberal arts college are often significant in the wider world as well as within our small college. We underline the real-world importance of what we do by submitting the results of the research to scientific publications, where it is reviewed by established scientists according to the professional standards of each field. Our pedagogical requirements are well satisfied every time we graduate an undergraduate with a publication record.

Those requirements are also well satisfied when we look at the Hampshire College Web site and see, listed under "Academic Programs," *Farm Center*. Within the School of Natural Science is an area of study called *Agricultural Studies and Rural Life*. The text goes:

> The study of food, agriculture, and rural life brings together faculty and students interested in the central intellectual, political, scientific, and cultural issues that dominate contemporary discussion of food and agriculture.
>
> The program combines a diverse academic curriculum with practical experience at the Hampshire College Farm Center, an organic working farm, and workshops with visiting writers, artists, and scholars. Students gain experience with the complex issues of sustainability through internships and apprenticeships with farms and advocacy groups.[4]

André Mayer and Jean Mayer would be pleased. So are we.

STUDENT REFLECTIONS

GOOD SOIL

MARADA COOK

When I came to Hampshire College, I already knew how to drive a tractor. After growing up on a family farm and working on organic farms on both coasts, I thought I knew a thing or two about growing vegetables, too. But I'd never seen broccoli like Nancy Hanson's.

Hampshire broccoli stands three feet high, glows with a blue-green verdant sheen, and produces head after head of perfect—and I mean perfect—worm-free, vitamin-rich, over-the-top, catalog-quality broccoli. When the admissions staff asked, "Why do you want to come to Hampshire?" I told them I wanted to learn the scientific reasons we should link soil health to the highest of mankind's achievements on earth. The broccoli, though, loomed large in my mind—I had to learn how to grow broccoli like that.

The Hampshire CSA farm manager, Nancy, proved to know more than a thing or two about broccoli. She was also the perfect blend of modern mentor and New England skeptic. She encouraged us to help with the next year's crop planning as well as pick vegetables with about forty of our friends. Being college kids, hunger was a common cause, the farm was full of edible rewards, the work was social, and, hey, why not get up early if it means the only shot at the community raspberry patch?

I picked vegetables with an intense and sensitive fellow student with no ability to teamwork. I taught him about how a large family like mine worked the land; he taught me about the importance of small things and stunning writing. We somehow stuck out several years of shared classes, farm shifts, and apartments. I learned how to grow broccoli, and he insisted that there was more to it all than broccoli. We stayed four years at Hampshire and the farm. One interest led to another; they all seemed to lead back to the land; the thrill of mental gymnastics along the field edges didn't get old. By the eighth semester there was still more to learn.

Hampshire's great broccoli came in part from the design work behind nurturing the soil. Nancy's farm plan fed the land; the land produced healthy soil and healthy crops. As we struggled to keep up with the harvests that flowed from such good land care, we ate the food we harvested, and we thought about how to change the world. I'm not saying we came up with any better answers than the generation that started Hampshire College, but we were there, and we ate of the earth of the place. And then we took it with us. In fact, we often went to classes wet, dirty, cold, and tired. We formulated our approach for the next five to ten years or more with a day that started in the dirt. Many of us still do.

Good ideas come from good soil. Each individual's every bite and every thought crafts a facet of the landscape of this new New England region. Those of us who work in the food and agricultural world see how fast and how furiously it is changing. The movement toward sustainable agriculture and locally produced, healthy food has sprung directly out of the mental seedbed of the 1970s. Hence the existence of Hampshire College and its unique Farm Center. Hampshire College was a good idea that landed on good soil.

A generation later, its soil feeds the minds of the movement.

Marada Cook is director of Crown O'Maine Organic Cooperative, a family business she owns and runs. She graduated from Hampshire College in 2007.

A FARM EDUCATION

NANCY HIRSHBERG

I can still remember the look on the faces of the schoolchildren who would tour the Farm Center. "Ick, what's that smell?" "Does it hurt them when you shave off their wool?" "You mean you're going to eat them?" For most it would be their first, and perhaps last, time on a farm. Their visit would connect them with the root of a daily ritual that is completely taken for granted—eating. As a young and aspiring educator, I knew that the students were more engaged than I had ever seen them in a classroom.

I was studying education and plant and soil sciences, specifically, "The Application of Piaget's Theories to a Middle School Science Curriculum." While agriculture was the theme, we weren't teaching farming. We were a testing ground for exploring how to reawaken minds that had been lulled to sleep, how to instill a sense of curiosity, excitement, and inquiry. What better place than a farm to awaken the senses and the mind? Farms are rife with teachable moments in the arts and sciences. Whether through exploring bacteria and molds in compost, learning about ecosystem sciences through the complex farm system, or studying the immigrant historical experience through the voices of farmworkers, farms provide rich resources for experiential study.

Democracy cannot thrive unless we have an informed citizenry capable of critical thinking. My studies at Hampshire taught me that, in many ways, the three R's of education had given way to the three C's: conform, comply, and consume. Yet, on the farm, I would witness the brightening eyes as the lights went on in the students' brains. It's hard not to be fascinated on a farm. The simple fact of understanding that food comes from somewhere beyond the back of the grocery store can have a profound effect on a child's understanding of the world. It connects him or her with the notion that all things come from somewhere. Maybe, then, things *go* somewhere, too. Students gain a greater appreciation of the world and how they are connected to it. After all these years I can finally fess up. We were a breeding ground for budding environmentalists! The Farm Center was a learning laboratory for all involved.

Nancy Hirshberg is vice president of natural resources at Stonyfield Yogurt. She graduated from Hampshire College in 1985.

STUDENT REFLECTIONS

TANGIBILITY

LISKA CLEMENCE CHAN

It was the Farm Center that attracted me from high school in Minneapolis to Hampshire College. The farm is where I learned to dock lambs' tails, drive a stick-shift truck, back a trailer, build fences, and plow with horse and harness. As a student with the dog project, I learned not only about the behavior of livestock-guarding dogs but also about evolutionary biology, animal husbandry, and ways of composing a scientific paper. Most importantly, I think, the farm and the people I encountered there taught me how to ask questions and how to pursue answers.

Almost twenty years later, a central part of the work I do each day is rooted in the hands-on mode of inquiry I gained at the Hampshire College farm. I am a landscape designer, and I teach in a university landscape architecture department. The parallels between what I do now and my days at the Farm Center seem distant, yet to me they are inextricable. My Div III was titled something like "Why Do Dogs Bark?" Under the guidance of Ray and Lorna Coppinger, it was an investigation of breed differences in vocal behavior. The path from there to teaching landscape architecture is linked through a desire to pass on ideas of cause and effect and my deep interest in the many facets of landscape change.

Dress in layers. Walk to my bike. Spin wheels from the dorms through the woods to the farm. The ground at the farm is lumpy. Each morning when I ride my green bike along the path, holes and lumps in frozen mud rattle fenders and knock the kickstand down. My memories are clear. I park my bike, march up the stairs to Ray's office, where, in stark contrast to the sharp morning air, I find the familiar warm haze of cigar smoke. After checking in for a couple of stories and instructions, I go down to the kennel, check on the puppies, take one five-month-old pup up to the Blazer, open the back, and load it in the crate. As I do this, she whips around and takes a chunk out of my sleeve. Ach! Damn dog.

The farm provided me—an idea-oriented city kid—with a controlled uncertainty and rare exposure to tangibility. The dogs were unpredictable, crafty, and often kind of horrible. The sheep escaped. The horses kicked, chewed, and breathed steam. When tart concord grapes popped out along the fence in late August, it meant school was starting again. I lead Jack, the Belgian draft horse, in a circle with my boyfriend (now husband) on Jack's back. Francis, who had left the city only one other time before going to Hampshire, floated, for a fleeting moment, five and a half feet in the air, gripping the mane and cringing. Hold on; if you surprise him, he will throw you.

Time on the farm is free from classroom abstractions. When it is cold, the sheep's troughs freeze, and that icy water is painful to fingers. Lambs born on a February night to a ewe with mastitis have a slim chance of surviving without hot water bottles and formula. When the baler breaks during haying, it's a crisis. Tomorrow there's rain. The hay has been tedded, and it'll mold if it gets wet. For me, the farm is where time fades. It's the place where a kid's idealism merges with dirt, bumps, bites, scrapes, stink, and joy.

Liska Clemence Chan is an associate professor and chair of the Department of Landscape Architecture at the University of Oregon.

NOTES

The authors thank the following individuals for factual and editorial assistance with this essay: Chris Jarvis, dean of natural science; Leslie Cox, farm manager; Nancy Hanson, CSA manager; Arthur Westing, former professor of ecology and dean of natural science; Lynn Miller, professor of genetics; Dula Amarasiriwardena, professor of chemistry; Paul Slater, adjunct professor of natural resource studies; and Laura Sayre and Sean Clark, for inviting us to tell the story and for editorial comments.

1. Franklin Patterson and Charles R. Longsworth, *The Making of a College: A New Departure in Higher Education* (Cambridge, MA: MIT Press, 1975), 108.

2. André Mayer and Jean Mayer, "Agriculture, the Island Empire," *Daedalus* 103 (1974): 83–95, 33.

3. *Hampshire College Catalog, 1985* (Amherst, MA: Hampshire College, 1984), 101.

4. http://www.hampshire.edu/admissions/agriculture.htm.

♦ Part 3 ♦

Coming of Age

8

University of Maine (1994)

Majoring in Sustainable Ag

MARIANNE SARRANTONIO

The first ceremonial spadeful of soil was turned over in Field F, belonging to the Black Bear Food Guild (BBFG), in the spring of 1995. The hand-dug field had symbolic importance to the first members of the guild. It represented their commitment to respect the needs of the land in their venture to learn how to farm sustainably. Field F, one of six fields they were to manage that year, was then mandated to be treated with special respect, remaining hand dug as a way of inspiring future guild members with the satisfaction gained from hard work and connection to the earth.

The BBFG was a natural offspring of the University of Maine's (UM) Sustainable Agriculture (SAG) Program, launched in 1988 as the first bachelor of science degree program in sustainable agriculture in the country. After several years of learning both theory and practice largely in a classroom setting, the students were anxious to put their knowledge to work in the field. A small group, led by a charismatic and persuasive older student, lobbied relentlessly for the right to farm, pushing their request repeatedly to the SAG Program coordinator, the chair of the department, the dean of the College of Natural Sciences, Forestry, and Agriculture, and the various UM Rogers Experimental Farm managers. In 1994, after nearly two years, the students were granted, in exchange for a land-use fee, a noncontiguous patchwork of underutilized fields on two sides of the road that splits the experimental farm in the town of Stillwater, some four miles from the main part of the UM campus in Orono. The soils on the three acres ranged from clayey and wet to sandy and droughty but also included a group of three half-acre fields with relatively good silt loam soil.

The name Black Bear Food Guild was chosen to give the group a university connection (the black bear is UM's mascot) and an identity as supposed apprentices within a skilled class of workpeople, namely, farmers, who share a common goal. In the first year, the students' idealism and enthusiasm were nearly boundless. In the fifteen years since the food guild's initiation, the field configuration, budget, and operating procedures have shifted several times, but the members' level of enthusiasm and idealism has remained high.

The first group of students to farm as the BBFG had to raise their operational budget almost entirely themselves, which they did with a mixture of fund-raising activities ranging from the sale of vegetable transplants to begging donations of seed and fertilizer from local farm supply stores. The university stipulated that students could be paid for their work that year only if they were eligible for work-study. The newly formed guild chose to run the farm on a community-supported agriculture (CSA) model, in which community members purchase a share of the farm's harvest in the spring and then receive a division of the produce each week during the season. In 1995, the students' farm sold fourteen full-share equivalents at $350 each, giving them slightly under $5,000 in cash with which to purchase equipment and supplies. They concentrated on seven staple vegetable crops plus basil and cut flowers. Share members in 1995 received roughly 1 pound of fresh produce for each dollar they paid, including 135 pounds of potatoes and over 50 pounds of onions. With the work-study program offsetting all labor costs, the guild finished the year with $332 to pass on to the following year's students.

The BBFG is rare among enduring college farms in that it is almost entirely student managed. To this day, there are no UM faculty or staff whose paid responsibilities include working with the BBFG. Student guild members are expected to carry out an extensive list of responsibilities, including forming a working team, developing a farm plan and budget, advertising shares to potential CSA members, collecting and depositing income, keeping detailed records for organic certification, and, of course, performing the majority of the field work. As lifelines, the students have a faculty adviser (me, since 2000), who is also the SAG Program coordinator; a research technician, who does some tillage and other field operations involving tractor work, such as laying black plastic; and a horde of other extension educators, faculty, and experimental farm managers, who help plan rotations, purchase inputs, install infrastructure, and deal with unexpected problems, such as the late blight that devastated potato and tomato crops in the Northeast in 2009. None of these university employees receive any financial compensation for their work with the guild, and none have it listed as a percentage of their job description. Although it has always been understood, and grudgingly accepted, that the university will not provide financial compensation to faculty and staff for their work with the food guild, those who work most closely with the students may receive some payment in kind in the form of produce.

The BBFG year typically starts in November or December, just as the previous season comes to a frozen end. Students interested in participating in the guild for the following year meet with the guild's faculty adviser, typically as a preformed group of people who feel that they can work together (long weeks in the field the following spring may disabuse them of their previous fondness for their coworkers, but more on that later). The BBFG crew generally consists of two to three students who work full-time for the summer, a few part-time students, and a handful of semireliable volunteers, all of whom must complete UM farm safety training to be allowed in the fields. The full-time student core must include at least one junior or sophomore who is a SAG major and ideally consists entirely of SAG majors. While many students across campus think that it would be enjoyable to have a summer farm experience, only those who have committed to the SAG major are likely to ever utilize the experience in their future career choice. Further, SAG majors will have been exposed to at least the rudiments of sustainable farming practices in the classroom before they put the hoe to the row in the field and will presumably make some effort to translate theory into practice. First-year students have occasionally been allowed to participate in the guild, but usually only if they have some previous farming experience and/or exhibit above-average maturity in terms of their academic and personal behavior. This is at the discretion of the faculty adviser.

At a more practical level, there is an issue of accountability in the selection process: participants are far more likely to adhere to their commitments and responsibilities if they anticipate an ongoing relationship with faculty and staff who may affect their future, both academically and in terms of future job and scholarship recommendations. The most difficult season on the UM student farm occurred when the number of SAG majors fell from an average of twenty to an all-time low of seven, only one of whom chose to participate in the guild, forming a working team with a gaggle of buddies who had no connection to SAG and who had romantic notions of bucolic frolicking in the fields but little genuine inclination toward long days of hard physical labor. When the SAG student dropped out of the guild early in the season, the remaining students gradually lost interest in the experience and simply walked away in early August, knowing that there would be no long-term ugly consequences for them. CSA share members were understandably furious, and the guild lost credibility on many fronts that year. It took several successful seasons to regain its good reputation.

At the initial fall meeting with prospective student farmers, the faculty adviser will generally lay out the expectations for the guild members, including the need for commitment, responsibility, and communication throughout the experience. Students are expected to make a decision about their commitment to the whole season, winter through fall, by the time the spring semester starts in January. Any student who subsequently changes his or her mind is required to find a replacement (subject to the faculty adviser's approval), unless the remaining members feel that they can carry on without additional help.

By late January, the reality of a student-managed farm operation kicks in as the newly formed crew meets weekly to (ideally) scour former BBFG planting records, analyze previous years' work logs and budgets, and begin the creation of a plan for the coming season. They will develop a budget based on the following information: total amount of labor available for the season, including any part-time labor they may hire to supplement their own effort; expected weeks of paid work; the hourly wage they anticipate; and the costs of seed, inputs, equipment, and miscellaneous other expenses. BBFG students no longer are required to have work-study status in order to participate and are, instead, paid from the general account created by CSA share money. The students are UM employees, and their pay rate is determined by university employment guidelines.

Each year, the enterprise is expected to leave at least $1,000 in the guild's budget for the next year's group to pay for potting soil, seeds, and other early-season expenses, including some labor. Costs incurred later in the semester have to be met with income from the CSA memberships. By late March, the students start their cool-season transplants in the greenhouse. The greenhouse that is available to them is conveniently located on campus next to Deering Hall, where the SAG Program is housed. It is the only greenhouse on campus that is certified organic and, at times, is in heavy demand for faculty and graduate student research projects as well. While the BBFG has never been denied space in the house, it has often had as close neighbors research projects that were not completely compatible with transplant production, such as entomology or pathology experiments involving pests of commonly grown vegetables.

Also in mid-March, applications are sent out for the CSA memberships. They are sent first to previous members, who have roughly one month to rejoin before membership opens to the general public. (Occasionally, difficult members from the previous year will be accidentally removed from the mailing list.) Membership goals vary from year to year according to budgetary needs but are generally in the range of thirty-five to fifty full memberships, intended to provide a family of four with sixteen weeks of produce. A full share in 2009 cost $425. Typically, much of the budget is composed of half shares, which are purchased by smaller families or individuals who partner to join the CSA. At forty-five full-share equivalents, the guild has nearly $20,000 for the season's expenses, which has normally been more than adequate to meet its needs and leave starting capital for the following year. All money collected is deposited in a dedicated university account under the experimental farm; as university employees, guild members are subject to all the regulations and expectations that involves. This sometimes irritates the students as they see themselves more as semiautonomous tenant farmers than as student employees.

One of the most difficult times for the student-managed farm comes when the late Maine spring finally begins to warm and dry the soil just as end-of-year projects and final exams overwhelm the student agenda. While not unique to the Maine student farm, the time crunch is exacerbated by the fact that all planting is done by the students themselves and that the window of opportunity for best spring sowing is truncated in the northern climate. This stress has led at times to suboptimal timing for the planting of early crops, especially when the weather is foul on the precious few days that students can clear their academic schedules for field work. Early-season activities that must occur before school gets out are almost all centered in the small sandy field that has drained and warmed up most quickly. These tasks include removing straw mulch from fall-planted garlic, planting and setting up trellises for peas, and transplanting leeks and other allium family crops as well as the first seedings of radishes, salad greens, and beets. Ideally, the previous fall's cover-crop residue (mostly oats and field peas) has been turned in by farm staff, and some secondary tillage has occurred. Most other field activities then take a back seat to course work for several weeks, although volunteers are sometimes recruited to fill in to help perform critical tasks.

In early to mid-May, when finals are over, the students will begin spending up to sixty hours a week intensively laying out, preparing, and planting the beds for the season. The research technician will generally help them lay black plastic for the solanaceous (tomato family) and cucurbit (squash family) crops. From this point on, the students are largely on their own in terms of field operations. They may do some additional bed preparation and amendment incorporation with a walk-behind rototiller, although this form of soil disturbance is discouraged because of the long-term detrimental effect it has on soil structure.

By early June, the BBFG fields will begin to take shape much as on any other vegetable farm around the world, with the varied neon shades of spring greens peppered with deep purples among the salad mixes and brassicas. The large hoophouse purchased by the BBFG in 1998 will fill by mid-June with precious frost-tender favorites such as heirloom tomatoes, murderously hot chili varieties, and at least five types of basil. The first pickup day for shareholders is usually in late June and is a day of frantic work and nervous excitement, even when the catch of the day is a mere handful of peas and radishes.

Midsummer field work can become a relatively laid-back routine of spot weeding, irrigating, and pest and insect scouting. It is common for each of the guild students to sneak away for a week's vacation sometime in July or early August. By mid- to late August, harvest has begun to accelerate, and the weekly pickups cap long days of hauling tubs of fresh vegetables back to the washing table for cleanup and weighing.

Classes often start at UM before Labor Day, causing the second wave of school-versus-farm stress for the guild members. Because of the cool climate in central Maine, crop harvest peaks quite late in the summer, and early September is the time of warm-season crop bounty—especially tomatoes and summer squash, which cannot be left past their optimum harvest time (share members are quick to point out that letting the zucchini reach eight pounds each hardly justifies saying that it is a heavy pickup day). Early frost is a constant worry: over the past ten years, frost has come as early as September 3 and as late as October 20. The hoophouse gives some protection but will prolong the season for the plants inside only by one to two weeks in an average year.

THE STUDENT-MANAGED FARM

The fact that the BBFG was established as a student-run enterprise under the auspices of both the SAG Program and the UM Experimental Station has molded the nature of the guild from the beginning, creating opportunities for student learning that go beyond those available on a college-managed farm, as well as spawning tensions that will probably never be resolved. Students, at times of stress, rail against the university machine that has failed to equip them with all the knowledge, experience, and tools needed to complete the field season successfully. In times of abundant harvests, the same students preen with pride at what they see as their personal achievement in delivering nature's bounty to the hungry masses.

The BBFG was established as a student- rather than staff-managed farm largely for economic reasons. In 1993, when students first began to petition loudly for a student farm, there were fewer than twenty-five students in the SAG Program and only two faculty members specifically allocated to the program. Economic activity in Maine is largely driven by wood pulp and paper, so forestry-based programs tend to receive the lion's share of the budget in the College of Natural Resources, Forestry, and Agriculture. Agriculture in the state focuses primarily on potatoes, dairy, and blueberries, and, although there is a thriving organic vegetable sector, organic vegetables are not an important export commodity for Maine, so there was scant economic impetus for the university to establish a well-funded organic student farm. The fact that the university agreed to rent the students almost three acres of land at one of its most accessible experimental farms is a tribute to the persistence of the students involved.

The choice of the student-as-manager model may have been a matter of convenience and cost savings for the university, but, for the students involved, it has a dramatic impact on the nature of their experience on the farm. Students report feeling far more confident about their abilities and accomplishments as farmers after having spent a year as guild comanagers. Many of the students who choose to work with the food guild have previously worked on a vegetable or mixed farm as an apprentice or as summer help during high school. But, in those previous positions, they have typically been given relatively menial tasks, and they may have spent almost their entire season hand-weeding root crops or picking beans without once being exposed to the larger decisionmaking processes that dictated why, when, and how crops were planted in particular places or at particular times. While the student BBFG manager may still spend much of her summer weeding, her outlook on the task may be one that better understands the urgency and appreciates the outcome than that of the mere student-as-laborer. As one food guild member put it, "They're still weeds, but they're *my* weeds." Mary Plaisted, a 2009 guild student, felt that she

Figure 8.1. Britta Jinson and the Zen of weeding. (Courtesy Michael Mardosa.)

had learned "about ten times as much by being part of the process" than when she had simply been told what to do in a farm experience the previous summer. The 30 percent or so of SAG students who go on to establish their own farms regularly cite the BBFG experience as being formative in their decision to farm for a living. Likewise, former guild members who choose careers that don't involve farm labor also cite the experience as having affected their choice to eschew farming.

Some of what Mary Plaisted learned in 2009 was, by her admission, "what *not* to do," which is a key to the learning experience as well. The student managers on a college farm can make a certain number of mistakes and be buffered from the negative outcomes far better than they will ever be again. They receive an hourly wage regardless of their total yield of broccoli and tomatoes. The CSA members are made aware before they join that the students lack the experience to provide maximum return for their investment. The price of a share is intentionally kept lower than average for the region as it is understood that the operation of the farm is in novice hands.

Much of the education gleaned by the student manager has little to do with planting, weeding, and harvesting. The development of the organizational skills needed to successfully complete a field season on any farm can carry over into nearly every aspect of the students' lives. Students must first plan the kinds and quantities of crops that they will grow, calculate their seed and amendment needs, and develop budgets and work plans. Then they must keep records of expenditures, work hours, and daily activities. For organic certification requirements, they need to keep details and receipts for every material brought into the field. Perhaps most difficult, they need to create the teamwork required for all guild members to be working to their best ability for the good of the whole, and each year the students struggle with decisionmaking by decree versus by consensus. Team projects are often loathed in the classroom, but they are imperative in many work environments, and in the field they are essential to the success of the production season.

A less obvious potential benefit of the student-manager arrangement is the cultivation within the students of the necessary maturity to know when to ask for help. This is a subtle but important aspect of being thrust into a situation of responsibility and self-rule. As a land-grant institution, UM employs many knowledgeable faculty and staff that students can access for recommendations on pests, weeds, fertility management, cover crops, and diseases. In 2009, the late blight would have taken all the BBFG tomatoes and potatoes had the students not gotten timely advice about how to avoid catastrophe. The test for the students is to recognize the opportunities for expanded and timely knowledge that lie within the extension, research, and technical staff whom they see on a weekly basis.

The student manager model also has some obvious drawbacks. The fact that farm activities overlap significantly with the academic year begs for a permanent staff person to oversee early- and late-season activities on the farm, particularly spring tillage and preseason cultivation for weed management as well as later-season farm cleanup chores. Of greater import have been the lack of continuity from one field season to the next and the lack of long-term planning. The hiring of a long-term manager who could report to faculty members or experimental station staff would give the farm more validity, more stability, and more opportunities for fund-raising during the off-season. Additionally, the necessary coordinated functioning of a group of students with no clearly defined leader often leads to personality conflicts that can cripple the farm operation in times of stress. Finally, lack of experience and the excitement of being in control can lead to poor decisionmaking and crop production plans that become too complex and unrealistic.

The problem of early- and late-season farm chores is ameliorated at the food guild farm to some extent by the services of the Rogers farm manager and the research technician who works for several SAG faculty members. As such, the tasks of spring plowing and cultivation are often incorporated into the schedule of general farm management activities, and the guild fields can quickly be plowed, harrowed, and cultivated on days when the needed implements are already hooked up. Similarly, at the end of the season, staff members will cultivate fallow fields and sow cover crops. Other pre- and postseason tasks are typically handled, sometimes hastily, by the guild members and a host of student volunteers who enjoy the outdoor physical labor during the spring and fall.

The issues of farm planning and continuity are harder to solve. Each group of students that commits to the guild believes that it is starting with a fresh slate, and the students are often inclined to seize the opportunity to act with little reference to the past or the future. Attempts by various faculty and staff to have students spend time studying the previous years' triumphs and disasters have been largely futile. In 2003, three SAG students who had worked with the guild the previous year used their senior capstone project to develop a handbook and five-year rotation plan for the food guild fields, including details of crop areas, crop variety recommendations, and planting dates needed to provide sufficient produce for each full share of the CSA. In spite of the handbook being a valuable and informative document and its being entirely accessible in both electronic and hard-copy versions, however, no subsequent food guild group has done more than briefly glance at it.

After several years of poor field planning early in the millennium, faculty imposed a nonnegotiable two-year rotation that put half the guild acreage in cover-crop fallow each year. The students now know which fields are available to plant to annual crops and which are sacrosanct. This imposed rotation is now so ingrained in the blueprint of the farm that it is no longer viewed by students as interference. The issue of long-term planning and crop rotations, then, has progressed to a two-year time frame but has not gone further than that. In spite of annual enthusiasm about including perennial fruit and vegetable crops such as berries, asparagus, and rhubarb in the field design, it is unlikely that any group will spend the extra work and money needed to benefit the farm two or three years down the road. The ultimate act of defiance against previous planning resulted in 2003, when guild members abandoned the edict of hand digging Field F and violated it with a rototiller in the name of time management. The following year, students quietly abandoned Field F altogether and never mentioned it again, like a disturbed relative of whom they were mildly ashamed.

The anticipated emergence of the well-functioning team of student managers each year often fails to materialize, and conflict can reach a critical flashpoint on the farm. Personality dynamics would probably have significantly less impact if there were a long-term manager who took a clear lead in decisionmaking. In the past, the faculty adviser sometimes designated an individual who would be responsible for ensuring that protocols, field activities, and communication occurred as planned. This person was typically an upper-level student in the SAG Program who had worked with the guild the previous year or who had significant experience in vegetable farming elsewhere. This model worked relatively well in some years but was entirely disastrous in others. In one season, a particularly domineering individual who was designated as liaison felt the responsibility so heavily that she pushed the guild more toward a queen versus worker bee model than anything remotely resembling a collective. Morale was quite low that season, and two of the "worker bees" subsequently dropped out of the SAG Program (although, ironically, the harvest was the best the farm has ever seen and share members were thrilled).

A different but potentially just as disabling set of problems arises when the entire team of students managing the guild in a given year has little or no farming experience and no clear leader emerges. The crew may spend an inordinate amount of time thinking, planning, and fine-tuning their season and miss the key opportunities to plant and weed. Such groups are far more prone to miscommunication about who is to perform which task at which time, and the farm operations can fall into chaos.

Guild enthusiasm, particularly in the planning stage, seems to be positively correlated with lack of experience. Innovation often takes precedence over tradition and practicality. Students are dazzled by the seed catalogs' promises of unconventionally colored and oddly shaped vegetables and the perceived political correctness of growing African heirloom root crops that have no ecological niche on any Maine farm. The farm planting scheme may begin to take shape in shamanistic swirls and pentangles that will never mesh with the linear cut of standard cultivating equipment. Seed order costs will quickly annihilate the guild's budget appropriations as the list of tiny, expensive heirloom variety packets containing twenty-five seeds each expands onto multiple pages.

In spite of the plethora of varieties ordered, the student managers tend to snub classic family fare, such as cucumbers or head lettuce, and focus more on what they perceive as a healthful, international, and flavorful vegetable selection. Piquant greens overwhelm the field, or they may plant up to a quarter acre of kale, in every color and leaf shape ever bred, much to the dismay of many families with fussy children. One year, share pickups became so consistently dominated by kale that the guild received a note, constructed from letters cut from the newspaper, that read, "NO MORE KALE OR ELSE!!" The note had been put together by the ten-year-old son of a share family. Attempts to have the students reduce their kale planting in subsequent years led to the appearance of "Save the Kales" T-shirts worn by guild members and their friends. The faculty adviser now requires that students submit the seed order for scrutiny and possible readjustment before funds are committed.

The student manager model for the BBFG operates most smoothly when advice and oversight are both offered and imposed early on in the yearly planning process. Afterward, advisers ideally step back and watch for signs of distress, stepping back in only when the guild is in danger of veering seriously off-course. For the adviser, knowing when this point occurs takes a certain amount of subtlety and a smidgeon of psychic ability, but, when the model works, the students maximize their learning experience while minimizing their risk of failure.

THE BBFG AND THE SAG PROGRAM

The BBFG has become such an integral part of the undergraduate SAG Program at UM that it is unlikely that the program could exist without it. It has been the single most effective recruiting tool for the program since 1996, and many potential new students show more interest in visiting the farm, even in the winter, when fields are captive under four feet of snow, than in hearing details about the courses offered in the academic program.

The connection between the BBFG and the SAG Program is more like a network of woolen threads than a thick rope. As mentioned previously, the guild cannot operate unless at least one member is a SAG major, and preferably most or all employed members are majors. To complete their degree requirements, all SAG majors must register for some form of practical training in a course called "Field Experience," which, while it does not literally specify field work, does require some hands-on effort and is most commonly fulfilled by student farm internships. About half of SAG majors choose the BBFG to meet their "Field Experience" requirement. To receive credit, they must perform a minimum of 240 hours of nonacademic labor, keep a daily journal, write a final three- to four-page summary of their experience, and give a short presentation to first-year students. Students may register for as little as one credit for "Field Experience" (thereby minimizing tuition costs) or as many as three credits for the same amount of work (thereby maximizing the credit toward their degree satisfied by their "Field Experience" work).

Students have periodically lobbied to obtain more credit for the BBFG experience while at the same time gaining greater access to the advice they need through a more formal classroom course to be taken before they begin working with the guild. This idea is impractical from an academic standpoint: the university has a strong bias against classes that have fewer than ten enrolled students unless they are critical to the degree program. On the other hand, there are several other relevant courses that guild students are likely to have taken before starting their field season. These include an overview course entitled "Principles and Practices of Sustainable Agriculture" and several more applied courses such as "Cropping Systems," "Weed Identification," "Applied Entomology," and "Organic Vegetable and Fruit Production" (first offered in 2008). While hardly the yeoman's complete education, these courses provide a rudimentary framework as well as many of the resources students will need to get started in the field. Faculty responsible for some of these courses have amended their curricula to include more topics that are of practical use for those starting to farm. For example, "Cropping Systems" now includes a series of lectures and a student team activity on optimizing crop variety selection when buying seed on a limited budget.

Most of the faculty and staff advisers who work with the students before and during the field season are associated with the SAG Program in some way. These advisers have mixed feelings about their role in ensuring student success in the field. UM faculty work on nine-month contracts but often are overtaxed with agricultural field research during the same months that the students need the most help. Tensions arise when students fail to understand that faculty are not on paid vacation from May through September and likely have multiple responsibilities to fulfill for grants, research, and the advancement of their own careers. One guild member recently complained that he felt like the SAG faculty had "thrown us to the woodchucks" once classes were out. Faculty can feel taken advantage of and unappreciated for the volunteer time they spend with the guild outside the academic year. These tensions can sometimes be ameliorated by open and regular communication between advisers and students before crises occur.

Figure 8.2. Mary Plaisted, Nick Costanzi, and Tracey LeFleur measure beds for the spring 2009 planting. (Courtesy Marianne Sarrantonio.)

THE BBFG AND THE UNIVERSITY

University administrators and the public relations office love to highlight the rural appeal of the student farm as a heartwarming example of the university's commitment to the land-grant mission and its recently professed goal of campuswide sustainability—as they did in a sumptuous photo essay in *UMaine Today* in 2008—but turn parsimonious when asked to contribute resources to the venture.[1] In fact, the university charges a land-use fee of as much as $1,500 to offset the labor, water, and electricity that the guild utilizes as part of the UM Rogers Experimental Farm. As such, the relationship between the BBFG and the university administration has never been particularly warm. But, despite students' near-universal and perhaps inevitable distrust of administrators, guild students have, in fact, been the beneficiaries of much largess via the university. Over the past fifteen years, the guild has accumulated a permanent storage shed/workspace of about 150 square feet, including a large walk-in cooler; an outdoor wash station under a canopy; a large array of hand tools, including every weed-destroying implement known to humanity; several walk-behind seeders; several hundred feet of drip-irrigation tubing; backpack sprayers dedicated for organic use; and the large hoophouse previously mentioned. (The hoophouse was destroyed in a windstorm in the spring of 2009, but two smaller replacements have been found that will cost the guild only $700 in materials to assemble.) Most of the larger capital items were purchased using small grants and department funds mediated by faculty in the SAG Program. Some, such as the new hoophouses, are recycled castoffs from other programs on campus. In addition, the BBFG fields regularly receive applications of organic dairy manure from one of the other university farms at no cost.

The BBFG also reaps the bounty of some of the other research and production fields at the Rogers farm: in most years, it receives enough potatoes to distribute more than twenty pounds per share as well as other excess vegetable and fruit produce from other fields. Some of this additional produce may not have been grown under organic certification, but share members are informed of the inputs the food may have received, and few turn it down. As mentioned already, advice and technical help is regularly donated by UM employees. While it may seem to the students that they are operating entirely on their own, they are, in fact, relatively well subsidized by the university in terms of labor and other resources. Relationships with the university administrators have often improved noticeably following the delivery of gift baskets filled with fresh organic vegetables. Some of these administrators have subsequently gone on to purchase shares in the BBFG and become ardent supporters.

THE BBFG AND THE COMMUNITY

The BBFG, as might be expected, also has extensive interactions with its share members. These members are primarily graduate students or employees of the university but also include community members who travel as much as twenty miles each week to pick up their shares of produce. The relationship between the student guild members and their clients has almost always been positive. Nearly 75 percent of the share members in any year have participated in previous years, and some have been loyal members for more than ten seasons.

Students generally put substantial effort into making their clients happy. They host a potluck dinner or pancake breakfast to start the sea-

Figure 8.3. Michael Bowman (*left*) chats with the Black Bear Food Guild graduate, now a successful organic farmer, Mark Guzzi at the Orono Farmers Market. (Courtesy Marianne Sarrantonio.)

son, and the twice-weekly pickup sessions can have a relaxed and congenial atmosphere. The guild publishes a periodic newsletter with recipes, humorous farm stories, and news of any upcoming changes to the weekly schedule. In 2009, the newsletter repeatedly informed share members of the impending late blight disaster that was likely to reduce or eliminate tomatoes from the weekly pickups to head off any criticism for poor management.

There are occasionally disgruntled share members who seek to receive compensation for what they feel were unsatisfactory returns on their investment. They may even attempt to damage the guild by taking their complaints directly to the university administration. In 2008 and 2009, spring and early summer rains were heavy and unrelenting, and crops were planted unusually late, through no fault of the students. Nevertheless, a handful of share members complained bitterly when pickups were scant for several weeks. In such cases, problems are generally best taken care of by intervention on the part of the faculty adviser or farm manager, who can lend some authority to the explanation of the well-established effects of weather on crop yields.

The original group of students who formed the BBFG were also key players in the establishment of the Orono Farmers Market, which convenes on Tuesdays and Saturdays on the UM campus. The BBFG brought excess produce to the farmers market weekly from 1995 until 2005, but the practice dwindled and eventually stopped. The BBFG is no longer a presence at the market owing partially to the additional stress participation put on student time and partially to community input. Share members sometimes complained that the vegetables the students brought to the market belonged to *them*—after all, hadn't they paid for a share of the harvest? Other farmers at the market were also uncomfortable with the competition from the BBFG, whom they perceived as having an unfair advantage owing to university subsidies. The combination of these pressures led the guild to shut down what was once a positive interaction with a wider set of community members who preferred to buy their produce through more traditional methods.

Conclusion

In spite of the many pitfalls of a student-managed farm, the BBFG has operated for fifteen years with many positive and few serious negative outcomes. Part of the reason it functions as well as it does lies in the fact that the premise that students are entirely in charge of the guild farm management is a myth. There are, in fact, many hands hovering around the guild to catch the students when they stumble and many eyes looking over their activities to ensure that university and farm policies are not breached. The tensions created by a student-managed farm overseen and aided by the labor of university employees uncompensated for their time will likely continue as long as the guild exists. Fortunately, the experience has been so overwhelmingly positive for the students who participate, as well as for the SAG Program, that the BBFG will undoubtedly continue in its current form for the foreseeable future.

STUDENT REFLECTIONS

The Adventures of the BBFG, 2009

Mary Plaisted

Expectations are funny things. When one thinks of what is involved in the production of vegetables and the managing of a CSA, the word *chaos* doesn't seem to become apparent until you are knee deep in mud in June. I knew I was going to learn what varieties of vegetables there are, when they are planted, and the other details of farming. I did not expect to learn the importance of adapting to the environment, through rain, wind, soil, and late blight.

The beginning of the year got off to an encouraging start. Snow was still on the ground in February, but we began contacting people who were involved last year in the BBFG to see if they'd like to continue for another year. E-mails were sent out with a comment box for suggestions, and it was unanimous for less kale. However, having Tracy on the team, we had to disregard these requests and plant three different varieties of kale.

The paperwork was not the most thrilling part of the BBFG experience, but it was necessary to be paid, so I didn't mind. It pretty much consisted of making receipts for the checks, mailing the receipts back to the share members, and finding out whom to give the checks to.

One of the frustrating things about this year was that we didn't have access to the account of our farm. It seemed like we had to go through a lot of people to find out how much money we had. It was definitely manageable, however, just less than convenient.

Once the paperwork was squared away, we began the process of picking out seeds, which I had absolutely no clue about. Thankfully, Nick and Tracy had a lot of experience with this, and we all got together and picked varieties out of the Johnny's catalog.

The week following spring break we started planting alliums (onions and leeks). We slowly put more and more in the greenhouse. Soon the better parts of two benches were full of young seedlings. Broccoli, basil, tomatoes, kale, and squash were all watered once or twice a day to make sure they grew big and strong.

Once summer began, it got off to a rocky (or, I should say, windy) start as the hoophouse blew over in a huge gust of wind. It landed about one hundred feet away from where it once stood. The metal supports were twisted and bent and, the plastic was barely usable. Morale still didn't seem to be dampened (just wait until June!) as we began the process of cleaning up. It took about a day and a half to get the wreckage cleared. If anything, this event brought the three of us closer as a group. Having an unexpected thing like this happen, we all came together as a team, which gave me high hopes for the rest of the summer.

Another challenge we met was that, in June, the rainy season never made way for summer. The fields were complete muck! This made it extremely difficult to direct seed anything because the seed would become rotten.

The third challenge that I wasn't expecting was the abundance of late blight in our tomatoes. It was heart-wrenching pulling up the mature plants that held this evil. Our yield was significantly lessened, which was unfortunate because tomatoes are usually plentiful in Maine.

Other than the obstacles, everything went smoothly all summer. It was interesting acting as my own boss for the summer. I had never had that opportunity, and the responsibility was an excellent learning experience. The goal from the beginning was to grow vegetables. The goal was met and, in my mind, exceeded with the ability to talk to the share members and build a better community. The whole summer has been the best one of my life, and I look forward to learning more about sustainable agriculture to continue to enjoy the outdoors as my occupation.

Mary Plaisted worked with Black Bear Food Guild in the 2009 and 2010 seasons and is now a junior in the Sustainable Agriculture Program at the University of Maine. She is a Maine native and became interested in the SAG Program after spending a year working on organic farms in Europe.

NOTE

1. Margaret Nagle, "Good Returns," *UMaine Today*, May/June 2008, 14–19.

9

Central Carolina Community College (1995)

Growing New Farmers

ROBIN KOHANOWICH

Central Carolina Community College (CCCC) is a three-county college with its main campus in Lee County, North Carolina. The Sustainable Agriculture Program—which in the fall of 2009 enrolled sixty-four full- and part-time students—is located on the Chatham County campus in Pittsboro, the county seat. Pittsboro is just fifteen miles south of Chapel Hill, home of the University of North Carolina, and twenty-five miles west of Raleigh, the main campus of North Carolina State University (NCSU). Duke University, in Durham, is also just thirty miles away.

Chatham County is one of the fastest-growing counties in the state. Nevertheless, residents of Pittsboro—with a population of fewer than three thousand—embrace small-town values of respect for one another and a strong sense of community. Pittsboro is home to a diverse group of artists and farmers, merchants and students, as well as to the North Carolina Zen Center. It supports software developers, biofuel research and production, antique shops, and art galleries. When sustainable agriculture students arrive in Pittsboro from other parts of the state and the country, they find a welcoming community that embraces sustainability.[1] The residents of Pittsboro support a local food co-op, the Chatham Marketplace, which is uncommon for a town of this size. The co-op has provided an opportunity for teaching about agricultural marketing and a place of employment for sustainable agriculture students.

As a community college, CCCC has no residential facilities. Students arriving from out of town and out of state find housing in local rentals and cohousing opportunities and sometimes choose to live closer to the larger population centers of Chapel Hill and Carrboro. Minimal public transportation is available in rural Chatham County, so students are encouraged to find carpool buddies early on in the semester. It is uncommon in this area for students to find housing on farms, although there are a few exceptions. One of these notable exceptions is the Celebrity Dairy, a goat dairy that makes award-winning chevre and has housed and employed a number of sustainable agriculture students.

CCCC is a tax-supported, public, nonprofit school under the control of a local board of trustees. Chartered in 1958 by the North Carolina State Board of Education, it became a part of the North Carolina Department of Community Colleges in 1963. The first curriculum classes were held on September 17, 1962. The Chatham County campus was built in 1992. The original two classroom and administrative buildings have been joined by two new buildings, both built to Leadership in Energy and Environmental Design (LEED) standards. A 16,500-square-foot sustainable technologies classroom and lab building, opened in August 2010, provides ample housing for the sustainability programs as well as space for arts instruction. A 24,000-square-foot joint CCCC–Chatham Community Library has also been constructed at the campus to serve both the college and the community.

In 1996, five acres of land on the Chatham County campus were allocated to the Sustainable Agriculture Program. For the past ten years, only two of these acres have been protected by a deer fence and, thus, have been available for growing. The college is in the process of expanding the production area of the farm to encompass two more of the five total acres. It is expected that, by the end of 2011, the farm will include at least one additional acre for annual production as well as perennial fruit crop production (Southern heirloom apples, pears, grapes, and various berries) and a site for a farm-scale compost/vermicomposting facility. Also on campus, a one-acre biofuel crop trial plot was initiated in the fall of 2009.

The land that CCCC purchased for the Chatham campus was originally a dairy farm, so much of the campus was formerly pastureland. The Sustainable Agriculture Program farm site, blessed with Georgeville series soils (deep, well-drained, moderately permeable soils formed in material weathered from the Carolina Slate Belt), has been organically managed since 1996. Year-round vegetable production takes place within a rotation of seasonally appropriate cover crops. The farm is divided into eight blocks, each of which is divided into eight hundred-foot beds, for a total of sixty-four beds (see fig. 9.1). At any given point in time, about a quarter to a half of that space is in cover crops. In addition, fourteen Java chickens (a heritage breeding project in conjunction with the American Livestock Breeds Conservancy) rotate through the farm as part of the overall eight-year rotation scheme. The student farm also has a pack shed, a wash and prep area for postharvest handling, a passive solar propagation greenhouse, and a hoophouse that has a three-year rotation in its own section of the cultivated area of the farm. Three beehives, managed by the Chatham Beekeepers, are also on-site. All the structures on the farm were built by students in associated classes (such as "Greenhouse Design," "Farm Structures," and "Basic Farm Maintenance").

FROM IDEA TO REALITY

The Sustainable Farming Program at CCCC grew out of a desire to address the needs of the farming community in Chatham County and the surrounding Piedmont region of North Carolina. Initiated by local growers in 1996, the program quickly formed into a one-of-a-kind collaboration of farmers, community members, CCCC, the North Carolina Cooperative Extension Service, the Carolina Farm Stewardship Association, the American Livestock Breeds Conservancy, REAL (Rural Entrepreneurship Action Learning) Enterprises, North Carolina A&T University (NCA&T), and NCSU. This group of state research and educational agencies, local nonprofits, and other individuals shared a desire to craft a new farmer-training program as a way of meeting the growing demand for locally grown food.

Early on, the program planners (visionaries!) knew that an on-campus farm would be needed to teach new farmers in the way they had envisioned. This group recognized that the probable student would most likely not have come from a farming background and, therefore, would lack familiarity with many basic aspects of farming.[2] Elementary practical farming skills, not just those directly related to production, would need to be taught. So the five acres that the CCCC student farm now occupies is part of the campus designated as the Land Lab, that is, a place where students can learn and practice skills in the field, and was initiated right at the beginning of this idea about starting a sustainable farming program. As Chuck Talbott, one of the program's early planners and instructors, remembered that period: "I can still see everyone sitting around the conference table at CCCC discussing the new small-scale farming program, knowing in the back of our minds the formidable task ahead: competing with cheap food and agribusiness, the only game in town. Is there really any consumer interest in small farms? Can small-scale farms survive? Are we taking our students down a dead end? I am glad we persevered. The seed has germinated and is growing."

One of the unique aspects about the origin of the student farm is the collaboration between the Chatham County Cooperative Extension Service and CCCC. These two entities saw the value of this local public farm as a way to satisfy the education-delivery needs of both organizations. Reading through the minutes of an April 1996 meeting to discuss the development of a small-farm curriculum at CCCC, one finds that the primary motivation for collaboration was the need for more extension outreach to small farmers as well as small-scale demonstration plots. In exchange for providing the land, CCCC would gain the benefit of both.

In 1997, CCCC began offering the initial credential, a continuing-education certificate of farm stewardship, within the area of sustainability. The original flyer advertising the certificate invited prospective new farmers to "become a certified farm steward" through the Sustainable Farming Program at CCCC. Students completed core course work, a production concentration, and an internship on a local cooperating farm. Course work was built around the idea of providing hands-on, practical training within a guiding framework of sustainability. The original group defined *sustainability* as economic profitability combined with environmentally sound farming practices. Today, the program is guided by the "triple bottom line" principles of sustainability, embracing economics, ecology, and social responsibility.

The original group of program planners included farmers, extension agents, consumers, and students who had begun taking the farming classes at CCCC. Their pioneering work and dedication (monthly meetings over the course of a couple of years) laid the groundwork for the current curriculum and envisioned the basic organization that the student farm has since evolved into. The beauty and challenge of a student farm is the constant stream of new people and ideas that flow through as different students make their journey toward their individual small-farm dreams. The key to stability and sustainability for us has been to have a farm manager who is not currently a student who can both manage the day-to-day farm operations and keep an eye on the overall picture of the health of the farm.

In the early days of the farm and the program, funds came from a variety of sources. Fund-raising efforts led by students included a benefit concert at a local nightclub and burrito sales during a regional farm tour. Program benefactors could make tax-deductible donations through CCCC's foundation, which has been key to the economic sustainability of the student farm. Not only can donors make charitable donations for endowments and scholarships, but some unrestricted funds are also made available, which has allowed the farm to be less tied to the restrictions of a typical curriculum program (which is important when running a farm—more about this later).

Community colleges are in general much more flexible and able to respond more quickly to shifting educational needs than universities. The mission of the community college in North Carolina is to open the door to high-quality educational opportunities, including workforce training, for the broadest possible population. People in Chatham County could see that small-scale sustainable agriculture was an emerging entrepreneurial opportunity. From proposing to inaugurating a new program at CCCC can take a year or less. Because universities have a much broader service area, among other reasons, it takes longer for them to develop new programs. This is evident if one looks at the past decade and the time that it has taken for universities to have degree programs in sustainable agriculture or agroecology or whatever they choose to title this genre of programs.

The transition from the collaborative creation of a demonstration plot site and hands-on facility for part-time students in the certified farm steward program to a year-round organic production student farm with a full-time manager, a student manager for the CSA (community-supported agriculture) program, and a thriving CSA took place over the course of several years. The key events that helped this transition happen included a $40,000 grant from the North Carolina Rural Center, which made it possible to increase the program coordinator position to full-time, create some student scholarships, and improve the farm's infrastructure, including the digging of a well dedicated to farm use. Prior to the installation of the well in 2000, the farm was irrigated by stretching a hose from the classroom building, across a parking lot, and into the field. Not very sustainable (or very convenient).

In the late summer of 2001, another infrastructure improvement maximized our potential for productivity more than any other: our eight-foot, high-tensile electrified deer fence was installed. The fence enclosed approximately two acres of land, of which a little over one acre is cultivated.

The final key event, actually a process, was to establish the curriculum program. Once the college has a credentialed program in place, funding is more stable. So, as the Sustainable Farming Program transitioned to become the A.A.S. (associate in applied science) degree in sustainable agriculture (beginning in the fall semester of 2002), some economic stability important for running the program was achieved. Prior to this transition, the farm tried to be self-supporting, through vegetable sales and other fund-raising events, as mentioned above. Donations of products, goods, and services were also essential to getting the farm up and running, as was the hugely significant amount of time donated by the people invested in making this a successful venture.

GETTING TO WORK

The nature of a student farm (especially on a community college campus) is such that the farmer is always training new farmers. An A.A.S. degree student is typically on campus for two to two and a half years. Many students come to earn the certificate, which is an even shorter time commitment. Therefore, the farmer spends much of his or her time in training/teaching, and the productivity of the farm (as an income generator) must be secondary to student learning.

CCCC has provided support for a part-time farm manager for most of the time that a farm has been on-site. That arrangement has varied from a ten-hour-per-week commitment paid through the office of continuing education, to a thirty-hour-per-week part-time permanent position, to our current full-time position with benefits. Justification for funding this position comes from the number of student hours generated by the Sustainable Agriculture Program and recognition of the important role a fully operational farm plays in the quality of education available to our students.

Full funding for a farm manager has always been desired but has proved difficult to achieve. In addition to using some income from produce sales, some of the strategies used to bolster the farm manager's ten-hour-per-week pay included additional teaching, with the farm manager offering workshops and teaching classes through CCCC's (noncredit) continuing-education offerings.

From 1997 to 2002, all labor, whether from students or the farm manager or the extension agent with his or her research-and-development plots, was very minimal (yet extremely significant—people worked extremely hard, but it was no one's full-time job). Continuing-education classes met once a week for a maximum of three to four hours per class. During that time, there were no full-time students who would be on campus anyway filling their nonclass hours by working on the farm. The key contributor to farm productivity was a continuing-education course in organic crop production, taught almost continually in some form or another since the program began. Students in the class and the instructor planted crops primarily in the spring and fall.

In spite of these challenges, the farm continued to develop during the 1997–2002 time frame. The greenhouse construction class built a twenty-by forty-foot hoophouse. The farm construction class built a shed. This farm was built on a shoestring, with every new building assembled as part of a class (whether a continuing-education class or one that is part of the formal curriculum), which means that you have a labor crew for four hours per class, one day a week, for approximately fourteen weeks (weather permitting). The first major purchase (outside a well) was our diesel tractor, which cost $15,000 in 2007. Prior to that, our tractor was a 1955 Massey that had been donated to the farm.

Various contributions were also made through the work of cooperative extension research plots and NCSU graduate student research. Each course or series of courses contributed in some way to the farm's infrastructure and productivity. An internship course allowed a local farmer/instructor to provide students with intensive, season-long study and experience on a working farm. Students from one of these internships created a permaculture garden on the farm site and planted the first perennial crops: two apple trees.

The first crop of A.A.S. degree and certificate students was welcomed into the Sustainable Agriculture Program in the fall of 2002. Eleven students ranging in age from eighteen to over fifty-five years enrolled in classes; the gender breakdown was 30 percent male and 70 percent female. Of the eight women, three had a degree of some kind already: one was a veterinarian, one a massage therapist, and one a Peace Corps returnee. The remaining five were all under thirty; two of these had access to family land. Four students arrived from out of state, with one having originally inquired about the program from Madagascar while still in the Peace Corps.

Our 2002 recruiting ad succinctly described the fledgling A.A.S. program: "In keeping with their strong commitment to sustainable agriculture in North Carolina, Central Carolina Community College in Pittsboro announces a new choice in sustainable agriculture education. Beginning in August 2002, CCCC will offer an Associate of Applied Science degree

Figure 9.1. The Land Lab at Central Carolina Community College: entrance gate and then a perennial flowerbed, four rows of potatoes, four rows of onions and garlic, and then trellising for tomatoes, with the chicken coop and hoophouse in the background. (Courtesy Mitch McCoy.)

in Sustainable Agriculture. This two-year degree will provide the skills for a variety of careers, including: farm manager for produce or livestock operations, agriculture research technician, and natural resources education. Unique course offerings will include Organic Crop Production, and Sustainable Livestock Management, as well as Marketing Strategies and Agricultural Mechanics." It is important to note that these course offerings were inspired directly by the original certified farm steward continuing-education program to address the whole range of education needs a new farmer would have.

I myself am the product of a traditional four-year university program in horticulture, and, after being here at CCCC for several years, this thought occurred to me: You can study horticulture for four years at a university and never get your hands dirty, whereas our students get dirty every day. Our motto has been "real farming, right now."

MARKETING MODELS

The student farm needs a way to market produce because it is truly a model of a small-scale market farm for the North Carolina Piedmont. Therefore, we produce saleable quantities of quality produce year-round. Students have access to some of this food, and some goes to the food bank, but, primarily, the produce is sold through the CSA.

The student farm CSA began in the summer of 2002, just before the first A.A.S. degree students arrived on the scene. The Sustainable Agriculture Program advisory group selected a restricted membership (faculty, staff, and students) CSA as our way of marketing produce so that the program would avoid direct competition with the local farms that had provided so much support for the development of the program. Researching this topic by looking at other student farms, it seems that student-grown produce is sold in many different ways and under many different circumstances. Feedback from local farmers varies in its concern about competition from student farmers, but, because of the potential for negative feelings, we tried hard to maintain very strict guidelines about whom we sell to.

In addition to the CSA, two student-run farmers market days are held each year on the CCCC campus. In the spring, organic crop production and farm business management students run a capstone project together that includes produce sales both at a farm stand and to a local wholesaler, Eastern Carolina Organics. In the fall, agricultural marketing students set up a farm stand on campus as a hands-on exercise in displaying, merchandising, and educating consumers about locally grown produce. Proceeds from all student-directed sales are contributed to a fund designated as seed money to help Sustainable Agriculture Program graduates start their own farming ventures.

The CSA marketing strategy has been successful and has endured through three farm managers. In addition to providing a very real marketing experience for the students (every aspect has student involvement, from planting to packing), the structure is such that the CSA manager rises from the ranks of student farmworkers. One of the challenges we have encountered is having the production aspect of the CSA run the farm—when, in fact, our mantra has to be education first, productivity second. This challenge had existed when the money generated from the CSA was needed to pay the farm manager and the students; now that that need has been removed from the equation, it is much easier to keep the focus on using the CSA for education, not the other way around.

The CSA also serves an invaluable outreach function for the farm within the campus community. Our CSA members are some of our strongest supporters. These testimonials from the 2009 season are typical:

The Sustainable Ag program is literally in my backyard. Every Friday I take in the sights and smells of the lush greenery, collect my box of goodies, and proceed directly to my kitchen. It is the purest form of food I have ingested since the days of my youth, growing up on a farm. It feels good knowing that I am feeding myself and my son food that was produced so close to home, without the hassle of maintaining my own garden.

My CSA ranks as one of the best things that *ever* happened to me in my life. I know I am putting safe, nutritious vegetables into my body. I am eating seasonal vegetables that are picked hours before I eat them. It thrills me to open the box each week to see the variety of produce. Fall is my favorite time since I love greens! My CSA offers our community the opportunity to learn about sustainable farming, which impacts many aspects of our environment. As the slogan says, "Eat Local." I have many blessings, and my CSA is one of them!

Getting a big box of food every week from a farm close to home is easier than shopping for it. My husband and I signed up for our share of CSA with this in mind. Inspired by the hundred-mile diet, we also loved the idea of eating food grown locally by people we knew. We have since discovered the wonderful world of culinary exploration that comes in every CSA box. We used to shop with a menu in mind, and now we open the box, and inspiration for a myriad of menus jumps out!

LABOR AND LEARNING

Work on the student farm provides the opportunity to apply the principles and skills being learned in the classroom to a production setting. Weather, pests, micronutrient deficiencies, and infrastructure all play a role in a farm's production capacity; these realities and how they interact are much more evident and memorable to students who integrate themselves into the farm on a regular basis. Students who work at the student farm are paid $8 per hour and can take home vegetables left over after the CSA is packed for the week. Students with just a few hours to spare each week may trade labor for a share rather than get paid an hourly wage. Recruiting workers for the student farm happens at the start of every semester. Recruiting for spring semester is a little more leisurely as true production doesn't crank up until sometime in February, but, in August, the farm is generally ready for some fresh recruits to assist with the ongoing CSA, summer crops, and the start of all the fall production.

The most difficult time for staffing the farm has traditionally been the period between late April and late May, from the last two weeks of the semester through the start of the summer intersession. Students fade out as the end-of-semester pressure builds, and then everyone needs a break or vacation, and so the farm gets a little lonely. Here in the North Carolina Piedmont, that period of time is critical in terms of farmwork. Spring crops are in full swing, strawberries need picking, tomato plants are going in, and other warm-season transplants need tending. The farm manager carries the farm through times like this, and, when we are lucky, a few students just want to stick around and work too.

Another staffing challenge that comes with a school-related enterprise is that classes come first: students work around their classroom schedules, and, at crunch time, when something has to give, it's often the farm shift that takes the hit. Classes do not meet Friday through Sunday, so usually only students who live nearby are available for work on those days. No class on Friday has been a scheduling tradition in the Sustainable Agriculture Program so that students who work on other area farms have that full Friday to help prep for weekend market activities.

A 160-hour on-farm work experience (COE111) is a requirement for completing the A.A.S. degree in sustainable agriculture. The student must work with a more experienced farmer and have some specific learning objectives outlined that can be met by working at the farm that he or she chooses. Sometimes students will do their work experience with the farm manager at the student farm, which is one way that we can fill that May/June labor gap. More often, a student finds a local farm to work with to complete COE111.

The importance of other sustainable, organic farms in the surrounding area and the role those farms play in the success story of the Sustainable Agriculture Program at CCCC and the life of the student farm cannot be overstated. They have played a critical role in presenting the reality of sustainable agriculture in our region. Student surveys always point to the value of real farmers and farm visits as highlights of the education offered here.

The success of the early continuing-education classes relied on full-time farmers to act as classroom instructors for courses meeting once a week for eight to ten weeks. Continuing-education instructors are paid an hourly rate calculated on class-time hours only; a class meeting for a total of thirty hours paid $450 in 1998. The continuing-education classes still have full-time farmers as instructors, although there are fewer courses offered in this way. The courses offered though the A.A.S. degree program still rely on farmer input, but in a way that is ideally more "sustainable" for the farmer in that he or she is not committed to leaving the farm for three to four hours every week for the duration of the eight- to ten-week course. Honoraria are provided to farmers who participate as guest speakers or as tour guides on their own farms.

Farmers are invited to be guest speakers to share with the students their particular area of expertise, whether it be producing cut flowers, fingerling potatoes, or organic peppers or marketing produce. Students find the openness and willingness of these farmers in sharing their trade to be a memorable benefit. Social responsibility is one of the components of the triple bottom line; these farmers demonstrate that principle, and, in turn, we expect our successful graduates to continue that pattern, giving back to their community.

To start naming all the farmers who have contributed to the development of the Sustainable Agriculture Program at CCCC and the creation of the student farm is to risk leaving someone out. So many have played an important role: whether through giving their advice, setting an example, contributing physical labor, and/or employing our students. Many of these farmers' names would be recognized around the country in sustainable, organic circles as they have been frequently tapped as conference speakers and resources for organic production in the Southeast. Truly, this program would not exist without them.

Classes are also welcomed on area farms. Field trips are the primary access that the program has to livestock production of species other than laying hens. In addition to privately owned farms, there are also university-run experimental stations, like the meat goat unit of NCSU, that students will visit as part of their education at CCCC. The geographic location of CCCC has facilitated cooperation with both NCSU and NCA&T researchers and professors and access to the working farms of both institutions.

Figure 9.2. Mary Beth Bardin, a student farmer 2008–2009. (Courtesy CCCC Marketing Department.)

Soil science, plant science, and animal science form the core of the basic sciences that are required for students enrolled in the A.A.S. degree. Successful completion of soil science is required by all credentialed programs for sustainable agriculture at CCCC. The student farm becomes the place to learn how to take soil samples, to see cover crops and green manures at work, and to learn how to operate a tensiometer and examine the structure of a productive clay loam soil. Organic crop production students learn how to drive the tractor, see firsthand what various cultivation and tillage implements can do, and learn when not to till or cultivate so as to avoid damaging the soil structure.

As far as class sizes are concerned, in courses where access to hands-on practice is a key instructional goal, the ideal class size is twelve to eighteen students. Two instructors work with a group of that size when they are on the farm. Typically, the students in crop production labs are split into two smaller groups, each with an instructor and a key set of skills to learn, and, after a designated time, the groups switch instructors to learn a different set of skills. A non-hands-on class, like "Introduction to Sustainable Agriculture," may have thirty students, still small compared to many university courses, but more typical of other courses in the community college setting.

On-farm research techniques are taught in plant science. Students learn the components of a research experiment and are encouraged to explore a topic of their own by conducting a small research project at the student farm. Likewise, biological pest management students are responsible for tracking the various pest management issues that occur during the semester at the student farm and explore currently recommended organic management practices for the pests that are present. The farm's flock of Java chickens provides some hands-on opportunity for the animal science and sustainable livestock management courses, but they are also good examples of pest management. The farm structures class has designed and built a variety of chicken coops and tractors, and having livestock integrated in the production scheme has helped us teach good agricultural practices in a real-life setting that is similar to that on many local farms.

LOOKING AHEAD

It seems like a simple thing, but one important strength of the CCCC student farm and Sustainable Agriculture Program has been the physical proximity between the lab and the student farm. The distance from the classroom to the farm can be covered in five minutes. Students leave the classroom, stop at their cars to put on their farm shoes, and dig in. Farm communication boards are located in the pack shed, where the farm manager has a white board system for posting need-to-know information. The boards are labeled *daily, weekly,* and *permanent.* Daily needs may include harvest tips, where to weed, or what kinds of goodies are available to feed the chickens. The farm manager is present most of the time classes are in session, which gives the students plenty of opportunities for working one-on-one with him or her.

All the farm managers have been sensitive to the need for students to be exposed to and practice a variety of tasks when they are working on the farm. This can sometimes be difficult as students' schedules may afford them only one day per week at the farm, and, if that happens to be harvest or pack-for-CSA time, the duties are pretty routine. Of course, it is also important for students to get a taste of that routine so that they know what to expect when working on a farm. One weeds until the task is done—the trick is to weed efficiently and to have a stimulating conversation with your coworker at the same time.

The current farm manager, Hillary Heckler, was recently asked, "What is your favorite crop to grow?" Her reply: "New farmers." The best index of the success of the CCCC Sustainable Agriculture Program is the number of successful new farmers emerging from its alumni pool. Some of these gain additional experience as CCCC student farm managers. Cheryl McNeill, our farm manager from 2006 to 2008, worked on the student farm while completing her course work in sustainable agriculture; Hillary was the student CSA manager during that same period. Others go on to start farms of their own. Shiloh Avery, a member of our first class of Sustainable Agriculture Program students (the Peace Corps returnee), is now a full-time farmer, she and her husband having bought a farm in North Carolina in 2008.[3] They are role models now and regularly give workshops and presentations at sustainable agriculture conferences. I heard them do an excellent session on marketing just this fall. What a reward as a teacher, to be able to attend your former student's conference session. That is probably common in the university world as grad students become Ph.D.s, but I'm not certain it is very common in the community college world. "I didn't come from a farming background," Avery explained responding to our survey. "I can say that I owe my entire farm to the college and the contacts I made there. I learned everything I know about sustainable farming from them."

The vision for the future of the CCCC Student Farm includes expansion of the farm production area with a new deer fence as well as additional new infrastructure, such as a student-built pack shed with walk-in cooler space. The farm has operated so far with a reach-in commercial cooler and two refrigerators, but the time has come for the step up to a walk-in cooler and the education associated with building and managing that premium space. Also in the works is a larger propagation greenhouse. The current passive solar structure comfortably allows about six students to work at a time. Larger class sizes and the need for more production have necessitated the requisition of a larger space.

The student farm is just one example of sustainability at work within CCCC's "Green Central" initiative. A solar hot water heater currently supplies water for handwashing, and plans are for hot water to be routed through the greenhouse benches to provide bottom heat for transplants.

A solar panel has been installed on the edge of the farm, part of the green building/renewable energy education taking place at CCCC. The tractor fuel used at the student farm is made from waste vegetable oil by CCCC students in the biofuels program. The waste vegetable oil comes from another innovative Green Central program, the Natural Chef, a culinary program with a focus on fresh, local, seasonal produce.

The Sustainable Agriculture Program at CCCC is making a contribution to the growing need and desire for people to have the skills to grow food locally and sustainably. As Richard Heinberg, the author of *The Party's Over, Peak Everything,* and *Blackout,* observes, "I think we will need lots more food producers over the years ahead. I have suggested the US will need 40–50 million new farmers over the course of the next two or three decades."[4] We just want to do our part at CCCC to help meet that goal.

STUDENT REFLECTIONS

IT'S THE DETAILS THAT COUNT

DAN SHIELDS

The most important benefit I gained from working on the student farm at CCCC is the knowledge of what crops to plant, how to plant them, and when to plant them in this part of North Carolina. This seems like a basic thing, but it has made a huge difference in my professional career. For example, arugula is one of our most profitable crops because we plant four rows per hundred-foot bed. We are able to harvest roughly fifty-five pounds per bed over a two-week period before we move on to the next succession with a minimal amount of labor. We charge $6.00 per pound retail and $4.25 per pound wholesale, so we're grossing on average $280 with very little labor and hardly any seed cost. Most folks I talk to at market plant two rows of arugula per hundred-foot bed. Their beds are more or less the same width as ours, so they're not able to maximize their bed space as efficiently as we do.

Another example of when to plant things that has greatly benefited us involves all our first fall successions of carrots, beets, arugula, turnips, and radishes. We always beat the competition to market with these crops because we are planting them the third week of July while others wait until mid- to late August. I remember how miserable it was the summer we planted carrots in late July at the Land Lab because it seemed strange to be planting a cool-weather crop in hundred-degree weather, but it has paid off for us many times over.

A final thing that I learned at the Land Lab is the concept of overwintering. We're able to have carrots, beets, spinach, kale, collards, etc. in mid-March because of this skill.

Dan Shields and his partner, Brittany Kordick, both attended the CCCC Sustainable Agriculture Program. They raise dairy goats, laying hens, meat rabbits, and a range of vegetables at Contrarian Farm in rural Pittsboro.

NOTES

1. Lyle Estill, *Small Is Possible: Life in a Local Economy* (Gabriola Island, BC: New Society, 2008). Estill is a Pittsboro resident.

2. See the new farmer typology, http://www.smallfarm.org/uploads/uploads/Files/GNF_PD_-What_does_the_term_new_farmer_mean.pdf.

3. Shiloh Avery and her husband, Jason Roehrig, are the owners of Tumbling Shoals Farm, a transitional organic farm near Miller's Creek, NC (see http://www.tumblingshoalsfarm.com).

4. "Exclusive to Transition Culture! An Interview with Richard Heinberg—Part Two . . . Powerdown and Transition Towns," *Transition Culture,* November 28, 2006, available at http://transitionculture.org. See also Richard Heinberg, *The Party's Over: Oil, War and the Fate of Industrial Societies* (Gabriola Island, BC: New Society, 2003), *Black: Coal, Climate and the Last Energy Crisis* (Gabriola Island, BC: New Society, 2009), and *Peak Everything: Waking Up to the Century of Declines* (Gabriola Island, BC: New Society, 2010).

10

Prescott College (1996)

Agroecology as the Cultivation of Soil and Mind

TIM CREWS

Prescott College is a small liberal arts college situated in the highlands of central Arizona, where ponderosa forests converge with chaparral scrub and desert grasslands. The college is known for its experiential pedagogies and for its dedication to the environment and social justice. Founded in 1966, Prescott has grown to serve a residential undergraduate student body of five hundred and an equal number of limited-residency students spread across bachelor's, master's and Ph.D. programs. In the residential undergraduate school, class sizes are small, with most capped at between twelve and fourteen students.

I was hired in 1995 to develop a curriculum in agroecology under the umbrella of the Environmental Studies Program. In the years since, faculty and students have started two farms and closed the gates on one, developed extensive campus gardens, initiated a cooperative CSA (community-supported agriculture) program, opened a college café dedicated to local foods, and spawned a food and agriculture curriculum that has found its way into most corners of the school's undergraduate and graduate programs. The college farm and gardens as well as those of local growers have been essential to this flowering of sustained interest in agriculture and food systems. Fitting a farm into a liberal arts college, both physically and pedagogically, has probably been easier at Prescott College than it might have been at many more traditional institutions. Yet acquiring land to farm and defining our curriculum as it relates to food and agriculture has entailed some difficult choices and trade-offs. Here I describe some of the journey.

A TALE OF TWO FARMS

The realization of a student farm at Prescott College was not the direct result of a student initiative per se so much as the combined outcome of faculty and college supporters recognizing a high degree of student interest in sustainable agriculture and a strong curricular fit within the Environmental Studies Program. In applying for the newly established position in agroecology and sustainable living, I was emphatic about one thing: if Prescott College wanted to extend experiential education into agroecology, it simply must acquire a farm. Moreover, I argued that the academic program that developed in agroecology around the newly acquired farm could take place only in the summer, to coincide with the height of the growing season. Part of the advantage of joining the faculty ranks of a small school like Prescott was that the college could—and did—decide to accommodate these somewhat challenging requests in a relatively short period of time. Moving much of my teaching obligation to the summer proved tricky because other important tasks, such as student advising, faculty meetings, and committee work, take place in the spring and fall. But the institution chose to be flexible and has struck a balance where I am able to fulfill most of my nonteaching obligations during the regular academic year while concentrating my teaching hours over the summer months.

The business of obtaining a farm was no less daunting. Prescott College was not in a position to purchase a piece of land with irrigation rights, so we were in need of a creative approach. Joel Hiller, the president of the college in 1995, rose to the challenge by putting together an agreement with the nearby farming town of Chino Valley, twenty miles to the north. Chino owned a large parcel of irrigable farmland and was interested in hosting a project that would highlight resource-conserving alternatives to the standard corn, alfalfa, and other hay crops of their struggling local farm economy. Thanks to President Hiller's efforts, the college and town signed a thirty-year lease on thirty acres with the agreement that the college would provide the infrastructure while the town provided the land at a nominal lease fee.

Excitement about the new farm spread rapidly throughout the college—mainly because we actually had a farm, not because of the land itself. The land was a treeless piece of former desert grassland that had become dominated by annual weeds after years of flood-irrigated row crop production. It was windy and dusty, and the Aridisol soil had negligible organic matter, turning to loose powder with cultivation. We named it Wolfberry Farm after the native perennial plant species *Lyssium pallidum*, a member of the tomato family. Pale wolfberry grows in the vicinity of most ancestral Puebloan ruins today and is thought by some ethnobotanists to have been planted by prehistoric peoples as a crop—a remarkable example of a well-adapted, enduring agriculture.

In 1996, the college received a matching grant challenge from a non-profit foundation in New Mexico to install infrastructure at Wolfberry. We also received a grant from the Greenville Foundation in Berkeley for a photovoltaic-powered water-pumping system. By the summer of 1997, Wolfberry Farm was able to host its first agroecology summer semester, with five acres of land served by a newly installed subsurface irrigation system, a garden area, a fruit tree orchard (yet to be planted), and an overall master plan researched and developed by Steve Ehrets for his senior project in ecological design.

Over the next decade, Wolfberry Farm served as the primary home for the Agroecology Program. Some farm improvements were undertaken by students enrolled in the summer semester itself: fencing the full thirty acres after pronghorn discovered our all-you-can-eat-salad-bar fields; constructing an open-air, three-walled straw bale classroom; and building an adobe chicken coop. In addition to projects completed by students enrolled in the summer semester, many of Wolfberry's major improvements emerged out of student-initiated independent studies or senior projects that were developed in consultation with me and other faculty members. For example, Dana Pauly researched and orchestrated the planting of a fruit tree orchard consisting of about eighty varieties of apples, apricots, plums, cherries, and almonds; Brad Elston and Tricia Biel-Gobel were inspired by the work of the landscape artist Andy Goldsworthy in their design and installation of a sunken, stacked sandstone meeting circle; and Matt Verson researched and planted hundreds of shrub and tree seedlings to form a twelve-hundred-foot shelter belt.

The most significant student-led initiative at Wolfberry Farm was the development of full architectural plans for a passive-solar, off-grid, straw bale caretaker's house by the ecological design student Julia Roll. Her plans were actualized into a building by a special topics in ecological design course taught by the local builder and artisan Don Routson. Overall, the model of student-initiated independent studies and senior projects moving new stages of farm development forward has been highly effective at Prescott. On occasion, I have inherited stalled, half-completed projects, and pushing them to fruition has been a challenge. At the end of the term, a simple, manageable initiative brought to completion is infinitely more appealing than a few odd parts of a grandiose vision.

But Wolfberry Farm was always a difficult place to grow. The wind and the exposure, the soil type, as well as gophers and birds, all seemed to conspire against all but the hardiest crops, and seedlings in particular were very difficult to protect and establish. Compared to cultivating the rich loamy soils of the University of California, Santa Cruz, Farm and Garden on the hills above Monterey Bay, where I apprenticed in 1981, Wolfberry Farm was boot camp. If the students could grow a tomato there, they could grow one anywhere. Many students were put off by the somewhat desolate landscape of the farm, while others seemed to thrive on its adversity.

In spite of all the human effort and financial investment in the property, the Wolfberry Farm chapter of Prescott College came to an end when the town of Chino converted a large portion of its water rights into a municipal status that prohibited irrigation for agriculture. Although it took a few years for the parties involved to realize it, this conversion included the water rights for Wolfberry Farm, and the college was accordingly instructed by the Arizona Department of Water Resources early in 2007 that irrigation, and, thus, all food production except wolfberry itself (which requires no irrigation), had to stop.

In the anxious months that followed, it became evident that a new farm was not going to be secured before summer, and, thus, it was unclear where the agroecology courses were going to take place. After much deliberation, we decided to expand on the work a handful of food-passionate students were doing by installing numerous small garden plots all over the downtown Prescott campus and use them in lieu of a farm for the agroecology summer semester. Forced on us by adversity, this decision turned out to have multiple benefits as the campus gardens were immediately embraced by the college community. The vegetables, flowers, and herbs were beautiful, and the plots were convenient for courses such as ecodesign, in which students researched rainwater catchment irrigation systems. Moreover, when students showed up for class at the beginning of fall semester, the plots immediately instilled interest in other food-related courses and activities. The scale and configuration of the plots did not, however, serve the agroecology courses well; we were still intent on locating a larger piece of good, farmable land.

THE JENNER FARM

In 2007, Prescott College was still not in a financial position to purchase irrigated acreage within a reasonable distance of campus. The college's experience in Chino Valley reflected a pervasive regional trend of converting irrigation rights to municipal uses. Thus, the value of arable farmland with water rights had skyrocketed over the previous decade. In the face of an overheated real estate boom in central Arizona, many farmers and ranchers opted to sell their land and water, make a windfall, and move their operation to another region or state. But there are also a growing number of land stewards who have responded to these real estate trends differently.

David and Kay Jenner have been ranching in Skull Valley, twenty miles southwest of Prescott, since the 1960s. They own over four thousand acres, encompassing scrub-covered volcanic hills, mesquite-dominated flatlands, and rich bottomlands lined with cottonwood trees that snake up the Skull Valley wash toward the Granite Mountain Wilderness. Rather than sell off some of the finest farm- and ranchland in the Arizona highlands to development, they opted in 2008 to place over 95 percent of their land in an agricultural conservation easement with the Central Arizona Land Trust. The Jenners are intent on keeping agriculture intact in Yavapai County. When it was clear that Wolfberry Farm would have to shut down, a group of college faculty and administrators approached Dave and Kay with the idea of establishing a new student farm on their land. After a year of discussions, they decided not only to preserve but also to promote agriculture by entering into a long-term agreement with Prescott College.

Today, Jenner Farm is the new home of the Agroecology Program. The site consists of twenty acres of rich alluvial soils and is bordered by towering cottonwood and mesquite trees. We have relocated the photovoltaic panels from Wolfberry Farm, added new panels to the array, and upgraded the inverter to power a hundred-gallon-per-minute solar water-pumping system. We then installed pipe to deliver water to three acres of drip irrigation, and we fenced the full perimeter of the twenty-acre farm as well as an interior three-acre section for draft horses and chicken tractors. As with Wolfberry Farm in Chino Valley, projects at Jenner Farm have been funded in part through external support, with about one-third of monies coming from donors and the remainder from Prescott College.

CRAFTING THE CURRICULUM

The primary purpose of the Jenner Farm at Prescott College is to provide an experiential classroom for studies in agroecology. The core of the agroecology curriculum consists of a series of six courses that span an entire growing season, from February to October. The series begins with "Plant Propagation" in the spring quarter; it continues in the summer semester with "Agroecology," "Field Methods in Agroecology," "Southwest Natural Systems Agriculture," and "Agroecosystems of the Arid Southwest," a travel course. The series culminates with a fall block course (a one-month intensive), "Food Preservation and Seed Conservation." These and a number of other courses in the natural and social sciences form the basis of a "competence" (similar to a major) in environmental studies. Agroecology will also form an important curricular component of a new sustainable community development competence emphasizing food justice and food security. At Prescott College, students work closely with faculty to design their own competences and "breadths" (similar to minors). Faculty have developed student advising documents for some of the more popular competence areas to help students develop their degree plan proposals.

The agroecology summer semester is an upper-division series, and, before students can enroll in it, they are required to take basic courses in biology, natural history, ecology, and earth sciences as well as social science courses such as "Issues of Global Food Production" and "Ecological Economics." Given the substantial list of prerequisites, most of the students who enroll in agroecology pursue a competence in environmental studies with an emphasis in agroecology or something similar. However, about a fifth of the enrolled students make agroecology their breadth. The best window for enrolling in the summer semester is between a student's junior and senior years. More often than not, students take a semester off either before or after the summer semester so as to avoid burnout and, in some cases, to retain eligibility for financial aid, which generally will not cover three consecutive semesters.

Aside from serving students interested in agroecology, the Jenner Farm and campus gardens are used by a broad range of other courses, including "Introduction to Soil Science," "Natural History and Ecology," "Botany," "Ethnobotany," "Ecological Design," "Permaculture," and "Field Methods for Plant Ecology." Beyond the social and natural sciences, several broader cross-disciplinary collaborations have taken place as well. One example involved a partnership between fine art and environmental studies students. For two years, the "Art as Public Expression" course taught by Julie Comnick has chosen to interpret food and agriculture themes on campus. In the first year, the students crafted sculptures depicting pioneers in sustainable agriculture. These beautiful and engaging pieces are nestled in gardens around the campus: Alan Chadwick, Rachel Carson, Liberty Hyde Bailey, Wangari Maathai, Barbara McClintock, and Gary Paul Nabhan are all creatively interpreted and represented. In the second year of the course, students painted a mural across the back of a recently constructed composting station depicting the "decomposition" of industrial society and subsequent rejuvenation of the natural world.

In designing the Agroecology Program at Prescott College, faculty and administrators have given a great deal of thought to which aspects of agricultural education the school is best suited to provide. Many students come to Prescott College with an interest in learning to grow food—not necessarily as a vocation, but more as a way of connecting with the earth and gaining personal satisfaction from eating freshly grown food. To meet this interest, the college offers hands-on courses in the spring and fall semesters in small-scale agriculture and permaculture—these are taught most semesters and have consistently filled for almost two decades. These courses help introduce students to basic practices and principles, but the fact that they are single course offerings scheduled outside the main growing season limits the depth of training that can be achieved.

Not surprisingly, many students emerge from introductory courses wanting to learn to farm. These students are highly enthusiastic and are seriously considering a vocation in growing food or pursuing related careers in education, research, or marketing. These future farmers look to the college for the next level of training, and it has been tempting to use Jenner Farm and the space dedicated to agriculture in the environmental studies curriculum to give them the training they want. We have had a good deal of internal debate over the years as to the scope of the agricultural education we are best able to offer. There are many outstanding student farms at colleges and universities that succeed in educating a new generation of farmers, and some of the gems are included in this book. But the prevailing view at Prescott College is that we should use our farm facilities for studies in agroecology rather than offering in-depth training in production agriculture. The reasons for this view can be summarized as follows.

1. The economic imperative. Simply put, financially successful farmers think as much about the market as they do about the soil. This economic imperative, the invisible weight that is always on farmers' minds, is difficult to capture and translate into a student farm setting. Part of what makes student farms so wonderful is that they do *not* try to maximize the economic efficiency of labor and that they can explore and celebrate crop diversity rather than focusing on targeted crop varieties to supply specific niche markets. Certainly, some student farms are under such pressure to be financially self-sufficient that they wind up embracing this economic imperative, but it is still rare for any student farm to cover the full costs of doing business. Land, labor, water, insurance, management, purchased inputs, and vehicles are almost always subsidized in one way or another.

2. Crops and methods of different bioregions. The crops grown and methods employed in the Arizona highlands do not always easily transfer to other regions of the United States or abroad. Colleges and universities that serve students from a local region are better suited to offer experiential training in regionally relevant production methods. Like many liberal arts colleges, Prescott draws students from all parts of the country. Concepts and issues explored in agroecology tend to be more universally relevant and more easily transferable to other growing regions than are specific growing practices.

3. Avoiding debt. Receiving in-depth training to farm at a private college or university translates into a considerable expenditure of tuition dollars. If that college experience can genuinely be said to represent the best place to learn to farm for a living, then the spending of those tuition dollars is entirely justified. But does it? A solid foundation in agroecology, on the other hand, will serve to inform students' decisionmaking acumen around a broad range of sustainability issues for their entire lives. It can, thus, valuably complement subsequent (or prior) training in production agriculture as well as in other vocations.

In response to the significant demand for in-depth farmer training that nevertheless exists, Prescott College currently encourages students to seek out internships, apprenticeships, or farm laborer positions with the best growers they can find in the regions where they ultimately want to farm. When successful, this approach delivers an affordable, high-quality, and regionally specific training, complete with the economic imperative.

THE PRESCOTT COLLEGE CSA

In 1999, students in the agroecology summer semester became strongly engaged in a conversation about the potential role of the student farm in supplying local produce to the Prescott College community. While the students were fully supportive of the use of the farm for studies in agroecology, they were disappointed at not having a consistent source of diverse local produce for the college. Yet, with further discussions, we realized that the issue was more about local food than the student farm. Moreover, we acknowledged that the growing season of the college farm ended in October, which did not coincide well with the academic year. By the end of the summer semester, after much brainstorming and debate, the students arrived at brilliance. What if college students, faculty, and staff decided to support local farmers to grow their food, rather than channel all their purchasing power into a college farm? What if we could take advantage of the unique geography in central Arizona, where food can be grown year-round at one location or another within a hundred-mile radius of Prescott College? Five students from the 1999 summer semester went to work to answer these questions through independent studies and senior projects.

The Prescott College Community Supported Agriculture (PCCSA) Program just celebrated its tenth year of delivering fresh local food from about ten growers to approximately two hundred eaters. The PCCSA coordinator works with a group of growers every season to determine what they will produce for the CSA. For the most part, farmers in Chino Valley, in close proximity to Prescott, provide produce in late summer and fall, whereas farmers in the warm Sonoran Desert near Phoenix provide food in the winter and spring. Every Tuesday, the coordinator will pick up produce from that week's growers, and, on Wednesday, the shares of food are available for pickup by PCCSA members in the college's café. The PCCSA shares a full-time coordinator with the Prescott Farmers Market. It serves the Prescott College community as well as residents of Prescott and nearby towns. At the same time, the PCCSA provides a perfect marketing outlet for the Agroecology Program: we are able to sell produce that is grown in excess of what students can eat, yet we are not obligated to farm specifically for the market. Aside from its primary role of providing food and supporting local growers, the PCCSA is a form of community outreach highly valued by the college administration.

AGROECOLOGY AND BEYOND

The term *agroecology* appears to have first been used by the Russian agronomist B. M. Bensen in 1928. The idea of agroecology spread throughout the world during the twentieth century, transforming agroecology into a scientific discipline, on the one hand, and a social movement, on the other.

Figure 10.1. An agroecology student feeds mesquite pods into the portable hammer mill to make flour. (Courtesy Tim Crews.)

Agroecology is inherently interdisciplinary. It crosses traditional agricultural disciplines such as soils and crop science with the science of ecology, but it also draws on the disparate disciplines of evolution, geography, anthropology, and economics to broaden the framework within which agricultural problems are assessed and solved.[1] Consider the definition of a weed. From a conventional agronomic perspective, a weed is a pest plant that steals water, nutrients, and even sunlight from a crop. Therefore, weeds need to be controlled in order to maximize crop yields. From an agroecological perspective, weeds are plants that very predictably colonize highly disturbed habitats that are rich in plant resources. To address weed competition in crops, conventional agronomists have historically focused on creative ways to kill them. Most recently, packages of genetically modified crops and herbicides are sold together, the crops engineered to survive when sprayed with the weed-killing herbicides. Agroecologists are more inclined to change the conditions that allow weeds to invade crops in the first place, rather than figure out how to kill them once they are present.

One of the most far-reaching examples of an agroecological solution that fundamentally addresses several major agricultural problems (including weeds) is the idea of developing perennial grain crops. This idea has been promoted by Wes Jackson and researchers at the Land Institute in Salina, Kansas, since 1980.[2] Jackson contends that agriculture will be far more sustainable if we pay attention to how native ecosystems function around us and model our farming systems to better mimic what we see. So important is this agroecological proposal that one of the agroecology summer semester courses, "Southwest Natural Systems Agriculture," focuses specifically on critically evaluating the potential gains and drawbacks of designing agriculture to more closely mimic natural systems. The farm-based dimension of this course revolves around the study of the natural history and domestication potential of wild food-producing plant species. Most of the plants of interest were used, and some continue to be used, by Native Americans in the Southwest. For example, agroecology students have for several years been evaluating mesquite, which grows on and around the Jenner Farm. In 2008, summer semester students researched different milling technologies for mesquite pods. Their findings eventually guided the purchase of a portable hammer mill for producing coarse- and fine-textured flours. Today, this mill will be towed to different parts of the Arizona highlands, where demand for mesquite flour is on the rise. People are able to collect the tasty leguminous pods and mill their own flour.

There are numerous reasons why a liberal arts education is enhanced with experience on a student farm, but possibly none is more important at Prescott College than the development of critical thinking around farming and food issues. If farming is anything, it is humbling. No sooner does a student succeed at raising a beautiful crop of chilies than blister beetles move through it like General Sherman's army, leaving complete destruction in their wake. I am convinced that, when examined from the classroom alone, some of the cardinal agricultural issues of our day are more easily viewed as black and white, issues like whether there is any place in sustainable agriculture for genetically modified organisms, or agrochemicals, or immigrant labor. Wes Jackson proposes that critical thinking ends where fundamentalism begins, yet there are certainly camps in sustainable agriculture open to accepting new fundamentalist converts. Moreover, as organic agriculture has become more profitable, the number of products sold to growers as beneficial, or even necessary, has risen. By learning to test claims, such as whether microbial inoculants accelerate or improve compost in any way compared to controls, students develop confidence in their own abilities to judge the sustainability of practices and products.

ALL THE HOURS IN THE DAY

The daily blend of rigorous academics with hard labor at Jenner Farm under the Arizona sun proves challenging for almost all students at some point during the fourteen-week summer semester. "Class" is held from 6:30 A.M. to 2:30 or 3:00 P.M., Monday–Thursday, and consists of field work, more structured field-based exercises, and discussions and lectures. Two days are dedicated to agroecology and field methods of agroecology, one day is dedicated to Southwest natural systems agriculture, and one day exists as "project day," a flexible day each week for catching up on time-sensitive tasks such as planting, weeding, or gathering data on research projects.

Specific daily schedules vary, but, generally, students meet in Prescott to make the twenty-mile drive to Skull Valley and Jenner Farm. Soon we hope to establish housing close to the farm so that students can enjoy a more rural life all summer. But, for now, they typically live in Prescott and commute to the farm. The first several hours of most days are spent doing the basics: planting, weeding, replanting, repairing drip lines, putting up fences, and, eventually, harvesting. In mid- to late morning, the group will often engage in a structured exercise pertaining to the curricular topic of the day, such as managing nutrient flows, insect or weed ecology, irrigation and water conservation, agriculture and ecosystem services, or farming and climate change. Around noon, the class breaks for lunch and then either meets up again in the shade of a tree to have a discussion or presentation or returns to the college if there are specific needs like a digital projector or microscopes. Students rotate farm caretaking responsibilities on the weekends. Academic work outside of class includes extensive reading and weekly study questions as well as literature-based and field experiment–based research papers.

This daily schedule is suspended for about one week each in May, June, and July for the course "Agroecosystems of the Arid Southwest." During this time, work-study students, or other faculty members, maintain crops at the farm. In this course, students travel in a fifteen-passenger van to visit a broad range of farms and food-related endeavors in Arizona, New Mexico, southern California, Utah, Colorado, and sometimes Kansas. At night, the class camps in campgrounds or on farms, and, during the day, activities range from hiking into prehistoric agricultural sites, to touring municipal composting facilities, to working on different farms or ranches in exchange for discussions and sometimes meals. Students are typically amazed at how their academic and hands-on training in agroecology enriches their abilities to understand and assess complex sustainability challenges faced by farmers and food-related businesses.

INEVITABLE TENSIONS

The agroecology summer semester schedule is designed to ideally balance thinking and doing, and, in many respects, it does. The pace and depth of the learning that occurs over the course of a long summer semester are qualitatively different from what happens in a more conventional classroom setting. Students have time to get out of their heads and make observations, reconsider assumptions, and, ultimately, link what might otherwise be perceived as abstract ideas with the very specific plants, insects, soils, and aquifers around them. But the schedule inevitably presents challenges as well.

There is always a range of learning styles in every mix of students, but, in an intensive and highly varied schedule such as that experienced by Prescott College agroecology students, these differences are intensified. Some students prefer to work rather than study. They are characteristically on time for early morning field sessions but late to hand in study questions. They are happy to dig irrigation trenches until the cows come home but struggle immensely to keep their eyes open during a discussion of crop genetic diversity. On the other end of the spectrum, I regularly encounter students who voraciously devour every intellectual challenge put in front of them but, when it comes time to hoe a half-acre sunflower/squash intercrop experiment, begin to question why they are paying tuition to work. "Why doesn't the college hire work-study students to do this? I have better things to do with my time." Of course, the labor provides essential lessons. It is when observations happen. It is when students internalize and calibrate ideals of farming without fossil fuels. It is when students most directly appreciate the contribution that undocumented workers make in providing citizens of the United States with abundant fruits and vegetables. But the reality is that there has to be a balance between labor and academics. It is an ongoing challenge that will not be solved because, in many respects, part of why this program is so successful is that it lures and sometimes drags students out of their comfort zones and into that more difficult terrain where some of the most valuable learning often takes place.

Another common question that student farms face is who gets to eat the food. While the primary purpose of the Jenner Farm is not to teach

Figure 10.2. Identifying insects at Jenner Farm. (Courtesy Shawna Yaussi.)

students how to grow the maximum amount of unblemished food for market (i.e., production agriculture), food is grown by the students and sometimes lots of it. When farms are told by college and university administrators that they have to be self-supporting, the pressure to channel produce to markets first, and let the student workers eat the leftovers, can be inescapable. Prioritizing the market can leave students feeling exploited and cynical and, indeed, deprived of one of the most rewarding and gratifying experiences of farming. Because Prescott College has included the Jenner Farm as part of its ongoing operating expenses, like a computer lab or a theater facility, we are not under pressure to generate income, and, thus, we can place students first in line to enjoy the food they grow, with other markets such as the college café, the college's CSA, the Prescott Farmers Market, and local restaurants queuing up afterward.

Even when the students are at the head of the line to eat what they have grown, the academic calendar can have a tendency to trump the growing season. Many crops do not finish maturing until well after the third week of August, when the summer semester ends. After several years of contending with the fallout of this abrupt ending to student involvement on the farm, including the labor vacuum left in the students' absence, a student named Colin Khoury stepped up and proposed a fall block course called "Food Preservation and Seed Conservation." He developed a marvelous curriculum and then helped teach the course for his senior project in 2000, and it has been offered ever since. "Food Preservation and Seed Conservation" allows students to complete the growing season and continue to learn within an academic context. Students harvest produce and seed from the Jenner Farm and college gardens while learning the culture, biology, and practical skills of preserving food and seeds.

VOCATIONS IN AGROECOLOGY

Approximately half the students who have studied agroecology at Wolfberry or Jenner farms have gone on to pursue a formal vocation in a food or farm-related field. There are many inspiring stories of how agroecology graduates are contributing to and transforming the food systems on which we all depend. The students Colin Khoury and Shanti Leinow Rade illustrate the range of vocations being explored.

Colin Khoury, the student who developed the course "Food Preservation and Seed Conservation," was hired shortly after graduating from Prescott College by the nonprofit Native Seed/SEARCH in Tucson, Arizona, as curator of its bean collections. After a time, he went on to earn a master's degree at the University of Birmingham in the United Kingdom, where he studied plant genetic resources. Following the completion of his M.S., he took a position with Cary Fowler's Global Crop Diversity Trust in Rome. Colin has recently started work on his Ph.D. at Wageningen University in the Netherlands, where he will conduct research on farmers' perceptions of climate change and how crop genetic diversity can help farmers adjust to climate change in Ethiopia, Zimbabwe, and Indonesia.

Meanwhile, back in Arizona, the agroecology student Shanti Leinow wrote her senior project on the history of agriculture in Chino Valley. Little did she know at the time that she would go on to help shape the future of agriculture in Chino Valley. She and her husband, Cory Rade, now run Whipstone Farm, which is among the most successful organic farms in central Arizona. They helped launch the Prescott College CSA program and have started another CSA of their own. They have both played pivotal roles in growing the region's farmers markets, and Shanti is one of just a handful of accredited organic certification inspectors in the Southwest.

Graduate research and farming are two of the most common pursuits of Prescott College agroecology graduates, but there are many others. Some have worked to integrate gardens into primary and secondary educational settings, where the garden becomes a tactile entry into science, health, history, art, and other subjects. Others have worked on food security projects in inner-city neighborhoods in the United States or in rural settings abroad. Still others have started businesses, from CSAs to heirloom seed companies.

The Jenner Farm and campus gardens at Prescott College play a vital role in academics as well as contributing to the campus community's sense of place, aesthetics, and sustainability. First and foremost, the gardens and farm facilitate experiential learning, contributing to the development of both pragmatic and critical thinking skills. Regardless of whether graduates go on to farm, teach, conduct research, breed seeds, work for nongovernment organizations, focus on food security, or simply consume food, the overarching objective of the college's food-and-farm programs is to nurture students with complex understandings of sustainability who can grapple with trade-offs at multiple scales and, ultimately, move society in positive directions both ecologically and socially.

While the gardens and farm produce significant amounts of food, one thing that differentiates Prescott College's agricultural program from those of some other schools is that food production per se is not the primary goal. Experimenting with how to produce food within particular ecological and social constraints is. College farms are in a position to push the envelope, exploring crop varieties, irrigation methods, fertility programs, and labor schedules that may be more sustainable. If the environmental educator David Orr is right, exploring these topics within the context of a liberal arts education can contribute to the transformation of how agriculture is both valued and practiced.[3]

STUDENT REFLECTIONS

WOLFBERRY REFLECTIONS

TARYN KENNEDY

The Arizona heat radiates through my straw hat, singeing my skin even through long sleeves and linen pants. Although the sun sits low in the east, the intensity of the summer day is building quickly. Noting the empty rain gauge, I join the group to divide up the morning chores. It is my turn for coop duty. I head across the farm to tend the chickens, beckoned by the clucks and coos of the hens, yet anxious about the rooster. Knowing his aggressive character, I slow down to build confidence for completing my task of feeding, cleaning, and collecting eggs. I wade through a field of mustard almost a meter high. Wolfberry Farm has a distinct look this season owing to unusually abundant spring rains that produced hectares of this beautiful wild annual weed. The colors of the farm—the tan of the twisty roads, the evergreen shelter belt, and the coral of the cobbed, straw bale buildings—stand in sharp, brilliant contrast to the lime-green mustards.

Putting off my confrontation with our feisty rooster, I wander through the natural systems agriculture plots to see how the transplants are faring. Collections of prickly pear (*Opuntia* spp.), lemonade berry (*Rhus trilobata*), four-wing saltbrush (*Atriplex canescens*), Indian ricegrass (*Oryzopsis hymenoides*), and currant (*Ribes inebrians*) are organized by species. The individual plants have been gathered from various parts over Arizona and transplanted here to see which ones would grow at Wolfberry Farm. The success of the transplants is mixed. Some have clearly taken hold, while others are barely hanging on. Observing these plants, I try to fathom living off the land in such an extreme environment, altering my diet to survive on these native sources of food. The stands of wolfberry plants undergoing propagation for seed and fruit trials provide a link to the agricultural history of the Southwest. The presence of wolfberry is connected to human habitation, often disclosing the location of prehistoric kitchen gardens and dwellings of the Hohokam or Ancestral Puebloans. I begin placing people in this region, wondering how a culture could secure perennial water sources and recalling our recent visit to Kykotsmovi on the Hopi reservation, where Eric and Jane Polingyuma farm maize without irrigation. My overall experience with Eric and Jane resonated with reverence for tradition, simplicity, and story. The depth that they planted each maize seed mirrored the rootedness of agriculture in the Hopi way of life. Jane's father gave Eric an ear of corn when they were married, saying, "Here, go make your life." The interrelation of culture and place was intimate.

With thoughts of Hopi maize sprouts growing through a foot of soil, I reach the coop door, pitchfork in hand. Irate, the aptly named rooster, greets me nonchalantly with a flip of his tail feathers rather than the spurs of his legs. As I take to my chores, he keeps an eye on my activities, but seems to condone my purpose there.

Taryn Kennedy was a Prescott College agroecology student in 2003 and is currently an M.S. student in the Soils and Biogeochemistry Graduate Group at the University of California, Davis.

NOTES

1. A. Wezel, S. Bellon, T. Dore, C. Francis, D. Vallod, and C. David, "Agroecology as a Science, a Movement and a Practice: A Review," *Agronomy of Sustainable Development* 29 (2009): 503–15.

2. Wes Jackson, *New Roots for Agriculture* (Lincoln: University of Nebraska Press, 1980); J. D. Glover, C. M. Cox, and J. R. Reganold, "Future Farming: A Return to Roots?" *Scientific American,* August 2007, 82–89.

3. David Orr, *Earth in Mind,* rev. ed. (Washington, DC: Island, 2004).

11

University of Montana (1997)

Agriculturally Supported Community

JOSH SLOTNICK

"I don't know much, but I know this: six months from now you'll wish you were here." Damian Parr's thick New York City brogue was the last voice in the closing circle of the 1991 season at the University of California, Santa Cruz (UC Santa Cruz), Farm and Garden. The ring of thirty-five or so grubby, all-age student farmers stayed quiet, eyes fixed back on Damian, the youngest person in the room. The words scorched themselves into my memory, but I did not know whether to believe them. Then I went ahead and spent the better part of my adult life attempting to re-create the experience for others as well as for myself.

What follows is an account of that work, the rough birth story and lessons learned from the place officially known as the University of Montana/Garden City Harvest PEAS (Program in Ecological Agriculture and Society) Farm. The project as an entity is much more the product of on-the-fly organizational evolution than it is the result of careful planning. Similarly, the kernels of wisdom I will relate are discoveries, not inventions. In helping create the PEAS farm, I pushed for an educational structure that looked a bit like the UC Santa Cruz farm, where I had been a student. Because that experience had been so powerful for me, I used it as a template. But, at the time of the inception of the PEAS farm, I could not have articulated why I believed it worked so well. Only now, after being part of years' worth of students' experiences, do I feel like I can accurately describe what happens and why. These are lessons learned over time, via observation. Like the student realizations I describe, these principles emerged organically. But first, the origin story and a description of the program.

After a school-year sojourn to Cornell University, I returned to Missoula, Montana, in the spring of 1995 with a newly minted master's degree that I earned studying student farms. I arrived in Missoula in late April and immediately jumped back into farming, in partnership with my wife. She had returned a couple of months earlier to get things going. On a national level, revolution was in the air, the Republican Revolution of 1994. Newt Gingrich had put forth a ten-point plan to right the country, the Contract with America. Essential to this contract was a pledge to end welfare as we knew it. Practically, this meant new regulations embedded deep in the farm bill. The new law, if enacted, would dramatically reduce the duration of access to food stamps for individuals while at the same time tying that access to a new series of work/training requirements. In Missoula, Mary Pittaway, the director of our local WIC (Women, Infants, and Children) program, looked into the near future and saw a tide of people descending on our food bank, an institution ill equipped to meet the needs of a massive influx of hungry people, newly cut off from food stamp support. Meanwhile, on the other side of town, the philosophy professor Deborah Slicer came out to our family farm wanting to trade work for food and a learning experience. We grew to know Deborah well, and, when she heard of my studies at Cornell, she asked, "Why don't we make a student farm here, at the University of Montana?"

At roughly the same time, Mary was driving past an ill-used chunk of public land when she noticed a grove of ripening plum trees. She understood from firsthand experience at the WIC office the narrow nutritional options available to people who have little money. She knew that the food bank couldn't handle the coming volume of people, and she understood what kind of nutrition emergency food shelters typically have to offer—past-date pastry, highly processed canned goods, ready-made food in a box. So Mary called a young activist, Caitlin Desilvey, and asked her if she could arrange for a crew of volunteers from her organization to pick the plums and bring them to the food bank. Caitlin went one better. She told Mary about the philosophy professor and the vegetable farmer who were trying to start a student farm and pointed out that the food would have to go somewhere. Maybe we could work together and create a supply of fresh food for the food bank beyond this year's plums?

Over the next year or so, we staged a handful of large community conversations, talking through our various understandings of the food/poverty situation in Missoula. Out of those conversations emerged a core group of people, a distillation of the problem, and a multifaceted solution. We called the central issue *food security*, by which we meant both the predictable access to high-quality food and the development of food production methods that, when repeated year in and year out, would yield suitable quantities of high-quality produce while maintaining the biological integrity of the land. One part of the solution was to offer the university a partnership: this new organization, Garden City Harvest (GCH), would run a student/community farm in affiliation with the university. GCH would start the farm, build the infrastructure, cover the operating expenses, and then distribute the food. The university would provide the labor, in the form of students and a teacher. GCH's food bank farm, in other words, could also be the university's student educational farm. In addition to the food bank farm, GCH would also begin a network of community gardens, strategically located in low-income neighborhoods. A GCH employee would staff each of the gardens and tend a few of the plots for the food bank. Anyone could trade hours of work for produce from the food bank plots—we called this *volunteer for veggies*. We went to the dean of the College of Arts and Sciences and made the following proposal: If we come back to you with enough money to start this project, will you cover the costs of hiring an adjunct to teach students on the farm? He signed off but didn't remember us when we came back with a $150,000 Community Food Security Coalition grant (a program built into the same farm bill as the new welfare regulations). He acquiesced but said, "Three years, the life of the grant, not a day more." He meant it.

In the fall of 1996, I stopped farming full-time with my wife and began a career as an adjunct professor in the Environmental Studies Program, running the PEAS farm. Deborah and I chose PEAS (Program in Ecological Agriculture and Society) because the name reflected the nature of the program—agriculture focused on land and community—and because we liked the acronym. We hit the ground running in the fall of 1996, and, by spring, we had tilled up two acres of university land near the edge of town, put up a greenhouse, and reinhabited an abandoned building on the property. That summer we grew beautiful food. The following year we added two nearby acres of county land and brought the CSA (community-supported agriculture) project up from thirty to sixty members. Three years into the project, when the USDA money dried up, the dean, true to his word, cut off his funding as well, smack in the middle of the semester. Luckily, the head of the Environmental Studies Program agreed to cover the position until the end of the semester but wasn't able to after that.

Our solution to this crisis was to offer the PEAS courses to students through the Continuing Education Department, which at the time ran on a fee-for-service model: instructors got paid though a cut of tuition. The university paid no benefits, offered no job security beyond the duration of the semester, and provided no services. The relative popularity of the farm allowed us to maintain the program through continuing ed, as students continued to sign up for PEAS. We had done a great job in the previous three years of providing students with worthy educational experiences, but the farm, on the edge of town and the far edge of the educational landscape of the university, was off the radar of most administrators as well as that of most Missoulians. The lack of public visibility at the outset allowed us to figure things out on the fly, but this same lack of scrutiny was almost our undoing—other than the students and a core group of proponents, few people among the administration or faculty really knew we were there. The PEAS farm did eventually evolve into an established entity, but this seems now like a happy accident. A handful of things, not all of them initially positive, had to happen for the project to continue, and most of these crucial developments were entirely serendipitous. These events, coupled with our success with students, allowed the program to evolve and, in time, to become stable and secure.

In 1999, we got word that the university land we had been working on was to be reappropriated for new research projects and that we needed to start looking for a new site. This dislocation, our biggest obstacle to date, in the end became our best opportunity. With help from City Councilman Dave Harmon, we found a new site in 2000 and began farming there in 2001. We moved the farm and didn't miss a season. The new land was a six-and-a-half-acre piece of school district property, a fifteen-minute bike ride from the university. Sandwiched between a popular walking trail and a well-traveled neighborhood road, the new farm had lots of visibility, the potential for expansion, and a great view of the Rattlesnake Wilderness. By the close of the twentieth century, moreover, local food and organic farming had wedged themselves into public discourse at the national level. In 2000, when the Environmental Studies Program was looking for a new professor, they hired a rural sociologist, Neva Hassanein, who focused her research on food, farming, and the environment. Neva noticed the good press the farm had received; she visited the land, talked with students, and then pushed for the farm classes to become an official part of the Environmental Studies Program. It took a few years, but, by 2003, we were in, though Neva and the environmental studies chair, Tom Roy, had to actively fund-raise to keep the program afloat.

PEAS has continued to grow since our initial institutional incorporation and physical move. In 2006, the current environmental studies director, Len Broberg, was able to get PEAS off of soft money and onto state funding, and, in 2007, we expanded the farm to nine and three-quarter acres. Though the farm has now become an established part of the university and the community, throughout its evolution its basic educational structure and schedule has remained the same. The Environmental Studies Program offers three PEAS courses a year, one each in spring, summer, and fall. In the summer, students spend Monday–Thursday from 8:00 A.M. to 12:00 P.M. working on the farm. Each day, two students make lunch, from the food we grow, for everyone else. On Fridays, we have a class in the morning and then go on a field trip to visit a farm in the area. In spring and fall, students work on the farm six hours each week, signing up for a section corresponding to a time slot—Monday/Wednesday 9:00–12:00, Monday/Wednesday 1:00–4:00, Tuesday/Thursday 9:00–12:00, Tuesday/Thursday 1:00–4:00—but all students come for a sit-down class at the farm on Wednesdays at 4:00.

The partnership nature of the farm—as a joint nonprofit/university venture—greatly facilitated our ability to solicit foundation grants, grants from local government, and donor gifts to fund the move to the Rattlesnake. That meant developing an existing irrigation well, putting up a greenhouse, building a toolshed, chicken coop, and farm center/barn, and paving a parking lot. We raised the money for this infrastructure primarily through GCH. Since the summer of 1997, GCH had been using the PEAS farm and the community gardens to successfully meet its mission of getting high-quality produce to low-income people while creating educational opportunities in sustainable agriculture. To fund-raise for the move, we built on this past success—past success being a good indicator of a wise community development investment. Interestingly, what on the university side of the partnership was marginal—an under-the-radar but excellent student experience—was, on the GCH side, the stuff of bragging rights: fifteen to twenty thousand pounds of produce delivered annually to the food bank, a ninety-member CSA, great local press, and national recognition. Following the move, we were a highly visible community farm in a beautiful landscape. A few more years of solid production and wonderful educational results, and we had become part of the cultural fabric of the town. Six hundred people regularly come out for our annual farm party in August, the CSA sells out before winter is over, and GCH has added two new programs to the farm: a community education program for school-

Figure 11.1. Josh Carter, a University of Montana Environmental Studies Program graduate student, prepares the CSA share pickup buffet. After earning his master's in Montana,
he began managing Vermont's Shelburne Farms' Market Garden (a full-fledged organic
farm). (Courtesy PEAS Farm/Garden City Harvest.)

children (more than two thousand students visited the farm in 2008) and a
"Youth Harvest" program where we host a small group of kids from Missoula's Youth Drug Court. We integrate these kids (five each season) into
the summer PEAS program.

We backed into cultural and institutional establishment, but, throughout this process, the educational structure and the quality of student experience has remained constant. Our work did not improve so much as our
permission to do it. Now, thirteen seasons in, I feel more certain about why
our model works educationally, as the catalyst for transformation, and as a
source of creating good in the world. Later in this chapter, I will offer a set
of principles for *designing* a student farm, not for getting one established
within the context of a university. If that's your goal, you can probably do
that more elegantly than we did.

As the years go by, I increasingly recognize the benefits of the organizational partnership between GCH and the Environmental Studies Program. It spreads the financial burden and does not cause either entity to
stretch beyond its realm of expertise. The Environmental Studies Program

can offer an educational experience without getting into the farming business, and GCH can grow food for the food bank, with student labor, and not have to promise higher education in the process. Each entity can work from its strengths and, by working together, combine to create something greater than either could do alone.

The Value of an Educational Farm

"What am I going to do? It can't possibly be over already!" A University of Montana PEAS farm student named June said this to me in the fall of 2009 while picking plums, ripe now after a few cold nights, gooey sweet and yellow on the inside, like dates. I had just told June and two other students working across the tree from me that we had only a few weeks left and that the season, and that meant the class, would soon be over. In her remark, June inadvertently acknowledged two key hoped-for outcomes from the student experience on the farm: (1) a high degree of attachment to the activity and the place and (2) a desire to maintain the feelings found at the farm, which implies the challenge of incorporating the personal changes gleaned from the farm experience into the next thing the students do. The best education transforms. A true educational experience should allow students to emerge changed; after the experience, they should, quite literally, feel the potential for creating a different type of relationship between themselves and the greater world. At its best, a student farm will act—effortlessly, organically—as host to just such an experience.

An educational farm is a medium for teaching sustainability via experience—even more than it is a vehicle for transferring the tools and techniques of a certain type of agriculture. Sustainability means relentless care, care for a place on its own terms and care for each other. In this way, sustainability is the opposite of exploitation; it is about tending, not reaping. In order for such tending to be possible, people must prioritize the health of their place and of their compatriots. The student farm provides the context for this type of care to emerge organically, and that is, I believe, its greatest strength. These expressions of care appear, so it seems, on their own and, consequently, have a sense of reality, of genuineness and authenticity, not typically found in academic settings. Care properly applied feels right, not because the teacher told you to, but because it actually is right. Though these expressions of ownership arrive authentically, I believe that they come as a result of a specific educational structure. The heart of this chapter details a version of that structure, a set of principles that will yield (apparently accidentally) the experience of sustainability.

Creating an educational context involving doing right by the place and by each other may not sound ethically controversial, but, in practical terms, it is radical. When thoroughly unpacked and realistically accounted for, most of what we do, and certainly what we buy, comes at a great cost to a specific group of people and a piece of land somewhere far from wherever here may be—this sore fact of modern life feels inevitable. An educational farm, properly structured, is dissent in action. A good student farm should inspire allegiance to the place, the activity, and all who share in its continual re-creation. That type of concern for particularity and community is full-on subversive in the modern world. Creating an educational context that is both real and academic, and that encourages the kind of care that sustainability implies, is more than a social coup; it is our educational obligation.

The primary goal of student educational farms, I believe, is not to create farmers. The goal must be to provide a transformational experience, a firsthand grasping of sustainability, a palpable sense of being bonded to a place and a group. This experience can deeply alter a student's sense of how he or she can potentially fit into the surrounding reality and, most importantly, how he or she can effect positive change. I believe that this type of learning can change the world.

Though once marginal, the PEAS farm has now become an integral part of the Environmental Studies Program. Since its inception, PEAS has offered students a unique and powerful educational experience and generated great benefits for the community. Tangible results and local popularity coupled with changes in both the local and the national context (Neva's arrival on the scene, our move to a high-profile site, and the ascendance of sustainable food as a topic of interest) greatly increased the odds for establishment within the university. The Environmental Studies Program now offers an undergraduate emphasis in sustainable food and farming, and prospective graduate students often cite the farm as one of the reasons they choose to apply to our program. The Environmental Studies Program now offers an array of innovative graduate and undergraduate courses related to food and farming. The community of Missoula, similarly, encourages the farm's continued presence because of its proven success in producing tangible results: public beauty, food for low-income folks, valued educational and social programs, and an overall recognition of the farm's power as a catalyst for community.

In offering advice on the design of a student educational farm, I would frame my responses around two questions: (1) How do we structure student educational farms so that care authentically emerges and students directly experience sustainability? (2) How can a student farm foster community support beyond the university? I will answer these questions through a description of a set of principles. However, these design principles must rest on a foundation of two truths. If these truths are ignored, a student/community farm will fail.

TWO TRUTHS

Locality

The first generalizable theme distilled from years of working on the PEAS farm and with the larger community is, ironically, sensitivity to local particularity. The farm fits neatly within the culture of this place and actively contributes to it and, by that grace, continues to exist. A cookie-cutter, template type of plan for a farm will fail. A farm must exist to further the interest of a specific community. I recommend the design principles below with confidence, but only if they are applied through a lens trained on a specific, particular locality.

Farming Is a Trade

"I want to start a community educational farm." I hear this statement often enough. I heard it today, in fact, from an earnest but soft-handed graduate student visiting from afar. He turned his recording device toward me like a baby bird opening its beak. I blathered on and on, and, as I was about to leave him and go back to work, he said it, clear as the poststorm blue sky above the hills behind him: "I want to start a community educational farm." I realized all that I had just told him would turn out insufficient without the next truth. "You want to start a community farm?" I said to the visiting graduate student. "Yes, an educational community-based farm in an urban area," said the graduate student. "Then you should go work on a farm or two or three of them. Learn from the mistakes of others. Ultimately, farming is a trade, like being an accountant or an electrician or a professor. Desire alone isn't enough. You need skills and experience; you must understand a set of tools and techniques. Get some of that down, then do it for a while, and then either all the other stuff I said will make sense or you'll be able to see it for bullshit."

So, if you are reading this and your interest goes beyond the merely curious—maybe you're contemplating starting a farm at your school?—understand that you must hire a farmer. Desire to do the job is not a sufficient qualification for managing a farm, and being a student of the student farm movement is nice, but it's also not enough. Hire a farmer—someone with real agricultural skills and experience—who can also teach. With this understood, we can move on to the meat of this chapter: How do you structure the program so that students experience sustainability as I described above, and how do you generate public support for your program? Here are three potentially replicable elements. The first two address student experience, the third community support.

THREE PRINCIPLES FOR DESIGNING A STUDENT EDUCATIONAL FARM

The Recipe

I first encountered an educational farm as a student. As I hinted at above, I was an apprentice at the UC Santa Cruz Farm and Garden in 1991. The experience working and learning on the farm was transformative, and it sent me strongly in a direction I continue on in today. Eden-like, with fruit trees, gardens, and fields, redwoods and the ocean, the farm was easy to slip into, but it was, I believe, more the educational/labor structure of the place than its beauty that led to its powerful educational effect.

After finishing the program, I returned to Missoula with my soon-to-be-wife and began farming à la Santa Cruz. A few years later, new-father panic inspired, I went to graduate school in New York while we kept farming in Missoula (our farm still exists today). As a graduate student, I studied educational farms at a handful of colleges in the United States. My experience as a student on the farm in Santa Cruz and farming on my own and the research I did in graduate school at Cornell led me to adapt the basic educational structure of the farm program at Santa Cruz to our specific context here in the Environmental Studies Program at the University of Montana. Though we changed some of the specific elements, the general form remained the same—a blend, heavy on the experiential, of real farm work and traditional pedagogy; this much I knew and felt confident of as an educational environment. A few years in, we noticed that, though our nascent success was apparent, our description of the essential form, and, therefore, our understanding of our own educational design, was incomplete. Through conversation and observation, we more carefully outlined the elements of our recipe, the key features of the form of our educational student farm. This isn't the only way, but it is one way, and it goes like this: In appropriate measure, blend small groups, humble labor, and tangible, beautiful, edible results.

When people work in small groups, engaged in humble labor—work that gets you dirty and doesn't require highly specialized abilities—the social barriers that naturally separate us from one another quickly erode. When you are weeding carrots across from someone, you both become dirty and sweaty, and you soon realize that you can work carefully and still have mental energy for conversation. One bed of carrots, and you will know where your partner is from, why he or she is here, and what he or she hopes to do next. The humility of the task creates common ground, and, once you are standing there together on common ground, a recognition of one another's humanity is inevitable. When working in small groups over time, bonding tends to spread across a group like a contagion, and what was once a mere collection of people becomes a tight little tribe. However, the bonding to each other is only half the magic here: just as important as being part of the group is recognizing one's relevance to that group. Students realize not too long into the season that they are personally necessary for the farm's success, that what they do matters. If they're not there to weed the carrots, there will be no carrots to harvest. For many students, regardless of background or access to privilege, this is the first time they have truly felt necessary. A few years ago, the writer and activist Frances Moore Lappé came to Missoula, and, in her talk, she observed that people need, on a primal level, to feel both personally effective and part of a group. So structured, a student farm can provide the context for both realizations to emerge, authentically, on their own.

Next in the recipe is beautiful, tangible, edible results—students reap what they sow and experience firsthand the value of their work. In our situation at the PEAS farm, it's not just the beauty of the carrots; it's also their ultimate destination—we grow food for an eighty-member CSA and for the Missoula Food Bank. In both cases we are obligated to deliver this food, and it meets a real need. The full experience of the food would be lost, however, if students didn't enjoy some of it themselves. As I described earlier, in the summer at the PEAS farm, students work from 8:00 A.M. to 12:00 P.M. each day, Monday through Thursday, and at noon we retreat to the barn and eat lunch, a lunch cooked by two students who spent the second half of their morning cooking food they helped grow. After working together all morning, eating together food grown together seals the deal. A profound sense of ownership is evident in the speech of students.

A third of the way through the summer, the pronouns have all changed from the second person to the first—when speaking to me, the students say, "Why doesn't *our* broccoli look as good as *our* cabbage?" or, "*We* need to fix the chicken fence." By August, the students effectively belong to each other, and the farm is theirs. On the third Thursday in August, we have our annual farm party, and the students show off their work, their farm, to the rest of the town. Typically, six hundred people or so come to the farm party. That's a lot of acknowledgment. The magic doesn't always work for all the students, but it always works for most of them. By autumn, a core group of students have bonded to each other, to the place, and to the activity. They've been working together on the farm for months and now feel both a group connection and a deep sense of ownership of the place, and *that* is the experience of sustainability that stays with them.

The Creative Tension between Production and Education

The PEAS farm has contractual obligations to eighty CSA members and to the Missoula Food Bank. We design the farm around meeting these obligations. We follow the tenets of traditional small-scale vegetable farming—composting, crop rotations, cover crops, and diversity—but we have determined what to grow and how much on the basis of the needs of the CSA and the food bank. Twice a week all summer long on Mondays and Thursdays, CSA members come to the farm between 4:30 and 6:00 P.M. to pick up their food. We display the vegetables on a twenty-foot table in the barn, farmers market style. We have the food harvested, washed, and set out with attention to color breaks and topographical changes to highlight beauty and limit confusion (it's a good idea not to put cukes next to zukes, e.g.). On harvest mornings, you can feel the intensity. We have a lot of food to get in by noon, when we eat that all-important lunch. After lunch, a small crew of graduate students, a few volunteer undergraduates, and I make flower bouquets and get the food laid out. On these days, there is no time for anything but getting the job done. Similarly, in the spring we get brief windows between seasonal rains when the ground is dry enough to work, and we have to plant quickly before the window closes. In the fall, when we know an untimely frost is imminent, we go at speed to harvest winter squash and pumpkins. In these situations (and many others), the class becomes a work crew. But this work crew is made up of students, people who have paid for instruction. Like the CSA members and the food bank, we have a contractual obligation here—these people have paid for a rich learning experience. There are times when the twin responsibili-

Figure 11.2. The PEAS Farm in full bloom, with Mount Sentinel in the background. The straw bale barn was completed in 2002. (Courtesy PEAS Farm/Garden City Harvest.)

ties of education and production chafe against each other. We may need to get the harvest in at the cost of a teachable moment, but I believe that this tension actually informs both halves of the dynamic and better allows us to meet both obligations.

Our economic dependence on results and, sometimes, the intensity of time pressure provide reasoning for instruction absent in a purely academic (even if it is hands-on) context. Why do we harvest carrots in bunches like this? Why do we plant successions of lettuce or grow spinach alongside the peas in early spring? The answers all relate to the ultimate destination of the food. If there were no one actually depending on the presence and quality of the produce, it would be a stretch to ask for, and to model, specific behavior related to its character. Educationally, the availability and quality of the food must matter. The reality of the situation creates a context for student investment that would seem inappropriate, or at least affected, in a mere academic context. Given that there are real expectations around the food, the students also get real feedback, not just the opinion of a professor. Twice a week people rave about the beauty of the food, ask for cooking suggestions, and openly wonder when the corn will arrive. The feedback enforces the sense of reality and obligation, which, in turn, informs the reasoning behind our agricultural choices.

Similarly, acting on teachable moments increases student investment. We may stop in the middle of the garlic harvest for an impromptu discussion of the relative merits of cutting off garlic scapes or leaving them on. Stopping the process to talk is recognition of the educational importance of the activity. Harvesting garlic is more than getting the garlic in so that we can distribute it; harvesting garlic is a medium for teaching about garlic, in a demonstrable way. This material expression of the importance of education deepens student investment and also has a positive influence on production. We all work better when we have a clear understanding of the underlying reasons for the tasks we're asked to do. Once the season is under way, we break the class into smaller groups, by task, first thing in the morning. These tasks and groups change daily as we move through the season, but the assignment of responsibility remains constant. In this small-group form, production and education truly merge. I bounce between groups, offer explanation, and then let them go. Firsthand experience, traditional explanation, and the successful assumption of responsibility blend seamlessly. The farm looks better, works better, and teaches better when education and production infuse one another.

A Public Farm Is a Catalyst for Community

The PEAS farm grows between fifteen and twenty thousand pounds of produce annually for the Missoula Food Bank. Most of this comes in the form of three crops: winter squash, carrots, and onions. The carrots get canned (at a facility at the Montana State Prison), and the food bank can store winter squash and onions without refrigeration. These large-scale harvests often attract attention and bring to the farm people who otherwise wouldn't be involved. There are volunteer organizations that want to see their efforts benefit the food bank directly in terms of high-quality food. Thousands of schoolchildren now come regularly to the farm for field trips. We have built an entire program, Community Education, around hosting classes and camps at the farm. The presence of the PEAS farm and the necessity of these fall harvests bring people together around an obvious good. Word of the coming onion harvest spreads quickly, often without spreading—since the farm is a public, visible place, people jog, walk, and bike by regularly. They notice for themselves what is happening, and I hear about it while in line at the post office. The visibility of the farm keeps people in touch with the agricultural process and, in turn, increases their understanding of this valley.

We all, I believe, have a pair of deeply buried needs that can be addressed in part via a public farm. We need to have a connection with what sustains us, and we need to be locals, to belong to a place. People see the farm from the nearby creekside trail or from the path on the ridge behind the farm, notice something agriculturally seasonal, and feel connected. Their speech reveals the farm's ability to passively meet both needs described above: they cross their arms on the other side of the fence and say, "These spring rains have been good for the onions, haven't they?" Only a wheat stalk hanging from the mouth and a pair of overalls separate the runner pushing a baby jogger from the farmer-neighbor next door. These people's comments show that they feel like they are in it too, that they understand this valley and understand the progression of plants that will become food, plants that live and die according to the gifts of this place. Knowing a place is a prerequisite for belonging. We all have a desire to live in a place worthy of our best assumptions about ourselves. When we are locals, when we believe that the place we live in is ours, we begin to care—the same way the PEAS kids grow into caring for the farm. Through its public, highly visible nature, the PEAS farm helps foster such private realizations. These realizations find expression in the large-scale attendance at our farm party. People come to the party to celebrate not just the farm but the season, the pleasures of high summer with fall around the bend, and, even more so, this place, Missoula. The event is an absolute demonstration of allegiance to locality. The PEAS farm operates a CSA—the well-known acronym stands for community-supported agriculture, but I believe we have the acronym backward. Because of the connection to the food bank, the PEAS farm's high-profile location, and the public events held at the farm, the PEAS farm informs local culture and has become a community institution. The farm agriculturally supports community and, consequently, enjoys great public support.

If, after muscling through all that, you have not lost your interest, by all means go forth and start a farm at your school. But please remember the following: any plan for the creation of an educational/community farm must first pass through your very own local filter, as the farm will exist, or not, according to the particularities, both biological and cultural, of your place. Take seriously the agricultural trade aspect of what you are contemplating and act accordingly. Small-scale vegetable farming, orchard-

Figure 11.3. Throughout the summer, students and Youth Harvest participants share in the duties of preparing a farm-fresh lunch for the group. (Courtesy PEAS Farm/Garden City Harvest.)

ing, and raising livestock are trades, complete with specific sets of tools, vocabularies, and techniques. The best plans will fail if the person running the farm can't do, or doesn't know, what needs to be done. The student farm's best educational result is an experience of sustainability on the part of students. Student work should yield the realization that the students are both personally effective and necessary and that they belong to the larger group and to the place itself. The farm should become theirs. This sense of attachment to a place and to a group comes only from care, carefully applied. That is sustainability. This experience will serve as a reference point for students for years to come. Encourage an economic reality and intensity within an educational context so that production and educational obligations can inform one another. Remember that the educational farm exists within a community: it should be a public place, open to passive experience of the agricultural process, the involvement of children, and celebration. In this way, the farm can become a force for the creation and maintenance of local culture. The farm can support community, even as the community supports the farm. Finally, acknowledge the privilege of such good work.

STUDENT REFLECTIONS

A PEAS Farm Journal

BRIANNA EWERT

August 21, 2009: It is my afternoon to water. Ethan and I were working in the fields after lunch, but he left to get a few more parts for the tractor. I have to move one more set of pipes and switch the water, but for now I am sitting on the porch, enjoying the quiet. There was a hawk flying over earlier, so I am also keeping an eye on the chickens. Those hens munched on quite a few of our vegetables, but I'd rather not see any of them get snagged.

Watering makes me remember the beginning of the summer. The first time I had weekend watering responsibilities, the very first week on the farm, I was so nervous that I made Josh give me a list of everything that needed to be watered, in what order and for how long. I marched around all weekend, moving pipes, clutching that list. Everything survived. Watering last weekend was an entirely different experience. Now I know what to look for, how to check the moisture in the soil, what the water needs of different crops are at different stages, how to consider the weather conditions, and I feel comfortable making the decisions myself. I can fix a stuck "rainbird" (and most of the other problems that come up) and have a whole new irrigation vocabulary: *handline, mainline, ball valve, riser, end cap.*

Every morning when I get to the farm, I swear you can see the changes in the fields. The pumpkins are bigger by the day. Tomatoes and peppers are ripening. Garlic is hanging in the barn rafters to cure. The killdeer nest that we carefully worked around in the corn field is long abandoned, and the last time I saw the chicks they were clear on the other side of the farm, no longer fuzzy puffballs. Already there are signs that the growing season is winding down. The pea trellises are long gone, replaced by a cover crop, and, one by one, other beds are going the same way. Watering is getting easier and easier now that the spring greens are done. We can no longer move the handlines in the pumpkin patch or the other squash beds. The leafy, prickly jungle is impossible to walk through. After I harvested zucchini this week, my arms were covered in tiny cuts. The CSA members are getting as tired of zucchini as I am of harvesting it, but are they thrilled with everything else! We had nineteen vegetables in the share this week. One of the members passed on a recipe for cold zucchini soup that I want to try, and Lori gave me the recipe for zucchini pizza crust she made for our lunch one day.

Cooking lunch for the crew is easy now with so many vegetables. Last week, a group of college guidance counselors visited the farm. Young Bri and I made a giant salad and dressing with our vegetables and herbs to serve them for lunch. (If she's Young Bri, I guess that makes me Old Bri.) She had all sorts of ideas for what to include in the salad. Quite a change from when the high school workers hadn't ever eaten most of the vegetables we grow.

Summer is almost over. Classes begin next week. It's hard to believe it has been almost two months since we camped out in the onion patch on the summer solstice, the turning point that tells the onions to stop growing bigger tops and start filling out their bulbs. But the days are still warm and long. I have been jumping in the creek behind the fields most afternoons in between weeding and harvesting. Last night the farm crew came over for a potluck at my house, and we hung out on the deck. After the sun finally set, we walked back over here and dipped in the creek again. Tonight we are going to hear Jeff's band play. When classes start, I know that I will still be up here two mornings a week and that I will still hang out with the farm crew, but I am going to miss the daily routine of outdoor work and the comfortable camaraderie we share. I am more settled in to Missoula than I ever could have expected in just three months. The rest of the farm crew have become my close friends and a support network. Anywhere I go in town, I bump into someone I know, whether it is a CSA member or a high school worker or a volunteer or a local farmer. I could not be better situated for starting graduate school in a new place on the other side of the country from home. I will miss being on the farm every day, but I am grateful for this place.

Brianna Ewert graduated from Harvard University in 2003. After five years working as a teacher and volunteering on small farms, she is currently a graduate student in the Environmental Studies Program, with a focus on sustainable agriculture, at the University of Montana and works at the PEAS Farm.

◆ Part 4 ◆

New Directions

12

University of British Columbia (2000)

The Improbable Farm in the World City

MARK BOMFORD

When the founders of the University of British Columbia (UBC) articulated the need for a university farm in 1910, their decision was based on simple math. Situated among more than 1 million acres of soils "as good as can be found in the world," on the doorstep of the rapidly growing port city of Vancouver, the commissioners assigned to find the best site for the university forecast what seemed to be an inevitable agricultural future. By their calculations, the future university would serve hundreds of thousands of agriculturists who would "maintain affluence" on the small but productive market farms, orchards, and dairies that the soils and climate could ably support.[1] "Canada will always be an agricultural country," the commissioners declared, adding: "The largest part of her wealth will always be derived from the products of the soil and the greatest number of her population will always be tillers of the earth."[2]

One hundred years after that forecast was made, it is clear that something didn't work out with the math. Out of 2.5 million residents in the Vancouver region, the 2006 census identified roughly four thousand farm operators whose incomes derived principally from farming, with an average age of fifty-four.[3] That's less than one-fifth of 1 percent of the region's population. So, when in 2008 more than fifteen thousand signatures appeared on a petition urging UBC's president to preserve the university farm, it was a powerful indication that the UBC Farm stood for something much more than farming as the census defined it. The UBC Farm had followed a tangled hundred-year path of fragmentation, displacement, and marginalization and, through a decade of student-led reinvention, had now gained a hopeful new identity at the forefront of an urban movement.

This chapter discusses some of the more prominent twists and turns of the UBC Farm's century-long journey and also provides a snapshot of how the current student-centered farm initiative specifically operates. In discussing the challenges and successes of the UBC Farm through time, a number of regionally and globally significant themes will be identified that have particular relevance to student-led farming initiatives across North America. Finally, in summarizing the aspirations of the farm's new academic plan, *Cultivating Place*, some key trends will be discussed that underscore the importance of maintaining working farms to engage urban populations.

BEGINNINGS

The importance of agriculture was indisputable when UBC was founded. In 1909, a group of commissioners recruited from established universities in eastern Canada, the United States, and Britain were tasked with finding a permanent site for a new provincial university. All the different disciplines had to be placed together, it was reasoned, in order to constitute a coherent whole. Since an agricultural college needed a rural location, the university as a whole needed to find a rural location.[4] When the commissioners recommended a site seven miles to the west of downtown Vancouver, perched above the Strait of Georgia on the Point Grey plateau, it was contingent on the agricultural suitability of the land. The commissioners recommended a site of at least seven hundred acres for agricultural teaching and research.[5]

The commissioners' recommendations were followed, though on a smaller scale. The seven-hundred-acre farm vision was pared down to two hundred acres, and land clearing and improvements for agriculture commenced well before any permanent academic buildings were constructed. When students made their 1922 "great trek" march to Point Grey from their temporary downtown classrooms to demand that the province kick-start the stalled construction of the university, the agricultural fields around the partially constructed buildings were already well established and in use for research work. When the province resumed construction of the campus in response to the students' efforts, the agriculture building was one of the first to be completed, amid the fields and orchards that defined the early campus landscape.[6]

Early growth on the university farm was set back during the Great Depression. Many horticultural plantings died or were abandoned. The dairy facilities were leased to the farm manager, formerly on the university payroll, who maintained the dairy herd as a commercial operation. By supplying milk to the nearby community, the farm was able to stay afloat through the 1930s even though all academic programs were severely cut back.

Following the Second World War, all faculties scrambled to meet the training needs of returning veterans. The Faculty of Agriculture's training in farm management included a mandatory practicum, often fulfilled at the UBC Farm.[7] The postwar boom also initiated the university's largest-ever expansion effort. The final phase of this two-decade expansion saw the relocation of the remaining farmlands to the "outer boondocks" of south campus, creating space for more than one hundred acres of parking lots, playing fields, and residences for the growing student body.[8]

ROOMS IN THE FOREST

When the move to south campus began, the university farm was allocated to different departments and divisions within the Faculty of Agriculture, with the Division of Plant Science, the Division of Animal Science, and the Department of Poultry Science all requiring new field sites. The Department of Plant Science was tasked by the university administration with choosing the most suitable area for future crop production somewhere in the 280-acre south campus triangle. The pioneering naturalist and one-time department head Bert Brink writes of bushwhacking over a period of five years in the dense second-growth forest in the area looking for the best location for potential crop production.[9] The complex of new research facilities on south campus was envisioned as occupying "rooms in the forest." Separated by treed walls, each discipline would have its own private enclave: animal science here, zoology over there; botany in this room, plant science in that room. Each discipline could pursue its particular specialization in its own area, planned according to the principles of a well-organized academic factory. *UBC Reports* relayed the sounds of progress—"the snarl of chainsaws, the crack of stump blasting and the growl of big clearing and log-yarding carts"[10]—as the forest came down in carefully delineated parcels. Work on animal barns, nursery facilities, and a high-energy physics research center proceeded shortly after the initial clearing. Faculty members whose work involved cultivating soil for crop production, however, still had nearly a decade of work ahead of them.

Coastal, upland forest soils represent much of British Columbia's land base.[11] It's possible for a farm to thrive on these soils, as Eliot Coleman's inspiring market garden guides attest, but the preparation involved is substantial.[12] These soils are formed from a glacial till. After clearing trees, stumps, and roots, you're left with something that is acidic, nutrient poor, and gravelly: a challenge for food crops and brutal for cultivation equipment. The cool, moderate coastal climate, however, creates ideal conditions for building up plenty of organic matter, and, with the right long-term cover-cropping strategies and stubborn rock picking, it is possible to grow a wide range of crops. The demanding preparations on south campus were completed by the Department of Plant Science in the late 1960s and early 1970s. Drainage tile and irrigation installation were followed by years of rock-picking work parties.[13] When students rediscovered the farm in 2000, they found a well-developed topsoil layer and organic matter levels in excess of 10 percent throughout the cleared areas: perfect to start growing in.

THE SHIFT TO SCIENCE

In the late 1960s, as the farm prepared for its move to south campus, a change was also happening in the organization of the Faculty of Agriculture. The increasing emphasis on laboratory-based specializations and deemphasis on farming led to a name change, from the Faculty of Agriculture to the Faculty of Agricultural Sciences.[14] Part of this shift reflected the general consolidation and industrialization under way in agriculture across the country. Canada's history of separating agricultural research, training, and extension services may have exacerbated this trend. Canada has no direct equivalent of the U.S. land-grant university system.[15] When the Experimental Farm Station Act was passed in 1886, most Canadian provinces did not yet have universities.[16] When the faculty changed its name in 1969, the university's formally sanctioned role was to train scientists, not to train farmers (now the responsibility of vocational colleges) or to provide extension services (now the responsibility of the provincial government). The vast majority of public research money available for agriculture was directed toward the federal experimental stations, leaving universities to pursue mostly industry-supported research.[17]

The momentum away from the field and into the lab had changed the tenor of the faculty by the 1990s. After a proposal to build a particle accelerator threatened to displace much of the farm once again in the early 1990s, new research projects and further soil improvement work tapered off.[18] The dairy herd was relocated from its south campus barn to a federal research farm one hundred miles away from campus in 1995. In 1997, the university's new Official Community Plan was finalized, designating the poultry and animal science barns as "housing reserve" and the plant science fields as "future housing reserve."[19] It looked as though the days of farming on campus were numbered.

SAVING THE FARM

In 1999, a confluence of factors turned this trend upside down, beginning a decade of sustained and effective student activism. The new dean of agricultural sciences had dissolved the faculty's departmental structure the year before, overhauling the undergraduate program, and creating new degrees in agroecology, global resource systems, and food, nutrition, and health.[20] Students in these new programs were encouraged to think broadly about sustainability issues and to engage themselves in real-world, practical, and often self-directed research problems. For these students, the south campus farm held the potential to bring all these pieces together in a meaningful way, blending sustainability theory with sustainability in practice.

On November 25, 1999, agriculture students filled a public meeting that detailed upcoming plans for housing development on campus. Students expressed the need to retain farmland for their education and raised the possibility of making the university town unique and forward looking by retaining and incorporating agriculture into its urban setting.[21] After this meeting, students formed a farm committee with faculty and staff members and, working with a graduate student whose thesis focused on south campus, published a vision paper: "Re-Inventing the UBC Farm." Fully endorsed by the dean, and published through the faculty, the paper examined the entire campus land base affiliated with agriculture and forestry, including the botanical gardens and the south campus farm areas, and proposed that they be managed in a unified way, providing a full suite of sustainability-related teaching and research activities.[22]

The livestock barns on the south campus farm were part of a housing reserve whose designation and fate were effectively finalized. The forest-ringed south fields, however, were designated as a *"future* housing reserve" and, as such, were protected from any housing development for a period of fifteen years. The process laid out in the official community plan was to wait until 2012, confirm that the site was not required for academic purposes, and, if this condition was met, proceed with the final build-out of the university town.[23] As students worked together in the field in a growing number of teaching and research projects, they also engaged the long-term-planning process directly. During the following years, an increasing number of farm advocates were successfully elected to executive positions within student government. They joined university planning committees and lobbied for the preservation of the farm at committee meetings. They launched an on-farm symposium and an annual "FarmAde" festival to highlight the integrated academic and community programs thriving at the farm. In 2005, after working for several years primarily under the umbrella of the Agriculture Sciences Undergraduate Student Society, they formed a formally constituted club, Friends of the Farm, as part of the university-wide Alma Mater Society. Friends of the Farm was now open to students and nonstudents alike, and, by 2008, it had grown in ranks to over seven hundred members.

As the 2012 deadline drew closer, Friends of the Farm shifted its activities from general outreach efforts to a more focused campaign to save the farm. During the summer of 2008, a new draft campus plan released three future scenarios for the UBC Farm, all of which implied significant reductions in the land available for farm-based programming and the consequent relocation of activities.[24]

The public consultations held that summer and fall were packed with students, faculty, staff, and community members. Preservation of the farm dominated the discussions.[25] Letters to the president's office swelled in number to the point where the fate of the farm became the single issue generating the most correspondence in UBC's recent history. Paper and online petitions were circulated. Letters of support arrived from both individuals and organizations, including the regional health authority, citizen advisory groups, influential nongovernment organizations, and elected officials. An "I ♥ UBC Farm" slogan soon appeared on bumper stickers, posters, buttons, and blogs around the city. Front-page newspaper coverage and attention from television and radio presented strong profarm messages. Three elections in late 2008 prompted candidates at the municipal, provincial, and even federal levels to issue statements in support of the farm. Student leaders presented a stack of petitions with fifteen thousand signatures to UBC's president shortly before a packed meeting of elected officials from municipalities through the region passed a unanimous motion of support urging the university to maintain the farm at its current twenty-four-hectare size (roughly sixty acres) and location.

Professionals from the community, mostly UBC alumni, including several internationally renowned architects, planners, landscape architects, and agrologists (licensed professional agricultural scientists in Canada), donated their time and expertise to organize a farm-specific visioning workshop. The workshop brought together more than two hundred expert stakeholders, including faculty, staff, students, aboriginal groups, and government and nongovernment representatives. Aided by eighty professional designers and artists from firms around Vancouver, the shared visions of attendees took shape as vivid plans, artistic renderings, and brainstormed notes filled over five hundred sheets of flipchart and vellum.

On December 3, 2008, UBC's Board of Governors requested a new academic plan for the twenty-four-hectare area on south campus.[26] As a twelve-member multifaculty academic committee began to assemble the new plan, students organized a spring "Great Farm Trek," in reference to the original 1922 student trek that persuaded the provincial government to build the new university on Point Grey. On April 7, 2009, over two thousand students and community members trekked from the Student Union Building to the UBC Farm. The atmosphere was upbeat, festive, and celebratory, with live music and supportive speeches from Vancouver's newly elected mayor, Gregor Robertson (a former organic farmer), and the prominent environmental scientist David Suzuki. Shortly after the crowd reached the farm, UBC's president unveiled a new permanent sign at the farm gates and joined student and community leaders in planting trees in a newly established hedgerow.[27] That summer, an outdoor talk and book signing by the author Michael Pollan, a steady stream of field dinners, and the most successful growing season to date buoyed spirits considerably, building general optimism that the farm had, indeed, been saved.

REINVENTING THE FARM

Early Challenges and Successes

Projects on the "new" UBC Farm took root in the summer of 2000. A team of students, working under the guidance of a graduate student and the south campus animal science farm manager, proceeded with an inventory and cleanup of the field site in the summer of 2000. Through the fall and winter leading into 2001, a small group of committed students worked on a range of farm-based class projects. One of these projects, completed as a term project for a business management course, was a business plan for a hypothetical market garden on the new south campus farm. In the summer of 2001, the student-led market garden followed this plan, broke ground, and began planting a range of crops. Plowing up sod that had been established for over twenty years, the garden suffered devastating losses from the voracious wireworm populations. Despite crop losses approaching 90 percent, spirits remained high as the community began to discover and enthusiastically embrace the new UBC Farm. Volunteers from campus and nearby neighborhoods joined students to work in the field. The public came to buy produce from students at sales from an old toolshed on Saturday mornings.

The combination of an economic downturn following the dot-com crash and a new provincial government pursuing massive program cutbacks meant that there were few grant opportunities from either public or private sources in 2002. The students who were employed to develop the farm's teaching and volunteer programs worked on month-to-month contracts, with no certainty of continued employment. The manager and technicians still working at the old south campus livestock barns did what they could to help, auctioning off animals and farm equipment, and retaining only a single tractor. By the summer of 2003, however, every source of funding that had supported the farm through its first three seasons had dried up. Faced with a large deficit of its own, the Faculty of Agricultural Sciences was forced to close the south campus livestock unit, laying off some key staff people who were instrumental in supporting the UBC Farm's early administration and operations. The farm's programming coordinator and family also found themselves homeless: their residence in the old milker's quarters at the dairy barn was now gone. With no money to pay students and the departure of staff, the farm was left with a field, a tractor, and a vision.

Fortunately, this vision proved far too compelling to wither and die. Even during a period of hibernation during the winter of 2003–2004, new people and projects came to the farm. The Faculty of Education was successful in securing funding to expand the children's garden and develop it into a busy intergenerational pedagogical research program. The Faculty of Science held an intensive field course, "The Science and Practice of Sustainability," at the farm, bringing students to study and live on-site in the summer. The university's Alma Mater Society was able to fund student positions to keep the volunteer program running, the Global Resource

Systems Program helped establish a fledgling practicum field course for its international students, and a grant from a community foundation helped keep the farmers market growing. Remarkably, amid the setbacks of funding cuts, layoffs, staff departures, and facility closures, the farm continued to grow on every front. Staffed entirely by students often working for little more than course credit, and operating like a hybrid small business and nonprofit society, the farm saw progress: more veggies were sold, more grants were written, more field area was cultivated, and more committed students, faculty, and community members pushed the UBC Farm on a steady upward trajectory.

The Farm Today

In ten years, this growth trajectory shows no indication of slowing, so describing the farm's operations today is a snapshot in time; a fleeting description of a quickly moving target. In 2010, the UBC Farm operates as an academic facility under the management of the Centre for Sustainable Food Systems, an academic subunit within the larger Faculty of Land and Food Systems. The center is currently led by a program coordinator, who fills financial and human resources management, fund-raising, stakeholder relations, and strategic planning roles. Three full-time and two part-time staff, five contract employees, and seventeen seasonally paid student employees made up the in-house staff at the UBC Farm in 2009. On a typical summer day, however, hundreds (and, on some days, thousands) of people come and go through the gates, including researchers tending their field work, apprentices and course attendees, children, and community groups and individuals arriving to volunteer, shop for produce, or just wander through the fields and forest. In 2009, the farm identified 150 active projects taking place on the twenty-four-hectare site, and each of these projects brought people to the farm.

The roles of the farm staff have shifted over the years as the programs have grown. All except one of the core staff began their careers at the farm first as student volunteers, then as student employees, transitioning into staff roles after graduation. In 2009, one staff member focused solely on academic support, helping students and faculty members with their project designs, scheduling, space allocation, and resource access. The field manager is responsible for overall farm operations, overseeing an integrated soil, crop, and livestock management strategy. A paid field crew takes direction from the field manager and works with volunteers and apprentices to complete field labor tasks. Instruction and coordination of the apprentice/practicum program is shared between two staff members. Finally, an administrative and marketing coordinator keeps the farm's business operations running smoothly, supporting the students and volunteers who operate the farm markets, the CSA (community-supported agriculture) box program, the children's programming, and the workshops.

Farm-gate sales and workshop fees generate roughly 60 percent of the farm's revenue, with the balance coming from grants and donations from many different sources. The farm's total revenues have increased tenfold since 2004, with average year-to-year growth rates of around 50 percent. Wages and benefits typically represent 85 percent of the farm's total expenses in a given year.

Facilities and Equipment

After the closure of the livestock facilities on south campus, the UBC Farm focused its programming on the twenty-four-hectare south field area allocated to the Departments of Plant Science, Forestry, and Botany in the late 1960s.[28] With agreements from each of the original tenants, who had largely abandoned the buildings, the farm gradually moved its programs into two field buildings and two greenhouses constructed during the 1970s and 1980s. After ongoing cleanup, upgrades, and repairs, the farm now houses its offices, kitchen, classroom, shop space, storage, cooler, and processing areas between the two small field buildings. The buildings are crowded and vibrant during the growing season, teeming with staff, students, children, and the general public. Two travel trailers provide homes for live-in caretakers who share a round-the-clock schedule for safety oversight and animal care. Two glass greenhouses and three soil-based polyhouses (high tunnels) provide plant propagation, season extension functions, and additional classroom space.

The UBC Farm inherited a fifty-five-horsepower John Deere tractor when the livestock facilities closed. Building a supply of field implements and tools has been an incremental process largely determined by year-end surpluses from market sales. The farm purchased a new Kubota compact tractor in 2006 and has been able to add a range of cultivation, planting, mowing, and spreading implements to its inventory on an annual basis.

Fields, Gardens, and Markets

Until 2007, adding new field projects was accomplished by turning over more sod to create new cultivated areas. The supply of readily arable land on the site having been exhausted, program growth is now accomplished through intensifying the use of existing fields or, increasingly, clearing blackberry (*Rubus armeniacus*) at the edges of the forest. As field activities continue to diversify and intensify, a detailed integrated land management plan is emerging, including the formalization of a long-term annual crop rotation into nine reasonably uniform quarter-hectare (roughly half-acre) fields. The rotation allows for a range of specific research and teaching projects to be integrated into an overarching planned annual cropping sequence. The gently sloping section in the center of the farm is now being planted to perennial crops, including a heritage orchard with seventy different apple cultivars and blueberry fields established in 2009. The remains of a vineyard planted in the early 1970s have been restored in the perennial area, and the vines are now flanked on either side by a truffle orchard and a hop yard, both undergoing soil preparation and awaiting planting in 2010. The farm maintains a flock of approximately 150 laying hens that rotate through the fields, with breeds and grazing configurations changing from year to year depending on the research objectives being pursued. Crop rotations are being planned to optimize continuity in forage for our honeybee hives, and a plan is under way to incorporate beef cattle into the rotation for overwinter grazing trials. The addition of diverse hedgerows throughout the farm is leading to a more dedicated forest management strategy. With the arrival of eager forestry classes at the farm in 2009, we envision more activity in the twelve-hectare forest perimeter that currently is used for botany and agroforestry courses and for traditional indigenous medicinal, ceremonial, and food plant harvests in the farm's land-based aboriginal programs.

A range of specialized gardens sit at the forest edge. The children's garden features permanent raised beds and wide pathways, a cob toolshed, oven, and archway, and shelters and washing stations for classes. Individual plots for our apprentices offer spaces to experiment with different plants and techniques independent of the main fields. Several medicinal plant gardens and garden spaces managed in partnership with the Musqueam First Nation, the Urban Aboriginal Community Kitchen Garden Project, and the Maya in Exile project incorporate traditional indigenous knowledge and practice into the farm landscape.

Most of our fields provide abundant harvests of high-quality produce in addition to their primary learning and research functions. Hundreds of varieties of vegetables, as well as fruit, berries, herbs, flowers, honey, and eggs, are all sold to the campus community through a variety of channels. The Saturday morning farmers markets and the expanding thirty-

Figure 12.1. The farm's honeybees pollinate our crops, produce honey for sale, form the basis of an immunology research program in the Faculty of Medicine, and have come to symbolize the integrative principle "no one thing does just one thing." (Courtesy Linda Fiechter.)

box CSA program both run from June to November. Campus food service outlets, nearby Vancouver restaurants, and some specialty retail outlets all buy from the farm. Our commitment to manage the entire site to meet or exceed provincial standards for organic certification and our high profile in the community typically means that demand for farm produce far outstrips supply. One of our largest challenges at the markets—now mostly resolved with three cash registers operating at all times—has been dealing with long lines and early sell-out times.

Academic Programming

Following the agriculturally centered vision of "Re-Inventing the UBC Farm," the farm added more course work, student-directed projects, community-service initiatives, and faculty-led research projects on an annual basis. With the publication and acceptance of a new academic plan, *Cultivating Place,* in late 2009, the proliferation of projects on the site now has a more focused framework and vision as well as some ambitious targets for further growth. *Cultivating Place* firmly positions the farm as a university-wide resource, still hosted administratively within the Faculty of Land and Food Systems, but with academic objectives that engage every discipline.

Perhaps because the students who rediscovered the south campus site in 2000 were struck by the destructive legacy left by the disciplinary fragmentation of the past, the farm has adopted the motto "no one thing does just one thing." The first principle of our academic programming is *integration*. To illustrate this principle, we often use the example of a farm-based butternut squash pizza sold every fall in the student union building. A bite of this pizza can be connected back to the farm's hives of pollinating honeybees on a multidisciplinary path that engaged business students in a marketing plan, food science students in a nutritional analysis, agroecology students in a cultivation and soil management plan, applied science faculty researchers in a biofertilizer field trial, and Faculty of Medicine researchers studying the immune system of the honeybees that were responsible for pollinating the squash blossoms. By layering and stacking multiple academic objectives into every component at the farm, the goal is to build a whole that is far greater than the sum of its parts.

Through curricular and cocurricular teaching and learning, more than twenty-five hundred students currently participate in on-farm activities annually. Students in fifty courses representing eight faculties as well as four UBC schools and both colleges actively used the farm in 2008.[29] On-farm learning is integrative—bridging multiple disciplines and traditions—and inherently applied, providing community service, participation in research projects, and active stewardship of the landscape. The farm's part-time, year-long practicum course caters to students enrolled in degree programs at UBC as well as the general public.

Among the farm's academic initiatives in 2009 were a range of research projects hosted by six different UBC faculties. These initiatives touched on topics of climate change, community health, food security, and ecosystem services. Research on-site included next-generation biofuel development and basic research in evolutionary biology (science), behavioral neuroscience (arts), mass spectrometry-based proteomics (medicine), biofertilizer development (applied science), animal welfare, avian genetics, and soil conservation (land and food systems).

The farm serves as an important point of connection and engagement for UBC. With farm visits reaching forty thousand in 2009, faculty and

students joined international visitors and the wider community to participate in courses and workshops, contribute to public events and festivals,
support student-led enterprises, and build important partnerships with
nonprofit, private-sector, and government organizations.

The farm's community engagement strategy blurs the traditional lines
between the academy and the community. Participating in a range of community service learning projects and community-based action research initiatives both on and off the farm, students and faculty act as agents of
change. The Urban Aboriginal Community Kitchen Garden Project that
takes place at the farm provides a good example of this kind of integrated
project. In 2009, the Urban Aboriginal Community Kitchen Garden Project brought more than seven hundred people from Vancouver's Downtown
Eastside and from coastal Aboriginal communities to the UBC Farm,
where they worked together in this comprehensive community health initiative. In collaboration with UBC's Institute for Aboriginal Health and
researchers in the Faculty of Land and Food Systems, participants cultivated and gathered foods in the fields and the forest, preserved salmon in
a smokehouse, and prepared food and feasts linked with cultural traditions
as a strategy to address a number of health challenges, including diabetes.
The individual and community health effects of the program have been
far-reaching and are being explored and replicated in other coastal BC
communities.

CULTIVATING PLACE

On the tenth anniversary of the packed community meeting in 1999, a
new academic plan for south campus was presented to the UBC Board of
Governors. *Cultivating Place: An Academic Plan for Applied Sustainability
on South Campus and Beyond* received full executive endorsement and was
warmly received by the board, followed by successful presentations to the
university senate. *Cultivating Place* recommended retaining the twenty-
four-hectare farm and forest site and using its interface with surrounding
areas as a "world class academic resource and a central part of UBC's sustainability aspirations."[30] The academic programming is envisioned to be
cross-faculty and collaborative in nature, utilizing the entire web of farm,
forest, and community connections as a living laboratory and an agent of
social change. The planning committee collected almost a decade's worth
of visioning material, including the plans that emerged from the 2008
design workshop, synthesizing a plan that reflected a broad range of inter-

ests. Students joined faculty members on the committee that prepared the new academic plan during the summer of 2009, continuing the strong tradition of student leadership that first sparked the vision for the UBC Farm. In contrast to the approach that carved out disciplinary "rooms in the forest" in the 1960s, *Cultivating Place* envisions a working farm that is much more than an agricultural enterprise and student leadership that works hand-in-hand with faculty, staff, and the wider community.

The *Cultivating Place* vision for the UBC Farm may seem ambitious for an organization that has spent much of its existence with an uncertain future. Its goals, however, reflect a recent history of rapid growth in a particular context. Our home university envisions itself as world leading, the city of Vancouver has branded itself as a "Green Capital" and positioned itself as a world city, and our province formally markets itself as, simply, "the best place on earth."[31] Our aspirations are in sync with this optimism. Ingrained in this vision is an appeal to the power held by the urban population: it's up to you to save your food supply. The privilege of dwelling in the world's most livable city is tempered with the responsibility of knowing what makes it livable and taking action to sustain and support that livability.

How Do We Value Land?

The programs and vision of the UBC Farm reflect its distinctly urban context, aiming to build a bridge between cities—in the global sense—and the rural footprints that sustain them. Urbanization is a global phenomenon and represents the largest human migration in history. The year 2007 marked the first time in history that a majority of the world's population resided in urban areas, and the next 2 billion people to live on this planet will live in cities.[32] For an urban consumer, food comes from an apparent "global everywhere, yet from nowhere . . . in particular," that defies easy visualization.[33] We are now four generations removed from the days when agriculture employed over one-third of the Canadian population. Fifteen years ago, when a UBC graduate student developed the "ecological footprint" tool to express complex data in a convenient land-based equivalent, firsthand understanding of the land and what it provided was already a distant memory to most of us living in cities.[34]

The UBC Farm's growth and success reflect the last decade's groundswell of efforts to reconnect urban residents with the source of their food. Ecological footprint analysis indicates that the food system's greatest impacts occur before produce leaves the farm gate, so the recent efforts to reconnect farms and cities though the growth of farmers markets, the reduction of food miles, and the expansion of community gardens may not offer city dwellers a complete picture of the impacts of their food choices.[35] A field in agricultural production looks and behaves very differently than an urban garden plot. The average Canadian's three-hectare "food-print" is composed of fields where native soils grow grains, forage, vegetables, fruit orchards, rangelands, and forests as well as uncultivated areas that can capture and balance the carbon in the system.[36] Bringing all these elements into one place in the midst of the city creates an improbable and essential hybrid, one that simultaneously brings the "global everywhere" and the "nowhere" back home.

In Vancouver's internationally acclaimed high-density residential areas, it is not uncommon for more than 150 people to live on a single hectare of land.[37] Living at these densities can be relatively energy efficient on a per-person basis, as each urban apartment dweller requires far less energy for heating and transportation than does a person living in a suburban or a rural setting. When it comes to food, however, living in a high-density city necessitates and reinforces the continued dependence on a rural food-producing hinterland. The global reality of increased urbanization goes hand in hand with a global imperative to carefully steward our remaining rural food-producing lands. Working at cross-purposes with this imperative is the pressure that urbanization exerts on the way we value land.

Perceived land value in an urbanizing society represents the UBC Farm's primary challenge. The question, "Can't this land be used for something better?" arises in many forms and demands an ongoing dialogue about how society values its agricultural land base. Critics contend that, by distorting the fair market value of land, our province's thirty-seven-year-old agricultural land reserve is to blame for Vancouver's status as Canada's least affordable city.[38] Proponents argue that the land reserve has made Vancouver the most livable city in the world, creating a containment zone that encourages a compact urban form and accessible green space.[39] The UBC Farm brings this dialogue away from the fringes of the city and into its core, engaging the dense concentration of people and policymakers who ultimately wield the greatest power. The farm's position as a change agent is highly leveraged, exposing it to the risks of speculative land valuation—but also to the rewards of changing an entire city's relationship with the land and food.

The UBC Farm and agriculture in the wider province of British

Columbia have shared one hundred years moving along largely parallel trajectories. With the UBC Farm and agriculture in general in British Columbia now surrounded by city, urbanization presents a serious threat at the same time as it offers a great opportunity. There is a growing understanding of the fundamental importance of agriculture to an urban population and agriculture's essential connections to health, ecology, global climate change, community, culture, and long-term urban viability. At the basis of the farm's reinvention is a belief that our role is to address not simply agricultural sustainability but rather the wide range of issues that underpin the continued existence of cities. As the UBC Farm engages urban people with a broad spectrum of interests, it aims to build urban-rural relationships that provide strong mutual benefits. If a city is to sustain its global life support systems, it must first understand what these systems are and how they work: not just where food comes from, but also how managed ecosystems capture and transform the energy needed to run cities, how they assimilate and productively recycle urban outputs, and how they can provide places for rich and transformative learning experiences. A working farm system in the midst of a city provides the essential microcosm to accomplish all this.

STUDENT REFLECTIONS

FIGHTING TO SAVE THE FARM

ANDREA MORGAN

The UBC Farm exhibits something that few universities can: a working, urban, organic research farm that displays and teaches some of the most fundamental components and practices of sustainability today. Though often undervalued at a university where life sciences, biotechnology, and business dominate, the farm is the heart of some of the most foresighted, creative, and essential research initiatives and programming on campus and, in my opinion, the world. The place is magnetic. It is one of the few remaining places on campus with soul and energy. The students and Vancouverites who come to the farm, whatever the reason may be, have a sparkle in their eyes and a refreshing eagerness in their demeanor. The farm makes youth, vitality, and the sweetness of food and nature feel abundant in a world that continues to degrade these fundamental gifts in life. When you are there, you can feel that it is special. When you survey the farm's diverse landscape, you know you're looking at an interconnected web of complex human and ecological bonds, the essential links we've managed to unravel to an overwhelming degree.

Some people have been telling me that the fight to save the farm is a lost cause. They tell me I should start going to class again and get more sleep. But, when I look into the eyes of the people I'm working with on this so-called campaign, I get choked up because I know they are my family, even though I barely know some of them. We are truly fighting for our futures together, and we are driven by something unexplainable. We also know we are right. Most of us are very young and inexperienced, and most of us are urbanites! But we are choosing to look beyond dominant paradigms and seemingly unbreakable powers-that-be because we know a better world is possible. For us, a little taste of that world begins at the UBC Farm.

Andrea Morgan graduated from the Faculty of Land and Food Systems at the University of British Columbia in 2010. She was president of Friends of the UBC Farm from 2008 to 2009 and is currently a UBC Farm staff member. These reflections were excerpted from a course assignment written in February 2009, in the midst of a decade of student efforts to secure a long-term future for the UBC Farm.

NOTES

1. Lower Mainland University Committee, *University Location in British Columbia: A Summary of the Arguments Presented by the Lower Mainland University Committee to the University Sites Commission Appointed to Fix the Location of the Provincial University of British Columbia,* June 1910, www.library.ubc.ca/archives/pdfs/misc/site.pdf.

2. John L. Todd, *Concerning the Choice of a Site for the University of British Columbia,* www.library.ubc.ca/archives/pdfs/misc/concerning_the_choice_of_a_site.pdf.

3. Statistics Canada, 2006 Census of Agriculture, "Farm Data and Farm Operator Data: Characteristics of Farm Operators," www.statcan.gc.ca/pub/95-629-x/2007000/4182410-eng.htm.

4. Todd, *Concerning the Choice of a Site for the University of British Columbia.*

5. Harry T. Logan, *Tuum Est: A History of the University of British Columbia* (Vancouver: University of British Columbia, 1958).

6. Robert Blair and Catherine Nichols, "Faculty History: UBC Faculty of Land and Food Systems," 2005, www.landfood.ubc.ca/faculty-history.

7. Ibid.

8. "Campus Spreading across Agronomy," *The Ubyssey* (University of British Columbia), September 14, 1965.

9. Bert Brink to Dr. Arthur Bomke, October 20, 1999, "Concerning the Lands Assigned to the Faculty of Agriculture," UBC Farm archives.

10. "UBC to Develop 60-Acre Botanical Garden," *UBC Reports* 12, no. 3 (June 1966): 1–4.

11. L. M. Lavkulich, "Soils: Soil Landscapes of BC: Part 2, The Major Soils and Soil Processes of British Columbia," 1978, www.env.gov.bc.ca/soils/landscape/part2.html.

12. Eliot Coleman, *The New Organic Grower: A Master's Manual of Tools and Techniques for the Home and Market Gardener* (White River Junction, VT: Chelsea Green, 1989).

13. Peter Garnett, interview with the author, 2006.

14. Blair and Nichols, "Faculty History."

15. Howard Steppler, "Agricultural Education," 2010, www.thecanadianencyclopedia.com/index.cfm?PgNm=TCE&Params=A1ARTA0000064.

16. Michael Shaw, "Aggies Look to the Future," *UBC Reports* 17, no. 17 (October 27, 1971): 6–7.

17. Ibid.

18. Derek James Masselink, *The UBC South Campus Farm: The Elaboration of an Alternative* (Vancouver: University of British Columbia, 2001).

19. The University of British Columbia, "Official Community Plan for Part of Electoral Area 'A,'" available at http://www.planning.ubc.ca/database/rte/files/UBC-OCP-only-05Nov.pdf.

20. N. Gudz, "Implementing the Sustainable Development Policy at the University of British Columbia," *International Journal of Sustainability in Higher Education* 5, no. 2 (2004): 2.

21. University of British Columbia, "Meeting Minutes—Public Information Meeting, 25 November 1999" (copy in author's files).

22. Moura Quayle, Derek Masselink, and Anthony Brunetti, "Re-Inventing the UBC Farm: Urban Agriculture and Forestry on the Point Grey Campus," University of British Columbia, Faculty of Agricultural Sciences, February 17, 2000.

23. UBC, "Official Community Plan."

24. Kirk & Co. Consulting, "UBC Vancouver Campus Plan Review Phase 4—Three Design Options," January 30, 2009, http://campusplan.ubc.ca/docs/pdf/Phase4_ConSumReport_Jan09.pdf.

25. Ibid.

26. UBC Public Affairs, "UBC Board of Governors Requests New Academic Plan for Sustainable South Campus," media release, December 1, 2008, www.publicaffairs.ubc.ca/media/releases/2008/mr-08-156.html.

27. UBC Public Affairs, "New UBC Farm Sign Unveiled at Preservation Celebration," media release, April 8, 2009, www.publicaffairs.ubc.ca/media/releases/2009/mr-09-farm.html.

28. Jordan Kamburoff, "Everyone Has a Stake in Planning," *UBC Reports* 20, no. 15 (November 20, 1974): 2.

29. Mark Bomford and Andrew Riseman, *Cultivating Place: An Academic Plan for Applied Sustainability on South Campus and Beyond* (Vancouver: University of British Columbia, 2010).

30. Ibid.

31. The University of British Columbia, "Place and Promise: The UBC Plan," http://strategicplan.ubc.ca/the-plan/vision-statement; City of Vancouver, "Vancouver Green Capital," 2009, http://vancouver.ca/greencapital/index.htm; Province of British Columbia, "British Columbia: The Best Place on Earth," www.gov.bc.ca.

32. C. Matthews, "Urban Farming against Hunger: Safe, Fresh Food for City Dwellers," *FAO Newsroom*, February 1, 2007, www.fao.org/newsroom/en/news/2007/1000484/index.html.

33. J. Kloppenburg, J. Hendrickson, and G. W. Stevenson, "Coming in to the Foodshed," *Agriculture and Human Values* 13, no. 3 (1996): 33–42.

34. Mathis Wackernagel, *Ecological Footprint and Appropriated Carrying Capacity: A Tool for Planning toward Sustainability* (Vancouver: University of British Columbia, 1994).

35. C. L. Weber and H. S. Matthews, "Food-Miles and the Relative Climate Impacts of Food Choices in the United States," *Environmental Science and Technology* 42, no. 10 (2008): 3508–13.

36. Global Footprint Network, "Footprint for Nations," www.footprintnetwork.org/en/index.php/GFN/page/footprint_for_nations.

37. Statistics Canada, 2006 Census, "2006 Census Tract (CT) Profiles," www12.statcan.gc.ca/census-recensement/2006/dp-pd/prof/92-597/index.cfm?lang=E.

38. Diane Katz, *The BC Agricultural Land Reserve: A Critical Assessment*, Fraser Institute Studies in Risk and Regulation (October 2009), www.fraserinstitute.org/Commerce.Web/product_files/BCAgriculturalLandReserve.pdf; Hugh Pavelitch and Wendell Cox, *Seventh Annual Demographia International Housing Affordability Survey: 2011*, available at http://www.demographia.com/dhi.pdf.

39. Smart Growth BC, "Agricultural Land: Home Grown Food Is Smart Growth," www.smartgrowth.bc.ca/AboutUs/Issues/AgriculturalLand/tabid/111/Default.aspx; "Liveable Vancouver," *Economist*, June 8, 2009, www.economist.com/blogs/gulliver/2009/06/liveable_vancouver.

13

New Mexico State University (2002)

Planting an OASIS

Constance L. Falk and Pauline Pao

The seeds were planted in the field, but nothing was ready to harvest yet. Without a well-developed class schedule, we had time to spare that day in early February 2002. I spaced the letters that spell *OASIS* across the top of the blackboard, and students began brainstorming words that began with each letter as I wrote them vertically underneath. Students began combining words to convert the name of the proposal that had created the class and project (the OASIS guild) into an acronym. None of the combinations generated much enthusiasm until, forty-five minutes into the exercise, one student put together "Organic Agriculture Students Inspiring Sustainability" and everyone recognized it was just right. We had captured the vision for the OASIS class and project in a catchy acronym.

For five years, from that beginning until the end of 2006, the authors of this chapter collaborated in teaching and managing an organic production and community-supported agriculture (CSA) class at New Mexico State University (NMSU), a land-grant university founded in Las Cruces in 1888. It was a profoundly moving and exhilarating, but also difficult, experience. Several years later, the effects the class and project had on this community in Doña Ana County, in southern New Mexico, are starting to become clearer.

The goals of the project were the following:

- Provide an experiential education opportunity for students to learn about organic farming and CSA management.
- Promote the CSA model to the community and to potential CSA farmers in the region.
- Establish a site where integrated teaching, research, and extension activities focused on organic farming could flourish.
- Conduct interdisciplinary research on sustainable and organic farming systems in a desert environment.

OASIS was the first certified organic garden on the NMSU main campus, the first organic vegetable production class to be offered at NMSU, and the first CSA venture in southern New Mexico. A key objective from the outset was to keep detailed production and marketing records in order to be able to precisely document the project's achievements. In five years, the project earned $115,201 in gross income and grew 554 varieties, including 372 cultivars of 39 different vegetables, 32 cultivars of 15 different herbs, and 150 cultivars of 72 flower species on approximately one acre of land (table 13.1). After the first year of production, gross annual income from the CSA memberships averaged about $23,000. One hundred thirty families were OASIS members during the five years of operation; about sixty to seventy full and half vegetable shares were sold each year. After the first two years, flower shares were sold separately from vegetable shares, which also included culinary herbs. Also after the first two years, OASIS did not have to advertise for members; a waiting list of about fifty families was never exhausted.

The class was taught for ten semesters, from spring 2002 through fall 2006. As an upper-division general education class, it was colisted in the Department of Agricultural Business and Agricultural Economics and the Department of Agronomy and Horticulture (now called the Department of Plant and Environmental Sciences). Initially funded by a $147,000 grant from the USDA Hispanic Serving Institutions (HSI) program, the class also carried an Honors College prefix and may have been the first organic CSA production class in any honors program in the country. The students, the CSA members, the Honors College dean, and the community organizations that benefited from OASIS student projects all enthusiastically embraced the class and the CSA. Nevertheless, the class struggled to find sufficient support among the college and university administration to provide the resources to continue the project, and, after five years, the class and project were suspended.

Table 13.1. Summary Statistics from OASIS, 2002–2006					
	2002	**2003**	**2004**	**2005**	**2006**
Gross income ($)	9,000	23,000	26,781	28,585	27,835
Total production of vegetables and herbs (lbs.)	20,111	16,460	18,329	20,620	19,614
Vegetable and herb production (lbs./ linear ft.)	2.07	1.20	1.29	1.21	1.32
Average cost for vegetables and herbs to members ($/lb.)	0.44	1.23	0.92	0.94	1.03
Flower production (no. of vegetables, flowers, and herbs)	1.64	1.15	0.88	1.01	1.01
Cultivars/crops (no. of vegetables, flowers, and herbs)	146/48	160/65	157/77	252/102	108/92
Water efficiency, vegetable and herb production (gals./lb.)	36.81	44.84	53.66	54.79	45.44
Water efficiency, gross income (gals./$)	82.26	32.09	36.73	39.52	32.02
Source: C. L. Falk, P. Pao, C. S. Cramer, and E. Silva, *OASIS: A Campus-Based, Organic, Community Supported Agriculture Farm*, NMSU–AES Research Report 760, May 2008, available at http://aces.nmsu .edu/pubs/research/economics/welcome.html.					

This chapter describes the practical management of and student involvement in the farm, its achievements, and its legacy.

HANDS-ON LEARNING

The classroom was located across the street from the main farm field, about a mile from the main campus, on the NMSU Fabian Garcia Research Center. In the first semester of OASIS (spring 2002), students in the class were all horticulture majors with the exception of one nutrition student. Because the class was not yet part of any official program requirements, the students signed up purely out of interest in the subject matter. Enthusiasm on the part of the instructors, the OASIS farm manager, and the students was palpable: we were all determined to make the project work. Because we had limited organic vegetable farming experience and no experience teaching an on-farm class using the CSA model, we obviously did not know all the answers. So, in the beginning, we tried to foster learn-by-doing attitudes, and students felt free to suggest ideas.

Before many routines were established, students asked questions like,

"Could we try to get landscape waste from the university grounds crew for our compost pile?" We facilitated their investigations and accepted their leadership, even though, in this case, the material turned out to be unscreened and full of debris and resulted in extra work to sift it. It was a learning experience for everyone. When a student suggested that we use laundry baskets as harvest baskets, we did. In these early cases, students were empowered and felt that their input was valued as it directly brought about change. They acquired a sense of accountability and ownership that propagated enthusiasm and dedication.

The classroom doubled as the CSA distribution room, and each Wednesday, for thirty-three to thirty-four weeks during the harvest season, the classroom tables were converted to a U-shape around the room where the vegetables, flowers, and herbs were displayed for the members to pick up, in an open-choice format. Students helped prepare the produce each week, staffed the distribution, and interacted with the members during the two-hour evening period when distribution was held. Because the classroom was on the farm, it greatly facilitated easy movement between the field and the classroom. Often a lecture would end up outside, by the compost pile, digging soil samples or searching for ladybugs.

Students in the class were required to participate in both group and individual creative projects, make an oral presentation about their creative project, and work thirty (later changed to twenty) hours per semester in the field outside class time. Honors students had to engage in an additional ten hours of service learning with a local social service agency or organization addressing hunger or poverty and write a short paper about their experiences.

Getting out into the community was particularly enlightening to the many students who were confronted with the economic and social situation in Doña Ana County, where NMSU is located. According to USDA data, 23 percent of the county population lived in poverty in 2008, including a third of all children under the age of seventeen, despite the fact that the county was (in 2007) the largest contributor to state agricultural income (18 percent). The county's agriculture is devoted primarily to the production of milk, pecans, and a few vegetables (onions, chile, cabbage), most of which is exported out of the region; very little truck farming or direct marketing of local foods existed in the region in 2002.[1]

After a few semesters of experimenting with the class schedule, we settled into a system in which class time was used for the group project, field work (mostly planting and harvesting), guest lectures, and hands-on farm lessons, such as double digging a garden bed or injecting drip tape.[2] The group project was a CSA planning activity in which students were asked to plan an OASIS CSA season on the basis of our preset number of shares. Their planning activity involved cultivar selection, bed and linear-feet allocation by vegetable cultivar, seed cost estimations, and field layout. They were asked to fit their plan into a set range of linear feet, were given a limit on seed costs, and had to justify all their choices in writing.

Paradoxically, this group exercise became increasingly complex but also easier from year to year. Accumulated historical yield information for certain cultivars provided insight into the better performers and simplified decisionmaking as repeating known winners became an accepted approach to farm planning. Deviations from just using the winners after the first few years became increasingly difficult to justify, but students did want to experiment. Students needed to think about how much cultivar differences in color, shape, flavor, and size actually mattered to CSA members. Without ever having actually seen or tasted most of the varieties, without ever witnessing a distribution or listening in on shareholder comments while they picked up their produce, this was hard for them to determine. They needed to consider the impact of days to harvest, seed cost, and crop spacing and crop rotation requirements. They also had to consider the relative cost of seed for trialing versus bulk amounts. That is, they had to determine which was more important: spending more money to trial small amounts of new varieties without any history of customer appeal or field performance or saving money by purchasing bulk amounts of proven winners. They were given copies of major organic seed catalogs and lots of support materials for converting seed units, estimating yields, etc. as well as (after 2002) field maps, planting schedules, and variety performance information from previous years.

In practice, the class planning project did not strictly determine the eventual field plan, but it did have some influence on cultivar selection. New crops such as stevia, edamame, fava beans, and ornamental corn as well as new cultivars were introduced to keep things interesting and broaden the experience of the shareholders. The field manager made final decisions about cultivars, space allocation, crop rotation, planting times, harvest quantities, and CSA share allocations. However, the students who worked for OASIS, especially those students who worked more than one summer or who both took the class and worked for the project, became quite skilled in many of the daily activities of the farm and developed a strong understanding of the project history and overall farm operations.

Figure 13.1. Pauline and sunflowers. (Courtesy Constance L. Falk.)

If the class had been structured in a two-semester series format with the field planning exercise included in the second semester, the students no doubt would have been better equipped to create a full-fledged seed order and field plan. However, we taught the class essentially the same way each semester, although naturally spring semester students participated in more planting activities for both spring and summer crops, while fall semester students experienced more harvesting activities, including both summer and fall season crops.

As one OASIS student worker described the experience:

During the summer months the workers of OASIS got a perspective on agriculture that was not provided anywhere else within the university. The classes in the agricultural college were largely geared toward large-scale agriculture, including monocropping, chemical calibrations, and reliance on GMOs (genetically modified organisms). With limited resources and support, the farm manager and staff managed to create a space that incorporated a diversity of crops, organic practices, and community outreach. The process was invaluable to us, and small-scale organic agriculture became a possibility as a career choice. It was a breath of fresh air to have a space and a group of people open to learning about a different method. For many of us, this was the first time being exposed to another way to farm and a new philosophy of life.

HANDS-ON MANAGEMENT

Without a highly organized and hardworking farm manager, the OASIS project and class would have been impossible, especially in the behind-the-scenes planning of the farm operation. Three seasons each year, she had to have seeds and supplies ordered, transplants started, and planting and harvesting scheduled on time. Each week, she also had to evaluate what needed to be harvested and prepare the harvest log sheet both so that we could fulfill our thirty-four-week CSA obligation and so that, on arrival at class, students would be able to check the log for instructions on what, how, and where to harvest. Although students were shown a new crop's location in the field and a method of harvest, the harvest log helped reinforce those lessons week after week. It ensured that each crop was harvested at the proper maturity and that not too much of a particular crop was harvested. In turn, this allowed distribution to shareholders in manageable amounts and maximized subsequent harvests over the season.

Students initialed the harvest log when they harvested particular cultivars to provide accountability and facilitate follow-up if something was harvested incorrectly, for example, lettuce cut too low or too high, bok choi cut too high (in which case the head falls apart), green chile harvested too early, beans harvested too young, eggplant harvested too small. Students were encouraged to harvest something different each week before repeating a crop so that they would have a well-rounded harvest experience. The manager also prepared yield logs, where counts and weights of crops harvested earlier in the week were recorded (such as beans or squash that required more than a once-a-week harvest). The main weekly harvest began early each Wednesday, and all produce harvested that day was weighed and counted before being stored in the cold room. In the early afternoon, the produce was taken to the classroom to prepare for distribution. All field production data were recorded and fed back into the next year's farm planning projects.

For the first few years, the work of the farm manager and one instructor and the hours supplied by the class in spring and fall were adequate to meet the labor required to plant, harvest, weed, and prepare for weekly distributions to the CSA members. We did, however, need to hire students in the summer, when the bulk of the labor was needed. First priority was always to hire class alumni. In later years, the paid student crew began working before May and after September to meet increasing needs for labor, especially after required classwork hours were reduced in response to student input and weed problems worsened. Hired student labor was also important because of the inherent inefficiencies of class labor. Students in the class were allowed to complete their required hours in small blocks of time, such as a half hour before class started, and sometimes failed to show up at all. Aside from the grade for completion of the work hours, there was little accountability. Some students waited until finals week to complete their work requirement, which eventually we had to disallow completely.

Consistent, paid help was always more valuable and reliable than volunteer help. The farm manager was able to provide good training and oversight to students coming to work on a consistent basis, which, over time, made them valuable assets to the program and allowed them to mentor other students or guests visiting the farm. Students who worked multiple seasons were most valued because they had a cumulative understanding of the program. Often these students came in with an interest in gardening, farming, horticulture, or agriculture and possessed a desire to learn more or develop their interests.

OASIS fostered tremendous curiosity and many epiphanies. As the farm manager's experience and cumulative knowledge increased over the years, balancing her perspective with students' desire to try out new ideas was challenging. Students new to the project didn't have a sense of the entire project and its history. They didn't know what had already been tried or what was unrealistic with the available labor. However, so as not to squash enthusiasm and the learning spirit of education, students were allowed to try out their ideas, even when they imposed extra work on the farm manager or were thought to be impractical.

For example, our compost pile was not managed in compliance with the organic standards for making compost because we did not have the time to do so. Compost as defined by the National Organic Program requires careful balancing of the carbon-to-nitrogen ratio, constant monitoring of the moisture content and temperature, and proper aeration. We did our best to make an "organically derived amendment" by piling organic materials from the farm onto the already-existing pile. (An initial load of ten tons of cow manure started the pile in 2002 and was augmented over the years with harvest and field waste, raked leaves, and onion waste from the adjacent breeding program.) The farm manager would dig a trough along the top of the massive pile and along the sides before watering it to aid infiltration (a major factor when composting in the desert), after which the research farm staff turned the pile with a front-end loader. Watering and turning were done whenever significant quantities of organic waste were added to the pile or when the pile required more moisture. When it was field preparation time, the most decomposed part of the pile was added to the field. However, one student insisted that we manage the pile more actively with hand labor and built a project around that, even though he was unable to follow up with the appropriate labor required to turn the pile by hand.

Lessons Learned

Perhaps the OASIS program could have fashioned a summer internship or certificate program in which students applied and received field instruction in the mornings and classroom instruction in the afternoons. As it was, all summer students worked just in the mornings from 7:00 A.M. to noon, during the cooler part of the day. The summer internship program could have supplied college credit and free housing with willing shareholder families. An alternative approach would be to charge a fee to be involved in a summer program; increasingly across the country, nonprofit and private farms are offering such programs. Either way, OASIS could have attracted more students interested and invested in the project during the summer months, when assistance was needed the most, while also generating income in the latter scenario. After the internship, chosen students could have been employed by the program and become the backbone of a truly student-run OASIS, taking a leadership role in the farm operations, decisionmaking, and mentorship to semester OASIS students.

In retrospect, OASIS could have also engaged the CSA shareholders more directly, involving them in the process while filling certain labor needs through a monthly labor requirement. This would have helped with ongoing tasks such as weeding or thinning and given the shareholders greater perspective about how and where their food was produced. Even though our shareholders were strongly supportive, many never set foot in our main field, although it was directly across the street from where they picked up their weekly distribution. Any such work requirement would have to have been expected and explained when shareholders first signed up for the CSA. We had voluntary weeding parties toward the end of the program, but only a fraction of the share-holders chose to attend.

Lack of funds or perceived lack of funds was always an issue with the OASIS program. Funds were available for supplies and student labor, but being frugal was always an implied mandate, especially as the three-year HSI grant ran its course. Tractor and water charges (billed to the project by the research farm) were carefully reviewed to make sure we were not overcharged, for example. The HSI grant included only two years of salary support for the farm manager, with the understanding that there would be ongoing institutional support thereafter (a requirement of the USDA HSI program); however, this support proved not to be forthcoming. Class lessons on the economics of the farm, which included discussions about the manager's salary, made an already frugal manager even more mindful of funds.

The farm manager worked sixty hours a week performing office and field labor, owing to her affinity for the work, dedication to the program, and passion for accuracy in record keeping. In hindsight, her workload could have been reduced had we purchased items such as a push planter, weed eater, weed flamer, motorized transportation to ferry produce from the fields, or a staking machine for tying tomatoes. We did obtain a golf cart toward the end of the program, which made harvest days a bit less stressful. It was a mistake to try to conserve funds at the beginning of the program by not purchasing labor-saving equipment.

Another outcome of the restricted budget was the decision to keep the entire OASIS field space (less than an acre total) in production each year in order to maximize the number of shareholders and, thus, income. As a result, soil building and weed management through cover cropping was not possible, and, ultimately, the weed buildup was, besides the departure of the farm manager and the second coinstructor, a major reason for shutting down the program after five years. With administrative support for additional land for rotation and the farm manager's salary, we could have continued the project. We considered raising the share price, but a full share price would have had to roughly triple to cover all operational and salary costs, a price increase we thought unreasonable. In the first two years, we also harbored the naive hope that we could get more land, and we did not foresee the aggressive advance of the nutsedge across the field. In retrospect, we should have planned the OASIS farm to include more space for rotations and cover cropping, although it would have shortened the number of years of the program by reducing our immediate income.

Figure 13.2. OASIS members pick up their produce at the weekly distribution. The OASIS classroom doubled as the OASIS CSA distribution room. (Courtesy Constance L. Falk.)

FOSTERING CREATIVITY

Initially, the class was taught as a special topics class, as no formal class existed in the catalog. After four semesters, the class obtained upper-division general education and honors class designations (partly in response to administrator complaints about the class's small size—typically around twelve students per semester). Students of all backgrounds and majors then began to sign up for the class, in part thanks to a university requirement for all students to take two classes outside their own college to fulfill upper-division general education requirements. Nonagriculture majors were encouraged and valued because they brought different interests to the class and because we needed to boost enrollment in order to legitimize the course in the eyes of university administrators.

Structured as an experiential education opportunity (no exams!), the class provided a learning platform for many different kinds of creative efforts. Students from art, geography, history, education, social work, English, journalism, engineering, anthropology, agricultural economics, Spanish, criminal justice, horticulture, agronomy, business, and agricultural extension and education all enrolled in the class. Because students came from a variety of disciplines, creative projects varied widely. Students in the class created gardens in town, including one at a pregnant and homeless teen shelter and another at a weaving cooperative for low-income Hispanic women. Other students built and explained the benefits of bat houses; one created a project using solar fencing to contain goats that weeded part of the field. A retired art teacher who took the class created original paintings of flowers and vegetables and donated them to the classroom/CSA distribution room. One student conducted an experiment to examine the feasibility of using organic cotton gin trash as a planting medium. Another student analyzed insect populations in the field; one student enacted the life cycle of an aphid in a memorably comic performance. A student translated the OASIS Web site into Spanish; another created a short documentary about a local farmer who started a CSA using the OASIS waiting list, which we had donated to him. A student majoring in English interviewed organic and conventional Pima cotton growers and analyzed their relative profitability. An anthropology student surveyed CSAs statewide about their operations; a criminal justice major investigated which local prison might be most interested in starting a garden. Students evaluated relative costs of organic produce in town; others organized OASIS member satisfaction surveys. One student dressed up as a professor in a smoking jacket and brought in puppets to demonstrate how *E. coli* bacteria go through the digestive tract.

An engineering student worked on our database for the OASIS production information. This database was designed and improved by three classes of computer information systems students under the supervision of two business college faculty members, who were also OASIS CSA members. With this database, we were later able to summarize the cultivar performance in great detail.[3] One of these business faculty members, who had not previously worked on agricultural projects, later obtained consulting work at the Stone Barns Center for Food and Agriculture in Pocantico Hills, New York, because of her experience with the OASIS database project.

A student who took the class later decided to dedicate her honors thesis project to building a garden at a local elementary school, which she did while seven months pregnant. One of our summer employees, an international student from Trinidad, created the Well-o-Gram program, in which our members generously paid for flower bunches to be donated to local organizations like medical hospices and cancer-care wards. At the end of the season, students and the farm manager mounted a harvest season festival, in which live music was brought in, a silent auction raised up to $1,000 one year, a local farmer demonstrated how to press apples for cider, pictures from the project were presented, and a delicious meal was shared with our members.

We also held several taste tests with our members to learn which cultivars of melons and tomatoes they preferred or which basil cultivar created the most flavorful pesto. We organized an herbal tea competition in which different students prepared teas from OASIS-grown herbs, which our members then rated. We marketed a variety of products for other local producers, including fruit shares, sparkling apple cider, contacts for local beef and pork, eggs for one of our CSA members, and squash. Once we had the opportunity to host the Independent Organic Inspectors Association, which used the OASIS farm site to train new inspectors. We took seriously our responsibility to foster more local food production and marketing and came to serve as a network for people in the community concerned about the food system. All these interactions between students, CSA members, local institutions, and the instructors deepened our commitment to community building, helpfulness, and healthy eating.

Several research projects emanated from or were related to what we learned at OASIS. For example, we got a small grant from the New Mexico Department of Agriculture to develop a root crop harvest washing station, which was eventually completed with the help of engineering students participating in an experimental program to teach engineering in cohort groups focused on practical projects. We also conducted preliminary investigations into methods to deter the beet leafhopper insect, which transmits curly top virus to tomatoes and other crops. We used both a kaolin clay spray product to confuse and deter leafhoppers from landing on the tomato plants and a mylar mulch product to create light conditions that would also confuse the insects plus help with weed control.

We obtained a USDA Risk Management Agency grant to examine season extension for lettuce and spinach and to investigate the potential for regional crop diversification. A grant from the Organic Seed Partnership, headquartered at Cornell University, enabled us to pay students and a portion of the farm manager's salary as we trialed organic seed varieties and identified farmers in New Mexico who could also participate in these trials. We worked with an engineering professor who developed an anaerobic digestion process, now patented, that he adapted for us to digest organic alfalfa, which we thought might make a local substitute for liquid

Figure 13.3. OASIS student employee Travis Romany delivers flower bouquets to a local hospice. Romany created the "Well-o-Gram" program, which enables OASIS members to purchase flower bouquets to donate to people in local health care facilities. (Courtesy Constance L. Falk.)

fish fertilizer purchased from the East Coast. (We were injecting the fish fertilizer in the subsurface drip-irrigation system to supplement fertility in the long growing season.) We got another grant to look at killed-mulch options in green chile systems to increase soil organic matter, retain soil moisture, and suppress weeds.

LONG-TERM BENEFITS

Although we have not maintained formal contact with students, the tight network that OASIS developed has led to many long-term friendships and support systems. Many OASIS summer crew students have gone on to attend graduate school in agricultural or food-related disciplines, to start their own farming operations, to join nonprofit farming endeavors, or to work for organic growers or other horticultural sectors. One of the former OASIS summer student employees now works at the Tucson Community Food Bank's Community Food Security Center as the manager of a twelve-acre sustainable farm. Another student who took the class began the first organic farm on the Navajo Nation, in northwestern New Mexico. A third now works in the Ministry of Agriculture in Trinidad.

In the fall of 2009, two NMSU staff members began compiling documents to prepare a request to the university that the class be reestablished. They solicited input from former students and polled OASIS CSA members for their opinions about the project. The responses demonstrate how deeply OASIS was valued by both students and community members:

> I'm glad to hear that someone is trying to get the class and CSA going again because it was an essential part of my education, so much so that I took the class in the spring and fall. I also worked at the farm in the summer and gave a few tours of the farm to groups of elementary classes. Although I did not graduate with a degree in agriculture, I do use the knowledge gained from those classes for my profession in early childhood intervention working with children with special needs and children with developmental delays. I try to engage every child to whom I provide services to participate in growing a plant of some kind and to learn where their food comes from.

> I took the OASIS course as an upper-division honors class, to fulfill a Viewing a Wider World requirement for my NMSU undergraduate B.S. degree, and it exceeded my expectations. I was introduced to local organic growers and the economic challenges they face, and I participated in the business of distributing produce to community stakeholders who invested in the farm. I appreciated the instructors' passion for sustainable agriculture and community service, and I even enjoyed the required field work hours. In addition, the writing project component to the class gave me an opportunity to approach organic farming from my own field of expertise, allowing me to research the microbiological activity of the organic fertilizers used and the effects of postharvest handling techniques on the safety of locally grown food. Also, I was able to follow the inspection process for National Organic Program certification, which gave me valuable insight into regulatory decisionmaking as I con-

tinue my postgraduate career in biology. The CSA program is an exceptional use of NMSU resources, offering students from diverse majors the ability to integrate education in good agricultural practices with community development programs.

The course was unique in that it showed students not from a farming background what it takes to raise crops from start to finish. The lectures were useful and informative, but the hands-on farming was the best part of the course. This was, by far, the most interesting Viewing the Wider World course that I took, and I would recommend the course to everyone. It's easy to disconnect the idea of food production from your own community, and I think this program really joins the two ideas together in a meaningful, realistic way. This unique program also directly supported the community in that people had a great source of fresh, delicious, in-season fruits and vegetables.

I was a former teacher assistant for the class. In all my years of learning, no class touched more on the business aspects of agriculture. From costs assessment to field planning, this class was one of the best hands-on learning experiences in my student career. In discussing the course with others, I found the research conducted during the duration of the project to be leaps ahead of other schools with similar sustainable agriculture courses.

I really enjoyed the OASIS veggies and flowers. The variety and flavors were amazing. I would often share the weekly distribution with my eighty-two-year-old mother—and she really misses OASIS. Please bring it back!

Before joining OASIS, I'd never even heard of Chinese cabbage, Japanese eggplant, or stevia. Now I'm addicted to some, still fighting with local grocers to carry others, and wishing I had the wherewithal to have my own garden. There were drawbacks. I learned I didn't like edamame or cilantro. But every week was an adventure, and the quality and freshness were impeccable. None went to waste as my neighbors helped relieve me of those items I couldn't acquire a taste for. The students weren't the only ones who learned something. The two years I participated, I lost lots of weight.

In the end, despite differences of opinion and struggles with the administration, the overwhelming sentiment about OASIS was positive. OASIS was a successful team effort that brought together the community, students, staff, managers, and instructors around food, labor, land, equity, fellowship, water, nature, diversity—in short, around all the endless issues and phenomena that make up life. It made us all slow down to appreciate and ponder the little things that sometimes go unnoticed, like freshly sown seeds pushing their way through the soil surface, the bees that worked alongside us quietly doing their jobs, or how fast yet surreptitiously weeds scatter their seeds and grow. It humbled us and brought awareness and gratitude that we were a small part of a greater system. With pleasure, we witnessed the delight of a city child who tasted for the first time the sweetness of English peas that she had just harvested.

In January 2008, about two years after OASIS was shut down, two students (one of whom had taken the class) approached Connie Falk about starting a student sustainability club on campus using the OASIS acronym with a slight alteration in its meaning so as to be more inclusive: Organization of Aggie Students Inspiring Sustainability. Falk agreed and also agreed to be club adviser. Later that spring, a second club adviser joined the effort.

Since that time, the club has gotten grant funding for and organized two citywide Earth Day celebrations and two fall sustainability film series. Members planted trees in public schools as part of Arbor Day. During spring break in 2008, they traveled to a vegan organic farm in northern New Mexico, camped out on the farm, prepared a strawberry field, and planted three thousand strawberry plants for the farmer.

The club also organized a presentation to the university president, urging her to sign the Talloires Declaration, which commits institutions of higher education to principles of sustainability in their curricula, operations, and student life. The president was so impressed that she not only signed the declaration but did so publicly at a World Café event that she funded at the students' request. (World Café is a large-group conversation facilitation technique that harvests the wisdom from many small conversations that take place in a café-type setting.) The student club organized the event to bring together faculty, students, staff, and community members to talk about what we can do together to promote sustainability. The president also declared at that meeting, in January 2009, that 2009 would be the Year of Sustainability at NMSU. She asked units across campus to create some kind of public event focusing on sustainability. A sustainability task force was created on campus, and one of the subcommittees focusing on the curriculum is the group that has turned its attention to reviving the OASIS class. That committee has approached the student senate at NMSU to endorse revival of the class and is at the time of this writing moving forward to make the same request to the faculty senate.

The time seems right in Las Cruces for increased focus on small-scale, diversified, local, organic food production. The city politics have shifted in a more progressive direction, a new university president has arrived, and many more people are aware of the need to localize and diversify the food system to make our community resilient in the long term. Although we have a few pieces of the puzzle remaining to put in place to reinstitute the OASIS class, with the right support we hope that it will be possible.

STUDENT REFLECTIONS

THE VALUE OF LABOR

TRAVIS ROMANY

Six o'clock in the morning is chilly in most places, even in New Mexico. I had just put down my coffee mug and was still savoring the fleeting warmth I held in my chest and my hands as I walked into our very small but fertile field. Today was going to be a different day because, after weeks of preparation and labor, we were to plant our first summer crop. Half awake, and with a breakfast burrito (a Southwestern staple for agricultural workers, as I discovered) still settling in my stomach, I thought how far I felt from everything I was accustomed to. To this point, I had lived my entire life in the city with its glistening newness, seas of people, and so many things to do. Through a long chain of events, I found myself studying agricultural economics in the relative wilds of Las Cruces, New Mexico, not because I loved agriculture, but because I hated the hunger that seemed so pervasive in the world and this seemed like a way to make some contribution toward the fight against it. After two years of studying in fluorescent-lit classrooms and sterile computer labs, I started wondering when I would get to the agriculture part of agricultural economics. I looked at my program's syllabus, and it dawned on me that I could, and most likely would, cross that graduation stage in two years without having any contact with a plant or vegetable or patch of earth.

To me there was a paradox: How could I help a farmer in the Caribbean or Ethiopia become a more efficient and productive grower if I didn't have any farming experience myself? It seemed that I might end up with all the technical knowledge supported by the best of modern theory but without any understanding of the life on the ground. If I made this mistake, I wouldn't be the first person to do so. In the very texts I studied and was being tested on, disastrous examples were given of various points in history where top-down, purely academic policies had been dictated to farmers without any consideration of what it meant to be a farmer in that place. I did not know what manual labor felt like as I freely allocated it as a resource in my homework assignments. I was not taking into consideration that the vines of Roma tomatoes cause your arms to itch and stain your clothes when you try to pick the fruit; I would factor in only the high price the tomatoes fetched in the global marketplace. I did not want to be that policymaker, so I signed up to work on a university farm. And here I was watching my breath become mist in front of my face as I settled on the damp ground with a box of zucchini seeds and a wooden ruler. I dug small holes and dropped a few seeds in them.

I still remember the soil between my fingers and the lingering disbelief that, one day, these little "pebbles" would become fruit. I remember the creeping heat as the day drew on and the eventual sweat running down the back of my neck. I remember the satisfaction I felt as I sat under an old tree eating lunch with coworkers who were fast becoming new friends while I looked at the forty-foot row of freshly planted squash. I remember feeling what it felt like to be a farmer, and I knew at the time, as I know now, that I would be a better agricultural economist because of it.

Travis Romany completed his undergraduate education at New Mexico State University in 2009. He now works as an agriculture policy consultant for a private firm in his native Trinidad and Tobago.

STUDENT REFLECTIONS

PRACTICAL FARMING

DAYNA LUZ HERNANDEZ

The OASIS course inspired me to become an organic farmer. I always knew I would develop a business in agriculture after graduating, but the OASIS course convinced me that the only responsible way to farm today is with organic, sustainable farming practices. My farming practices include the use of organic seeds, all-natural fertilizers and soil amendments, and crop rotations for sustainable farming. I take great pride in the quality organic vegetables and herbs that I supply to my local community.

The OASIS course provided more practical experience than any other course I took during my bachelor's degree. The principles of efficient land use, water conservation through drip irrigation, and biological insect control are some of the agricultural techniques from the OASIS course that are still in practice on my farm today. I also learned about the specific vegetable cultivars that are successful in this region. The course covered all aspects of organic farming from the planning stages, to planting, cultivating, and maintaining the crops, and eventually to the harvest.

All students were required to spend at least thirty hours working in the field. While much of this time was spent on the OASIS farm itself, it was a very valuable experience to spend some of this field time at other local farms. This exposed me to alternate views of farming and allowed me to gain many more farming skills. One aspect of the course that has stuck with me was the requirement for each student to develop a project related to organic farming or sustainable agriculture. I built a bat house. The bats not only act as pollinators but also supply biological insect control to my farm.

The OASIS course also taught me how to organize a successful CSA program, and I will be developing my first CSA program this year. I'm not sure I would have had the confidence to develop a CSA on my farm if it weren't for the experience I gained in the OASIS course. I'm very excited to take my farm into this new endeavor.

Dayna Luz Hernandez took the OASIS organic vegetable production course in the spring semester of 2006 and graduated from NMSU that year with a bachelor's degree in horticulture. She owns and operates Gard-N-Hers Farm in Las Cruces.

NOTES

1. See http://www.ers.usda.gov/StateFacts/NM.htm.

2. For a more detailed discussion of the class structure and the tensions between class and CSA project goals, see C. Falk, P. Pao, and C. S. Cramer, "Teaching Diversified Organic Crop Production Using the Community Supported Agriculture Farming System Model," *Journal of Natural Resources and Life Sciences Education* 34 (2005): 8–12.

3. C. L. Falk, P. Pao, C. S. Cramer, and E. Silva, *OASIS: A Campus-Based, Organic, Community Supported Agriculture Farm*, NMSU-AES Research Report 760, May 2008, available at http://aces.nmsu.edu/pubs/research/economics/welcome.html.

14

Michigan State University (2003)

Four-Season Student Farming

JOHN BIERNBAUM

How do you tell the story? From what perspective? With which facts? How much from the head, and how much from the heart? Is it a narrative grounded in the academic literature, or is it rather a story about place, people, process, and transformational change? The history of the Michigan State University Student Organic Farm (MSU SOF) can be told in many ways. The account offered here is from the perspective of a tenured faculty member and professor who partnered with students, staff, and other colleagues to cultivate what has developed into a thriving student organic farm at a land-grant university. The intent is to paint an instructive picture for those seeking to start similar farms at other schools as well as for those walking the path of personal growth in a learning-farm culture.

The MSU SOF started as a location for organic high-tunnel research and quickly expanded to a forty-eight-week community-supported agriculture (CSA) program to research and demonstrate year-round vegetable production and to provide students with organic farming experience. From the beginning, the goal of the MSU SOF has been to incorporate student requests for practical organic farming opportunities with the additional need for research, outreach, and service to the campus and local communities. Creating an integrated program has been a key objective, as well as a budgetary imperative, for the SOF from the start. A research project established the site and funded the first two high tunnels, providing a foundation for later expansion. Undergraduate employees of the research program later became undergraduate farm crew employees of the SOF. The connection to a research project and to specific teaching programs (the Horticulture Department and the Residential Initiative for Study of the Environment [RISE] specialization) provided additional funding and a clear direction for development while enabling students to take an active and defining role.

MSU's tag line is, "Advancing knowledge. Transforming lives." The story of the MSU SOF also includes the theme of transformational change. Our experience has shown that the most important aspect of the MSU SOF is not necessarily the horticulture or the farming; it is the opportunity for transformation that students experience daily. Finding the words to describe this transformation is more challenging than bringing people to the farm to see it. But it is a story that needs to be told.

Another theme that will emerge in the story that follows is the importance of four-season farming for local food. For the educational farm, four-season farming allows for expanded learning within an already condensed academic experience. There are more opportunities to practice and more opportunities to consider the principles of balance and discipline. Summer on the farm does not have to be all work and no fun if production and sales are extended across the year.

The first fifteen years of the MSU SOF have seen continuous growth that I like to characterize with a horticultural metaphor of five phases: (1) preparing the soil, (2) sowing the seeds, (3) developing roots and a healthy plant, (4) flowering, and, finally, (5) fruiting and dispersing seeds. In the first part of this chapter, I will trace this developmental process of growth; then I will describe the MSU SOF's current configuration in more detail.

PREPARING THE SOIL: 1994–1999

The MSU SOF grew out of the fertile ground prepared by the Michigan Sustainable Agriculture Network (MSAN), a cross-disciplinary, joint graduate and undergraduate student organization founded in 1994. Graduate assistantship funding for a coordinator position for MSAN was provided by Richard Harwood, who then held the C. S. Mott Endowed Chair for Sustainable Agriculture. The extension specialist Susan Smalley worked with the coordinator and other students to invite outside speakers, establish a for-credit seminar class, and stimulate learning with an emphasis on participatory processes. A motivated core group of students representing multiple departments used a steering-team structure with a rotating meeting facilitator and note taker to foster shared responsibility and leadership.

Two other student programs that would later affect the SOF also emerged at this time. One was RISE, an undergraduate specialization with students from seven colleges coming together as a cohort. A second was the Bailey Scholars Program, a specialization in "connected learning" that emphasizes personal identification of learning goals, course conveners in place of instructors, and a strong focus on dialogue and listening.[1] The two programs provided opportunities for students, staff, and faculty to work together with an emphasis on participatory education and a common theme of food.

I was doing my own soil building during this time following my first sabbatical, moving to a new home with land to plow, and becoming a full professor after my first ten years of teaching and research in production and fertility management for greenhouse ornamentals. MSU funding for a minority graduate student assistantship combined with funding from the Organic Farming Research Foundation for a project on organic production of edible flowers started my shift from flowers to food and from non-organic to organic production systems.

Another essential step in preparing the ground for me was meeting Laura DeLind, a colleague at MSU, and learning about CSA. With more than a decade of experience as an early CSA pioneer, Laura convinced me that horticulture was only part of what was necessary to make the farm a success. People and community skills were equally important. Two books she recommended, Brian Donahue's *Reclaiming the Commons* and Trauger Groh and Steven McFadden's *Farms of Tomorrow Revisited,* had a major impact on my understanding of what the MSU SOF could achieve and how to make that happen.[2] The authors offer important, thought-provoking explorations of how agriculture and farming depend on access to land and engaging people.

SOWING THE SEEDS: 1999–2002

With the ground prepared, the seeds of the MSU SOF were sown in a variety of ways. The first MSAN meeting to discuss a student farm was held in April 1999. Over the next two years, a dedicated group of ten to twenty students worked as the Student Organic Farm Initiative (SOFI) to collect information from outside and inside the university, to build a vision, and to seek funding for a farm. We continued the MSAN tradition of offering a selected topics class with a focus on learning about and understanding organic farming. The students also spent time contacting and visiting existing student farm projects around the country. Valuable information was obtained from programs at Iowa State University, Colorado State University, Middlebury College, Warren Wilson College, and others. An independent study course the following semester provided the focus to move the idea forward.

I too was studying and traveling during this time. Attending the Upper Midwest Organic Farming Conference for the first time in 1999 opened my eyes to the dynamic, innovative, welcoming community of organic and sustainable producers across the Midwest. Participating in a season extension and cold storage workshop in Albany, New York, where I met the legendary high-tunnel producer Steve Moore and made a trip to Eliot Coleman's Four Season Farm in Maine, got me thinking about the possibilities of a year-round CSA. Gradually, my edible flower research grew into organic transplant research, which grew into high-tunnel and compost research. A USDA sustainable agriculture research grant at MSU funded construction of high tunnels and organic winter salad greens research at the Horticulture Teaching and Research Center (HTRC) in early 2001.

Up until the point of starting the research program at the HTRC in 2001, we were all looking for a place for the student farm that would be close to campus and more visible to the public. But, once we built the first research high tunnels at the HTRC, we realized that the site had many advantages as a place for the SOF. An orchard of forty-year-old fruit trees was being removed, and a ten-acre area was becoming available. The organic high-tunnel research was placed on the west side of the HTRC to avoid spray contamination. While we started with one acre, once the site was selected for the SOF the area gradually increased to three, then five, and, finally, ten acres.

The W. K. Kellogg Foundation inaugural Food and Society Conference in 2001 was important for the students because several from the MSU SOF attended and spoke directly with Kellogg program directors about funding. The students worked with Laurie Thorp, another MSU colleague, to prepare and submit a concept letter to start a student farm. I submitted a separate research proposal for high tunnels for year-round local food. Thanks to creative thinking, we were asked to combine the proposals, and the idea of setting up three sixteen-week CSA sessions to align with the two academic year semesters and one summer session was born.

Figure 14.1. Student organic farm entrance and high tunnels in early 2006. (Courtesy John Biernbaum.)

The funding was approved for the summer of 2002 and provided for the first graduate student farm manager, some basic equipment, and three high tunnels. The required plan for sustainability of the project was provided by growing the CSA and, thus, farm income over time.

Because MSU is a land-grant university, a key measure of program success is the ability to extend new knowledge to off-campus audiences. In 2001, I submitted a proposal to the North-Central Sustainable Agriculture Research and Education program that would form the foundation for future outreach efforts. We received funding to build one high tunnel at a local farm and a second at a local school. After a year of experience, the "farmer" at each location helped present a one- or two-day workshop for other farmers. The farm and school were less than five miles apart, and the intent was that parents of students eating salad greens at the school would become buyers for the salad greens from the farm. The educational materials developed for these workshops provided the foundation for later outreach efforts, and many workshop participants now have high tunnels of their own.

So, by early 2002, we had people, a site, a program, and funding. With these essential features in place, it was time to get growing.

Developing Roots and a Healthy Plant: 2002–2005

The fall of 2002 was an exciting time, with the construction of three high tunnels by students providing a sense of success after several years of preparation. Every Saturday and several evenings for a ten-week stretch, as many as twenty students worked on building the structures and forming the planting beds. More than half the students had little or no prior experience with tools. I look back on this as one of the most rewarding times in my academic career. I usually have the image of the students standing in front of the newly completed high tunnel in my mind. The dedication of the students was obvious. I remember asking some of them why they came every Saturday, and the answer was a clear and obvious, "We had to!" They had to because of their own enthusiasm for and commitment to what they were building.

In parallel with and just prior to the Kellogg Foundation proposal submission in 2002, a USDA Higher Education Challenge Grant was submitted that was based on the proposal that students could learn about organic farming during the academic year by growing in high tunnels. The proposal was funded on a second try in 2003, and the $100,000 over two years funded an undergraduate student farm crew as well as an additional graduate assistantship for an assistant farm manager who focused on working with class instructors to bring their students to the SOF. Students learned about organic farming, season extension, CSA, and local food.

The forty-eight-week MSU SOF CSA was launched in May 2003 with twenty-five memberships. As part of another for-credit selected topics class, graduate and undergraduate students worked together from January through April to formulate a planting and distribution plan and to recruit the first CSA members. They gathered information from a variety of sources, including Laura DeLind and another local farmer, Susan Houghton. Starting in January 2003, the day-to-day farm management was directed by the graduate assistant Michele Ferrarese. She had previous CSA and farming experience and, equally important, a passionate commitment to experiential learning and group dynamics. Michele's combination of plant and people skills was essential to both the short- and the long-term success of the farm. She worked with the students to establish a culture of cooperation and respect for the place, the process, and the people. The first year she was assisted by five paid students who had interned on small-scale organic vegetable farms the summer before.[3]

However, managing a year-round farm while completing courses and writing an extensive report is not conducive to personal health and sanity for a graduate student. It was done because that is how the funding was available and perhaps because we didn't know any better. In retrospect, the process was not consistent with the principles we wanted to promote at the SOF. The next farm manager position was developed as a full-time, technical staff position and provided a more reasonable set of expectations.

The dynamics of the MSU student groups and what they were learning—MSAN (sustainable agriculture), RISE (environmental awareness), and Bailey Scholars (self-directed learning)—had a significant influence on the students that shaped the early years of the SOF. A few students were involved in all three programs. It was also important because the programs had directors or coordinators (as opposed to faculty) who were able to focus on student learning and cultivating student activities as well as funding to support those activities.

Looking back, the use of one-credit selected topics courses to move the discussion of the initiation of the farm from the evening, registered student organization meetings (MSAN and SOFI) to the daytime classroom sessions was important and, likely, essential. The consistent meeting time and student participation, the focus, and the efforts of students to complete graded activities that advanced the group consensus all contributed to the realization of the goal. The third one-credit course became the first SOF practicum class in the fall of 2005, which provided the initial experience of how to blend classroom self-directed learning and working at the SOF for credit and not a paycheck. Going forward, we would learn that having students paying to work next to students working for pay would require a new process.

FLOWERING: 2005–2008

As the farm, the CSA, and organic production expanded, we kept looking for the opportunity to provide undergraduates with organic farming courses. We also found that there was plenty of demand for providing farmer workshops about season extension and organic farming. The original plan was to focus more on classes first and then outreach, but the outreach opportunities grew so quickly that the two happened in parallel.

The discussion of how to start classes began in the fall of 2005 and early 2006. A proposal was developed within the MSU system, and funds were requested to focus on developing classes rather than continuing to increase the size of the CSA. Simultaneously, a team of MSU faculty submitted a multidisciplinary proposal to the organic research and outreach program that included a request for funding to develop courses using a modular approach that could be used both for students and for farmers. A new academic specialist was hired (Corie Pierce) to help launch and coordinate the program. Over a year was spent developing the courses and going through the necessary MSU approval process. A year-long, forty-credit organic farming certificate program was approved in mid-2006, and the first cohort of certificate students arrived in 2007. To help teach the courses, the SOF farm manager (Jeremy Moghtader) was reappointed as an academic specialist, and additional farm income from a summer-only CSA and an on-campus farm stand was used to employ a new assistant production manager (Tomm Becker).

For outreach presentations, the main topic was season extension using high tunnels. The soil and crop management methods presented just happened to be organic because it made sense. The method of leading with season extension and providing information about organic farming as a method that makes sense has been a successful outreach strategy that we continue to use today. All our high-tunnel work is based on four principles:

1. Build soil organic matter for long-term fertility and water conservation.
2. Increase crop or product diversity to minimize risk.
3. Develop diverse markets that maximize return to the farm.
4. Use season-extension techniques to spread work and income.

Additional workshops were developed on organic transplant production, compost production and use, managing soil organic matter and health, and the basics of vegetable selection, scheduling, and production. The information originally developed for workshops later became the curriculum for the organic farming courses on campus. Organizing workshops takes time and funding. The Michigan Food and Farming Systems (MIFFS) project (a Kellogg Foundation–funded nonprofit located at MSU) was willing and able to organize and fund season-extension, high-tunnel, and soil-building workshops. MIFFS's own funding from the USDA Risk Management Agency (RMA) Community Partnership Program provided a focus on reaching underserved audiences. After several years of presenting workshops with MIFFS, in 2006 additional support from RMA funded a half-time outreach academic specialist position (Adam Montri) for high-tunnel education within the domain of the MSU

SOF. The other half of the position was funded by a research grant to study the economics of high-tunnel production and to assist farmers with construction and crop production. The now-full-time outreach position is supported by the RMA Community Partnership Program, with additional support for urban agriculture education in Flint and Detroit. In addition to regular high-tunnel workshops at the SOF and for regional groups working on new farmer development, the high-tunnel outreach specialist is working with farmers in Flint and Detroit.

The impact has been extended by partnering with at least eight other outreach organizations or conferences addressing farmer or new farmer education. This visibility provided an important opportunity for recruiting students for the on-campus teaching program. Another part of the story is developing outreach programs that will eventually be self-supporting through program fees. The current effort focused on underserved audiences does not provide that opportunity or focus yet, but the value we are creating in our programs will keep that door open.

FRUITING AND DISPERSING SEEDS: 2008–2010

The basic model for research at the SOF is to provide opportunities for small- to medium-sized undergraduate and graduate student projects (not large replicated trials) and the testing of ideas identified in faculty research. Here is an example of what can happen. Students doing an independent study on the campus food system determined that MSU was purchasing twenty tons of lettuce per year. Further calculations estimated that one hundred thirty- by ninety-six-foot high tunnels would be needed to produce that amount of lettuce. Dr. Mike Hamm, who currently holds the C. S. Mott Chair for Sustainable Food Systems, sponsored a high-tunnel project at the SOF to begin growing lettuce for the campus with a goal of eventually having twenty to twenty-five local farms with four or five high tunnels each producing lettuce for MSU and other institutions. In the winter of 2008–2009, the SOF produced thirty-five pounds of salad greens a week for the university. Students assessed the perceptions of other students about local and organic salad greens. This project has grown into a key partnership with the Division of Residential and Hospitality Services, which organized a fund-raising event for the SOF in the fall of 2009 that brought in over $16,000 for a student scholarship endowment. The local and organic dinner was held under a tent at the SOF and featured five courses prepared by five MSU chefs; it is now envisioned as an annual event.

Initially, there was no fee for use of the land, equipment, and cooler at the HTRC. As funds became available, the SOF has made an annual payment of $2,000, increasing over time to $5,000, to the HTRC. The energy and maintenance costs of the coolers and cold storage are significant and must be budgeted. A class project during the fall of 2008 completed a carbon footprint analysis of the SOF and identified refrigeration as at least 90 percent of the farm's energy use. Protected classroom, work, and tool storage areas were initially (2003) provided with a high-tunnel/greenhouse structure. A much-needed washing and packing structure and shaded work/teaching area were provided in 2007 with funding from the MSU Mott Group Chair.

The SOF farming activities that support the base income have continued to expand and diversify. From the original CSA of twenty-five memberships in year 1 and fifty memberships in year 2 the program has grown to currently include sixty year-round shares (at roughly $480 for sixteen weeks, or $30 a week), forty summer-only shares, an on-campus farm stand open from April to October, and the sale of produce for student dining programs. Each program grew gradually, with students and farm staff developing ideas for how to expand programs in a way that funded the necessary farm activities. The budget in table 14.1 provides an overview of current income and expenses.

A common question is, "How many people are at the farm each day?" The number continues to grow. In addition to staff, there are normally three student employees working forty hours per week during the summer; during the academic year, this shifts to eight to twelve students working eight to sixteen hours per week. In addition, twelve to fifteen certificate-program students have been at the farm part-time for the last three years. The number of volunteers at the farm also continues to grow. The current process for selecting paid undergraduate farm crew employees favors students who have volunteered at the SOF and already learned basic planting, cultivation, and harvesting methods.

The Organic Farming Certificate Program completed its third cycle in 2009. Techniques for integrating farm production and student learning have been developed, practiced, and refined.[4] A key was continuing to develop methods in which students paying to "learn/work" shared the farm with students working for pay. It is reasonable to say that the farm employees who were the focus of attention prior to the teaching program got less attention as time went on. The system developed with three people (Jeremy, Corie, and Tomm) who worked together well and were dedicated to

Table 14.1. Sample MSU SOF Annual Budget	Dollars	Assumptions
Income:		
Carryover	$15,700	
Produce and sales:		
60 membership, 48-wk. CSA	$86,400	$30/wk.
40 membership, 24-wk. CSA	$28,800	$30/wk.
26-wk. farm stand	$15,600	$600/wk.
Campus dining	$6,000	
Subtotal	**$136,800**	
	(36%)	
Outreach:		
Grants	$100,000	
Program fees	$10,000	
Subtotal	**$110,000**	
	(29%)	
Training program:		
15 students @ $7,500	$112,500	
Subtotal	**$112,500**	
	(30%)	
Total income	**$375,000**	
Expenses:		
Personnel:		
Farm manager	$56,000	$40,000 @ 40% fringe
Outreach specialist	$72,500	$50,000 @ 45% fringe
Training specialist	$72,500	$50,000 @ 45% fringe
Second-year students	$54,000	three at $18,000
Undergraduate labor	$35,000	
Subtotal	**$290,000**	
	(77%)	
Fees:		
HTRC fee	$5,000	
HTRC office support	$1,750	
1% tax on income	$3,750	
Subtotal	**$10,500**	
	(3%)	
Other:		
Farm materials and supplies	$15,000	
Infrastructure/equipment	$5,000	
Outreach materials and supplies	$10,000	
Outreach travel	$17,500	
Training materials and supplies	$10,000	
Training travel	$2,000	
Web page, marketing	$5,000	
Carryover	$10,000	
Subtotal	**$74,500**	
	(20%)	
Total expenses	**$375,000**	

figuring out how to make it work. When Corie took the opportunity to go back home to family in Vermont in 2009 and Tomm left to get married and start his own farm, Jeremy became the farm and training program coordinator and Dan Fillius the new production manager, responsible for hiring students and managing the planting and harvesting. So we now have two people to do what was covered by three while the system was being developed. Three years of a fairly constant farm production and marketing plan helped make the development of the teaching program more realistic (but still a challenge). The training program coordinator is primarily responsible for the CSA and farm stand. A shared understanding of responsibilities is important, as is hiring and accepting students who can work as a team.

Students learn to take responsibility for key tasks—from field or high-tunnel management to CSA and farm stand harvest and distribution—and an emphasis is placed on helping them think like a farmer. In addition to the course work and on-farm experience, the development of personal learning plans has evolved as a successful teaching tool. Program coordinators meet with students one-on-one on a regular basis to identify personal learning goals and to assess progress.

FARM MANAGEMENT DETAILS

The current setup of the MSU SOF includes three 20- by 96-foot high tunnels, two 30- by 96-foot high tunnels, and one 30- by 144-foot high tunnel with a mobile 30- by 96-foot high tunnel to be built in 2010. The spaces between the high tunnels are used for intensive seasonal salad crop production. Two heated 20- by 96-foot greenhouses are used for transplant and vegetable production. We have ten acres for field production, with approximately five of those acres in production each year. Initial soil fertility was primarily from animal manure compost produced on campus; current fertility is a combination of compost, cover crops, and green manures integrated into the crop rotation. Seven, half-acre fields are used for the rotation. One 0.6-acre plot is used for research and demonstration of temperate-climate edible forest gardening based on permaculture principles.

Over fifty vegetable and herb crops are produced together with at least twenty cut flower crops. In addition, small quantities of berries and tree fruit are produced as part of the edible forest garden planting. The farm has also maintained a flock of laying hens in a mobile coop and four hives for honey production and practiced small-scale shitake mushroom and maple syrup production. The 11,500 square feet (roughly 6 percent of total space) of high-tunnel area yielded 10,500 pounds of produce (approximately 25 percent of total yield) compared to 28,000 pounds of produce from approximately 175,000 square feet of field production.

One of the unique aspects of the MSU SOF is the year-round farming process. Through a combination of high tunnels for season extension of summer fruit crops and winter harvesting of salad, leafy greens, and root crops and refrigeration for longer-term storage of potatoes, squash, onions, cabbage, carrots, beets, and garlic, local produce is provided year-round. The details are in the scheduling of crop production and the management of the high tunnels and cold storage. The high tunnels are passive solar greenhouses (not heated), a steel frame covered with one or two layers of polyethylene film that protect crops from wind, rain, and snow and trap the heat of the soil just as clouds keep the earth warmer than a clear sky.

After a three-year transition, the farm was certified organic in 2004 by the Organic Growers of Michigan and has been certified since then by the Ohio Ecological Food and Farming Association. Tractors are used for primary and secondary cultivation in the fields and for application of compost. Transplants are grown in a heated greenhouse on-site using a compost-based potting medium in plastic cell trays (50 or 128 cells). Drip irrigation is used in all fields and some high tunnels with primarily hose and breaker watering in the high tunnels. High-tunnel production is maintained by adding a five-gallon bucket of high-quality compost to each twenty square feet of bed space at each planting (two or three times per year). The compost is made from hay, decomposed vegetable residues, straw, wood shavings, sphagnum peat, and soil. Additional minerals are added on the basis of annual soil tests and may include gypsum for calcium, sulfur to lower pH, and potassium sulfate.

We start with the premise that there is no one right way to farm. Farming is about choices: what to grow, how much to grow, when to plant, how to keep crops healthy. Each decision requires more knowledge. Is the process a battle with the elements or an orchestration of varied components in a dynamic environment? Is it about working with nature or against nature? The answer is simple for us. Organic farming is not going backward, and it is not simply farming without pesticides and chemicals. Organic farming is ecological farming based on managing the farm as a complex living organism, starting with the soil. Slowly soluble mined minerals and certain nonsynthetic pest management materials are allowed. However, compost, green manures, and cover crops provide the bulk of the fertility. Pest management strategies include crop rotations, diverse plantings, exclusion with crop covers, physical removal by hand or vacuum, and, occasionally, targeted pesticide sprays with biological or short-lived materials.

CHALLENGES AND ACHIEVEMENTS

After fifteen years of planning, analysis, growth, and experimentation, of building infrastructure and soil fertility, relationships, and alliances, the MSU SOF has much to be proud of. We are still learning and adjusting, still juggling multiple, mostly complementary objectives, and still seeking long-term financial stability and institutional permanence. Providing students with opportunities to learn and grow is the heart of what we do and is more important than our food production. We know that what we are doing is working. We see the SOF recruiting students to MSU and positively affecting the retention of students at MSU. We see what participants at the SOF are doing when they move to other communities and the growing influence of MSU SOF alumni and their activities as teachers and agents of change.

Future projects under discussion for the MSU SOF include increased incorporation of livestock into our production systems, the development of an adjacent woodlot for woodland herb wild crafting and mushroom production, and the construction of a pond for aquaculture. The potential value of animals at the SOF was first demonstrated when a graduate student brought sheep from the Animal Science Sheep Farm to graze down cover crops in 2003. Over the years, Laurie Thorp and the RISE program have brought chickens, bees, and pigs to the SOF. There is a spot suitable for a pond and/or for animal housing and pastures. Aquaculture is also possible in the high tunnels or greenhouses, and donors have expressed interest in supporting such projects. The limitation lies in finding faculty or staff to provide the expertise and leadership for enthusiastic students.

As indicated above, after three years of offering the Organic Farming Certificate Program, staffing transitions and the funding realities of the university prompted a reformulation of teaching strategies. While fifteen students in a forty-credit program at approximately $300 per credit generates $180,000, there is no way for tuition dollars to come directly back to the certificate program. It does not appear that recurring funding would be provided for a teaching position. For the 2010 season, I will continue to teach on-campus organic farming classes for degree students, but the on-farm training portion will shift from a for-credit to a noncredit on-farm experience, similar to the long-standing six-month farm apprenticeship program at the University of California, Santa Cruz. Rather than two days on campus and two days at the SOF each week, students will be full-time at the SOF, independent of the academic schedule. The newly renamed Organic Farming Training Program will be reduced from eleven to nine months (March–November), which will still provide experience with four-season farming while giving the program coordinator and lead instructor down time for annual program revisions. The other benefit is that for the noncredit program the cost is the same for in-state and out-of-state students (out-of-state tuition doubled the original certificate program cost). With a program cost (for 2010) of $7,400 per participant and fifteen participants, the program will become a nearly self-supporting outreach program when combined with the nearly self-supporting farm operations.

Most of the classroom courses will continue for undergraduate students as long as enrollment can be maintained. A sustainable and organic concentration in the horticulture major has been developed in response to the growing student interest. Some of the workers and volunteers at the SOF have changed majors to horticulture.

A strategic planning process begun in the fall of 2007 sought to identify options for recurring funding and to take the SOF to a broader platform in the university. Ten other student farms were contacted in an effort to identify practices at other farms or a model familiar to MSU administrators. One recurring question that emerged during the strategic planning process was whether a name change might facilitate the SOF's transition from a project to a program. Many possible names were considered, most including the word *center*. The name Student Organic Farm may not adequately represent the full range of current activities, but it is a reminder of the project's origins as a student-driven initiative. There may be an institute or center in the future of the SOF, but there is a clear consensus that the physical place of the program's activities will always be the SOF.

In June 2008, twenty-five SOF students and alumni were surveyed regarding transformative learning outcomes, as distinct from farm skill competencies. The results showed that students placed a high value on the learning community they found at the SOF. This community was often described as empowering students to effect change on a larger scale. The SOF was described as a safe place where students were able to test ideas, think freely, and gain self-confidence. As one student put it, "It has transformed me into more of an active, intentional, engaged human being." The

Figure 14.2. End of spring semester and graduation party at the SOF, including fourth-year and certificate program students and staff in 2009. (Courtesy Patricia Biernbaum.)

ability to engage in real work emerged as a key theme. Another student said, "That kind of responsibility is very different from writing a paper, and it repeatedly helped me create new habits of thinking." This developed sense of responsibility was mentioned both in the context of caring for plants and animals and in the sense of caring for and respecting fellow students. Repeatedly, students mentioned valuable lessons learned from being a responsible member of a group.

Overall improved health and well-being were also mentioned by numerous students as a result of their time spent at the farm. This included both mental and physical health. Students spoke of improved eating habits, shifting to more plant-based diets, and increased physical activity as outcomes of working at the farm. The farm was frequently described as a place that provides students with a refuge from the stresses of academic life. Nearly every respondent mentioned the farm as providing a much-desired community with a common set of values.

Students at the MSU SOF organize an end-of-semester farm graduation and recognition ceremony. The graduating student testimonials invigorate the steering team and make the case for why student farms are so important. They say things like, "I would not have survived MSU if it was not for the farm and all of my friends at the farm," "I learned more at the farm about what is really important than in my classes," "My memories of the farm and all of you that helped me through my MSU years will sustain me as I move on to new challenges," and, "I hope that those of you who are new to the SOF understand how important this place and this program are and that you care for it as passionately as those of us graduating have learned to care for it."

Farming and nurturing plants and animals while learning to manage season and climate variability is an exercise in discipline, wisdom, and experience that nurtures self-confidence. Self-confidence and self-respect foster personal growth. Personal growth fosters personal responsibility and democracy. Food independence is an essential component of democracy.

In the early days of the Michigan Agricultural College (the forerunner to MSU), all students had to work for three hours per day. The 1862 report of the national commissioner of agriculture included a report on agricultural colleges in Europe and the United States that might serve as models for the emerging land-grant colleges. The Michigan Agricultural College model of students working alongside faculty in the fields was described as a unique model worth emulating. Given our experience, this is as true today as it was a century and a half ago.

NOTES

1. For more information on the Bailey Scholars Program, see http://www.bsp.msu.edu.

2. Brian Donahue, *Reclaiming the Commons* (New Haven, CT: Yale University Press, 1999); Trauger Groh and Steven McFadden, *Farms of Tomorrow Revisited* (Junction City, OR: Biodynamic Farming and Gardening Association, 1998).

3. For additional details about the start-up of the MSU SOF, see Michelle Ferrarese's thesis and other publications at www.msuorganicfarm.org.

4. For more details, see John Biernbaum, Laurie Thorp, and Matthieu Ngouajio, "Development of a Year-Round Student Organic Farm and Organic Farming Curriculum at Michigan State University," *HortTechnology* 16, no. 3 (July–September 2006): 432–36.

15

Yale University (2003)

A Well-Rounded Education

Melina Shannon-DiPietro

The Yale Sustainable Food Project is a one-acre organic market garden, a collaboration with Yale Dining Services to bring local, seasonal, and sustainable food into Yale's dining halls, and a set of extracurricular and academic programs related to food, agriculture, and the environment. Located at one of the nation's tweediest, brainiest institutions, we have an unlikely mission: to create opportunities for undergraduates to experience food, agriculture, and sustainability as integral parts of their education and everyday life. In the words of one undergraduate participant, Nat Wilson (class of 2008): "The Yale Farm stands out because it is concerned not so much with things remote and far away . . . as with what good we could do here and now."

What follows is an account of how we got started, the values that have guided our work, and the strategies we have found most effective. But the truth is that we created this organization by the seat of our pants. Some of the tools and methods outlined here were encouraged by our more experienced mentors; others we stumbled into and, in so doing, felt we had discovered truths that fundamentally changed our work. To the extent that these strategies can be useful to you, I hope you'll take them on.

I came to Yale when the Sustainable Food Project was still just an idea. I was three years out of college, had spent time farming in Italy, Maine, and Massachusetts, and had traded in my fancy management consulting job for the opportunity to connect high school students to the land as a teacher at the Chewonki Foundation. I had planned to begin working on improving school lunch offerings for public school students around the nation: Yale offered a different opportunity. It seemed like a way to join my experience and my passions and to keep my hands in the dirt while building a strong organization that could positively affect the way Yale students understood and interacted with food, the land, and the environment for the rest of their lives. I began my work with an incredible group of colleagues, including Ernie Huff, Josh Viertel, who is now president of Slow Food USA, John Turenne of Sustainable Food Systems, Lucas Dreier, and Laura Hess, and throughout my time here have been blessed with great collaborators across the school.

Yale is an Ivy League school. While the league is technically an athletic conference, these schools are better known for their academic rigor and social elitism. Each of the schools has its own character, and the competition among them for students and stature is intense. Within the Ivy League, Yale is known for producing civic-minded graduates, future presidents and politicians. The campus is awash in debate clubs and political societies. Yale wasn't the first Ivy League to establish a college farm: both Dartmouth and Cornell had beaten us to the punch. But both Dartmouth and Cornell are located in relatively rural communities, and their students are known for being outdoorsy and down-to-earth. Yale's are not.

Yale's campus is urban. Gritty city streets butt up against gothic buildings that visitors and tour guides often compare to those at Harry Potter's boarding school. College guidebooks, as well as the administration, caution students not to walk alone after dark. Neighborhoods change rapidly, and, while New Haven and Yale now have a mostly productive, positive relationship, tensions ran high for decades. This is where we began our work: it proved to be fertile ground.

GETTING STARTED

The Sustainable Food Project was dreamed up by a determined and visionary group that included students, Yale's president, Richard C. Levin, and the chef and entrepreneur Alice Waters. Alice Waters, affectionately known as the mother of America's sustainable food movement, had founded Chez Panisse, one of the nation's best restaurants, and established the educational food and gardening program known as the Edible Schoolyard in Berkeley, California. When her daughter enrolled at Yale, Alice saw an opportunity to begin a similar program at the college level. Her arrival coincided neatly with the advocacy work that had already begun on campus: a group of students, having studied the impact of pesticides on children's health, had begun conversations with President Levin about improving food in the dining halls. Levin, who would go on to create sweeping environmental initiatives across campus, was enthusiastic and suggested a campus farm in addition to the dining initiative. Together, President Levin, Alice, and students agreed that Yale would build a program that would strive to change the way the nation eats.

Charged with building this program, we hit the ground running in early 2003. A sizable gift from an anonymous donor fueled our work. It also raised the stakes, as did Yale's visibility. While many of our colleagues at other schools say that funding is the first challenge they faced when establishing their programs, our challenge was different: we had to get Yale's (and the nation's) minds around the radical notion that students at an elite, urban, liberal arts Ivy League institution could benefit from a farm, that food in the dining halls mattered, and that food and farming were worth thinking about at all.

We identified a one-acre plot on the edge of campus that had been sitting unused and secured permission to transform it into the Yale Farm. We began training dining hall workers to forgo frozen, precut vegetables and instead use fresh local produce. We planned a conference that would publicize Yale's commitment. Throughout that first year, we worked tirelessly on each of these fronts, regularly clocking eighty-hour workweeks as we began to revamp how the school thought about food, agriculture, and the land.

Steadily, we expanded each of our initiatives. By the summer of 2003, the empty acre was taking shape as a productive market garden. We collaborated with CitySeed, a local nonprofit that was working to bring a farmers market to New Haven, and students began selling Yale Farm produce at a new downtown market established that fall. Over the next two years, we built passively heated greenhouses and a wood-burning hearth oven. When we planted a small orchard of fruit trees two years later, we knew we were here to stay. In 2008, a hundred students, alumni, and staff turned out to help us raise a timber-frame pavilion on the site. It had been four years in the planning, approvals, and construction.

The dining program began as a pilot in Berkeley College, one of Yale's twelve residential undergraduate "colleges," each of which has its own dining hall. We needed to demonstrate that students wouldn't riot at the introduction of a menu that some tenured faculty imagined as "rabbit food" and that Yale's unionized staff—known for their propensity to strike—wouldn't head to the streets in protest of the changes. We set out to make great food, and as it turned out, students lined up for it. Some even counterfeited identification cards so that they could enter the Berkeley College dining hall. The dining staff liked working with real ingredients; they proclaimed they finally felt like not just cooks but chefs. After a while, students did threaten to riot—if we didn't expand the menu and purchasing innovations to the other eleven dining halls on campus. And so, in 2004, we began an incremental expansion into the other college dining halls. Today, Yale Dining spends about 20 percent of its budget on local, seasonal, and sustainable food.[1] Though most of the Sustainable Food Project's other activities have been funded by alumni gifts, the incremental cost of sustainable food purchasing in the dining halls has become part of the university's general budget. As you might expect, growth was easier in a time when the economy was flush; the rate of improvement has slowed since the economic downturn in 2008.

We had held a national conference on campus in 2003, and the attention it garnered got us thinking about how to spark regular conversations on campus about food and agriculture issues.[2] We began joking that our aim was to make these topics as pervasive at Yale as the a cappella singing groups that have been popular here since the early twentieth century. With the help of another alumni gift, we established a series of student internships and began hosting workshops, lectures, and discussions on campus. Today, these lectures and events happen at least once every week. In 2006, we took on the administration of Harvest, a fledgling preorientation program that put incoming freshmen to work on local farms. Through this program, one of a handful of preorientation options offered by Yale, incoming freshmen spend the week before school begins on family-owned farms in Connecticut. Farmers appreciate the enthusiastic, if unskilled, labor, and students make some of their first friends at Yale. And, while we had been cautioned that we shouldn't think about touching the academic realm, the strong student enthusiasm for these issues began bringing faculty members interested in food and agriculture out of the woodwork. There are currently about thirty courses related to food and agriculture at Yale. The undergraduate program in environmental studies was a natural ally: students in that program can now graduate with a concentration in sustainable agriculture.

That is the bare-bones description of our work as it stands today, in early 2010. And, while each of these programs is worthy of its own description, in the remainder of this chapter I'm going to focus on the farm and the good it does in a university setting. Then I'll share some of the foun-

Figure 15.1. Student volunteers Daniel Fromson '09 and Daniel Sussman '07 harvest carrots at the Yale Farm for the Yale-Harvard game (November 2006). (Courtesy Sean Fraga '10.)

dational strategies we used to strengthen the program within the institutional setting and make it part of the culture here at Yale. Finally, I'll touch on how we have grown the program over time.

VALUE OF AN EDUCATIONAL FARM

The Yale Farm is a fifteen-minute walk uphill from the undergraduate campus. Students can walk, bike, or take the free campus shuttle. From the way students sometimes talk about this distance, you would imagine we were a state or two away. We manage to entice them to make the trip—once they've made their first visit, they almost always return—but, if you want a college farm that is constantly booming with activity, find a location that is convenient for your students.

People in the neighborhoods north and east of the Yale Farm are mostly white and upper-middle-class or above. People in the neighborhoods west of the Yale Farm are mostly not white and mostly middle-class or poor. South of the Yale Farm, the neighborhood is Yale: the School of Forestry and Environmental Studies, various administrative buildings, and the "Whale," a hockey rink designed by the architect Eero Saarinen. People from all these neighborhoods use the Yale Farm on a regular basis. On spring days, the farm teems with activity. The low rumble is a rototiller, the shrill voices are the children of grad students and young professors. Undergrads, middle-aged neighbors, and emeritus professors weed the beds. I'm reminded often that the farm is a leveler. Working around a garden bed quickly creates a minisociety, and that is precisely what makes the farm radical at this ivory tower institution. Working-class New Haven moms from the neighborhood nearby express the same surprise at seeing broccoli growing—pre–freezer bag—as the tenured white male faculty members who make their homes in the suburbs around New Haven.

Ask parents or grandparents what their child or grandchild should learn at college, and farming is not likely to be on their list. For the vast majority of Americans, a college education is about upward mobility. Farms, and physical work more broadly, are not part of that equation. So, when I took on a position at Yale in which I was to encourage students to put down their books and pick up a hoe, I asked myself the same question alumni regularly ask me: "Why should Yale students spend time on a farm?"

Yale was founded in 1701. It's worth noting that it later became the first land-grant school in the state of Connecticut and quite possibly the first institution to teach agriculture in the state. Today, however, the bias against the agricultural and vocational is pervasive on most Ivy League campuses. At Yale, as at many liberal arts schools, there is a belief that a well-rounded education produces the best citizens. But a well-rounded education has been understood to mean one that gives students a range of theoretical or academic knowledge and all but ignores both practical and preprofessional skills.

We decided to take our lead from our own experience on farms as well as from thinkers like Thomas Jefferson, Wendell Berry, and David Orr. Our goal was threefold: first, to give Yale students and the community a genuine appreciation for agriculture through ready access to a farm; second, to create opportunities for learning that would generate in students a belief in their abilities, a strong environmental ethic, and a visceral connection to the land; and third, to inspire students to act on that connection in some capacity for the rest of their lives.

With these goals in mind, we designed a student farm that would welcome the community and provide easy access to all comers. Our acre butts up against a heavily trafficked city street where cars back up during rush hour. We dug our beds right up to the sidewalk. Most fences on campus are made of wrought iron. Ours is made of a light wire mesh that allows passersby to see straight into the garden. Clematis, roses, and espaliered apples grow along the fence. People look in, lean over, and get pulled into the farm.

The farm gates are always unlocked. On hearing this, visitors ask: Doesn't your produce walk off? Some of it does. Once, for example, a Yale employee stealthily began a side business selling our "Sun Gold" tomatoes. Mostly, however, I assume that, if you're hungry enough to steal food, you need it. Keeping the gates unlocked builds trust and implicitly asks the whole community to steward the acre.

Having a farm on campus teaches passively as well as actively: everyone who passes by learns through simple observation. In December, the street-side beds are full of cabbages, radicchio, Brussels sprouts, and broccoli. Whether I'm in meetings at the dean's office or picking up a bottle of wine at a nearby shop, people have stopped me to say, "You're still pumping out food. I didn't know you could grow past fall." Through observing the farm, our neighbors learn about seasonality, locality, and food from their own experience. I believe that this experience and the appreciation that results can reconnect people with the source of their food. Most of the modern American food system is far away or hidden, and this distance breeds ignorance and neglect. Humans tend not to care about what they don't see. The Yale Farm brings the connection between land and food home to everyone who visits it.

Closing the gap between young people and nature is critical. The stretches of green, the light on leaves: these views are hard to come by on an urban campus and are important to our individual and collective well-being. The architect Louis Kahn pointed to great campus architecture as the thing that would remind students that they have the power to do great work.[3] I'd argue that great campus farms do the same work. The structure of an apple tree in winter, the bold color of spring's first tulips, the experience of pulling a tiger-orange carrot out of the ground, all these things connect us to natural beauty, thus reminding us of the potential and possibilities of life. The chance to realize that connection at a farm or garden nearby, where we can roll up our sleeves and interact with the environment, turns us into stewards of the land over time.

Louise Glück, the former U.S. poet laureate who is currently teaching at Yale, once stopped me and said, "Thank goodness you're starting a farm here." One of her undergraduate students had written a poem for her class in which two dozen stanzas on the autumn season ended with a daffodil bursting into bloom. Glück knew that a poet who is going to write about nature needs to have experienced it.

Undergrads show up at the farm to work, play, flirt, and eat pizza. Every year, some students claim the farm as their own. They become dedicated volunteers or take on paid positions as farm interns who manage the workdays we hold three afternoons a week; they become *pizzaiola* (pizza-makers) at our wood-burning hearth oven. All of them learn something at the farm, and, after six seasons of watching this transition, I believe that the farm rounds out their liberal arts education and makes them better versions of themselves. All of them, volunteers and interns, engage in work that is real and in work that needs doing. The harvest needs to come in; the carrots need to be sown; the fire needs to be lit so that volunteers can be fed. For many students, it is the first time that they experience physical work that needs doing or the mastery of a physical skill. Whether students are building a fire or planting a crop, work at the farm gives them a way to evaluate what they are learning and to know almost immediately whether their technique works. Watching your hands transform the land transforms you, and this is where college farms provide a critical education: meaningful action builds a sense of agency, competence, and efficacy. This is where our students become Jefferson's students. We tend to think of the life of the mind and the life of the body as opposed—as representing different arenas of endeavor, different tools, and different labors. Yet a full education comes from putting these realms together, thus helping students develop their capacity for meaningful action.

As students master these skills, they are brought into a different relationship with the land. We aren't, to the relief of a lot of alumni and parents, raising Yalies to be the next generation of farmers for the United States (although we may be raising a few). But the farm allows them to independently and authentically realize the connection between their actions and the natural world. This sense of satisfaction and purpose stays with them. Our alumni plant gardens and shop at farmers markets. They may buy organic sheets, or get involved in farm bill politics, or start baking their own bread. Their acts are simple, radical, and joyful. Taken together, their actions have the potential to change economies and communities. Rebekah Emanuel (Yale College, class of 2007) says of her work at the farm, "It was the first time I really felt that living could be a movement."

Other students involve a sense of mission in their everyday life. Dan DeBoer (Yale College, class of 2007) started working at a traditional investment bank after college. He was dissatisfied with the position: "Working

Figure 15.2. Community children visiting the Yale Farm. (Courtesy Sean Fraga '10.)

on the farm gave me a greater connection with my responsibility to change the world for the better, particularly with regards to the environment. I felt I needed to get back in touch with that responsibility. I began to look for a new job that would give me an opportunity to utilize the skills that I had in a way that would help the environment." Dan now works for a firm investing in wind technology.

Our students' parents, families, and friends have also felt the farm's influence. One set of parents is keeping chickens now. Others are shopping at farmers markets; many are composting in their backyards. In this way, the impact of the Yale Farm extends beyond its student population to the communities across the nation from which those students hail.

FOUNDATIONAL PRINCIPLES

Getting a farm established at a university takes a lot of heavy lifting. The work of navigating a bureaucracy and its politics can make bucking hay bales look easy. You'll want to be ready for this lifting and choose someone who is game to do it. Four foundational principles guided our work in establishing the program: the first two of these are about our approach to designing our organization at Yale; the other two are embedded in our approach to food and the farm.

Respect the Culture of Your Institution

Our first principle was to pay attention to the culture of our institution and establish programs that would thrive in that culture. Good farmers plant crops that are suited to their site, climate, and soil. In establishing a college farm and its accompanying programs, you need to do the same. Yale places a premium on student leadership, community service, and alumni outreach. Our internships and Harvest program reflect those interests. We host two special community events during the summer and a harvest festival in the fall. About two hundred community members turn out for each event. We run programs that change students' lives, but I believe that we continue to thrive at Yale because we've found a way to talk about those programs in a way that aligns with the university's priorities.

Another component of this philosophy was to look to the university calendar—the high holy days of Yale life—to identify strategic occasions for outreach to demonstrate our value to the school. We opened the Yale Farm for tours and receptions on Parents' Weekend, Bulldog Days, and alumni reunions. This helped us significantly along the way. After a couple of prospective students wrote application essays claiming that they chose Yale because of our work, the admissions office put a two-page spread about the farm in its viewbook. To us, this was as good as a front-page article in the *New York Times*.

Cultivate Key Supporters

Our second principle was to find strong advocates for our programs. We couldn't have asked for a more stellar cabinet of supporters than President Levin, Alice Waters, and my boss, Ernie Huff, the associate vice president of finance. But there were plenty of other players who needed to be wooed. Every college has influential players. Find them and make them champions of your program. Each summer, we invite a targeted list to the Yale Farm for lunch: the wood-burning hearth oven is a powerful tool for building allies! Having groups like the president's office, the dean's office, the provost's office, and the Office of Development understand the farm on a personal level is important to advancing our goals. This twofold approach has built strong, natural support for our work.

Seduce Your Audience

Our third principle came to us from Alice Waters, who instructed us to seduce the entire campus. "Seduce them," she said, "through taste." This ethic of seduction pervades our work. We grow the best produce in town, and, in a city known for its pizza, we give the competition a run for its money. Varsity athletes and suburban parents alike stamp their feet at the taste of a "Sun Gold" tomato. Taste is primary, pleasurable, and direct.

After a few seasons, I came to understand how critical Alice's mantra is. College farms and urban gardens offer some of the most promising connections city dwellers have to the land today. We all eat. And, because we do, food is the sweet spot of the environmental movement. It drives home—in a pleasurable way—the notion that our everyday actions affect the environment and that those actions can put either more or less wear and tear on the ecosystem. Food is a broadly appealing entryway to environmental stewardship, community, and everyday political action.

So, when we draw up our planting list, we ask, "What would Alice Waters think?" We do this because we figure that, if we can get a celebrated chef excited about our produce, we can probably make an impression on our undergrads and neighbors. OK-tasting varieties are culled from our planting list. Some days, this philosophy makes me feel like a taste dictator, as students suggest one more time that we grow the visually stunning but bland tasting "Green Zebra" tomatoes. Then the "Sun Gold" reminds me that this approach is worthwhile.

Food and cooking also build community. Eating the food we've grown together reinforces our work in the field. Students who are strangers to one another stretch pizza dough, top pizzas, and serve one another; they come away with a sense of camaraderie and generosity. The wood-burning hearth oven provides a rare space on campus where students learn to make food from scratch. We host a series of workshops here on topics such as canning tomato sauce, culturing sourdough bread, and making pickles. These workshops are regularly oversubscribed. Students are hungry for this knowledge, and that's because the act of feeding oneself is an important act of self-reliance and self-sufficiency. At a time when more and more people are eating out, cooking at home is a radical, simple act of community.

Alice's wisdom also influences how we set up the farm: the physical space itself is seductive. We edge beds and fences with nasturtiums, roses, and hyacinth beans to make the space lush. One summer evening, I walked into the farm to discover a student sprawled out on the central grassy green

Figure 15.3. Justin Freiberg, a graduate student at Yale's School of Forestry and Environmental Studies and an intern with the Yale Sustainable Food Project, plants garlic during a fall workday at the Yale Farm (October 2008). (Courtesy Sean Fraga '10.)

walkway reading Heidegger. When I offered him a bench, he gestured to the stand of "Casa Blanca" lilies above him, saying that he had found the best-smelling place in the city. Along with these pretty touches, we are relentless about getting weeds out and having orderly beds. We are constantly overturning stereotypes of what an organic farm looks like. Visitors express surprise that we're not knee-deep in weeds. I once watched a group of M.B.A. students grinning in delirious surprise while listening to our interns talk about efficiency and productivity. Every other journalist who visits asks where the marijuana patch is. Constantly confronting these stereotypes can be frustrating, but the effort is worthwhile for the larger change we are making.

Grow as Much as You Can

The superstar organic grower and author Eliot Coleman visited us late in the summer of 2003. He looked at our artistic trellises and big-headed sunflowers. And he made a simple point: you need to be productive and prove that this is a worthwhile economic venture. This logic struck me as odd at first. Our college farm isn't a good economic model: if you were trying to run a profitable farm, you wouldn't hire unskilled students or even grow the wide range of crops we do. Now, I've come to understand that the focus on productivity is important because managing a farm this way makes it a better resource for students and the community. This has become our fourth principle. The best learning a college farm can offer is generated from the work itself. A focus on productivity—efficient work habits, high yields, and economic profit—when balanced by the taste ethic and a sense of joy in work generates both care and discipline. High standards make it clear when one has mastery, and the challenge of living up to these standards builds student learning and ambition. Our growing beds are thirty inches wide; we grow intensively, planting crops densely. Salad greens, for example, grow in twelve rows to a thirty-inch bed. We think of every square foot of bed as real estate that can yield profit: the beds are rarely empty as a result.[4]

This attitude extends to the pace of the work. Our summer internship program, through which six Yale students spend fifteen weeks learning the theory and practice of sustainable agriculture at the Yale Farm every summer, always reminds me that instilling pride in skill and productivity is important. Every year, about three weeks into the summer, I struggle: I'm excited that our student interns are starting to take ownership of the farm but frustrated that their pace, on average, is more bucolic than agricultural. I was trained on a production farm, where lollygagging wasn't tolerated. When teaching, I put an emphasis on productivity because this helps us find the speed at which work is both fast and pleasurable. This doesn't mean that we sacrifice teachable moments, playful moments, or real rest. We just do each of these consciously.

PARTNERSHIPS AND ACADEMICS

The four principles I laid out above—pay attention to the institution's culture, find strong advocates, highlight taste, and keep a focus on productivity—gave our work a strong foundation. As the program grew, we built in other ideas. If you're aiming to get a program started, you might find it useful to know how we expanded the number of people dedicated to this work and how, on a college campus, we work within the academic realm.

Yale has five thousand undergraduates and six thousand graduate students. Some will try their hand at farming with us. Others will come to try the pizza. Others will consider the whole project laughable. I understand that, yet I'm personally driven by the idea that everyone deserves good food and that the nation is better off if everyone has spent some time on a farm. It's important to me, and to our work, that the sustainable food movement not be confined to the granola-loving set. So we plan as if we could get each and every one of Yale's students to stop and examine their relationship with food and the land. Our Harvest preorientation program, run out of the Yale College dean's office, is a feeder program that gets them while they're young. This year, 6 percent of the freshman class signed up, and we felt jubilant at the program's steady growth. We also develop on-campus partnerships to help bring others into the fold. We've created a series of events on class, race, and food access with the Afro-American Cultural Center. We've partnered with the Center for British Art, bringing their student interns out to draw in the garden. We've worked with the Humanities Center to create a food and film festival. Events like these can bring out a hundred people who have never been to the farm before.

Yale is a college, and students are supposed to mostly study during their time here. Last year, 850 undergraduates enrolled in courses related to food, agriculture, and the environment. The Yale Farm would be doing great work even if it only offered students the chance to physically engage with the land. Connecting it to the academic realm further enhances and strengthens students' experience of the space.

In the last few years, there has been a dramatic shift in course work, and we're still trying to get our heads around it. It's exciting, for sure: the classes reflect a growing consensus that the world's most pressing questions regarding health, culture, the environment, education, and the global economy are related to the food we eat and the way we produce it. Yale has an important contribution to make to the field, bringing together the natural sciences, humanities, and social sciences. Today, the idea of creating a program for studying food and agriculture at Yale is a radical one— but so was the American studies program before it was established in the 1960s, or the women's studies program before it was established in the 1980s. Developing a full-fledged course of study on food, agriculture, and the environment will take equal time and experimentation.

For now, we publish a course guide that explains Yale's academic offerings in food and agriculture. With faculty members in environmental studies, we built a track, similar to a minor, devoted to food and agriculture, and, with a broader group, we are now discussing the merits of a similar track in international studies. Students have yet to receive formal academic credit for their time at the Yale Farm. Nevertheless, professors in various

Figure 15.4. The Yale Farm's Lazarus Pavilion is a timber-frame structure that was raised by Yale students in October 2008. The farm's wood-fired oven is a main feature of the pavilion and is used weekly in cooking demonstrations and pizza tastings. The pavilion also hosts classes, pizza evenings, and special events at the farm throughout the year (October 2009). (Courtesy Sean Fraga '10.)

disciplines use the farm to teach. A women's studies class uses the hearth oven to re-create the first scribed recipes, while the chemistry department uses farm spinach in its research on improving photovoltaic cells. Courses from the School of Forestry and Environmental Studies use the farm to examine soil structure. I can't predict how use of the farm will change as it becomes more deeply involved in the academic work; my goal has been to continue to create an experience that produces genuine attachment to the land and real satisfaction in the work done because rich learning happens there.

So that's the adventure of our farm so far. Go forth. Create your farm. Know that, if you create a beautiful, productive space that honors community, hard work, and play and that fits your institution, it may not be easy, but you will be successful. You will build a place that will receive a lot of love and attention and that will change many people's everyday lives, making them stewards of the land. That is the power of a college farm.

STUDENT REFLECTIONS
_____

SEEDING SCALLIONS

NOZLEE SAMADZADEH

I spent the summer of 2009 working as a full-time intern on the Yale Farm. There were six of us, and, as we learned, laughed, and weeded all summer, we each changed and grew stronger in more ways than we could realize. It was an amazing three months. I'm a computer science major used to speeding through college and spending too much time checking my e-mail, so the farm lifestyle was a welcome change. I woke up earlier, went to bed earlier, became constantly aware of the food I was so lucky to eat, and grew tan and muscled shoveling dirt in the sun instead of typing code in the lab.

Eventually, the summer had to end. We ambitiously decided to build a new set of compost bins during our last week, but alongside our mini-construction project was the normal weekly cycle of the farm: seeding head lettuce in soil blocks, suckering the tomato plants, and planting longer-term crops as the season dictated. That final week it was scallions, which replaced the bush beans we'd ripped out two weeks before. I was more than a little bit wistful as I pulled the four-row seeder back and forth across the bed. These scallions would be harvested after my time at the farm was over.

School began, and, predictably, it became hard to make time for the farm's workdays. I was still eating locally and sustainably, but something was missing. Finally, one Tuesday in late October, I made time to go to the farm. Walking in was a revelation: It was fall! The trees' leaves had turned, and the air was crisp, so different from the summer beauty of the Yale Farm I had known so well, but just as amazing.

I was put to work in the very bed of scallions I'd planted in August. They weren't doing so well. I'd never anticipated that the falling leaves from the chestnut tree overhead would smother the plants and that purslane, our most prevalent summer weed, would shrivel at the first sign of cold. After discussion with the farm manager, we decided to plant sorrel seedlings among the gaps in the rows of scallions.

We started working, and I remembered how good it felt to get dirty and use my hands, clearing away weeds and replacing them with plants that would feed and sustain people I might never see. Yes, we wished that the scallions had yielded a better harvest, but both the farm and the earth are flexible and forgiving—you can try again if a crop doesn't work out.

I left that day for class with dirt under my fingernails and a clear head. The lessons I learned from farming have a far broader scope than merely the beds of plants and vegetables. From within a world of papers, tests, and deadlines, I remembered that it's important to slow down to rethink, reassess, and maybe even reorient your goals, as we had with the bed of scallions. And, while intellectual thought is a wholly worthy activity, stopping to use your hands to complete a concrete task can make thoughts flow that much more easily when you return to the library. It turns out that agriculture and a university education have more in common than I thought: that October day on the farm, I learned that I benefit much more from each when I spend time doing both.

Nozlee Samadzadeh interned at the Yale Farm during the summer of 2009 and now edits the Yale Sustainable Food Project's student blog.

NOTES

1. For more information on Yale Dining's long-term sustainability initiatives, visit http://www.yale.edu/dining/about/sustainability.html.

2. The full schedule of the conference can be found online at http://www.yale.edu/opa/arc-ybc/v32.n10/story6.html (*Yale Bulletin and Calendar*, 7 November 2003).

3. "Every time a student walks past a really urgent, expressive piece of architecture that belongs to his college, it can help reassure him that he does have that mind, does have that soul" (Louis Kahn).

4. This requires regular amendments of compost. For more on the intensive method, see Eliot Coleman's *The New Organic Grower* (White River Junction, VT: Chelsea Green, 1995).

Conclusion

Starting a Student Farm

Laura Sayre and Sean Clark

So you want to start a student farm? Maybe you're a student or a recent graduate, maybe you're a tenured faculty member, maybe you have a staff position linked to a newly established campus sustainability initiative. Individuals in all of these situations have started student farms, including several of those described in these pages. One of the themes of this book is that student farms seem frequently to have gotten started thanks in large part to the persistent efforts of a single, dynamic individual with a vision of how a student farm could fit into his or her campus community. It often takes several years to get the farm established—so, if you're starting this project as a student, be aware that you may be working to create opportunities for your successors, rather than for yourself and your peers. Often, too, there is an element of serendipity, with multiple factors—a previously overlooked piece of land, a new faculty hire, a successful grant application—suddenly falling into place at once.

As the previous chapters suggest, there's no single set of rules for starting a successful student farm. Certainly, there are conditions and resources that, if present, will improve your chances for success: a good piece of land, well placed; faculty and staff with the right expertise; ample funding; supportive administrators; a strongly committed group of students; interest among the wider local community. But no one starts out with all these things; and, in some cases, even in many cases, not having some of them—or at least not having them right away—has turned out to be a blessing in disguise. Several of the student farms profiled in this book, for instance, started out in one location only to lose their land a few years later. As difficult as the move may have been, with more experience they were in a better position to choose and develop an improved site the second time around.

Grant funding, too, can be perilous, sometimes bringing with it the temptation (even the obligation) to make big expenditures before the specific nature of what's needed becomes clear. Depending on grants to operate your farm is not only risky but also stressful, as someone must continually search for the necessary support for the farm's survival.

There is a certain paradox here: while most of the chapters in this book point to the importance of experience—of expert, preexisting farming skills and knowledge as essential to the creation and maintenance of a successful student farm—many of the participants in the student farm projects described here learned that lesson the hard way. In hindsight, they would have done this or that differently, managed expectations better or foreseen and headed off potential conflicts. All the student farms whose histories are told here, from the oldest to the newest, have evolved and changed continually over the years: adding acreage or enterprises or getting rid of them; experimenting with different marketing strategies; changing management structures; reconfiguring the relationship between the farm and the academic curriculum; forging new partnerships or spinning off projects to other entities. A student farm, like any farm, is a living thing; it will not stay still.

So, while we would like to be able to offer you a blueprint for student farm establishment—and while there are many useful lessons offered in the chapters of this book, lessons born of experience and stamina and sweat and, no doubt, even some tears—the truth is that there is no blueprint, no absolute set of requirements. Even the most experienced farmer, starting out on a new piece of land with a new group of workers or a new suite of crops, will have some things to learn. Transitioning a property to organic management, too, usually involves a few years of adjustment as soil quality improves and ecological interactions shift. But the marvelous fact about living things is that, generally, if you give them half a chance, they grow. And soon you figure out how to make them grow better. If there is one essential ingredient, it may be unconquerable enthusiasm—and enthusiasm, as Marianne Sarrantonio observes in chapter 8, "particularly in the planning stage, seems to be positively correlated with lack of experience."

Taken together, the chapters of this book show that there are many different ways to organize a successful student farm. One unifying principle, as Josh Slotnick emphasizes in chapter 11, is that a student farm needs to be developed within the context of its specific location, both geographic and institutional. It should serve the needs and interests of the students at that school and, whenever possible, those of the local community as well. Obviously, it should feature crops and livestock and other enterprises typical of its region, but it should also, as Stephen Bramwell, Martha Rosemeyer, and Melissa Barker argue in chapter 4, be trying out new ideas and new farming systems that may prove typical in the future. Some student farms are focused specifically on the training of new farmers; some teach organic gardening skills; some serve as sites for undergraduate and graduate student research; some provide an experiential underpinning for an academic program in sustainable food and farming systems. Some do all these things at once. Many produce large quantities of good food for their local communities. Many have served as loci for innovations that have spread across the entire campus or even beyond. All, it seems safe to say, teach both a wide range of practical skills—how to sharpen a chainsaw, how to read a soil test, how to recognize a sick lamb, how to save seed for next year's planting, how to butcher a chicken, how to apply for organic certification, how to cook fresh vegetables, how to work in the cold and rain or in the blazing sun—and a host of equally useful but less tangible skills, such as leadership, teamwork, tolerance, resilience, flexibility, organization, responsibility, ethics, and communication.

Diversity, in short, is key. In lieu of a set of rules, then, we've assembled the following list of ten key steps to student farm formation. These steps are based on the combined wisdom emerging from the essays in this book as well as on our own experiences both farming and teaching, on visits to dozens of student farms, and on discussions with other individuals involved in student farming. These steps don't exist in a fixed order: you'll probably find yourself looping back repeatedly to certain steps, perhaps skipping over others. A few years from now, you may have others to add to the list. As Marada Cook observes in her contribution to chapter 7, "Good ideas come from good soil."

1. Form your core group. You may have already done this, but the first step is to identify a core group of three or four or six people who are not just interested but willing to work to make this thing happen. Many community-supported agriculture (CSA) programs work on the core-group principle. You need to be able to brainstorm ideas, tag team on specific tasks while you're all juggling various other commitments, and mobilize a range of skills and contacts that will be essential in the steps ahead. One of the hazards of student farms is that they can become magnets for idealism, expected to serve too many worthy objectives at once, so try to be as specific as possible in articulating your shared vision: What are your goals, and what priority order will you give them? What needs are you trying to meet? Whose needs are they?[1]

2. Identify your allies. Once you have your core group, start thinking about whom you need to convince and who can help you. Faculty members, deans, provosts, the president? Alumni? Student organizations? Someone in the facilities department or in buildings and grounds? Some of your most useful allies may not necessarily be the first people who spring to mind or the ones who officially have the most power. Still, get acquainted with the organizational chart for your school so that you can understand who reports to whom. Most important, consider all disciplines: there may be someone in the business school or the engineering department or the American studies program who has a keen interest or deep background in farming and can offer you expertise and support.

3. Hunt for land. Sure, it's early in the process, but this is one of the best parts, and you'll probably find yourself doing it anyway. Walk or cycle around campus and consider possible open patches of land, small or large. Study local maps. Find out the names of the best agricultural soils in your area, what they look like, and where they can be found. If you think you may have found a possible site, remain skeptical. Think about how easy it is to get to without a car, whether there's water for irrigation available, whether there's storage and electricity nearby. Think about drainage and slope and aspect and shade, not just now, but throughout the year. Think, too, about history: What did your campus look like fifty years ago? A century ago? Where were the farms in this area? What were they known for? Are there any signs of them remaining—barns, sheds, farmhouses, fruit trees? History can be useful for uncovering possible problems (contamination, compaction, flooding) as well as for understanding the potential of a given soil or field. Some student farms, on the other hand, are originally suggested by the existence of an old farm property within the current campus boundaries, in which case a new farm enterprise can also serve a historic preservation function. Many land-grant institutions are rich in underutilized agricultural experiment station land and/or greenhouses on or near campus. You may be able to barter space in exchange for providing educational and outreach opportunities later on.

4. Do your homework. This step applies to the entire process, of course, but it's also a step in its own right. Many student farms have gotten their start as a class project of some kind and/or have evolved as a series of class or individual student projects. You might start with a simple mission statement or a full-blown feasibility study, including, for instance, a site plan, a business plan, a marketing plan, and field plans. Later projects may include designs for individual buildings or other facilities such as root cellars, hoophouses, greenhouses, biodiesel facilities, wind towers, composting toilets, or photovoltaic arrays. There are lots of great resources available on all these topics—the Web sites for the Sustainable Agriculture Research and Education program within the US Department of Agriculture (www.sare.org) and ATTRA, the National Sustainable Agriculture Information Service (http://attra.ncat.org), are a good place to start. At a large university, doing your homework can also mean simply getting acquainted with what's going on in different parts of the institution. What challenges does your school face? What's the budget situation? Is there a long-range campus-planning document? What new initiatives are in the works? How many different ways can you add academic rigor to your work?

5. Seek funding. Alas, these are tough economic times, and grant funding can be hard to come by. Alas, too, a proposal for a student farm may no longer be novel enough to immediately wow potential funders. On the other hand, at least they'll have a sense of what you're talking about. The good news is that the projects described in this book have gotten under way and even continued and expanded with widely varying amounts of financial support. Some kind of financial commitment from the institution will be critical for the stability of the farm, but it's important to recognize that this can take many forms—land, buildings, vehicles, utilities, personnel, work-study allocations, compost—and to acknowledge the value of what you do receive. Be realistic about how much you can bring in from the sale of farm products alone, especially in your first few seasons. Even well-established, thriving student farms typically cover only operating expenses (seeds, supplies, other inputs) from their sales revenue, not salaries. Finally, the flip side of seeking funding is just as important: be frugal with the funds that you have. Solicit donations, whether in cash or in kind. Welcome volunteers. Bargain hunt. Shop for tools at yard sales. Recycle. Reuse. Scavenge.

6. Start small. If key resources—especially farming expertise—are in short supply, don't hesitate to start your farm as a garden, even a small garden. A small garden well stewarded is going to be worth more to your cause than several acres planted and overgrown (see step 7). In the same vein, keep your cropping plan simple, limiting crops and varieties to a manageable number. If things go well, you can expand and diversify next year and again the year after that. Once you have something up and running, you may be in a better position to hire the farm manager who can help take things to the next level (or someone in your group may have become qualified to be that farm manager). This bit of advice applies to infrastructure projects as well. As Tim Crews puts it in chapter 10, "At the end of the term, a simple, manageable initiative brought to completion is infinitely more appealing than a few odd parts of a grandiose vision."

7. *Keep it weeded.* The importance of this step cannot be overemphasized. Yes, we know about biodiversity and refuge areas and all that, but, if you're trying to win over an entire campus community, it will help to keep things tidy. Aesthetics matter, especially if you're in a highly visible location. And, if you want good yields—which you should—weeds will likely be your most important obstacle. Sure, there are insects and diseases to manage, but, if you're using organic methods, aggressive weeds will be your greatest pest challenge. Use mulches to suppress weeds, and walk your gardens or fields often to see what's going on. Use stakes and string and tape measures if you want your beds and rows straight and even. Clean your tools when you are done with them and put them away where they belong. Mow. Turn the compost, and cover it to keep odors from offending passersby. Don't let piles of used plastic mulch or other debris stack up in the corner of some field. Plant flowers, both annuals and perennials. Wash out the harvest buckets at the end of the day, and set them to dry. A well-kept farm is not only more appealing to outsiders; it's also usually a safer and more pleasant place to work. Above all, it demonstrates a sense of commitment.

8. *Read.* You are in school, after all. A key rationale for student farming is that book learning and hands-on learning are complementary. If you don't have assigned reading as part of a course or courses associated with the student farm, come up with your own reading list or form a reading group with some friends or colleagues. Remember that not all knowledge is to be found on the Internet or even in books published within the past ten years: troll the stacks of your school's library, poke around in secondhand bookshops, ask older farmers what sources they have found most valuable over the years. One of the things that's unique about organic and sustainable farming is that it reconsiders traditional farming practices and finds new ways to mix old wisdom with new technologies. An outstanding portal for relevant resources both old and new is the Alternative Farming Systems Information Center housed at the National Agricultural Library (http://afsic.nal.usda.gov).

9. *Write.* This applies not just to the early, planning stages of the student farm (see step 4) but to its later, everyday functioning as well. Com-

mitting what you've done and what you plan to do to paper on a regular basis will help you develop your ideas, facilitate communication among current student farmworkers, and provide an indispensable record of what worked, what didn't, and how much it all cost for student farmers in years to come. Good recordkeeping is essential for organic certification and makes it possible to analyze and assess the value—both budgetary and otherwise—of different farm enterprises or experiments from season to season. Note that writing can take many forms, from blogs, e-newsletters, and twitter updates to personal journals, financial accounts, yield records, and academic papers. Many student farms find it useful to keep a whiteboard list of field work chores or items to harvest so that anyone arriving at the farm with an odd hour to work will know where to start. Others maintain an online or hard-copy farm handbook to keep track of favorite varieties, planting schedules, and other accumulated bits of local knowledge.

10. Think very carefully before adding livestock. Animals are great, but they require an entirely different order of care than plants: daily attention regardless of whatever else is going on in your life, and, if they pine and die, everyone is going to feel horrible. They require water and food and shelter (including fencing); water that is heavy, food that can quickly become expensive, and shelter and fencing that require maintenance. Above all, animals are time-consuming, easily eating up two to three hours of someone's day, every day, especially if they assume the role of pets or mascots. Ideally, moreover, any livestock or poultry on the property will be not just existing side-by-side with the plant part of your agricultural enterprise, but integrated with it in some fashion and have some purpose: grazing the fields as part of your rotation, supplying fertility in the form of manure (which, however, may need to be hauled and composted before it can be applied to your fields), controlling invasive weeds, or providing traction. The cute factor supplied by livestock needs to be balanced against all these more tangible realities.

11. Cultivate partners and supporters beyond campus. Several of the chapters in this book illustrate the value of developing partnerships with the wider local community. Student farms can be terrific venues for improving town-gown relations. Remember that you have as much to gain as to offer in these relationships. Also keep in mind that farmers in your area may see you as competition for their business, particularly if you sell your produce at the local farmers market or start a CSA. Offering gardening or farming workshops and field days as well as sponsoring community educational events will increase awareness of your activities and promote an appreciation for your efforts. Get to know your local organic and sustainable farming community if you don't already: its members will constitute one of your most valuable resources. This point connects to steps 2 and 4 above as well: get input from multiple stakeholders, and think about how you can work together. The more people you have on your team, the more you'll be able to do in the long run.

12. Don't forget to socialize. Last but not least, enjoy the rewards of what you are doing, and share them. This takes many forms. There's a story about how, in the early days of the UC Santa Cruz Farm and Garden, Alan Chadwick and his apprentices used to make bouquets of flowers and put them out in buckets in a central spot on campus for passersby to take away. You may be focused more on immediate profitability, but generosity can be an excellent long-term investment. Another essential point, as Ann Bettman notes in chapter 5, is that, when designing your farm and garden, you should include areas to hang out when the work is done for the day. Ideally, your farm will have a kitchen, even if it's an outdoor kitchen, so you can cook and share what you have grown. You'll have an easier time attracting and keeping workers if the farm is a place where people enjoy spending time. Hosting events where you invite others to the farm—potluck suppers, harvest festivals, open houses, summer barbecues, commencement celebrations—is also key to the life and continued survival of the farm. Some students complain that student farms can become cliquish, can come to be perceived as places where only a certain group of students feels welcome: your goal, as Melina Shannon-DiPietro emphasizes in chapter 15, should be to get as many different members of the campus community to visit the farm in the course of a year as you can. That way, the farm will become part of the identity of the school and all who are associated with it.

This book has demonstrated that, far from being merely a recent fad on college and university campuses, student farms have deep roots in North American higher education, stretching back not just to the countercultural trends of the 1960s and 1970s but to nineteenth-century ideals of pragmatism, progressivism, and democracy. While every campus farm is unique, the histories recounted in these pages are representative of dozens of other student farms, past and present, that have challenged and nourished the lives of thousands of individuals over the generations. Long-standing student farms must weather major transformations within the agricultural economy while remaining relevant to their individual institutions and the regions they are a part of. But your work here today can also help shape that agricultural future. The process begins with that first spadeful of compost, that first seed placed in the ground.

You want to start a student farm? The lessons of this book can be summed up in three words. Go for it.

NOTE

1. The phrase *magnets for idealism* was suggested to us by Suzanne Morse of the College of the Atlantic.

Appendix

An Inventory of Student Farm Projects in the United States and Canada

The following list of student farms is based on a directory assembled by Laura Sayre in association with "Farming for Credit," an article about the student farm movement originally published on NewFarm.org in 2004 and updated at several points over the following two years. Information in the directory was then verified and expanded in the fall of 2009 with the help of a group of Sean Clark's students at Berea College: Iris Bahr-Winslow, Lilly Belanger, Jeff Bowling, Frances Buerkens, Adrienne Hamilton, Libby Kahler, Jean Majewski, and James White. Entries are organized by region (Midwest, Northeast, Southeast, West, Canada) and then by state or province. For each entry, the listing includes the name of the school, the name of the farm, the year the farm was established, its size in acres, the kinds of crops grown, the types of livestock raised (if any), whether there is certified organic acreage, and, finally, the marketing strategies employed. While every effort was made to ensure the accuracy of this list, the student farm movement is continually evolving—with new projects appearing, new acreage coming under cultivation, marketing strategies continually being refined, etc.—making any inventory of this nature necessarily provisional. We beg tolerance for any errors that may remain.

State/ province	University/ college	Farm name	Year established	Size (acres)	Crops*	Livestock*	Certified organic acreage?	Marketing*
Midwest								
Illinois	Illinois State University	University Farm		610	H, F	Ca, S		
Indiana	Earlham College	Miller Farm	1970s	2				CSA
Indiana	Goshen College	Merry Lea Environmental Center			H	Pi		

State/ province	University/ college	Farm name	Year established	Size (acres)	Crops*	Livestock*	Certified organic acreage?	Marketing*
Iowa	Iowa State University	ISU Student Organic Farm	1996	2	H		Yes	CSA, FM, DH
Michigan	Michigan State University	MSU Student Organic Farm	2003	10	H		Yes	CSA, DH, FS
Minnesota	Carleton College	Carleton Farm Club Organic Gardens	Late 1980s	1	H		Yes	DH, LM
Minnesota	St. Olaf College	STOGROW Farm	2005	1.5	H		Yes	DH
Minnesota	University of Minnesota	Cornercopia, the Student Organic Farm	2004	1	H		Yes	FM, R, LM
Missouri	College of the Ozarks	College of the Ozarks Farm	1906		H, F	Ca (beef, dairy), Pi		
Ohio	Oberlin College	George Jones Farm	1995					CSA, LM, FM
Ohio	Wilmington College	Academic Farms	1946	300	F, H	Ca, Pi, SG, Po		FB
Wisconsin	Lawrence University	Sustainable Lawrence University Garden (SLUG)	2005	0.25	H		Yes	DH, FM
Wisconsin	Northland College	Mino Aki Community Garden	mid-1990s					
Wisconsin	University of Wisconsin, Madison	F.H. King Students of Sustainable Agriculture Demonstration Garden	1979	0.5	H		Yes	FB, FM
Wisconsin	University of Wisconsin, Oshkosh	Student/ Community Garden	2006	1	H		Yes	FB
Wisconsin	University of Wisconsin, Platteville	Pioneer Farm	1957	430	F	Ca, Pi		
Wisconsin	University of Wisconsin, River Falls	Campus Farm and Mann Valley Farm	1912	290	H, F	Ca, Pi, S		

State/ province	University/ college	Farm name	Year established	Size (acres)	Crops*	Livestock*	Certified organic acreage?	Marketing*
Northeast								
Connecticut	Yale University	Yale Sustainable Food Project	2003	1	H			FM
Maine	Bowdoin College	Bowdoin Organic Garden	2004	1	H		Yes	CSA, DH
Maine	College of the Atlantic	Beech Hill Farm	1999	5	H		Yes	DH, FS
Maine	Unity College	Unity College Garden	1997	<1	H			FS, FB
Maine	University of Maine, Orono	Black Bear Food Guild at Rogers Farm	1994	3	H		Yes	CSA
Maryland	University of Maryland	Master Peace Community Farm	2007	0.5	H			FM
Massachusetts	Hampshire College	Agricultural Studies Farm Center	1978	90	H, F	Ca (beef, dairy), Pi, SG	Yes	CSA, FS
Massachusetts	Mount Holyoke College	MHC Student Garden Project	2004					
Massachusetts	University of Massachusetts	Stockbridge School of Agriculture	1918					
New Hampshire	Dartmouth College	Dartmouth College Organic Farm	1996	2	H			FS
New Hampshire	University of New Hampshire	Campus-Community Farm	2003	30	H	Ca (dairy)	Yes	DH, FS
New Jersey	Rutgers University	Cook Student Organic Farm	1993	5	H		Yes	CSA, FB
New York	Cornell University	Dilmun Hill Student Farm	1996	12	H, F		Yes	DH, FS, R
Pennsylvania	Delaware Valley College		1896		H	Ca (beef, dairy), Pi, bees		

State/ province	University/ college	Farm name	Year established	Size (acres)	Crops*	Livestock*	Certified organic acreage?	Marketing*
Pennsylvania	Dickinson College	Dickinson College Farm	1999	30	H			DH, FM, FB, LM
Pennsylvania	Slippery Rock University	Robert A. Macoskey Center for Sustainable Systems Market Garden Project	1992	1	H		Yes	FM
Pennsylvania	Wilson College	Fulton Farm	1994	7	H			CSA, FM, DH
Vermont	Bennington College	Bennington College Community Farm	1996	5	H	Po	Yes	DH, LM
Vermont	Green Mountain College	Farm and Food Project	1997	12	H	Ca, SG, Po, bees	Yes	CSA, FM, DH
Vermont	Middlebury College	Slow the Plow Organic Garden	2001	3	H			DH
Vermont	Sterling College	Sterling College Farm	1962	156	H, F	Ca, SG, Pi, Po, horses	Yes	DH
Vermont	University of Vermont	Common Ground Student-Run Ed. Farm	1995	3	H		Yes	CSA, FB
Vermont	Vermont Technical College				H	Ca (dairy)		FM
Southeast								
Arkansas	Southern Arkansas University	SAU Farm		660		Ca, Po		
Florida	Miami Dade College				H			
Georgia	Berry College		1902	740		Ca (beef and dairy)		
Kentucky	Berea College	Berea College Farm	1871	500	F, H	Ca, SG, Pi, bees	Yes	DH, LM, FM
Kentucky	University of Kentucky	Sustainable Agriculture Program	2003	11	H		Yes	CSA

State/ province	University/ college	Farm name	Year established	Size (acres)	Crops*	Livestock*	Certified organic acreage?	Marketing*
North Carolina	Appalachian State University	Goodnight Family Teaching and Research Farm in Valle Crucis	2001		H	Pi		
North Carolina	Central Carolina Community College	The Land Lab	1995	5	H	Po		CSA, FM
North Carolina	North Carolina State University, Goldsboro	Center for Environmental Farming Systems	1996	15	H			CSA
North Carolina	Warren Wilson College	Warren Wilson College Farm	1894	275	H, F	Ca, Pi		LM
South Carolina	Clemson University	Student Organic Farm	2001	15	H		Yes	CSA
Tennessee	Tennessee Tech University	Tech Farm				Ca, Pi, SG		CSA
Virginia	Ferrum College	Agriculture Club Beef Farm		42				
Virginia	Virginia State University	Randolph Farm		416	F, H			
West Virginia	West Virginia University	WVU organic research farm project	1998	62	H		Yes	
West								
Arizona	Prescott College	Jenner Farm	1996	20	H, F	Po	Yes	CSA, LM
California	Butte College	Butte College Farm		85			Yes	CSA
California	California State Polytechnic University	John T. Lyle Center for Regenerative Studies	1994	16			Yes	CSA
California	California State Polytechnic University	Swanton Pacific Ranch	1987	3,200	F, H	Ca, SG	Yes	LM

State/ province	University/ college	Farm name	Year established	Size (acres)	Crops*	Livestock*	Certified organic acreage?	Marketing*
California	California State Polytechnic University	Cal Poly Organic Farm	1989	11	H	SG	Yes	CSA
California	California State University, Chico	Agricultural Research and Teaching Center		800	H, F	Ca, Pi, SG		
California	College of the Redwoods	Sustainable Agriculture Farm	2001	38	F, H		Yes	CSA
California	Deep Springs College	Deep Springs Ranch	1997	152	F, H	Ca	Yes	DH
California	Humboldt State University	Arcata Educational Farm	1993	2				CSA, FM
California	Mt. San Antonio College				H	Yes		
California	Rudolf Steiner College	Raphael Garden	1987	3	H	Po, Ca, SG		CSA
California	Santa Rosa Junior College	Shone Farm	1970	365	H	Ca, SG	Yes	
California	Stanford University	Stanford University Community Farm	1997	1				
California	University of California, Davis	Davis Student Experimental Farm	1977	21	H	Po	Yes	CSA, R
California	University of California, Santa Cruz	The Center for Agroecology and Sustainable Food Systems	1967	27	H		Yes	CSA
Colorado	Colorado State University	The Rocky Mountain Small Organic Farm Project	1998	8	H		Yes	
Colorado	Naropa University	Hedgerow Farm		20				

State/ province	University/ college	Farm name	Year established	Size (acres)	Crops*	Livestock*	Certified organic acreage?	Marketing*
Idaho	University of Idaho	Soil Stewards Club	2003	0.25	H		Yes	CSA, FS
Montana	Montana State University	Towne's Harvest Garden	2006	3	H			CSA, FB
Montana	University of Montana	PEAS Farm	1997	9.75	H	Po		CSA, FB
Nevada	University of Nevada	EnAcT Environmental Action)	2008	1	H		Yes	
New Mexico	New Mexico State University	OASIS	2002	1	H			CSA
Oregon	Oregon State University	OSU Organic Growers Club	2001	1.5	H	Po	Yes	LM
Oregon	University of Oregon	The Urban Farm	1976	1.5	H			LM
Texas	Texas A&M, Kingsville	Kingsville Teaching and Research Farm	2008	545		Ca, Go, Pi, Rabbit		
Washington	Evergreen State	Evergreen Organic Farm	1972	5	H	Po	Yes	CSA, LM, FB, DH
Washington	Fairhaven College	The Outback Farm	1972	5	H		Yes	FB
Washington	Washington State University	Organic Teaching Farm at Tukey Orchard	2004	3	H		Yes	CSA, DH, LM
Wyoming	University of Wyoming	ACRES (Agricultural Community Resources for Everyday Sustainability)	2007	1.5	H			FM, LM
Canada								
British Columbia	University of British Columbia	UBC Farm	2000	60	H			CSA, FM, LM, R
Nova Scotia	Nova Scotia Agricultural College	NSAC Farm				Po, Ca, SG		

State/ province	University/ college	Farm name	Year established	Size (acres)	Crops*	Livestock*	Certified organic acreage?	Marketing*
Ontario	University of Guelph, Guelph	Guelph Centre for Urban Organic Farming	2008	2.5	H			
Quebec	Cégep de Victoriaville	Jardins bio du Cégep	2002	4.5	H		Yes	CSA, LM

* **Crops:** F = field crops; H = horticultural crops. **Livestock:** Po = poultry; Ca = cattle; SG = sheep/goats; Pi = pigs; **Marketing:** CSA = community-supported agriculture; DH = dining hall(s); FM = farmers market(s); FB = food bank/donations; FS = farm stand; LM = other local market(s); R = restaurant(s).

Further Reading

Given the highly interdisciplinary nature of student farming and the recent proliferation of books and articles related to sustainable agriculture and food politics,
the list of titles here could be extended almost indefinitely. We have limited ourselves to a handful of practical manuals for small-scale organic farming and market gardening combined with a few key titles relating to the social, educational,
ecological, and economic contexts of sustainable agriculture. The reader is also
encouraged to consult the endnotes to each chapter of this volume.

Aber, John, Tom Kelley, and Bruce Mallory, eds. *The Sustainable Learning Community: One University's Journey to the Future.* Durham: University of New
Hampshire Press, 2009. An account of sustainability efforts at the University
of New Hampshire, including curriculum development, an organic research
dairy, and a student organic gardening club.

Berry, Wendell. *Bringing It to the Table: On Farming and Food.* Berkeley, CA:
Counterpoint, 2009. A collection of some of Wendell Berry's most important
essays (and selections from his fiction) relating to food and agriculture, with
an introduction by Michael Pollan.

Bornstein, David. *How to Change the World: Social Entrepreneurs and the Power
of New Ideas.* Rev. ed. New York: Oxford University Press, 2007. Not about
agriculture, but Bornstein's concept of social entrepreneurism and the characteristics of innovative organizations holds relevant insights for student farm
undertakings.

Byczynski, Lynn. *The Flower Farmer: An Organic Grower's Guide to Raising and
Selling Cut Flowers.* Rev. ed. White River Junction, VT: Chelsea Green, 2008.
The single best guide to organic cut-flower production, written by the editor
of the excellent monthly newsletter *Growing for Market.*

———. *The Hoophouse Handbook: Growing Produce and Flowers in Hoophouses and
High Tunnels.* 2nd ed. Lawrence, KS: Fairplain, 2006. By the same author, a
useful guide to organic hoophouse production.

Coleman, Eliot. *The New Organic Grower: A Master's Manual of Tools and Techniques for the Home and Market Gardener.* White River Junction, VT: Chelsea Green, 1995. The classic beginner's guide to small-scale, "plant-positive"
organic vegetable production.

———. *The Winter Harvest Handbook: Year Round Vegetable Production Using
Deep Organic Techniques and Unheated Greenhouses.* White River Junc-

tion, VT: Chelsea Green, 2009. Coleman's most recent book, describing in detail his system of all-season vegetable growing, no matter the climate or latitude.

Dean, Andrea Oppenheimer, and Timothy Hursley. *Rural Studio: Samuel Mockbee and an Architecture of Decency.* New York, NY: Princeton Architectural Press, 2002. Design ideas and inspiration for building useful and creative structures from recycled materials, based on an innovative, community-based educational project linked to the School of Architecture at Auburn University.

Donahue, Brian. *Reclaiming the Commons: Community Farms and Forests in a New England Town.* New Haven, CT: Yale University Press, 1999. An eloquent case for the value of community farms, presented via an account of the author's involvement in the development of Land's Sake, a community farm outside Boston.

Groh, Trauger, and Steven McFadden. *Farms of Tomorrow Revisited: Community Supported Farms, Farm Supported Communities.* Kimberton, PA: Biodynamic Farming and Gardening Association, 1997. A call for a radical new approach to agriculture based on greater community control of the food system, simple living, and a respect for nature.

Grubinger, Vernon P. *Sustainable Vegetable Production from Start-Up to Market.* Ithaca, NY: Natural Resource, Agriculture, and Engineering Service, Cooperative Service, 1999. A very practical, illustrated manual on the tools and methods for vegetable production.

Henderson, Elizabeth, and Robin van En. *Sharing the Harvest: A Citizen's Guide to Community Supported Agriculture.* Rev. ed. White River Junction, VT: Chelsea Green, 2007. An essential resource for planning and starting a CSA operation.

Jack, Zachary Michael, ed. *Black Earth and Ivory Tower: Essays from Farm and Classroom.* Columbia: University of South Carolina Press, 2005. Reflections on farming and teaching by Victor Davis Hanson, Linda Hasselstrom, John Hildebrand, and others.

Jackson, Wes, Wendell Berry, and Bruce Colman, eds. *Meeting the Expectations of the Land: Essays in Sustainable Agriculture and Stewardship.* San Francisco: North Point, 1984. A classic collection of articles by the likes of Stephen Gliessman, Amory Lovins, and Gary Paul Nabhan.

Lawson, Laura J. *City Bountiful: A Century of Community Gardening in America.* Berkeley and Los Angeles: University of California Press, 2005. A well-researched history of community gardening, a tradition with many parallels to and intersections with the student farm movement.

Louv, Richard. *Last Child in the Woods: Saving Our Children from Nature Deficit Disorder.* Chapel Hill, NC: Algonquin, 2005. The journalist Richard Louv's influential call-to-arms regarding the long-term impacts of young people's increasingly structured and sheltered lives.

Magdoff, Fred, and Harold Van Es. *Building Soil for Better Crops.* Beltsville, MD:

Sustainable Agriculture Network, 2000. A clear and detailed guide to the basic principles of soil science and their relationship to sustainable farming techniques.

M'Gonigle, Michael, and Justine Starke. *Planet U: Sustaining the World, Reinventing the University.* Gabriola Island, BC: New Society, 2006. A wide-ranging, provocative look at the role of universities in the sustainability movement, and vice versa. The authors are affiliated with the University of Victoria, British Columbia, and ground their discussion in UVic's own experience balancing sustainability and growth.

National Research Council. Committee on a Leadership Summit to Effect Change in Teaching and Learning. *Transforming Agricultural Education for a Changing World.* Washington, DC: National Academies Press, 2009. Available online at http://www.nap.edu/catalog/12602.html. An official report on the changing demographics, imperatives, and innovations of agricultural education in the United States.

————. Committee on Twenty-First Century Systems Agriculture. *Toward Sustainable Agricultural Systems in the 21st Century.* Washington, DC: National Academies Press, 2010. Available online at http://www.nap.edu/catalog/12832.html. The follow-up to the landmark 1989 report *Alternative Agriculture.* Includes a section on "Knowledge Institutions" as well as numerous farm case studies.

Ngouajio, M., et al. "Proceedings of the Workshop 'Curriculum Development for Organic Horticulture,' Sponsored by the American Society for Horticultural Science's Organic Horticulture Working Group, July 21, 2005, Las Vegas, Nevada." *HortTechnology* 16, no. 3 (July–September 2006): 413–45. A collection of short articles from researchers and educators at ten state universities reflecting on the growing demand for courses in organic horticulture; student farms are considered as a key element in emerging organic curricula.

Orr, David W. *Earth in Mind: On Education, Environment and the Human Prospect.* Washington, DC: Island, 1994. An important set of essays (including "Agriculture and the Liberal Arts") based in part on Orr's experience directing the environmental studies program at Oberlin College, which launched a community-based student farm project in 1995.

Raps, Beth, and Dennis Jacobs. "Work, Learning and Belonging at the Six U.S. Work Colleges: Results of the Work Colleges Consortium Collaborative Research Project, 2002–2005." A detailed study of the functioning and benefits of the work college system, including several college farms.

Contributors

MONTE ANDERSON received a B.S. and an M.S. from Southern Illinois University, where he focused mainly on agronomy and horticulture, and a Ph.D. in agriculture education and administration from the Ohio State University. He has been director of agriculture at Wilmington College since 1985.

MELISSA BARKER grew up in the greater Seattle area, graduated with a B.S. from Evergreen State College in 1999, and went on to manage livestock and a forty-member CSA at Oyster Bay Farm for five seasons. She was the farm manager at Evergreen State College from January 2004 to 2010. She and her husband manage Homegrown Pastures, a small-scale livestock and vegetable farm located just outside Olympia, WA.

ANN BETTMAN holds a B.A. in fine arts from Boston University and a B.L.A. and an M.L.A. from the University of Oregon. She has been responsible for the University of Oregon's Plants Program within the Landscape Architecture Department since 1979 and was director of the University of Oregon Urban Farm from 1983 through 2007. She has self-published two books, *The Green Guide: Eugene's Natural Vegetation* (1982) and *The Urban Farm* (2002).

JOHN BIERNBAUM earned horticulture degrees from North Carolina State University (B.S.), Pennsylvania State University (M.S.), and Michigan State University (Ph.D.) and is a professor of horticulture with twenty-five years of service at Michigan State. In addition to coordinating the SOF, he teaches courses in organic farming principles and practices, greenhouse management, compost production and use, organic transplant production, and passive solar greenhouses for protected cultivation and advises undergraduate and graduate students. He presents regular farmer and urban agriculture workshops on organic high tunnel production. His current research is focused on composting and vermicomposting for the small-scale farm including recycling of campus food residuals.

MARK BOMFORD has been immersed in food system sustainability for fifteen years, founding and coordinating local and international projects focused on urban agriculture, community food security, food and health education, and food system modeling and research. In 2009, he was recognized with the University of British Columbia's inaugural President's Service Award for Excellence and with the Alma Mater Society's highest honor for alumni contributions to UBC and the community, the "Great Trekker" award. He currently serves as the director of the Centre for Sustainable Food Systems at the UBC Farm.

STEPHEN BRAMWELL is a visiting faculty member at Evergreen State College, where he teaches the practice of sustainable agriculture. He received his B.A. in international studies from the University of Washington and an M.S. in soil science from Washington State University. Since 2003, he has combined his own education with teaching and farming. His teaching and research interests focus on mixed crop-livestock agriculture, sustainable agriculture and social justice issues, and curriculum development for agrarian experiential education.

SEAN CLARK is associate professor in and chair of the Department of Agriculture and Natural Resources at Berea College in Kentucky, which operates a five-hundred-acre student educational farm. He holds a B.S. and an M.S. from Virginia Tech and a Ph.D. from Michigan State University. Prior to teaching at Berea, he was research manager of the Sustainable Agriculture Farming Systems Project at the University of California, Davis. His research, which has focused mainly on organic crop production, has been published in journals such as *Environmental Entomology; Agriculture, Ecosystems and Environment;* the *American Journal of Alternative Agriculture;* the *Agronomy Journal;* and *BioCycle.*

LORNA COPPINGER was a research associate at Hampshire on the Livestock Dog Project. She is the author of *The World of Sled Dogs* (Howell, 1977) and coauthored, with Ray Coppinger, *Dogs: A New Understanding of Canine Origin, Behavior and Evolution* (Scribner, 2001). Lorna holds an A.B. from Boston University and an M.S. from the University of Massachusetts. She is the coauthor with Ray of many scientific publications.

RAY COPPINGER began his career at Hampshire College in 1969 and was one of the founding science faculty members. He helped design the Environmental Quality Program and steered part of that program into the evolving Farm Center. As a professor of biology, he centered his teaching on the behavior and evolution of domestic animals. He holds an A.B. in American literature and philosophy (Boston University), an M.A. in zoology (University of Massachusetts), and a Ph.D. in biology. He has published dozens of articles in a variety of scientific journals.

TIM CREWS, a native of New Mexico, has been developing the agroecology program and related offerings at Prescott College since 1995. For his doctorate at Cornell, he studied how traditional farmers in Mexico maintained long-term productivity without fertilizer inputs, and, for a postdoc at Stanford, he studied how soil fertility changes with soil age in Hawaii. He received his B.A. in agroecology and environmental studies from the University of California, Santa Cruz, and was an apprentice at the UC Santa Cruz Farm and Garden in 1981.

CONSTANCE L. FALK has degrees in English, business (M.B.A.), and agricultural economics (Ph.D.) from Oklahoma State University. She has been on the faculty at New Mexico State University in the Department of Agricultural Economics and Agricultural Business since 1988. She cowrote the grant that created the OASIS project at NMSU and cotaught the OASIS class from 2002 to 2006. She is also a returned Peace Corps volunteer, having served in Honduras from 1982 to 1985.

FREDERICK L. KIRSCHENMANN shares an appointment as a distinguished fellow for the Leopold Center for Sustainable Agriculture at Iowa State University (ISU) and as president of the Stone Barns Center for Food and Agriculture in Pocantico Hills, NY. He also oversees the management of his family's thirty-five-hundred-acre certified organic farm in south central North Dakota and is a professor in the ISU Department of Religion and Philosophy.

ROBIN KOHANOWICH was hired in 1999 as the curriculum developer for Central Carolina Community College's Sustainable Agriculture Program and since 2002 has served as the program's lead instructor. She holds a B.S. in horticulture from Clemson University, a teaching certificate for high school biology from the University of North Carolina, Greensboro, and a master's in extension education from North Carolina State University. She has also worked as a high school science teacher, a microbiologist for a pharmaceutical company, and a farmworker on organic farms in New York and North Carolina.

PAULINE PAO has a bachelor's degree in horticulture from the University of California, Davis. Since 1992, she's worked in biological control, propagated plants for a public estate garden, managed a university research greenhouse, and, for five years, managed all field, distribution, and data-gathering operations for the OASIS CSA at New Mexico State University. Currently, she runs a small vegetable operation and manages the Aztec Farmers Market in Aztec, NM.

MARTHA ROSEMEYER has been a member of the faculty in environmental studies at Evergreen State College since 2001. At Evergreen she teaches ecological agriculture; food, health, and sustainability; and the practice of sustainable agriculture. After her doctorate at the University of California, Santa Cruz, she lived and worked in Costa Rica for eight years, teaching tropical agroecology field courses for the Organization for Tropical Studies and the University of California while conducting research on soil ecology and nutrient cycling of traditional dry bean systems and working in participatory rural development. After that, she was a visiting faculty member at the University of Wisconsin, where she taught tropical sustainable agriculture and coordinated the Wisconsin Integrated Cropping Systems Trials.

MARIANNE SARRANTONIO is associate professor of sustainable cropping systems at the University of Maine and the coordinator of the undergraduate B.S. in sustainable agriculture program. She has a Ph.D. in soil fertility from Cornell University and has been working in the area of sustainable and organic agriculture for more than thirty years. Her publications include *The Northeast Cover Crop Handbook* (Rodale, 1996).

LAURA SAYRE holds a B.A. from Simon's Rock College and an M.A. and a Ph.D. from Princeton University and was a postdoctoral fellow with Yale University's Program in Agrarian Studies. She has been a research associate at the Land Institute, a senior writer and editor for NewFarm.org at the Rodale Institute, and a farmworker on several organic farms. She is currently based in Dijon, France, where she is a researcher with the Institut national de la recherche agronomique, working on a study of traceability issues in contemporary farming systems.

MELINA SHANNON-DIPIETRO earned a bachelor's degree in social studies from Harvard University in 2000 and joined Yale in 2003 to help found the Sustainable Food Project. From 2008 to 2010, she was the project's director. Her publications include a set of sustainable food purchasing guidelines.

JULIA SHIPLEY has a B.S. in environmental education from Lesley University and an M.F.A. in creative writing and literature from Bennington College. She served as director of writing studies and faculty in sustainable agriculture at Sterling College for four years. Her writing about agriculture has appeared in *Alimentum, Farming,* the *Small Farmers Journal,* and *Vermont Life,* among other publications. Her chapbook of poems, *Herd,* won the Sheltering Pines Press Award.

JOSH SLOTNICK is lecturer in the Environmental Studies Program at the University of Montana, where he manages the PEAS farm and teaches students on the farm and in the classroom. He has a master's in professional studies in agriculture extension and adult education from Cornell University, a B.A. in philosophy from the University of Montana, and a certificate in ecological horticulture from the University of California, Santa Cruz. He is also a returned Peace Corps volunteer, having served in Thailand from 1988 to 1991.

ROY JOE STUCKEY completed a Ph.D. in dairy science and an M.S. in agriculture economics at the Ohio State University. His B.S. is from Wilmington College, where he eventually became the first director of agriculture and later served as vice president for institutional relations and planning. In 1969, he accepted an appointment as president of Jamestown College, in Jamestown, ND. Presently, he is retired and a member of the Board of Trustees at Wilmington College.

MARK VAN HORN has been the director of the student farm at the University of California, Davis, for more than twenty years. He also teaches courses at UC Davis and is involved in extension efforts in sustainable agriculture and organic farming. His publications focus on sustainable production methods and systems and sustainable agriculture education. He is a founding member of the Sustainable Agriculture Education Association and was cochair of its steering committee from 2007 to 2010.

Index

CPSIA information can be obtained at www.ICGtesting.com
Printed in the USA
245492LV00002B/1/P

9 780813 133744